The UN Guiding Principles on Business
and Human Rights

# The Raoul Wallenberg Institute
# Human Rights Library

VOLUME 39

*The titles published in this series are listed at* brill.nl/rawa

# The UN Guiding Principles on Business and Human Rights

Foundations and Implementation

*Edited by*
Radu Mares

LEIDEN • BOSTON
2012

This book is printed on acid-free paper.

Library of Congress Cataloging-in-Publication Data

ISSN 1388-3208
ISBN 978 90 04 21051 6 (hardback)
ISBN 978 90 04 22579 4 (e-book)

Copyright 2012 by Koninklijke Brill NV, Leiden, The Netherlands.
Koninklijke Brill NV incorporates the imprints BRILL, Global Oriental, Hotei Publishing, IDC Publishers, Martinus Nijhoff Publishers and VSP.

All rights reserved. No part of this publication may be reproduced, translated, stored in a retrieval system, or transmitted in any form or by any means, electronic, mechanical, photocopying, recording or otherwise, without prior written permission from the publisher.

Authorization to photocopy items for internal or personal use is granted by Koninklijke Brill NV provided that the appropriate fees are paid directly to The Copyright Clearance Center, 222 Rosewood Drive, Suite 910, Danvers MA 01923, USA.
Fees are subject to change.

# Table of Contents

|   | | |
|---|---|---|
|   | Preface | vii |
| 1 | Business and Human Rights After Ruggie: Foundations, the Art of Simplification and the Imperative of Cumulative Progress<br>*Radu Mares* | 1 |
| 2 | The Ruggie Rules: Applying Human Rights Law to Corporations<br>*John H. Knox* | 51 |
| 3 | The Development of the 'UN Framework': A Pragmatic Process Towards a Pragmatic Output<br>*Karin Buhmann* | 85 |
| 4 | Contextualising the Business Responsibility to Respect: How Much Is Lost in Translation?<br>*Fiona Haines, Kate Macdonald and Samantha Balaton-Chrimes* | 107 |
| 5 | Remodelling Responsible Supply Chain Management: The Corporate Responsibility to Respect Human Rights in Supply Chain Relationships<br>*Sune Skadegaard Thorsen and Signe Andreasen* | 129 |
| 6 | Human Rights in the Supply Chain: Influence and Accountability<br>*Karin Lukas* | 151 |
| 7 | Responsibility to Respect: Why the Core Company Should Act When Affiliates Infringe Human Rights<br>*Radu Mares* | 169 |
| 8 | The Monster Under the Bed: Financial Services and the Ruggie Framework<br>*Mary Dowell-Jones and David Kinley* | 193 |

| | | |
|---|---|---|
| 9 | Human Rights Norms for Business: The Missing Piece of the Ruggie Jigsaw – The Case of Institutional Investors<br>*Rory Sullivan and Nicolas Hachez* | 217 |
| 10 | Pushing the Boundaries: The Role of National Human Rights Institutions in Operationalising the 'Protect, Respect and Remedy' Framework<br>*Meg Brodie* | 245 |
| 11 | Ruggie's Diplomatic Project and Its Missing Regulatory Infrastructure<br>*Christine Parker and John Howe* | 273 |
| 12 | Protect, Respect, Remedy *and Participate:* 'New Governance' Lessons for the Ruggie Framework<br>*Tara J. Melish and Errol Meidinger* | 303 |
| | List of Authors | 337 |
| | Index | 343 |

# Preface

This book originates from a meeting convened under the auspices of the Association of Human Rights Institutes (AHRI) in Copenhagen, in June 2010. By then it became obvious that John Ruggie's work as UN Special Representative for human rights and business was being favourably received by the UN Human Rights Council, and a formidable coalition made up of the Organisation for Economic Co-operation and Development (OECD), the European Union, the World Bank's International Finance Corporation (IFC), and the business-heavyweight International Organization for Standardization (ISO) was aligning behind it. The 'Protect, Respect and Remedy' Framework (2008) and the soon-to-be-released Guiding Principles on Business and Human Rights (2011) were thus likely to become the reference point for corporate social responsibility (CSR) for the next decade.

At the conclusion of the Ruggie mandate in June 2011, a momentous event in the CSR field, interested observers from diverse walks of life would inevitably ask: What value did this mandate add to the CSR field? Are the foundations of this work solid? Will Ruggie's efforts be consequential in practice for the benefit of rightholders? What are the implications for business and policymakers? How would Ruggie's argumentation fare with professionals interested in regulation and governance issues? The demand for a quality academic publication was obvious.

Most fortunately for this project enough authors that have left their mark in the area of corporate responsibility opted in. As the chapters bear witness, the contributors took on the task of looking back critically at the foundations and creatively forward to the challenges of following up Ruggie's mandate. Authors were invited to submit advanced drafts by early May 2011 and present them at a two-day seminar at the Raoul Wallenberg Institute of Human Rights and Humanitarian Law (RWI), in Lund, Sweden. Fortunately, a majority of the authors were able to travel to RWI in mid-May 2011. At this meeting two commentators were appointed for each paper in a first round of feedback, followed by a discussion involving the rest of the authors. The same format with two commentators was employed to offer feedback to non-attending authors, via email. After further revision, each chapter was subjected to external review during June. The final manuscripts were sent in by late August 2011. John Ruggie received the entire manuscript in September and, on behalf of all authors, I would like to thank him for his expeditious comments that allowed some inaccuracies to be addressed.

On a terminological note, some writers in this volume refer to the *Ruggie* Framework while others to the *SRSG* Framework or the *UN* Framework. The editorial decision was to leave each author the discretion to use the preferred formulation. Some of those using the SRSG/UN formulation intend to emphasise that, rather than being a work simply associated with its author, this is work that the UN has sanctioned and therefore carries the weight and full authority of the UN. Other writers refer to the Ruggie Framework for simplicity while still others use it to impress the idea that the normative choices reflected in the Framework and Guiding Principles reflect the world view of their author, an outlook which is not necessarily the best way forward for business and human rights. Such subtleties notwithstanding, SRSG and Ruggie can herein be read interchangeably and refer to the same work that John Ruggie presented to and which was endorsed by the Human Rights Council.

Other terms that are used herein interchangeably concern businesses. Such is the case with regard to "multinational enterprises" (MNEs), a term preferred by the OECD, and "transnational companies" (TNCs) used in UN and International Labour Organization instruments. Similarly, unless otherwise indicated by the context, the terms "corporation", "company", "business" and "enterprise" refer to for-profit business organisations.

Finally, legal professionals might be puzzled by references to corporate "obligations", "duties" and "responsibilities". Ruggie's reports affirm a corporate *responsibility* to respect human rights and he actually explained the choice of words: "The term 'responsibility' to respect, rather than 'duty', is meant to indicate that respecting rights is not an obligation that current international human rights law generally imposes directly on companies, although elements may be reflected in domestic laws. At the international level, the corporate responsibility to respect is a standard of expected conduct acknowledged in virtually every voluntary and soft-law instrument related to corporate responsibility, and now affirmed by the Council itself." (A/HRC/14/27, 2010)

This project has been aided in important ways by numerous colleagues and friends. Among them, Timothy Maldoon, Publications Officer at RWI, processed the manuscripts thoroughly and rapidly. Martin Rosell, master student at RWI, was determined that the authors' seminar and an associated public event should run smoothly, and also perused manuscripts for imperfections. External reviewers swiftly offered valuable comments on manuscripts. Finally I would like to thank the authors that strove for high quality contributions while abiding to very tight deadlines and thus made this one of the easiest and most pleasant editorial jobs one could wish for.

Radu Mares
Lund, Sweden

# 1 Business and Human Rights After Ruggie: Foundations, the Art of Simplification and the Imperative of Cumulative Progress

Radu Mares*

## 1. Introduction

The United Nations (UN) Special Representative of the Secretary-General (SRSG) on the Issue of Human Rights and Transnational Corporations and Other Business Enterprises has now concluded his work.

Professor John Ruggie who was entrusted with the SRSG mandate expects his work, laying down the needed foundational work and now carrying the authority of the Human Rights Council (HRC), to mark 'the end of the beginning': the "Council endorsement of the Guiding Principles, by itself, will not bring business and human rights challenges to an end. But it will mark the end of the beginning: by establishing a common global platform for action, on which cumulative progress can be built, step-by-step, without foreclosing any other promising longer-term developments."[1] Let us hope that this 'end of the beginning' paraphrase of Churchill after the crucial El Alamein battle will mark a turning point in business and human rights as it did in WWII.[2]

The HRC endorsed unanimously Ruggie's reports, first in 2008 and finally in 2011. This marks a breakthrough in itself by being the first time the UN member states adopted a common position laying down standards of expected behaviour from business with regard to human rights. This mandate on business and human rights (2005–2011) came on the heels of an ill-fated standard-setting effort in the UN – the Draft

---

* Senior researcher, Raoul Wallenberg Institute of Human Rights and Humanitarian Law, Lund, Sweden.
1 *Guiding Principles on Business and Human Rights: Implementing the United Nations 'Protect, Respect and Remedy' Framework*, A/HRC/17/31, 2011, para. 13 (hereinafter 'Guiding Principles').
2 Churchill said: "This is not the end. It is not even the beginning of the end. But it is, perhaps, the end of the beginning." W. Churchill, 'The End of the Beginning', The Lord Mayor's Luncheon, Mansion House, 10 November 1942, <www.churchill-society-london.org.uk/EndoBegn.html>.

Norms (1998–2004).[3] While the Norms chose a more direct path to corporate accountability, to a large extent relying on international treaties and monitoring, and national regulations, the SRSG conceived a broader and less centralised template aimed at leveraging the responsibilities and roles of various social actors and relying on legal and other rationalities to move markets towards a more socially sustainable path.

This represents an exciting moment for the debates on corporate social responsibility (CSR): two different visions of social change and global governance are on the table. The Draft Norms' more traditional state-centric, international law-based approach meets the less centralised, governance-based outlook of the SRSG. In an unavoidably multifaceted treatment to the issue of corporate accountability, the two diverging visions rely, not surprisingly, on many common elements and building blocks that were however arranged and balanced differently. Ruggie went for a strategy of preparing a siege instead of leading a cavalry charge.

This volume aims to capture this moment in time: a moment of tacking stock of a successfully concluded mandate and of preparing for the massive task of following-up with more operational guidance, more detailed standards, more effective governance mechanisms and more finely grained conceptual treatments. It is a book delving into what the contributors perceive as the accomplishments of a mandate as well as its deficiencies and outstanding issues. The chapters that follow offer a detailed though selective treatment of the SRSG's work, with a special emphasis on its regulatory and governance features and implications.

The SRSG work, with the 'Protect, Respect and Remedy' Framework (2008) and Guiding Principles (2011) as its peak, is multilayered and comprehensive. Instead of a dry, tedious description this introductory chapter will give the floor often to the SRSG: readers will find numerous quotations and references that will allow him or her to follow Ruggie's reasoning. Ruggie should be commended for the way he explained many of his choices through accessibly-written reports, working papers, academic journal articles, speeches, interviews and private exchanges with countless individuals. Many of these documents will be referenced herein. Annex 1 to this introduction lists all the SRSG reports for easy reference. The intention here is to provide some context to the arguments contributors to this volume make and emphasise some issues of special relevance to those interested in a regulatory and governance perspective on CSR.

Although Ruggie has refused to call for an encompassing treaty on business and human rights and he concluded that businesses currently do not have legal obligations under international human rights law (IHRL), it would be a grave mistake to overlook his work as of marginal relevance to legal academics and professionals, to presume that his thinking was not informed by law. Instead there is a wealth of materials, analyses and entry points for lawyers interested in international law, human rights law, criminal law, company law, securities law, investment law, transparency laws and law of contracts. Also the broader issue of what role the law could and should play in international governance and in complex regulatory regimes is at the core of Ruggie's work.

---

3   *Norms on the Responsibilities of Transnational Corporations and Other Business Enterprises with regard to Human Rights 2003*, UN Doc. E/CN.4/Sub.2/2003/12/Rev.2 (hereinafter 'Draft Norms').

## 2. Mandate

Ruggie was appointed SRSG following the stalemate in the Commission on Human Rights in 2004. After the Sub-Commission on the Promotion and Protection of Human Rights submitted the Draft Norms to the Commission, the later decided not to endorse them; instead it asked the UN High Commissioner for Human Rights to conduct an in-depth study on "the scope and legal status of existing initiatives and standards" relating to the corporate responsibilities with regard to human rights.[4] Following the receipt of that study,[5] the Commission decided to set up the SRSG mandate for a two-year period, later prolonged with a third year. That mandate asked the SRSG to identify standards of corporate responsibility, to clarify often used CSR concepts such as 'complicity' and 'sphere of influence', to focus on human rights impact assessments, to compile best practices of states and corporations, and to elaborate on the regulating role of states.[6]

In 2008, Ruggie presented the 'Protect, Respect, Remedy' Framework. The Human Rights Council, which has replaced the Commission on Human Rights in 2006, endorsed unanimously the Framework and asked the SRSG to continue his work for another three years. The new mandate required him, among other issues, to provide concrete guidance regarding the obligations of states and responsibilities of businesses, to elaborate on the scope and content of corporate responsibility, to explore effective remedies to corporate abuses, and to continue his work in a broadly consultative manner.[7]

In 2011, Ruggie concluded his work by issuing the Guiding Principles, a set of 31 recommendations containing foundational and operational principles. The HRC adopted unanimously this document and also decided the follow-up to the SRSG mandate.[8] Thus a multistakeholder-forum on business and human rights will meet annually and a Working Group of five experts will be established for a three-year period with a multitude of tasks: dissemination, promoting implementation, best practice identification, capacity-building, country visits, recommendations on access to remedies, and dialogue and cooperation with relevant actors.[9]

---

4   Commission on Human Rights, *Responsibilities of transnational corporations and related business enterprises with regard to human rights*, Decision 2004/116.
5   *Report of the United Nations High Commissioner on Human Rights on the responsibilities of transnational corporations and related business enterprises with regard to human rights*, E/CN.4/2005/91, 2005.
6   Commission on Human Rights, *Human rights and transnational corporations and other business enterprises*, Resolution 2005/69, 2005.
7   Human Rights Council, *Mandate of the Special Representative of the Secretary-General on the issue of human rights and transnational corporations and other business enterprises*, Resolution 8/7, 2008.
8   Human Rights Council, *Human rights and transnational corporations and other business enterprises*, A/HRC/17/L.17/Rev.1, 2011.
9   Ibid.

## 3. Framework and Guiding Principles

The 'Protect, Respect, Remedy' Framework can be succinctly summarised, in Ruggie's own words, as follows:

> The Framework rests on three pillars. The first is the State duty to protect against human rights abuses by third parties, including business enterprises, through appropriate policies, regulation, and adjudication. The second is the corporate responsibility to respect human rights, which means that business enterprises should act with due diligence to avoid infringing on the rights of others and to address adverse impacts with which they are involved. The third is the need for greater access by victims to effective remedy, both judicial and non-judicial. Each pillar is an essential component in an inter-related and dynamic system of preventative and remedial measures: the State duty to protect because it lies at the very core of the international human rights regime; the corporate responsibility to respect because it is the basic expectation society has of business in relation to human rights; and access to remedy because even the most concerted efforts cannot prevent all abuse.[10]

Specifically on corporate responsibilities, the responsibility to respect (RtR) contained in Pillar 2 calls for "an ongoing process of human rights due diligence, whereby companies become aware of, prevent, and mitigate adverse human rights impacts. The four core elements of human rights due diligence [are]: having a human rights policy, assessing human rights impacts of company activities, integrating those values and findings into corporate cultures and management systems, and tracking as well as reporting performance."[11]

The normative orientation of the RtR is provided by international law standards. In explaining which rights the due diligence process should encompass, Ruggie wrote:

> The answer is simple – in principle, all internationally recognized human rights ... because companies can affect the entire spectrum of rights ... [C]ompanies at a minimum should look to the International Bill of Human Rights – the Universal Declaration and the two Covenants – as well as the ILO Declaration on Fundamental Principles and Rights at Work. They should do so for two reasons. First, the principles these instruments embody are the most universally agreed upon by the international community. Second, they are the main benchmarks against which other social actors judge the human rights impacts of companies.[12]

---

10   Guiding Principles, *supra* note 1, para. 6.
11   *Business and human rights: Towards operationalizing the 'protect, respect and remedy' framework*, A/HRC/11/13, 2009, para. 49 (hereinafter 'Towards operationalizing').
12   *Ibid.*, paras. 52–54.

## 4. Approach and Results of the SRSG Mandate

In the pursuit of his 2005 mandate, Ruggie set himself to deliver not an international code of conduct containing corporate responsibilities and an implementation mechanism. Instead he conceived a broader framework able, in the words of the High Commissioner for Human Rights, "to guide the understanding of, as well as responses to, the issue of business and human rights".[13] His premise has been that

> The root cause of the business and human rights predicament today lies in the governance gaps created by globalization – between the scope and impact of economic forces and actors, and the capacity of societies to manage their adverse consequences. These governance gaps provide the permissive environment for wrongful acts by companies of all kinds without adequate sanctioning or reparation. How to narrow and ultimately bridge the gaps in relation to human rights is our fundamental challenge.[14]

In his effort to challenge that 'permissive environment' Ruggie demonstrated his ability to simplify and reframe CSR discussions. 'Simplify' because he appears to have extracted three key aspects (the three 'pillars') that have been familiar in CSR debates, structured the analysis around them and got the acceptance of key stakeholders.[15] However, as it often happens, the devil can be in the details, where controversies have erupted and linger on. However this simplification and streamlining has been important in securing the buy-in for the Framework from diverse stakeholders. Ruggie himself wrote about his pursuit for a shared understanding and securing support from various constituencies:[16]

> Two main achievements are widely attributed to the SRSG's mandate:
> 1. Generating a profound shift in the dynamic of the business and human rights debate, from deep polarization among stakeholder groups in 2005 to a greater shared understanding of business and human rights challenges;
> 2. Securing wide multi-stakeholder support for the 'Protect, Respect and Remedy' Framework and the Guiding Principles for its implementation as the foundation for better managing those challenges going forward.[17]

---

13  N. Pillay (United Nations High Commissioner for Human Rights), 'The Corporate Responsibility to Respect: A Human Rights Milestone', *Annual Labour and Social Policy Review* (2008), <www.ohchr.org/Documents/Press/HC_contribution_on_Business_and_HR.pdf>.

14  *Protect, Respect and Remedy: a Framework for Business and Human Rights*, A/HRC/8/5, 2008, para. 3 (hereinafter 'Protect, Respect and Remedy').

15  See the chapter by Melish and Meidinger in this volume, arguing in favour of a forth pillar – the 'Participate' pillar – that Ruggie should have recognised.

16  *See especially* the chapter by Parker and Howe in this volume, analysing Ruggie's diplomatic project.

17  *Recommendations on Follow-Up to the Mandate*, Mandate of the Special Representative of the Secretary-General (SRSG) on the Issue of Human Rights and Transnational Cor-

A prime example of reframing is the well-known state obligation to protect human rights.[18] By offering a Framework instead of a code of conduct, Ruggie ensured that the CSR discussion is not carried in a vacuum. There is a difference in emphasis which reflects different thinking: while most other CSR instruments affirm and stress in the preamble and first article the obligations of states under international human rights law,[19] the rest of the text tends to be devoted to corporate responsibilities. Ruggie employed a different structure: state duties and corporate responsibilities would both be 'pillars' under a construction that stands precariously if a pillar is too weak. In other words, treatments of CSR that do not lose sight of the duties and roles of states have more potential to solve human rights problems in practice. Furthermore, in the economy of the SRSG reports, each pillar takes quite an equal space; there is no imbalance here either. In addition, not only are the duties of states restated, but they are detailed to point at inconsistencies in state practice,[20] they cover both host and home states of multinational enterprises (MNEs), and they account for states as both regulators and economic actors. This reframing and comprehensiveness pays dividends: the result is a governance template that discusses responsibilities and roles and aims to prompt diverse actors into (concerted) action. Ruggie strives to leverage influence from different quarters by showing how inaction, inconsistencies and irresponsibility feed on each other to allow impunity.

Linked to the task of securing stakeholder buy-in, Ruggie employed a participatory approach throughout his mandates. He has arranged seminars, conferences, field studies and other engagement avenues that he used to collect views and communicate his work.[21] Make no mistake, this approach was also clearly outlined in the UN mandate as a reaction to some criticisms that the Draft Norms process had received.[22] Furthermore, Ruggie networked widely and commissioned studies from various organisations, law firms and experts in an attempt to leverage expertise on punctual

---

porations and other Business Enterprises, 2011, <www.business-humanrights.org/media/documents/ruggie/ruggie-special-mandate-follow-up-11-feb-2011.pdf>.

18   For a discussion about the nature of a state's obligation to protect, *see* M. Hakimi, 'State Bystander Responsibility', 21:2 *The European Journal of International Law* (2010) pp. 341–385.
19   For example, the Draft Norms read: "States have the primary responsibility to promote, secure the fulfilment of, respect, ensure respect of, and protect human rights recognised in international as well as national law, including assuring that transnational corporations and other business enterprises respect human rights." Draft Norms, *supra* note 3, para. 1.
20   Ruggie referred to "'vertical' incoherence, where governments take on human rights commitments without regard to implementation; and 'horizontal' incoherence, where departments – such as trade, investment promotion, development, foreign affairs – work at cross purposes with the State's human rights obligations and the agencies charged with implementing them." Protect, Respect and Remedy, *supra* note 14, para. 33.
21   *See* the chapter by Buhmann in this volume detailing the participatory process throughout the SRSG mandate.
22   Commission on Human Rights, *supra* note 6, para. 3.

issues.²³ This approach has generated a remarkable effervescency and engagement in the legal community, for example. Finally, Ruggie engaged with countless individuals, critics and supporters alike, through open letters or private exchanges. At the end of his mandate the HRC commended Ruggie for "the broad range of activities undertaken …, including in particular the comprehensive, transparent and inclusive consultations conducted with relevant and interested actors in all regions".²⁴ Echoing this perception, the European Union stated that "there is no doubt that the success results from the inclusive approach of a process where States, business actors and civil society were fully associated".²⁵

Ruggie has made a deliberate push to key organisations in an effort to scale up the impacts of his work in the UN.²⁶ Notable has been his promotion of the human rights 'due diligence' idea to the Organization for Economic Co-operation and Development (OECD), the World Bank's International Finance Corporation (IFC) and the European Commission (EC). All these organisations had CSR policy instruments preceding the SRSG mandate; these instruments have or will be updated in light of the SRSG work. Ruggie also influenced the International Organisation for Standardisation (ISO) as it was preparing its first Guidance on social responsibility, the ISO 26000, which is an important document given the ISO's broad reach into the business community.

Ruggie defined his approach as a "principled form of pragmatism: an unflinching commitment to the principle of strengthening the promotion and protection of human rights as it relates to business, coupled with a pragmatic attachment to what works best in creating change where it matters most – in the daily lives of people".²⁷ It is in relation to principled pragmatism where the discussion of policy choices and surrounding controversies fits in: Should Ruggie have proposed to the HRC the pursuit of an international treaty on CSR? Should he have maintained that companies have legal responsibilities under IHRL? Should corporate responsibilities extend beyond 'respecting' towards 'securing' human rights? Do states have an obligation to reach extraterritorially as part of their duty to protect against corporate abuses? It is now

---

23   See the SRSG website at <www.business-humanrights.org/SpecialRepPortal/Home>.

24   Human Rights Council, *Human rights and transnational corporations and other business enterprises*, A/HRC/RES/17/4, 2011.

25   *EU comments on the draft Guiding Principles for the implementation of the UN 'Protect, Respect, Remedy' Framework*, D(2011) 702 246, 31 January 2011, <ec.europa.eu/enterprise/policies/sustainable-business/files/business-human-rights/eu_statement_final_en.pdf>.

26   Ruggie said: "At the same time as I've been working through UN, I've also been working with a number of other international institutions to make sure that their policies become aligned with the UN Framework and Guiding Principles … It is important for such convergence to take place, and because it makes it more likely that there will be a level playing field for all." 'Business and Human Rights: Together At Last?', A Conversation with John Ruggie, *Fletcher Forum of World Affairs*, Summer 2011, pp. 121–122.

27   *Interim Report of the Special Representative of the Secretary-General on the Issue of Human Rights and Transnational Corporations and Other Business Enterprises*, E/CN.4/2006/97, 2006, para. 81 (hereinafter 'Interim Report').

clear that the element of pragmatism has been vindicated by the HRC's unanimous endorsements in 2008 and 2011. But the principled part will be unmistakably dependent on how effective Ruggie's strategy of change will prove to be, as Ruggie himself rightly noted in his sobering 'end of the beginning' remarks.[28]

Ruggie has enriched the field of business and human rights as a result of his six-year mandate. This is partly due to him not shying away from controversy; his choices and explanations have offered at least a reasoned reference point for supporters and dissenters to reflect upon. He came forward with painstaking explanations when, for example, he dismissed the conceptual approach taken by the Draft Norms or when he refused to call for a encompassing treaty on CSR. The battle of ideas could only benefit from such opportunities for frank and reasoned discussions, which are bound to continue after the mandate was concluded. In connection with this, the SRSG reports sometime strike as models of learned yet accessibly-written argumentation. While all sides – Ruggie and his diverse contestants – agreed that individuals everywhere require better protection against human rights abuses occurring in business operations, Ruggie's elaborations presented with unprecedented clarity some tensions, complexities and choices. While various actors predictably and legitimately disagree on some of the choices made in the Framework and General Principles, there is little doubt that the business and human rights discourse is now at another level than it was in 2005.

Another contributor to Ruggie's 'enrichment' legacy in the field has to do with the broad governance outlook he adopted. Ruggie sought to identify key tensions crisscrossing the CSR body, and to impress a system of interlocking roles and responsibilities. Getting hold conceptually of such a polycentric governance model is significantly more complicated than the state-centric, treaty-driven model offered by the Draft Norms. Ruggie did not offer, neither could he within the format of the SRSG reports, a fine-grained model of governance in the CSR area. He limited himself to discard, impress and outline. Delving deeper into the dynamics of CSR regimes to understand their functioning and how to design for effectiveness is surely the next step if governance-based conceptualisations of CSR are to deliver on their promise. As Ruggie decided to remain involved with the business and human rights field after the conclusion of his mandate, including writing a book, it is hoped that he will refine further the polycentric governance regime in the business and human rights area.[29]

In a few years Ruggie developed a broad portfolio of materials that could be readily accessed and referenced to support and clarify his position.[30] He has methodically covered punctual issues through his reports, addendums, scholarly articles, conference speeches, interviews, and commissioned studies from prestigious organisations. Based on this approach, Ruggie's credentials as a top thinker in his academic field,[31]

---

28  See text associated with *supra* note 1.
29  J. G. Ruggie, *Post-Mandate Plans*, 18 July 2011, <business-humanrights.org/media/documents/ruggie/ruggie-post-mandate-plans-18-jul-2011.pdf>.
30  See Annex 1 in this chapter for his reports, and the SRSG website (*supra* note 23) for additional studies commissioned or submitted during the SRSG mandate.
31  See the chapter by Melish and Meidinger in this volume where they discuss Ruggie's background and his sociological institutionalist approach to system transformation.

his experience in high positions in the UN allowing for navigation of the treacherous currents in the UN,[32] his astonishing energy of making contact with diverse audiences, and the counter-instinctive fit of a political scientist asked to bring clarity to a domain – human rights – traditionally occupied by lawyers have all conspired to deliver through the last six years the first UN-endorsed global instrument on business and human rights and the most advanced conceptual elaboration on business and human rights carried out in an international governmental organisation to date.

## 5. Draft Norms versus Framework: Between Polarisation and Similarities

As mentioned before, the SRSG mandate was set up because work on the Draft Norms came to a standstill as business opposition intensified and state support in the Commission on Human Rights proved to be lacking. Non-governmental organisations (NGOs) championed the Draft Norms for a few key reasons: the promise of legally binding obligations on business, through an international treaty and subsequently national laws; the sweeping obligations on companies expected not only to 'respect' human rights, but to 'promote', 'protect', 'secure' and 'ensure respect' of human rights;[33] and the monitoring and verification to be provided by international organisations, such as the UN, and national mechanisms.[34] Although nobody – including the drafters and supporting NGOs – harboured any doubts that the Draft Norms were a work in progress that required further refinement, they sensed the importance of kick-starting an international rule-making process to hold companies accountable. To put it differently, no matter the possible shortcomings of the Norms initial draft in concept or formulation, they would pale in comparison with the importance of kick-starting the process.

Ruggie however was concerned, policymaking-wise, by the states' lack of willingness to adopt and then to actually enforce an international legal instrument. Concept-wise, he was critical in regard to the perceived lack of foundations, boundaries and specificity characterising the Draft Norms' approach to corporate responsibilities. In this regard Ruggie explained extensively his decision to dismiss the Norms; he questioned, among other aspects, why different actors would have similar sweeping obligations[35] and how the resulting overlap of state and corporate obligations would affect the governance system.[36] These aspects, Ruggie felt, have derailed the Draft Norms

---

32   Ruggie served as Assistant Secretary-General and Chief Adviser for strategic planning to UN Secretary-General Kofi Anann (1997–2001).
33   Draft Norms, para. 1, *supra* note 3.
34   *Ibid.*, paras. 15–17.
35   Ruggie drew attention that "[w]hile corporations may be considered 'organs of society', they are specialized economic organs, not democratic public interest institutions. As such, their responsibilities cannot and should not simply mirror the duties of States." Protect, Respect and Remedy, *supra* note 14, para. 53.
36   The overlap of responsibilities would invite "endless strategic gaming by states and companies alike". Interim Report, *supra* note 27, para. 68. Further Ruggie wrote: "The corpo-

and would do so again with regard to his mandate.[37] If the Norms process was actually delivering just an illusion, Ruggie chose to outline what he thought could conceptually and feasibly move the debate closer to a path of improved business practices and ultimately accountability for rights violations. Ruggie summarised well the interests of some key stakeholders in the controversy surrounding the Draft Norms:

> It would be surprising if all major actors in the 'Norms' debate, quite apart from the substantive merits of their arguments, did not also behave strategically, in keeping with their perceived interests. Business typically dislikes binding regulations until it sees their necessity or inevitability. Governments often support the preferences of corporations domiciled in their countries and/or compete for foreign investment. And the imprimatur of 'UN Norms' would have provided NGOs with a powerful campaign tool: declaring certain corporate acts to be 'illegal' has far greater social purchase, even in the absence of viable enforcement mechanisms, than merely claiming corporate 'wrongdoing.'[38]

The fate of the Draft Norms continues to polarise writers almost a decade after their peak in 2004,[39] including contributors to this volume. The Norms versus Ruggie controversy is fading in importance, particularly now that the SRSG project was endorsed by the HRC while the Norms were not. Also the thinking behind the SRSG approach has been refined and presented in much more detail than the drafters of the Norms had or could have done. In the same time, and without overlooking the fundamental disagreement on the social change process at hand, there are some surprising similarities that invite us to leave behind some of the controversy.

For example, the Draft Norms mention the 'due diligence' concept that came to define Ruggie's approach to corporate responsibilities. The Commentary to the Norms reads: "Transnational corporations and other business enterprises shall have the responsibility to use due diligence in ensuring that their activities do not contribute directly or indirectly to human abuses ..."[40] Further elaboration of what due diligence

---

rate responsibility to respect exists independently of States' duties. Therefore, there is no need for the slippery distinction between 'primary' State and 'secondary' corporate obligations – which in any event would invite endless strategic gaming on the ground about who is responsible for what." Protect, Respect and Remedy, *supra* note 14, para. 55.

37  Ruggie outlines in detail the conceptual flaws of the Draft Norms, as he perceived them, in J. G. Ruggie, 'Business and Human Rights – The Evolving International Agenda', *American Journal of International Law* (2007) p. 822. (hereinafter 'Evolving Agenda').

38  *Ibid.*, p. 822.

39  The OHCHR summarised in 2005 the main arguments against and in favour of the Draft Norms. Report of the High Commissioner, *supra* note 5, paras. 20–21.

40  *Commentary for the Norms on the Responsibilities of Transnational Corporations and Other Business Enterprises with Regard to Human Rights*, E/CN.4/Sub.2/2003/38 (2003), para. A.1.b), <www1.umn.edu/humanrts/links/CommentApril2003.html>.

entails has been welcomed both by Ruggie himself[41] and by supporters of the Norms.[42] Another commonality revolves around the value of transparency. While the Norms expected businesses to 'periodically report' on the implementation of the Norms (paragraph 15), Ruggie expects companies to 'know and show' that they respect human rights (Guiding Principle No. 21). Finally, although the role of law seems to be the supreme polariser in the Norms-Ruggie debate, a more nuanced understanding is needed. As a later section will show, Ruggie did not endorse an *international* and *overarching* legal instrument on CSR at *this moment in time*, while he explicitly affirmed the necessity or at least encouraged states to consider a *specific* international treaty (on international crimes), *national* laws in various fields, and that all these interventions are called for *now*. In the coming years it will be important to attempt to focus on such commonalities between the Norms and the Framework without obscuring their different visions of social change and the role of law in the process.

## 6. Ruggie on Voluntarism

Ruggie's opinion on corporate voluntarism cannot be deduced from two of his decisions that antagonised many NGOs: international human rights law by itself does not currently impose legal obligations on companies,[43] and the SRSG will not recommend the HRC to pursue an international treaty laying down corporate obligations. Indeed, on a number of occasions Ruggie made explicit remarks about the potential as well as the inherent limits of corporate voluntarism and multistakeholder CSR initiatives.[44]

The inherent limits of voluntarism have to do with participation and accountability and are well-known: voluntary approaches alone cannot coerce unwilling companies to adopt CSR policies or to join multistakeholder initiatives; neither could they thereafter force companies to abide by their stated CSR commitments. To achieve uni-

---

41  Ruggie wrote: "Had the Norms exercise confined itself to compiling such an inventory [of human rights instruments], coupled with a set of benchmarks of what practices business must or should avoid, and what it could help to achieve, the subsequent debate might have focused on substantive issues: What belongs on the list, what doesn't, and why? What are the different categories of business responsibilities, ranging from the mandatory to the desirable? How can broad principles best be translated into management practices and tools? In short, the relevant stakeholders might well have focused on the sorts of operational issues that have been taken up by a group of ten companies known as the Business Leaders for International Human Rights (BLIHR), which are engaged in a constructive effort to explore whether and how some of the concrete provisions of the Norms can be turned into company policies, processes and procedures." Interim Report, *supra* note 27, paras. 57–58.

42  The chapter by Sullivan and Hachez in this volume indicates that there is value in re-using the Draft Norms' orientation in the guise of the BLIHR's detailed list of corporate responsibilities.

43  For an analysis of corporate responsibilities under international human rights law, *see* the chapter by Knox in this volume.

44  For examples of corporate voluntarism, *see* United Nations Global Compact and Office of the High Commissioner of Human Rights, *Embedding Human Rights in Business Practice*, 3 volumes (2004, 2007, 2009).

form coverage and coercion, law has a privileged position due to its unique ability to systematically tackle wrongdoers. As Ruggie wrote, "[a]t the risk of sounding like a heretic, I would contend that private governance arrangements, no matter how successful, can take us only so far. They will remain relatively small islands of progress unless their achievements are rooted in, and generalized through, the sphere of public authority."[45] Elsewhere Ruggie asked the key question: "How can current CSR initiatives be scaled up and connected, in order to establish an interlocking network of regulatory instruments and governance structures?" In a sobering view of the limits of CSR he remarked:

> At the end of the day, none of these efforts of aggregation and leveraging can be successful without governments, because governments are the global embodiment of representative politics. Yet, at the same time, when devising strategies for change, it is not always wise to begin with governments. Now that I am no longer at the UN, I can confess to that heretical thought.[46]

## 7. Ruggie on Law

Ruggie stated that he understood that his "mandate is intended to be primarily evidence based".[47] Through the years he took note of laws and contracts, both of which create legal obligations for businesses. He covered numerous bodies of law at national and international levels. There are recent legal developments of high relevance to human rights and a few should be succinctly discussed here.

### 7.1. Recent Legal Developments

Ruggie concurs with an assessment of globalisation often voiced in civil society circles. He acknowledged that "the backlash [against globalization and global market integration] is triggered by a growing imbalance in global rule making. Those rules that favour global market expansion have become more robust and enforceable ... [b]ut rules intended to promote equally valid social objectives, be they labor standards, human

---

45   J. G. Ruggie, *The Global Compact and the Challenges of Global Governance*, Annual Meeting, Global Compact Learning Forum, 11–13 December 2002, p. 3. See also R. Mares, *The Dynamics of Corporate Social Responsibilities* (Martinus Nijhoff Publishers, 2008) pp. 158–164.

46   Carnegie Council on Ethics and International Affairs, *The Impact of Corporations on Global Governance*, A Report of the Empire and Democracy Project (Carnegie Council, New York, 2004), pp. 11 and 23.

47   Interim Report, *supra* note 27, para. 7. "But insofar as it involves assessing difficult situations that are themselves in flux, it inevitably will also entail making normative judgments. In the SRSG's case, the basis for those judgments might best be described as a principled form of pragmatism ..." *Ibid.*, para. 81.

rights, environmental quality or poverty reduction, lag behind and in some instances actually have become weaker." [48]

### 7.1.1. Transparency

The bulk of recent laws adopted at national level aim to enhance transparency; corporations are required to disclose information on various aspects of their operations with direct or indirect implications for human rights. For example, the Dodd–Frank Act (2010) in the US has two relevant sections.[49] Section 1502 refers to conflict minerals that are used to finance violent conflicts in the Democratic Republic of Congo (DRC). It asks companies to disclose annually whether their products are 'DRC conflict free' or not, and to describe the due diligence measures the company takes to track such minerals in its supply chain. Preliminary data indicates the dramatic effect of this transparency law.[50] Section 1504 requires extractive companies (oil, natural gas and minerals) to disclose the payments (taxes, royalties, license fees, production entitlements and bonuses) they make to foreign governments.[51] This allows investors to assess better the risks entailed by their investments.[52] The Securities and Exchange Commission (SEC) is about to issue detailed rules for implementing the law.[53]

---

48  J. G. Ruggie, 'Taking Embedded Liberalism Global: The Corporate Connection', in J. G. Ruggie (ed.), *Embedding Global markets: An Enduring Challenge* (Ashgate, 2008) p. 234 (reference omitted).

49  Dodd–Frank Wall Street Reform and Consumer Protection Act (2010).

50  A World Bank source reported that "[a]lmost everything came to a standstill" following the passage of the US law. "Increased scrutiny of companies working in the region has caused mineral buyers including Traxys SA, Malaysia Smelting Corp. and Amalgamated Metals Plc to curtail or eliminate their purchases, and most trade from eastern Congo ground to a halt April 1. That month, electronics-industry groups implemented new guidelines for mineral smelters to ensure their products were 'conflict-free'." M. J. Kavanagh, 'Congo Government Asks U.S. to Use OECD Guidance for Conflict-Mineral Rules', *Bloomberg*, 28 July 2011, <www.bloomberg.com/news/2011-07-28/congo-government-asks-u-s-to-use-oecd-guidance-for-conflict-mineral-rules.html>; Motorola: "The law created a de facto ban on minerals in the Congo." J. Bardelline, 'Motorola Seeks a Conflict-Free Electronics Supply Chain in the DRC', *Greenbiz*, 12 July 2011, <www.greenbiz.com/news/2011/07/12/motorola-seeks-conflict-free-electronics-supply-chain-drc>.

51  K. M. Martorana, *Legislating Transparency in the Extractive Sector: Will the Securities and Exchange Commission take the lead?*, Oxfam America, 12 July 2011, <www.policyinnovations.org/ideas/innovations/data/000196>.

52  For how investors factor tax information in their decisions, *see* C.t Investments, *Materiality of disclosure required by the Energy Security through Transparency Act*, 2010, <www.calvert.com/NRC/literature/documents/10003.pdf>.

53  *See* the debate before the SEC with diverging submissions asking the SEC to require detailed data, as NGOs and some institutional investors prefer, or more aggregated data, as the industry argues. Examples of the former position are Revenue Watch International (K. Lissakers, Submission to SEC, 6 December 2010) and Calvert Asset Management Company (B. Freeman *et al.*, Submission to SEC, 15 November 2010). Examples of the latter position come from Shell (Submission by M. J. ten Brink, Executive Vice President Controller,

Along the same lines, California adopted in 2010 a law requiring disclosures on goods tainted with slavery and human trafficking. The law states that "[c]onsumers and businesses are inadvertently promoting and sanctioning these crimes through the purchase of goods and products that have been tainted in the supply chain". Therefore it requires "retail sellers and manufacturers doing business in the state to disclose their efforts to eradicate slavery and human trafficking from their direct supply chains …".[54] Stronger yet is the EC approach to combat illegal logging by tackling the trade in illegally harvested wood. The regulation to come in force in 2013 imposes a traceability obligation on traders and a due diligence system on operators to prohibit entry.[55]

The European Union (EU) has endorsed Ruggie's Framework and Guiding Principles and emphasised that it "was highly supportive from the outset".[56] The European Commission is currently considering amending the Directive on annual and consolidated accounts[57] to enhance the disclosure of non-financial information by enterprises.[58] A recent, large report from the EC wrote: "For public policy, when a company is obliged, coaxed or encouraged to report on its CSR activities, it is a key means of 'leveraging' more CSR."[59]

### 7.1.2. Company Law and the Corporate Governance

Transparency, augmented by 'comply or explain' requirements, has been a trademark of the corporate governance area.[60] This approach was introduced first in the UK. Since

---

Royal Dutch Shell plc, 25 October 2010) and American Petroleum Institute (Submission by K. Isakower and P. Mulva, 9 December 2010). All submissions are available on the SEC website, *Specialized Disclosures: Title XV Provisions of the Dodd-Frank Wall Street Reform and Consumer Protection Act*, <www.sec.gov/comments/df-title-xv/specialized-disclosures/specialized-disclosures.shtml>.

54  California Transparency in Supply Chains Act of 2010, <info.sen.ca.gov/pub/09-10/bill/sen/sb_0651-0700/sb_657_bill_20100930_chaptered.html>.

55  Regulation (EU) No 995/2010 of the European Parliament and of the Council of 20 October 2010 laying down the obligations of operators who place timber and timber products on the market, *Official Journal of the European Union*, 12 November 2010.

56  In addition, the EU showed that "[t]he European Commission has recently completed a guide on the social considerations in public procurement, launched an ongoing public consultation on non-financial reporting and expects to put forward a new policy initiative on corporate social responsibility later this year, including proposals on how to implement further the UN Framework". EU Comments, *supra* note 25.

57  Directive 2003/51/EC on the annual and consolidated accounts of certain types of companies, banks and other financial institutions and insurance undertakings.

58  For submissions received during the public consultation period, and other documents *see* <ec.europa.eu/enterprise/policies/sustainable-business/corporate-social-responsibility/reporting-disclosure/index_en.htm>.

59  V. Wensen *et al.*, *The State of Play in Sustainability Reporting in the European Union*, European Union, 2011, p. 5.

60  As a definition, the OECD writes that "[c]orporate governance involves a set of relationships between a company's management, its board, its shareholders and other stakehold-

1993, companies listed on the London Stock Exchange are required to include in annual reports a narrative statement of how they apply the principles of the 'Combined Code'. The 'comply or explain' provision requires a statement as to whether or not the company has complied with the Code and, if not, to give reasons for any non-compliance.[61] Since 2006, the EU also has a 'comply or explain' provision to promote better corporate governance. A Directive requires listed companies to include a corporate governance statement in its annual report containing a reference to the corporate governance code to which the company subscribes and to the extent to which the company departs from this code an explanation as to the reasons for not applying it.[62]

The regulations above exhibit mandatory reporting coupled to an authoritative and detailed code, or 'soft law' instrument. Simpler versions that, at least for the time being, lose the soft law component exist in the US. There, the Sarbanes Oxley Act (2002) requires, among others, that companies either adopt and then disclose a 'code of ethics' addressing compliance with law and ethical conduct by key corporate officers, or explain publicly why the company has not adopted such a code.[63] As Catá Backer explains, "the object was not to impose ethics codes but to create a legal framework within which stakeholders could negotiate the extent and terms of such codes".[64] There is an evolutionary component built in this regulatory strategy as there is always the possibility to add later the authoritative and more detailed soft law standards.

To remain in the corporate governance area, some states have adopted regulations asking institutional investors themselves, rather than the companies they invest in, to be more transparent on their investment decisions. Back in 1999, the CSR community welcomed the UK's Occupational Pension Schemes Regulations which asked pension funds to state "the extent (if at all) to which social, environmental or ethical considerations are taken into account in the selection, retention and realisation of investments".[65] This example was quickly replicated in Australia, with more detail

---

ers. Corporate governance also provides the structure through which the objectives of the company are set, and the means of attaining those objectives and monitoring performance are determined." *OECD Principles of Corporate Governance*, OECD, 2004, Preface, p. 11.

61   Para. 12.43A of the *London Stock Exchange Listing Rules*.
62   Amendments to Directive 78/660/EEC, Article 46a, Directive 2006/46/EC amending Council Directives 78/660/EEC on the annual accounts of certain types of companies, 83/349/EEC on consolidated accounts, 86/635/EEC on the annual accounts and consolidated accounts of banks and other financial institutions and 91/674/EEC on the annual accounts and consolidated accounts of insurance undertakings, *Official Journal of the European Union*, 16 August 2006. See also European Commission, *The EU corporate governance framework*, Green Paper, COM(2011) 164 final, 2011, p. 2.
63   *Sarbanes–Oxley Act*, Section 406 (a)(b) 'Code of Ethics for Senior Financial Officers' in Title IV 'Enhanced Financial Disclosures'.
64   L. Catá Backer, 'From Moral Obligation to International Law: Disclosure Systems, Markets and the Regulation of Multinational Corporations', 39 *Georgetown Journal of International Law* (2008) p. 138.
65   *Occupational Pension Schemes (Investment, and Assignment, Forfeiture, Bankruptcy etc.) Amendment Regulations 1999*, Article 11A. The effects of the law can be gleaned from the

required from a broader range of institutional investors.[66] These laws clearly legitimise a discussion of CSR among corporate governance stakeholders. But they also remove explicit prohibitions or implicit understandings prompting investment managers to ignore CSR considerations. Indeed a study commissioned by Ruggie described how some investment funds in Australia and the US are not allowed to take CSR into account.[67] Such apparently 'mild' legal provisions thus serve a useful purpose, and Ruggie noted in relation to the UK law that "the government recently confirmed that pension fund trustees are not prohibited from considering social, environmental and ethical issues in their investment decisions, provided they act in the fund's best interests. This guidance stemmed from calls to reform legislation governing pension funds to explicitly allow, and in some cases require, consideration of social and environmental issues, including human rights."[68]

There should be no mistake when assessing the flurry of corporate governance regulations relevant to CSR: these regulations aim to enlarge managers' margin of manoeuvre and guide them to a better identification of new types of risks. The purpose though remains the same: high return on investment and corporate profitability. Clarifications in company law, as done extensively in the UK in 2006, are meant to dispel misunderstandings and eliminate express prohibitions for taking CSR into account, but clearly they are not meant to have human rights trump profitability. The UK Companies Act clarifies what the duty of care that business directors have under company law entails:

> A director of a company must act in the way he considers, in good faith, would be most likely to promote the success of the company for the benefit of its members as a whole, and in doing so have regard (amongst other matters) to –
> (a) the likely consequences of any decision in the long term,
> (b) the interests of the company's employees,

---

biennial survey on responsible investment practices of UK corporate pension funds that the USKIF publishes. See UK Sustainable Investment and Finance, *Responsible Business: Sustainable Pension*, 2011, <www.uksif.org/cmsfiles/281411/25_Aug_UKSIF_Pensions_Report_2011.pdf>.

66  For how the Australian regime has delivered transparency in the last decade, especially the effectiveness of the guidance provided by the Commission and the compliance response from the industry, see E. Banasik, M. Barut and L. Kloot, 'Socially Responsible Investment: Labour Standards and Environmental, Social and Ethical Disclosures within the SRI Industry', *Australian Accounting Review*, No. 55 Vol. 20 Issue 4, 2010.

67  For example, and SRSG report noted that "[i]n the U.S. the Department of Labor has guidelines which formalize the ambit of a fund manager's discretion. Under these guidelines, the managers of employee benefit plans may 'never subordinate the economic interests of the plan to unrelated objectives, and may not select investments on the basis of any factor outside the economic interest of the plan.'" *Human rights and corporate law: trends and observations from a crossnational study conducted by the Special Representative*, Addendum 2 to the Report, A/HRC/17/31/Add.2, 2011, para. 175 (hereinafter 'Human rights and corporate law').

68  Ibid., para. 176.

(c) the need to foster the company's business relationships with suppliers, customers and others,
(d) the impact of the company's operations on the community and the environment,
(e) the desirability of the company maintaining a reputation for high standards of business conduct ... [69]

To promote the respect of this duty, the law requires a report ('the business review') with the purpose "to inform members of the company and help them assess how the directors have performed their duty under section 172 (duty to promote the success of the company)".[70]

When company laws in other jurisdictions do not refer explicitly to the interests of the shareholders and instead use formulations such as the 'best interests of the company', an opening seems to appear to play up the interests of stakeholders. "One could interpret 'the company' as a reference to a social institution, creating a duty to act in the interests of all stakeholders instead of just shareholders alone", an International Commission of Jurists study remarked.[71] But it rightly warned that "[e]nthusiasm for these possibilities should remain cautious ... More inclusive fiduciary duties do not respond to *the danger that victim's interests will be recognised, but outweighed. Responding to this means imposing specific legal duties to respect certain interests.*"[72]

Ruggie commissioned a study investigating the obstacles as well as the potential of company laws in promoting CSR.[73] His correct starting point was that "[c]orporate and securities law directly shapes what companies do and how they do it. Yet its implications for human rights remain poorly understood."[74] For this reason, there are calls to rewrite the company laws on the managerial duty of care in order to promote stakeholder interests, including the protection of human rights. Ruggie's study of 39 jurisdictions found in this respect that "[m]ost surveyed jurisdictions do not expressly require any recognition of a duty to society or respect for human rights as a condition of incorporation or listing".[75] The problem is that even if they would do it, such duties of care are hardly legally enforceable in courts.[76] Stevelman wrote about the duty of care owed by corporate managers and directors to the company and shareholders: "[A]s an enforceable legal standard, as opposed to an essentially hortatory, normative one, the duty of care is essentially moribund. Charter exculpation provisions, corporate indemnification, and corporate-funded directors' and officers' insurance have

---

69 Article 172(1), Companies Act 2006.
70 Ibid., Article 417(2).
71 *Access to Justice: Human Rights Abuses Involving Corporations, South Africa*, International Commission of Jurists, 2010, p. 9. <www.icj.org/dwn/database/SouthAfrica-ElecDist.pdf>.
72 Ibid., p. 10. (emphasis added).
73 Human rights and corporate law, *supra* note 67.
74 Ibid., para. 10.
75 Ibid., para. 50.
76 Mares, *supra* note 45, ch. 2.

generally limited, or eliminated, the potential for holding these managers personally liable in suits alleging breach of due care."[77]

The solution would be to say that companies owe the society a duty of care, but this is a matter of general tort law offering compensation for harm done, or otherwise commonly done in other specialised legal fields such as environmental law or labour law that protect specific interests. But such duty of care would *not* be a duty of care under company law which deals basically with duties that managers owe to the corporation for the purposes of profit-making. Therefore revisions of corporate duties have to be performed in other bodies of law if one counts on *judicial* enforcement and on managers not having the discretion (and responsibility) to *balance* corporate success and stakeholder protection. One such body of law is tort law, as illustrated with litigation under the US Alien Tort Claims Act and British tort law in the next section.

Ruggie values these developments in corporate governance and places them in the context of 'corporate culture'. He elaborated on three types of laws able to foster 'rights-respecting corporate cultures': reporting requirements, directors' duties, and legal provisions specifically recognising the concept of 'corporate culture' such as the US Sentencing Guidelines.[78] He deems that "[g]overnments are uniquely placed to foster corporate cultures in which respecting rights is an integral part of doing business ... Sustainability reporting can enable stakeholders to compare rights-related performance."[79]

In conclusion, recent developments in corporate governance hold at least two implications for CSR. First, they present a complex regulatory approach to shaping corporate behaviour. The limits of judicial coercion prompted the corporate governance regime to try to shape behaviour through an interesting mix of authoritative codes (soft law) and legally-binding disclosure requirements working in tandem to put the spotlight on sub-par, careless managerial practices and empower beneficiaries (primarily shareholders, but also indirectly some other stakeholders). This approach in national corporate governance parallels nicely Ruggie's understanding and attempt to strengthen a global governance regime that is not entirely dependent on state action, hard law and judicial enforcement.[80] In both corporate governance and CSR there is a strong emphasis on transparency and soft law. The important difference between the two regimes lies, of course, in the self-help capacities of the beneficiaries: the shareholders have a legally-sanctioned power over the management and access to the huge

---

77  F. Stevelman, 'Globalization and Corporate Social Responsibility: Challenges for the Academy, Future Lawyers, and Corporate Law', *New York Law School Law Review*, 2008/2009, p. 837 (reference omitted).

78  *Business and Human Rights: Further steps toward the operationalization of the 'protect, respect and remedy' framework*, A/HRC/14/27, 2010, paras. 36–43 (hereinafter 'Further steps').

79  Protect, Respect and Remedy, *supra* note 14, paras. 29–30.

80  The EU endorsed Ruggie's orientation and suggested that "[t]he so-called 'smart mix' of regulatory and voluntary policy instruments is a pragmatic approach which is already followed to a greater or lesser extent in many States." EU comments, *supra* note 25.

leverage of financial markets while human rights holders lack this type of power and markets working for them to keep business executives in check.

The second implication is that corporate governance and CSR travel on the same road, but only part of the way. Recent clarifications of managerial duties of care and legal requirements for disclosure of non-financial information are two engines slowly aligning corporate governance with CSR objectives. And they serve to prevent corporate governance from severely shortcutting CSR efforts, as shown above. But corporate governance has inherent limitations given the fundamental orientation towards interests of the company and/or shareholders and the wealth-creating function of the enterprise. The boost from corporate governance is notable but needs to be maintained through other engines if the rocket is to keep flying. Laws outside of the corporate governance regime, contracts and other non-legalistic rationalities must play their part to deliver accountability towards stakeholders.

### 7.1.3. Tort

The Alien Tort Claims Act (ATCA) in the US offers the main litigation arena against MNEs[81] of interest to CSR due to its peculiar reference to international law.[82] Ruggie has followed it closely and borrowed the legal definition of complicity from the ATCA courts' rulings on 'aiding and abetting'.[83] He openly spoke against a recent decision of a US court that imposed an impossibly high 'knowledge standard' for companies to be held liable as accomplices.[84] While no plaintiff has so far succeeded on the merits in an ATCA court, a few settlements have been reached and some procedural hurdles hindering access to justice have been cleared.[85] Not all is going uphill for the ATCA plaintiffs as exemplified by two notable setbacks taking place in 2009 and 2010.[86]

---

81   For a comprehensive source of materials and news on corporate human rights litigation, see the Corporate Legal Accountability Portal, <www.business-humanrights.org/Legal-Portal/Home>.

82   "The district courts shall have original jurisdiction of any civil action by an alien for a tort only, committed in violation of the law of nations or a treaty of the United States." *Alien Tort Claims Act*, 28 USC 1350, 1789. For more on the ATCA, see M. Gottridge et al., *The Alien Tort Statute: An Introduction And Current Topics*, Litigation and Administrative Practice Course Handbook Series, Practising Law Institute, 2010.

83   Protect, Respect and Remedy, *supra* note 14, para. 74.

84   Brief of *Amicus Curiae* International Law Scholars, *Presbyterian Church of Sudan v. Talisman Energy, Inc.*, on petition for a writ of *certiorari* from the Supreme Court to the US Court of Appeals for the Second Circuit, 2010 WL 1787371 (2010), p. 24.

85   For a list of cases, see Center for Constitutional Rights et al., Universal Periodic Review (United States of America), *Stakeholder Submission on United States Obligations to Respect, Protect and Remedy Human Rights in the Context of Business Activities*, 19 April 2010, <www.earthrights.org/sites/default/files/documents/escrnet-upr-april-19-2010.pdf>.

86   For a detailed discussion of recent developments under ATCA *see* the chapter by Knox in this volume.

Overseas plaintiffs have approached British courts to hold corporations accountable by using general principles of negligence law. The pioneering work[87] done by the law firm Leigh Day & Co and Richard Meeran has resulted in recent high profile settlements with companies such as Trafigura for dumping toxic waste in the Ivory Coast (settled in 2009), Monterrico Metals for its involvement in repressive actions in Peru (settled in 2011) and Shell for pollution in Nigeria (Shell accepted responsibility in 2011).[88] A court case started in 2011 pits Columbian farmers as plaintiffs against BP for its alleged negligence that resulted in an oil spill that poisoned water, destroyed crops and killed livestock.[89]

Host country courts have recently surprised transnational corporations (TNCs) with high awards. An Ecuadorian court ruled in 2011 that Chevron has to pay USD 18 billion for Texaco's pollution decades ago.[90]

Ruggie has consistently emphasised the importance of judicial mechanisms throughout his reports. His elaborations of Pillar 3 on access to remedies have highlighted the legal and practical barriers that plaintiffs face,[91] and called upon home states to keep their courts open to plaintiffs from abroad. In this respect he recommended that "States should strengthen judicial capacity to hear complaints and enforce remedies against all corporations operating or based in their territory, while also protecting against frivolous claims. States should address obstacles to access to justice, including for foreign plaintiffs – especially where alleged abuses reach the level of widespread and systematic human rights violations."[92] In his 2009 he detailed:

> Where the company is a subsidiary of an overseas parent, additional factors can compound these barriers. The parent company may use its own leverage with the host Government or mobilize the home Government and international financial institutions. The alternative of filing a suit in the parent company's home State for the subsidiary's actions, or for the parent's own acts or omissions, can raise jurisdictional questions about whether it is the appropriate forum, and may trigger policy objections by both home and host State Governments. Moreover, the standards expected of parent companies with regard to subsidiaries may be unclear or untested in national law. Such transnational claims also raise their own evidentiary, representational, and financial difficulties.[93]

---

87 *Lubbe* v. *Cape Plc* [2000] 1 WLR 1545, 2 Lloyd's L. Rep 383; *Connelly* v. *RTZ* [1996] 3 WLR 373; *Sithole & Ors* v. *Thor Chemicals Holdings Ltd & Anor* TLR, 15 February 1999.
88 For a detailed account of how a transnational liability case is litigated, *see* J. McCulloch, 'Beating the odds: The quest for justice by South African asbestos mining communities', *Review of African Political Economy* (2005).
89 D.Taylor, 'BP oil spill: Colombian farmers sue for negligence, *The Guardian*, 11 January 2011.
90 For documents on this long-running case, see <chevrontoxico.com>.
91 Guiding Principles, *supra* note 1, Principle No. 26.
92 Protect, Respect and Remedy, *supra* note 14, para. 91.
93 Towards operationalizing, *supra* note 11, para. 95.

### 7.1.4. Contract

Ruggie has emphasised the importance of commercial contracts incorporating CSR provisions. The economic leverage of governmental agencies, banks and large companies is considerable.

The issue of public procurement is a key contractual means through which states, as economic actors, can influence corporate behaviour. 'Socially responsible public procurement' has trailed developments in responsible supply chain management with which large private companies have experimented since the mid-1990s.[94] Now governments are more explicit on their role in "setting an example and influencing the market-place", as the European Commission recently stated.[95] In the United States, all contractors doing significant business with the Federal Government must certify that they have compliance programmes rooted in ethical and legally compliant cultures, based on those required in the Sentencing Guidelines.[96] Also in the US, an Executive Order from 1999 targets goods produced by forced child labour. Accordingly, public federal procurement shall include special provisions in contracts to the effect that the contractor has to certify that a good faith effort was made to determine whether forced or indentured child labour was used, and to cooperate in providing access to the contractor's records, documents, persons or premises. The sanctions on contractors are termination of contract, debarring from eligibility for future contracts and inclusion on a List of Parties Excluded from Federal Procurement.[97]

Contractual provisions on CSR are also increasingly incorporated in the financing and guarantees states offer to companies. Ruggie noted that the law in the US now directs the Overseas Private Investment Corporation to issue "a comprehensive set of environmental, transparency and internationally recognized worker rights and human rights guidelines with requirements binding on the Corporation and its investors".[98] Likeminded regulations are targeting national export credit agencies (ECAs) in the EU through new transparency requirements. Recently, EU countries agreed that they will submit yearly reports explaining how effectively their ECAs assess the environmental

---

94 See C. McCrudden, 'Corporate Social Responsibility and Public Procurement', in D. McBarnet, A. Voiculescu, T. Campbell (eds.), *The New Corporate Accountability: Corporate Social Responsibility and the Law* (Cambridge University Press, 2007)

95 European Commission, *Buying Social – A Guide to Taking Account of Social Considerations in Public Procurement*, 2010, p. 5.

96 United States Federal Register, Vol. 73, No. 219, 12 November 2008 (referred to in Further steps, *supra* note 78, para. 31)

97 Executive Order 13126 Prohibition of Acquisition of Products Produced by Forced or Indentured Child Labor (12 June 1999). For the effects of this regulation, see R. Woodard, *Sourcing: US labour 'blacklisting' a wake-up call to India?*, 20 July 2010, <www.just-style.com/analysis/us-labour-blacklisting-a-wake-up-call-to-india_id108351.aspx>; 'US Sees Big Drop in Child Labour Use by Indian Carpet-Makers', *Sify News*, 20 July 2010, <sify.com/news/us-sees-big-drop-in-child-labour-use-by-indian-carpet-makers-news-international-khunacfgihg.html>.

98 Further steps, *supra* note 78, para. 29.

and human rights risks of the commercial ventures they back.[99] At the international level, the IFC has for years had Performance Standards; these have been updated recently and make direct reference to Ruggie's due diligence recommendations.[100]

Contracts between private companies have long been seen as a key lever in the CSR area. For example, the discussions on supply chain management are premised on the leverage that influential companies have over their suppliers and distributors, leverage that can be formalised in contractual provisions.[101] CSR provisions have found their way into contracts through which one party communicates its codes of conduct and expectations, outlines due diligence measures and provides that non-compliance can be a ground for termination of contract.[102] Outside the area of supply chain responsibility there are interesting developments taking place. For example, regarding access to medicines, a pharmaceutical company expanded access to medicines by signing an immunity-from-suit agreement with a generic company enabling the latter to manufacture and sell the medicine in sub-Saharan Africa and India.[103] Such an approach goes a long way from the practices a decade ago of pharma companies protecting fiercely their HIV/AIDS medicine patents in developing countries.[104]

### 7.1.5. Soft Law

At the international level, there have been important standard setting efforts through which states have crystallised their expectations regarding responsible business behaviour. Major international governmental organisations took the lead in the 1970s and recently they sought to bring into line their human rights provisions with Ruggie's due diligence recommendations. It can be said that a battery of soft law currently exists.

---

99   Amnesty International, ECA-Watch and Eurodad, 'Giving human rights credit: EU countries agree to toughen export loan scrutiny', *Press release*, 29 June 2011.

100  Its general Performance Standard reads: "Business should respect human rights, which means to avoid infringing on the human rights of others and address adverse human rights impacts business may cause or contribute to." IFC, Assessment and Management of Environmental and Social Risks and Impacts, Performance Standard 1, 2012, para. 3.

101  M. P. Vandenbergh, 'The New Wal-Mart Effect: The Role of Private Contracting in Global Governance', 54 *UCLA Law Review* (April 2007) p. 913.

102  For an example, *see* GlaxoSmithKline, *The GSK standard contract clause for Ethical Standards and Human Rights*, 2011, <www.gsk.com/responsibility/cr-report-2010/supply-chain/supplier-standards/human-rights-clause.htm> (accessed 7 September 2011). For a discussion, *see* B. Martin, *Can transnational corporations legally apply conditions to companies that supply them with contract and agency labour?*, Report for International Federation of Chemical, Energy, Mine and General Workers' Unions (ICEM), 2007, <www.publicworld.org/files/icemlegal.pdf>.

103  *Bristol-Myers Squibb Signs New Agreement to Expand Access to Reyataz(R) (atazanavir sulfate) in sub-Saharan Africa and India*, Bristol-Myers Squibb Press Release, 28 June 2011.

104  M. Heywood, 'South Africa's Treatment Action Campaign: Combining Law and Social Mobilization to Realize the Right to Health', 1:1 *Journal of Human Rights Practice* (March 2009) pp. 14–36.

The OECD has revised in 2011 its Guidelines for MNEs originally adopted in 1976,[105] and additionally it adopted due diligence recommendations pertinent to the trade in conflict minerals, also in 2011.[106] The International Labour Organization (ILO) still has its 1977 Declaration for MNEs outlining relevant labour rights, a document that is periodically updated. The IFC has updated its Performance Standards for project finance in 2011.[107] In late 2010 the ISO released a detailed guidance on social responsibility.[108] The European Commission has applauded Ruggie's Framework and will reference it in its next CSR policy paper.[109] Regarding sustainability reporting, the Global Reporting Initiative is working on its fourth generation of Reporting Guidelines to be released in 2013.[110] And now the HRC has sanctioned Ruggie's Framework and Guiding Principles. Numerous other multistakeholder initiatives exist in diverse industries such as extractives, labour intensive industries, information technology, agriculture and many others.[111]

Ruggie wrote in relation to soft law:

> [T]he standard-setting role of soft law remains as important as ever to crystallize emerging norms in the international community. The increased focus on accountability in some intergovernmental arrangements, coupled with the innovations in soft law mechanisms that involve corporations directly in regulatory rulemaking and implementation, suggests increased state and corporate acknowledgment of evolving social expectations and a recognition of the need to exercise shared responsibility.[112]

### 7.2. Ruggie's Legal Questions and Answers

These legal developments have been duly noted in the SRSG reports. Throughout his mandate Ruggie sought to answer many questions of immediate relevance to lawyers.

---

105   OECD, *Guidelines for Multinational Enterprises*, 2011.

106   OECD, *Due Diligence Guidance for Responsible Supply Chains of Minerals from Conflict-Affected and High-Risk Areas*, OECD Publishing, 2011.

107   There are eight Performance Standards, effective from 1 January 2012.

108   International Organisation for Standardisation, *Guidance on Social Responsibility*, ISO 26000, 2010.

109   See EU Comments, *supra* note 25. Already in its 2006 White paper on CSR, the Commission wrote that it was following the progress of the SRSG. European Commission, *Implementing the Partnership for Growth and Jobs: Making Europe a Pole of Excellence on Corporate Social Responsibility*, COM(2006) 136 final (Brussels, 2006), p. 6, <www.coess.org/documents/com_2006_0136.pdf>.

110   <www.globalreporting.org>.

111   See R. Mares (ed.), *Business and Human Rights – A Compilation of Documents* (Martinus Nijhoff Publishers, 2004).

112   *Business and Human Rights: Mapping International Standards of Responsibility and Accountability for Corporate Acts*, A/HRC/4/035, 2007, para. 62 (hereinafter 'Mapping Standards').

Does international law impose obligations on corporations, that is, private actors? He concluded that "the treaties do not address direct corporate legal responsibilities explicitly, while the treaty bodies' commentaries on the subject are ambiguous … In conclusion, it does not seem that the international human rights instruments discussed here currently impose direct legal responsibilities on corporations."[113] Is there a principled obstacle for international law doing that? He wrote that "[n]othing prevents states from imposing international legal responsibilities for human rights directly on corporations".[114] Were the Draft Norms a restatement of international law as its authors claimed? Ruggie understood that "restatements 'reflect the law as it presently stands or might plausibly be stated by a court.' The idea that the Norms project amounted to no more than a 'restatement' of legal principles was contested by business and also questioned by academic observers."[115]

What is the relation of the Guiding Principles with international law? Ruggie thought that "[t]he Guiding Principles' normative contribution lies not in the creation of new international law obligations but in elaborating the implications of existing standards and practices for States and businesses; integrating them within a single, logically coherent and comprehensive template; and identifying where the current regime falls short and how it should be improved".[116] Further, "[n]othing in these Guiding Principles should be read as creating new international law obligations, or as limiting or undermining any legal obligations a State may have undertaken or be subject to under international law with regard to human rights".[117]

What is expected from companies where domestic law conflicts with international standards? Ruggie deemed that "[o]ne of the toughest dilemmas companies face is where national law significantly contradicts and does not offer the same level of protection as international human rights standards. National authorities may demand compliance with the law, while other stakeholders may advocate adherence to international standards, as might the company itself, for reasons of principle or simple consistency of policy."[118] He recognised that such situations leave companies caught in the middle – in regard to for example freedom of association, gender equality, freedom of expression and right to privacy – and they should seek to "find ways to honour the spirit of international standards without violating national law".[119]

Does international law have a role in the emerging CSR regime? Ruggie decided that "international law has an important role to play in constructing a global regime to govern business and human rights. The effectiveness of its contributions will be maximized if it is embedded within, and deployed in support of, an overall strategy of increasing governance capacity in the face of enormously complex and ever-changing

---

113   *Ibid.*, paras. 41 and 44.
114   *Ibid.*, para. 36.
115   Evolving Agenda, *supra* note 37, p. 827 (references omitted).
116   Guiding Principles, *supra* note 1, para. 14.
117   *Ibid.*, page 6.
118   Towards operationalizing, *supra* note 11, para. 66.
119   *Ibid.*, paras. 67–68.

forces of globalization."¹²⁰ In outlining his strategy of achieving social change, Ruggie addressed the key question coming from civil society: "[W]hy not start the treaty-making process now, while simultaneously taking shorter-term practical steps?"¹²¹ Is a general international treaty on CSR the better way forward at this moment in time?

> There is one thing the report does not do: recommend that states negotiate an overarching treaty imposing binding standards on companies under international law. Treaties form the bedrock of the international human rights system. Specific elements of the business and human rights agenda may become candidates for successful international legal instruments. But it is my carefully considered view that negotiations on an overarching treaty now would be unlikely to get off the ground, and even if they did the outcome could well leave us worse off than we are today … It is essential to strengthen the international human rights regime to bridge protection gaps in relation to business. But more readily achievable alternatives to the status quo exist, involving both mandatory and voluntary measures …¹²²

Can home states regulate their companies operating internationally? Ruggie thought that "home states are already legally permitted, if not necessarily willing, to take more extensive action to regulate overseas human rights harm by corporations based in them without arousing host state ire".¹²³ Does the home state's responsibility to protect human rights extend extraterritorially? Ruggie concluded that

> [t]he [UN] Committees have not expressly interpreted the treaties as requiring states to exercise extraterritorial jurisdiction over abuses committed abroad by corporations domiciled in their territory. But nor do they seem to regard the treaties as prohibiting such action, and in some situations they have encouraged it … In general, international law permits a state to exercise extraterritorial jurisdiction provided there is a recognized basis: where the actor or victim is a national, where the acts have substantial adverse effects on the state, or where specific international crimes are involved.¹²⁴

How does a host state's duty to protect human rights fit in Ruggie's vision? He wrote:

---

120  Evolving Agenda, *supra* note 37, p. 840.

121  J. G. Ruggie, 'Business and human rights – Treaty road not travelled', *Ethical Corporation*, May 2008 (hereinafter 'Treaty road not travelled').

122  *Ibid.* Ruggie was more positive to an intergovernmental process of drafting a narrow international legal instrument dealing with gross human rights abuses potentially amounting to the level of international crimes. Recommendations on Follow-Up to the Mandate, Mandate of the Special Representative of the Secretary-General (SRSG) on the Issue of Human Rights and Transnational Corporations and other Business Enterprises, 2011, <www.business-humanrights.org/media/documents/ruggie/ruggie-special-mandate-follow-up-11-feb-2011.pdf>.

123  Treaty road not travelled, *supra* note 121.

124  Evolving Agenda, *supra* note 37, pp. 829–830.

[A]ny 'grand strategy' needs to strengthen and build out from the existing capacity of states and the states system to regulate and adjudicate harmful actions by corporations, not undermine it. Currently, at the domestic level some governments may be unable to take effective action on their own, whether or not the will to do so is present. And in the international arena states may compete for access to markets and investments, as a result of which collective action problems may restrict or impede their serving as the international community's 'public authority.' This observation drives the desire to impose direct obligations on corporations under international law. But doing so can itself have adverse effects on governance capacities, as we have seen – leaving aside the question of any such proposals' current political feasibility and legal enforceability. Therefore, it seems more promising in the first instance to expand the international regime horizontally, by seeking to further clarify and progressively codify the duties of states to protect human rights against corporate violations: individually, as host and home states, as well as collectively through the 'international cooperation' requirement of several UN human rights treaties. This will also establish greater clarity regarding corporate responsibility and accountability, and create a broader understanding among states about where the current regime cannot be expected to function as intended, and its vertical extension, therefore, is essential. International instruments may well have a significant role to play in this process, but as carefully crafted precision tools complementing and augmenting existing institutional capacities.[125]

What implications for the duty to protect follow from the state-business nexus exemplified by state-owned enterprises,[126] privatisation of public services[127] and public procurement[128]? What features of investment agreements and international arbitration are problematic from a human rights perspective?[129]

What legal obstacles and opportunities for CSR exist in various bodies of law? For example, do directors' duties under company laws allow, encourage or require directors and senior management to consider a company's social impacts, including on human rights?[130] Are human rights risks 'material' for purposes of financial reporting regulations?[131] Would following Ruggie's recommendation actually increase the danger of corporate liability with businesses incriminating themselves "by providing external parties with information they would not otherwise have had to use against

---

125   Ibid., pp. 838–839 (references omitted).
126   Guiding Principles, *supra* note 1, Principle 4.
127   Ibid., Principle 5.
128   Ibid., Principle 6.
129   Towards operationalizing, *supra* note 11, paras. 28–37. See also *Principles for responsible contracts: integrating the management of human rights risks into State-investor contract negotiations: guidance for negotiators*, Addendum 3 to the Report, A/HRC/17/31/Add.3, 2011.
130   Further steps, *supra* note 78, paras. 39–41. *See also* Human rights and corporate law, *supra* note 67.
131   Further steps, *supra* note 78, paras. 38 and 69–76.

the company"?¹³² Or on the contrary, does due diligence offer a defence to companies unwilling to improve their performance and human rights impacts? Ruggie noted:

> Conducting due diligence enables companies to identify and prevent adverse human rights impacts. Doing so also should provide corporate boards with strong protection against mismanagement claims by shareholders. In Alien Tort Statute and similar suits, proof that the company took every reasonable step to avoid involvement in the alleged violation can only count in its favour. However, the Special Representative would not support proposals that conducting human rights due diligence, by itself, should automatically and fully absolve a company from Alien Tort Statute or similar liability.¹³³

What procedural obstacles and other hindrances exist that prevent victims from accessing judicial remedies?¹³⁴ What is the state of currently available remedies? In this respect, as he accounted for recent CSR and regulatory developments, Ruggie warned that "this patchwork of mechanisms remains incomplete and flawed. It must be improved in its parts and as a whole."¹³⁵ What is the role of state-based, non-judicial mechanisms, like national human rights institutions (NHRIs)?¹³⁶ Ruggie observed that "[n]on-State mechanisms may be linked to industry-based or multi-industry organizations; to multi-stakeholder initiatives ensuring member compliance with standards; to project financiers requiring certain standards of clients; or to particular companies or projects. Non-State mechanisms must not undermine the strengthening of State institutions, particularly judicial mechanisms, but can offer additional opportunities for recourse and redress."¹³⁷ Would a global ombudsman that could receive and handle complaints be a way forward? Ruggie indicated that

> [s]uch a mechanism would need to provide ready access without becoming a first port of call; offer effective processes without undermining the development of national mechanisms; provide timely responses while likely being located far from participants; and furnish appropriate solutions while dealing with different sectors, cultures and political contexts. It would need to show some early successes if faith in its capacity were not quickly to be undermined. To perform these tasks any such function would need to be

---

132   Towards operationalizing, *supra* note 11, para. 80.
133   Further steps, *supra* note 78, para. 86.
134   Protect, Respect and Remedy, *supra* note 14, para. 89. See also Towards operationalizing, *supra* note 11, paras. 93–98; Further steps, *supra* note 78, paras. 103–113. See also Ruggie's letter to UK on the issue of legal aid reform, <www.business-humanrights.org/media/documents/ruggie/ruggie-ltr-to-uk-justice-mininster-djanogly-16-may-2011.pdf>.
135   Protect, Respect and Remedy, *supra* note 14, para. 87.
136   For an analysis of Ruggie's treatment of NHRIs, see the chapter by Brodie in this volume.
137   Protect, Respect and Remedy, *supra* note 14, para. 86.

well-resourced. Careful consideration should go into whether these criteria actually can and would be met before moving in this direction.[138]

What is the danger of looking at CSR mainly through legal lenses? He wrote:

> [M]any elements of an overall strategy lie beyond the legal sphere altogether. Consequently, the interplay between systems of legal compliance and the broader social dynamics that can contribute to positive change needs to be carefully calibrated. No less of a human rights authority than Amartya Sen warns against viewing rights primarily as 'proto legal commands' or 'laws in waiting.' Doing so, he argues, would unduly constrict – he actually uses the term 'incarcerate' – the social logics and processes other than law that drive the evolving public recognition of rights. The implication of Sen'[s] insight for the business and human rights agenda is that any successful regime needs to motivate, activate, and benefit from all of the moral, social, and economic rationales that can affect the behavior of corporations. This requires providing incentives as well as punishments, identifying opportunities as well as risks, and building social movements and political coalitions that involve representation from all relevant sectors of society, including business – much as has been occurring in the environmental field.[139]

## 8. The Bigger Picture

Ruggie took note of a multitude of legal developments. He also regarded the importance and limitations of corporate self-regulation and multistakeholder initiatives. There seems to be no arguing that at the end of the day coercion will need to be amassed from various sources to deal with corporate laggards. Often gathered (and sometimes dismissed) under the catch phrase of 'voluntarism', *non-legally binding standards* – laid down by states, private actors or a combination of both – and their *enforcement* obtained from other sources than judicial coercion have an important role to play. From a governance perspective, the dichotomy binding/non-binding is hardly productive for grasping the dynamics and evolution of norm-making processes in the CSR area.[140] The question still is how we get sufficient coerciveness. Where states have failed – unable or unwilling – in their responsibility to establish a regulatory framework, can corporate voluntarism play a facilitating role in getting the states to act, to regulate? And in complex regulatory situations can voluntarism complement and work in combination with hard law?[141]

---

138   *Ibid.*, para. 103.
139   Evolving Agenda, *supra* note 37, pp. 839–840 (references omitted).
140   See R. Mares, 'Global Corporate Social Responsibility, Human Rights, and the Law: An Interactive Regulatory Perspective on the Voluntary-Mandatory Dichotomy', 1:2 *Transnational Legal Theory* (2010) pp. 221–285.
141   See the chapter by Melish and Meidinger in this volume discussing the 'New Governance' scholarship and the need for 'orchestration'.

### 8.1. Role of Voluntarism in the Norm-making Process and in the Functioning of Governance Regimes

The first aspect refers to the role of voluntarism in facilitating law-making and law enforcement. Ruggie mentioned briefly, on a number of occasions, that "[a]s companies internalize the responsibility to respect, they will *increasingly support State efforts to bring laggards along*".[142] Elsewhere he noted:

> A related criticism is that voluntary initiatives undermine the prospect for more robust regulations or other public sector roles. But this claim is premature at best. There is little chance of transnational firms becoming subject to legally binding regulations at the global level any time soon; the political will or even capacity simply is not there, and much of the corporate world would unite to fight it. In contrast, *voluntary initiatives over time may build an interest among leading firms for* a more level playing field vis-à-vis laggards, thereby realigning the political balance in the corporate sector.[143]

On another occasion Ruggie anticipated that

> at the end of the day the accumulation of experience inevitably will lead to a desire for greater benchmarking, for moving from 'good' to 'best' practices and even formal codification, so that some of the 'soft law' products of voluntary initiatives are likely to become 'harder' law down the road. The advocates will include industry leaders to lock in their own first-mover advantages, or wanting a level playing field vis-à-vis laggards – as happened when several major energy companies lobbied the US Congress for some form of greenhouse-gas limits after President Bush rejected the Kyoto Protocol. Laggards have a harder time opposing standards based on actual achievement of their peers than ex ante standards.[144]

These however are quite lapidary and optimistic views. It would have been valuable, in order to cut through the voluntary-mandatory controversy, to have Ruggie explain in more detail this process, key dynamics, key interactions, how norms get institutionalised in the regulatory sphere and so on. Maybe this is a task for which the academia is better positioned to pursue than the SRSG mandate was, but it would go a long way to address well-founded concerns of NGOs that voluntary approaches displace much needed regulation. For example, Vogel reviewed contributions from political science, law, sociology, management, business ethics and international and development studies in an effort to account for "scholarship that is relevant to understanding

---

142  Further steps, *supra* note 78, para. 123 (emphasis added).
143  J. G. Ruggie, 'Reconstituting the Global Public Domain – Issues, Actors, and Practices', 10:4 *European Journal of International Relations* (2004) p. 518 (emphasis added).
144  Ruggie, *supra* note 48, pp. 251–252 (reference omitted).

the emergence, structure, and impact of civil regulation, and its significance as a new and evolving dimension of global economic governance".¹⁴⁵

Some insights could nevertheless be gathered from a seminar convened by the SRSG and summarised in a 2008 SRSG report. It addresses explicitly the relationship of multi-stakeholder initiatives (MSIs) to regulation:

> Critics often portray MSIs and voluntary standards generally as providing alternatives to or even means of escaping binding regulation. For most MSIs, however, the regulatory interface is much more complex. Some seek eventual public policy integration as a way of achieving scale, bringing in smaller firms, producers of commodities and other unbranded products, and companies and Governments from emerging markets which do not have other incentives to join. For others, the whole point is to get Governments to implement regulation they already have on the books.
> 
> Participants predicted that MSIs would need to focus more explicitly on their relationships to regulation in the future, for a variety of reasons. First, many leadership companies actually prefer regulatory solutions in some areas, where 'level playing fields' are business-critical. Second, MSIs are proving to be interesting platforms for joint policy advocacy. And third, to the extent that MSIs begin to shift entire markets, they are more likely to come under scrutiny from regulators at the national and international levels on competition and trade policy grounds.
> 
> While participants agreed that different MSIs would necessarily have different 'end games', they also felt that MSIs share an opportunity to use their experience to feed into smart regulation in the areas in which they work.¹⁴⁶

It might be the case that Vogel articulated a key insight regarding CSR: "The long-term effectiveness of private labor codes may well lie in public recognition of their limitations, leading them to be *replaced* or *complemented* by more effective national and international public regulations."¹⁴⁷ Such an evolutionary perspective could capture an essential dynamic associated to CSR.¹⁴⁸

Rather than delve on the qualitative dynamics of a long and sinuous process, Ruggie seems at times content with quantitative references to the 'tipping point': "[A]s is true of all voluntary – and many statutory – initiatives, determined laggards find ways to avoid scrutiny. This problem is not unique to human rights, nor is it unprecedented in history. But once a tipping point is reached, societies somehow manage to mitigate if not eliminate the problem. The trick is getting to the tipping point – a goal to which this mandate is dedicated."¹⁴⁹

---

145   D. Vogel, 'Private Global Business Regulation', 11 *Annual Review of Political Science* (2008) p. 262.
146   *Summary of five multi-stakeholder consultations*, Addendum 1 to the Report, A/HRC/8/5/Add.1, 2008, pp. 257–259.
147   Vogel, *supra* note 145, pp. 274–275.
148   The chapter by Skadegaard Thorsen and Andreasen in this volume analyses the evolution of voluntary initiatives covering labour standards in supply chains.
149   Mapping Standards, *supra* note 112, para. 81.

A more promising angle that Ruggie employs to cover this aspect has to do with the 'scaling-up' of various existing initiatives. He took note of industry and company self-regulation, multi-stakeholder initiatives, public-private hybrids combining mandatory with voluntary measures, various regulatory measures to promote a corporate culture respectful of human rights, and the potential of corporate liability for international crimes in some national courts. Then he deemed that "[w]ithout in any manner disparaging these steps, our fundamental problem is that there are too few of them, none has reached a scale commensurate with the challenges at hand, there is little cross-learning, and they do not cohere as parts of a more systemic response with cumulative effects."[150]

It is commendable that Ruggie made the cumulative process the supreme ambition of his mandate:[151] it emphasises the need to scale-up and impresses a much needed evolutionary perspective. For Ruggie international law and national laws have a clear role to play in this cumulative process even though law does not hold the answer to everything when it comes to the responsibilities and roles of businesses. He cautioned states to "not assume that businesses invariably prefer, or benefit from, state inaction, and they should consider a smart mix of measures – national and international, mandatory and voluntary – to foster business respect for human rights".[152] And he firmly affirmed that

> markets work optimally only if they are embedded within rules, customs and institutions. Markets themselves require these to survive and thrive, while society needs them to manage the adverse effects of market dynamics and produce the public goods that markets undersupply. Indeed, history teaches us that markets pose the greatest risks – to society and business itself – when their scope and power far exceed the reach of the institutional underpinnings that allow them to function smoothly and ensure their political sustainability.[153]

While Ruggie felt the need for many qualifications in his treatment of the role of law – at what level (international or national), by who (host or home states), on what issue (overarching or specific CSR instrument) and at what time (now or later) – he was trenchant on the role of states. Not only did he dedicate a pillar of his Framework to this issue, but he wrote: "The role of states in relation to human rights is not only primary, but also critical … [T]he repertoire of policy instruments available to [host and home] states to improve the human rights performance of firms is far greater than most states currently employ."[154] Elsewhere he considered that

---

150   Protect, Respect and Remedy, *supra* note 14, para. 106.
151   See the quotation referenced by *supra* note 1.
152   Human rights and corporate law, *supra* note 67, para. 206.
153   Protect, Respect and Remedy, *supra* note 14, para. 2.
154   Interim Report, *supra* note 27, para 79.

not all state structures as a whole appear to have internalised the full meaning of the state duty to protect, and its implications with regard to preventing and punishing abuses by nonstate actors, including business. Nor do states seem to be taking full advantage of the many legal and policy tools at their disposal to meet their treaty obligations. Insofar as the duty to the protect lies at the very foundation of the international human rights regime, this uncertainty gives rise to concern.[155]

In his academic treatment of the global public domain, Ruggie wrote that "[T]he effect of the new global public domain is not to replace states, but to embed systems of governance in broader global frameworks of social capacity and agency that did not previously exist".[156] It is in this respect that Ruggie simultaneously qualifies the role of law as merely one of the rationalities shaping behaviour and unequivocally affirms the role of states. The result is what Catá Backer referred to as a 'polycentric (multi-layered and intertwined) system of governance'.[157] In his assessment of the SRSG's efforts at coordination, leverage and scaling-up, Catá Backer wrote:

> We move here from vague notions of corporate social responsibility applied in an ad hoc basis by individual corporate and state actors to the elaboration of a multi-level system of polycentric governance. The process from conception to elaboration has been complicated by the need to challenge the basis for conventional governance – one grounded in the idea of the singularity of the state. The SRSG has proposed a set of principles for the governance of economic actors operating within and beyond the state that is grounded on both public and private power. The coordination of these two sources of authority, and their development of systems of behavior control will be the great challenge for the emerging system of economic globalization in the coming decades.[158]

Thus Catá Backer concluded that "if there is no one silver bullet for the governance of the human rights obligations of business, then it will be necessary to produce a polycentric (multi-layered and intertwined) system of governance."[159] States have a key role to play in the functioning of this governance system, and have to strive for consistency with their obligations and interests in other legal domains where economic interests assert themselves powerfully. With his 'duty to protect' pillar Ruggie forcefully drew attention to unacceptable inconsistencies in state practice.

The struggle to eliminate such inconsistencies can be placed against Fischer-Lescano and Teubner's writings on the fragmentation of global law. He warned that "[l]egal fragmentation is merely an ephemeral reflection of a more fundamental, multidimensional fragmentation of global society itself"; that "[a]ny aspirations to a nor-

---

155   Mapping Standards, *supra* note 112, para. 86.
156   Ruggie, *supra* note 143, p. 519.
157   L. Catá Backer, 'On the Evolution of the United Nations' "Protect-Respect-Remedy" Project: The State, the Corporation and Human Rights in a Global Governance Context', 9:1 *Santa Clara Journal of International Law* (2010) p. 126.
158   *Ibid.*, p. 156.
159   *Ibid.*, p. 126 (reference omitted).

mative unity of global law are thus doomed from the outset. A meta-level at which conflicts might be solved is wholly elusive both in global law and in global society"; and finally that "[l]egal fragmentation cannot itself be combated. At the best, a weak normative compatibility of the fragments might be achieved. However, this is dependent upon the ability of conflicts law to establish a specific network logic, which can effect a loose coupling of colliding units."[160]

Consistent with Ruggie's refusal to reduce the CSR discussion to a hierarchical, legalistic take, Teubner and Fischer-Lescano wrote eloquently about legal dynamics at the global level, especially about the plurality of law-making mechanisms, and the complex landscape featuring the legal centre, the legal periphery and the social environments of law:

> What, however, will take the place of hierarchy of legal norms? The center-periphery divide. While courts occupy the center of law, the periphery of the diverse autonomous legal regimes is populated by political, economic, religious etc. organizational or spontaneous, collective or individual subjects of law, which, at the very borders of law, establish themselves in close contact to autonomous social sectors. Once again, it is the fragmentation of global society that establishes the new schisms between the legal center, the legal periphery and the social environments of law. In the zones of contact between the legal periphery and autonomous social sectors, an arena for a plurality of law-making mechanisms is established: standardized contracts, agreements of professional associations, routines of formal organizations, technical and scientific standardization, normalizations of behavior, and informal consensus between NGOs, the media and social public spheres. By virtue of their independent secondary norms that differ fundamentally from those of national or international law, genuinely self-contained regimes can establish themselves in line with the following technical definition: A regime is a union of rules laying down particular rights, duties and powers and rules having to do with the administration of such rules, including in particular rules for reacting to breaches. When such a regime seeks precedence in regard to the general law, we have a 'self-contained regime,' a special case of *lex specialis*.[161]

Such writings generate a more nuanced understanding of the reach and operation of law when it comes to globalised business operations. Such treatments resonate with Ruggie's elaboration of 'new global public domain' defined as "an increasingly institutionalized transnational arena of discourse, contestation, and action concerning the production of global public goods, involving private as well as public actors. It does not by itself determine global governance outcomes any more than its counterpart does at the domestic level. But it introduces opportunities for and constraints upon both global and national governance that did not exist in the past."[162]

---

160   A. Fischer-Lescano and G. Teubner, 'Regime-Collisions: The Vain Search For Legal Unity In The Fragmentation Of Global Law', 25 *Michigan Journal of International Law* (Summer 2004) p. 1004.
161   *Ibid.*, pp. 1012–1013 (references omitted).
162   Ruggie, *supra* note 143, p. 504.

The governance regime for CSR will have to be mindful of the danger that some businesses will play the RtR strategically. Ruggie made the RtR operational through the idea of due diligence. However a focus on procedures, and process-oriented regulations, runs the well-known danger of decoupling or symbolic conformity as a strategic response. Decoupling or ceremonial conformity, a form of opportunism, implies that "organizations under pressure to adopt particular structures or procedures may opt to respond in a ceremonial manner, making changes in their formal structures to signal conformity but then buffering internal units, allowing them to operate independent of these pressures".[163] Jamali further elaborated that decoupling "is more likely in loosely coupled organizational fields, characterized by ambiguity, uncertainty, multiple conflicting expectations, high transaction costs, limited regulatory commitment, and the absence of mechanisms to monitor compliance".[164] These features are strikingly present in the business and human rights area.[165]

Institutional theory has for some time dealt with the diffusion of organisational practices. However, as Jamali writes, awareness has grown that "conformity may have been exaggerated and that there are important elements of variation in terms of degree of agency, choice, proactiveness and self-interest in responding to institutional pressures".[166] From several contributions to this volume transpires uneasiness with the process orientation that Ruggie, through the due diligence component, has impressed on his corporate responsibility treatment. They would have preferred a different approach able to deliver accountability and ensure real change through, for example, more specific, detailed definitions of corporate responsibilities for each right;[167] a right of participation for civil society;[168] and more radical changes in corporate decision-making structures.[169] In brief, Parker and Howe charge that Ruggie "underestimates the capacity of business to neutralize, deradicalize, individualize and formalize critique".[170]

When all is said and done, did Ruggie downplay the need for law? Was he in favour of keeping companies deregulated?[171] Will his work have facilitated or hindered

---

163   R. W. Scott, *Institutions and Organizations: Ideas and Interests* (Sage, Thousand Oaks, CA, 2008) p. 171.

164   D. Jamali, 'MNCs and International Accountability Standards through an Institutional Lens: Evidence of Symbolic Conformity or Decoupling', 95 *Journal of Business Ethics* (2010) p. 625 (references omitted).

165   For an example, *see* the chapter by Haines, Macdonald and Balaton-Chrimes in this volume documenting corporate strategies of resistance on tea plantations in India.

166   Jamali, *supra* note 164, p. 618 (references omitted).

167   *See* the chapter by Sullivan and Hachez in this volume.

168   *See* the chapter Melish and Meidinger in this volume.

169   *See* the chapter Parker and Howe in this volume.

170   *Ibid.*, p. ??

171   Weissbrodt, the main author of the Draft Norms, wrote: "The Special Representative of the Secretary-General was supposed to develop standards, but has instead attempted to derail the standard-setting process and bow to the corporate refusal to accept any standards except voluntary codes." D. Weissbrodt, 'Keynote Address: International Standard-Setting

the emergence of much needed stronger regulatory frameworks? The law has clearly been the great polariser in the Norms/Ruggie controversy.[172] Two different visions of social change collided. Law as the preeminent and indispensable mechanism for social change versus law at the right time, in the right quantities and in the right combination with other factors. Law, especially international law, as the 'silver bullet' versus a belief in the non-existence of a silver bullet. For Ruggie "there is no single silver bullet solution to the very complex business and human rights challenges. Instead, all social actors – states, businesses, and civil society – must learn to do many things differently. But those things must cohere and generate an interactive dynamic of cumulative progress – and that is precisely what the Protect, Respect and Remedy framework is intended to help achieve."[173]

The framing and mapping performed by the SRSG mandate are remarkable. Ruggie broadened the debate and eloquently wrote about the puzzle in front of the CSR movement:

> [W]hat we needed to focus on were exactly these gaps between an increasingly integrated global economy and the fragmented political and regulatory systems and how to bridge those gaps, which involved states, it involved businesses, it involved other actors, it involved preventative measures, it involved remedial measures, it would involve law, it would involve voluntarism – it was just a much bigger puzzle that had to be put together.[174]

---

on the Human Rights Responsibilities of Businesses', 26 *Berkeley Journal of International Law* (2008) p. 373, at p. 390.

172 Just refer to HRW's critical assessment of the HRC decision on Ruggie: "[T]he council endorsed the status quo: a world where companies are encouraged, but not obliged, to respect human rights … Guidance isn't enough – we need a mechanism to scrutinize how companies and governments apply these principles." Human Rights Watch, *Global Rules Needed, Not Just Guidance*, 16 June 2011, <www.hrw.org/node/99908 UN Human Rights Council: Weak Stance on Business Standards>. *See also* FIAN arguing in favour of binding international and national regulation and asking the HRC to "avoid promoting ineffective mechanisms … such as the UN Global Compact and the OECD Guidelines on MNCs have proved largely ineffective to address human rights abuses by TNCs. They have frustrated the hopes of victims to obtain remedy, wasted the resources of civil society organisations and have been misused by some corporations as public relations vehicles vis-à-vis public criticism and as cover up for their real human rights performance." FIAN, *Statement to the Delegations on the Human Rights Council 2011*, 17th Session, 2011, <www.fian.org/news/press-releases/CSOs-respond-to-ruggies-guiding-principles-regarding-human-rights-and-transnational-corporations/pdf>.

173 J. G. Ruggie, 'Engaging Business: Addressing Respect for Human Rights', *Keynote Address to the U.S. Council for International Business, U.S. Chamber of Commerce, International Organization of Employers*, Atlanta, 25 February 2010, <www.reports-and-materials.org/Ruggie-keynote-address-in-Atlanta-25-Feb-2010.pdf>.

174 J. Sherman, 'Business and human rights: joining the dots', Interview with Ruggie, International Bar Association, July 2010.

Elsewhere Ruggie reverted to his famous concept of the 'embedded liberalism compromise' and considered that

> private governance produces only partial solutions, and its own unfolding brings the public sector back in. It is difficult at this early stage to be more precise, and thus it is doubly imperative not to exaggerate either the virtues or the effects of these institutional developments ... [T]he skewed distribution of agential capacity between North and South is too pronounced, accountability problems too pervasive and the distributional consequences of these kinds of global governance instruments too poorly understood for us to believe that they reflect some new stable equilibrium. What we can say is that a fundamental recalibration is going on of the public-private sector balance, and it is occurring at the global level no less than the domestic. Haltingly and erratically, something akin of an embedded liberalism compromise is being pulled and pushed into the global arena, and the corporate connection is a key element in that process.[175]

Ruggie comprehensively mapped voluntary initiatives as well as relevant bodies of law. With his governance outlook he discouraged a dichotomous understanding of voluntary and mandatory initiatives, and drew attention to their interactions in governance regimes. Hopefully, now that he is relieved from the constraints of his SRSG mandate, Ruggie will outline his understanding of how the CSR regime will slowly tighten the grip around laggards, a job for which political scientists are particularly well placed to explain.[176] He compellingly framed the issue as caused by a 'governance gap' and mapped the field comprehensively, but the dynamics of closing this gap need further analysis. Ruggie already hinted at this when he observed that

> [t]he terrain is fraught with strategic manipulation and the potential for shirking. But it also opens the door to more firmly institutionalizing an emerging global public domain by bringing the public sector in ... Now we are slowly beginning to come full circle: business wants to channel some of the pressure [from civil society actors] it faces into the construction of at least minimally effective public sectors, including at the global level. This sets up the possibility of a very different political dynamic than existed as recently as the 1990s.[177]

Institutional theory approaches seem able to cut through the voluntary/mandatory debate and explain deinstitutionalisation, diffusion and reinstitutionalisation of norms, such as the due diligence norm.[178] It seems that the CSR debate is now ripe to begin

---

175  Ruggie, *supra* note 48, p. 253.
176  Vogel noted that: "'Governance without government' has long been observed and theorized by political scientists [describing] a 'postmodern world of multiple and overlapping authorities: sovereign and nonsovereign, territorial and non-territorial'." Vogel, *supra* note 145, p. 263 (references omitted).
177  Ruggie, *supra* note 48, p. 252.
178  G. Mantilla, 'Emerging International Human Rights Norms for Transnational Corporations', 15 *Global Governance* (2009) pp. 279–298. R. Greenwood *et al.*, 'Theorizing Change:

exploring complementarities and leave behind the voluntary/mandatory divisiveness: through his work Ruggie has placed the interaction law/voluntarism higher on the agenda.[179] As Vogel wrote:

> One key research question has to do with the relationship between civil regulation and public or state regulation. Civil regulations and state policies can interact in many ways. Private regulatory standards can function to avoid additional state regulations, to complement or better enforce state regulations, as a precursor to more stringent state regulations, or as a substitute for state regulations. Under what conditions and how frequently has each outcome occurred?[180]

### 8.2. Role of Home States in the CSR Governance Regime

The home states where transnational companies are headquartered have a key role in the global CSR regime. Ruggie has emphasised this role but resisted calls to acknowledge that the state's duty to protect in Pillar 1 applies extraterritorially to benefit populations overseas. NGOs have criticised Ruggie's choice because it leaves it to home states' discretion, instead of being an imperative, to regulate their TNCs through national laws and contracts, and through state-to-state instruments such as investment and trade agreements.[181]

De Schutter argued in favour of an obligation on the home States of TNCs to provide a remedy for victims abroad, which could take the form either of parent-based extraterritorial regulation imposing a due diligence obligation on parent companies, or foreign direct liability imposing prescriptions directly on the foreign subsidiaries. The former alternative appears preferable, he thought. As to the status of such a state obligation, "[w]hile this would build on current developments in the international law of human rights, it would also go beyond them in obliging the home State to exercise a form of extraterritorial jurisdiction over the corporations which have its nationality for their operations overseas".[182]

In her thorough analysis of the state's obligation to protect, Hakimi noticed that extraterritorial obligations to protect have received little attention in the academic lit-

---

The Role of Professional Associations in the Transformation of Institutionalized Fields', 45:1 *Academy of Management Journal* (2002) pp. 58–80.

179  K. Webb (ed.), *Voluntary Codes: Private Governance, the Public Interest and Innovation*, 2004, <www2.carleton.ca/sppa/research/publications>, (especially ch. 5: K. Webb and A. Morrison, 'The Law and Voluntary Codes: Examining the "Tangled Web"').

180  Vogel, *supra* note 145, p. 275.

181  For a detailed treatment *see* Kinley's discussion of three important avenues – trade, aid and corporate responsibility – that developed states have at their disposal to strengthen the protection of human rights in less developed countries. D. Kinley, *Civilising Globalisation, Human Rights and the Global Economy* (Cambridge University Press, 2009).

182  O. De Schutter, *Extraterritorial Jurisdiction as a tool for improving the Human Rights Accountability of Transnational Corporations*, Background paper to seminar in Brussels on 3–4 November 2006, pp. 51–52.

erature compared with the obligation to respect.[183] Augenstein looked closely at the jurisprudence of the European Court of Human Rights and found few and rather isolated instances pointing towards states' obligation to regulate their companies regarding impacts abroad.[184]

Ruggie has dealt with the issue of extraterritoriality at length in his reports[185] and organised seminars on this theme. In his 2008 report he concluded:

> Experts disagree on whether international law requires home States to help prevent human rights abuses abroad by corporations based within their territory. There is greater consensus that those States are not prohibited from doing so where a recognized basis of jurisdiction exists, and the actions of the home State meet an overall reasonableness test, which includes non-intervention in the internal affairs of other States... Further refinements of the legal understanding of the State duty to protect by authoritative bodies at national and international levels are highly desirable.[186]

The 2010 report, while still not characterising the duty to protect as extending extraterritorially, explained:

> In the heated debates about extraterritoriality regarding business and human rights, a critical distinction between two very different phenomena is usually obscured. One is jurisdiction exercised directly in relation to actors or activities overseas, such as criminal regimes governing child sex tourism, which rely on the nationality of the perpetrator no matter where the offence occurs. The other is domestic measures that have extraterritorial implications; for example, requiring corporate parents to report on the company's overall human rights policy and impacts, including those of its overseas subsidiaries. The latter phenomenon relies on territory as the jurisdictional basis, even though it may have extraterritorial implications.[187]

### 8.3. Role of Financial Actors in the CSR Governance Regime

The last decade has witnessed increased attention to the responsibilities and roles of financial actors. The main focus has been on the more direct relationships involved in project finance through which banks support projects, usually infrastructure projects. Large institutional investors, such as pension funds, supposedly taking a longer term

---

183   Hakimi, *supra* note 18, p. 376.
184   D. Augenstein, *State Responsibilities To Regulate And Adjudicate Corporate Activities Under The European Convention On Human Rights*, Submission to the SRSG on the issue of Human Rights and Business, April 2011.
185   For example, Mapping Standards, *supra* note 112, paras 10–18.
186   Protect, Respect and Remedy, *supra* note 14, paras. 19 and 21 (reference omitted).
187   Further steps, *supra* note 78, para. 48.

outlook on their investment than other more speculative investors,[188] have also attracted attention and sometimes regulatory interventions, as discussed before. Among the international initiatives in this area are the UN-backed Principles for Responsible Investment Initiative for institutional investors (2006)[189] and the Equator Principles for banks, basically applying the IFC performance standards (2003).[190] The financial crisis of 2008 brought to the forefront the tremendous complexities that came to characterise financial markets' vehicles and operations.[191] The CSR movement is yet to come to grip with such complexities.

The SRSG portfolio of reports cover export credit agencies, stock exchanges, financial products such as socially responsible investment (SRI) indices, financial regulations requiring transparency, company law and securities law aspects and so on. And, as highlighted previously, he wrote eloquently about markets: "The challenge we face is a big one: we are caught up in a fundamental institutional misalignment in the world between economic forces and actors on the one hand, and the ability of societies to adapt to the adverse consequences of the economic forces and to take full advantage of the opportunities of the economic forces on the other hand."[192] Still Ruggie's treatment in this area is tentative in the meaning that he took note of key actors and CSR initiatives but fell short of a fuller understanding of the responsibilities of investors and financial institutions. Except for the case of project finance, where the direct relationship between the financier and the specific project is straightforward and resembling complicity, the talk seems to be more about roles rather than responsibilities of financial institutions.[193]

Ruggie does not frame the relationship between investors and the companies they invest in as one of complicity: their offering of capital to companies is not seen as assistance or contribution to the commission of harm. The financiers' responsibilities are not discussed in the same breath with value chain responsibility either, despite clear similarities. In this respect, Catá Backer observed that

> [t]here is something of a disjunction between the SRSG's discussion of supply chain obligations of corporations, and the discussion of the obligations financial institutions involved in the financing of corporate activity ... It seems odd to suggest that an industry with such a sophisticated approach to the monitoring and control of borrowers would be incapable of adding another layer of monitoring and review – that centered on human

---

188  J. P. Hawley and A. T. Williams, *The Rise of Fiduciary Capitalism: How Institutional Investors Can Make Corporate America More Democratic* (University of Pennsylvania Press, Philadelphia, 2000).

189  <www.unpri.org>.

190  <www.equator-principles.com>.

191  *See* the chapter by Dowell-Jones and Kinley in this volume.

192  J. G. Ruggie, 'Introductory Remarks', in *Corporate Responsibility for Human Rights: Concepts, Examples, Approaches*, Summary Report (Berlin), 21 January 2010, <www.human-rights-business.org/files/report_thats_right.pdf>.

193  *See* the chapter by Sullivan and Hachez in this volume on the role of institutional investors in CSR.

rights – to an already well established list of risk assessment protocols. Indeed, it would seem that banks are in a better position to monitor compliance form their borrowers than companies might be able to monitor the conduct of their down chain supply chain partners.[194]

The idea on which an investor's responsibility to act seems to build comes less from CSR's notions of complicity[195] and more from corporate governance where the emphasis in the last 15 years has been on active shareholding, active ownership.[196] The view here is that uniformed and passive investors allow corporate managers to employ risky approaches that can harm business prospects and societies alike. As noted previously in the corporate governance section, the thrust here is the success of the business in the long term which requires a proper identification and management of all types of risks, including the risk that careless handling of human rights will backfire on the company. Having to rationalise the protection of human rights in terms of a company's own success is of course inherently limited, as discussed in a previous section.

Given the numerous intermediary financial institutions entangled in a web of inscrutable financial relationships and dealings, the way forward for CSR seems to point to the idea of 'shared responsibility' and the need for multistakeholder governance initiatives as a way of discharging it. For example, Keenan and Ochoa argue in favour of a 'shared duty to protect', meaning that "states, private actors, and international institutions should share the duty to protect those rights that are violated in connection with business and financial activity".[197] They "propose a fairly bright line: when states and investors knowingly engage with host states that are unable to protect their own citizens against harms that may be committed or facilitated by the investment, they undertake to share this duty with the host state. In short, arrangements that result in investors benefiting from the dysfunctional nature of host states should give rise to the investor's obligation to share in the duty to protect human rights."[198]

Ruggie himself considered that "soft law hybrids have made a singular contribution by acknowledging that for some purposes the most sensible solution is to base initiatives on the notion of 'shared responsibility from the start'."[199] At one of the sem-

---

194 L. Catá Backer, 'The United Nations' "Protect-Respect-Remedy" Project: Operationalizing a Global Human Rights Based Framework for the Regulation of Transnational Corporations', Conference Paper, Symposium: Corporations and International Law, Santa Clara University, 12–13 March 2010, p. 181.

195 A. Clapham and S. Jerbi, 'Categories of Corporate Complicity in Human Rights Abuses', 24 *Hastings Int'l & Comp. L. Rev.* 339 (2001). International Commission of Jurists, *Final Report of the Expert Legal Panel on Corporate Complicity in International Crimes* (2008).

196 The OECD deems that "[t]he corporate governance framework should protect and facilitate the *exercise* of shareholders' rights". OECD Principles of Corporate Governance, *supra* note 60, Section II, p. 19 (emphasis added)

197 P. J. Keenan and C. Ochoa, 'The Human Rights Potential of Sovereign Wealth Funds', 40 *Georgetown Journal of International Law* (Summer 2009) p. 1151, at p. 1158.

198 *Ibid.*, p. 1158 (references omitted).

199 Mapping Standards, *supra* note 112, para. 87.

inars Ruggie convened, as the transcript reads, Ruggie observed that the notion of shared responsibility

> recognizes that the challenges arising from globalization are structural in character, involving governance gaps and governance failures. Accordingly, they cannot be resolved by an individual liability model of responsibility alone but also need to be dealt with in their own right. This requires a model of strategically coherent distributed action focused on realigning the relationships among actors, including States, corporations and civil society.[200]

### 8.4. *Role of Core Companies in the CSR Governance Regime*

#### 8.4.1. Responsibility of Parent and Buyer Companies Regarding their Affiliates' Operations

Through his RtR, Ruggie has simplified diverse expectations of what companies should do by distilling a responsibility to 'do no harm'. From the inflation of verbs used by the Draft Norms[201] Ruggie has retained just one: 'respect' human rights meaning 'do no harm', 'do not infringe on human rights'. And this RtR is applied to all business, including TNCs and other large companies. Such complex business groups and networks have *blurred boundaries* and operate lawfully in accordance with the principle of *legal separation* of entities. The OECD observed that "[m]ultinational enterprises, like their domestic counterparts, have evolved to encompass a broader range of business arrangements and organisational forms. Strategic alliances and closer relations with suppliers and contractors tend to blur the boundaries of the enterprise."[202] Unfortunately, Ruggie's treatment of the RtR is affected in insidious ways.

Ruggie and other voices in CSR of course have not overlooked these two aspects. Thus Ruggie recognised that "[t]he worst alleged corporate-related human rights abuses typically have involved third parties connected to a company's operations, such as security forces or suppliers, with the company being accused of complicity in whatever act was committed by that third party. In a number of cases the allegations have included war crimes and crimes against humanity."[203] Further Ruggie took note of the doctrine of limited liability and of arms-length market exchanges as he discussed network-based and hierarchical business structures. He acknowledged that "[t]ransnational corporate networks pose a regulatory challenge to the international legal system".[204] This legal separation is no small obstacle as Catá Backer signalled: "As a matter of corporate law in virtually every jurisdiction, the essence of legal personal-

---

200 *Corporate responsibility under international law and issues in extraterritorial regulation: summary of legal workshops*, Addendum 2 to the Report, A/HRC/4/35/Add.2, 2007, para. 34. See also Evolving Agenda, *supra* note 37, p. 839.
201 *See* text associated with *supra* note 33.
202 OECD Guidelines for Multinational Enterprises, *supra* note 105, p. 11.
203 Ruggie, *supra* note 173.
204 Evolving Agenda, *supra* note 37, p. 824.

ity, and the autonomy of separately chartered corporations serve as the bedrock any approach to the obligations of corporations to monitor and control the behavior of others."[205]

The question is whether Ruggie should have isolated, for reason of clarity, the case of business groups and networks as distinguished from individual enterprises, and then disaggregated the RtR to explain what it requires from core companies.[206] Is the core company only under a responsibility to 'respect', asking it to make sure its decisions do not harm directly or indirectly human rights, or is it also under a responsibility to 'protect' the human rights that affiliates infringe? Without using these words, in his explanations and illustrations of due diligence Ruggie clearly covers both the 'respect' and 'protect' situations. This broad scope of the RtR is commendable and in tune with social expectations. But Ruggie chose not to come forward with a principled way of attributing responsibility to the core company in the 'protect' case. Conceptually, this is a question of attribution of responsibility well-known in jurisprudence in determinations of liability.

Ruggie did screen jurisprudence and explicitly took note of available legal doctrines. Overall Ruggie makes extensive use of the notion of complicity, in both its legal meaning (such as 'aiding and abetting') and a non-legal meaning (such as 'association' or 'involvement').[207] His 2007 report referred to some legal doctrines: "The international tribunals have also imposed liability for 'aiding and abetting' a crime, or for engaging in a 'common purpose' or 'joint criminal enterprise'."[208] In 2010 Ruggie further wrote:

> [O]ne legal challenge is the attribution of responsibility among members of a corporate group. Many corporate-related human rights violations also violate existing national civil or criminal law, but applying those provisions to corporate groups can prove extremely complex, even in purely domestic cases.
>
> A range of legal arguments has been advanced in cases involving the responsibility of parent companies for harm caused by subsidiaries. Some rely on the parent company's alleged 'negligence' with respect to its subsidiary (primary liability), focusing, for example, on whether the parent has established key systems or processes, like those dealing with hazardous activities. Other arguments invoke 'complicity' (secondary liability) or the concept of 'agency' (vicarious or third party liability), which are found in both common and civil law jurisdictions. The responsibility of partners in joint ventures and other

---

205 Catá Backer, *supra* note 194, p. 74.
206 *See* chapter by Mares in this volume.
207 He wrote: "The corporate responsibility to respect human rights includes avoiding complicity. The concept has legal and non-legal pedigrees, and the implications of both are important for companies. Complicity refers to indirect involvement by companies in human rights abuses – where the actual harm is committed by another party, including governments and non-State actors." Protect, Respect and Remedy, *supra* note 14, para. 73. *See also Clarifying the Concepts of 'Sphere of influence' and 'Complicity'*, Companion report, A/HRC/8/16, 2008.
208 Mapping Standards, *supra* note 112, para. 23.

contract-based relationships raises even more complex questions, though the theory of multi-agency liability has gained traction in some jurisdictions. In short, far greater clarity is needed regarding the responsibility of corporate parents and groups for the purposes of remedy.[209]

However Ruggie covered jurisprudence only in a descriptive manner: doctrines were noted, their relevance acknowledged but not analytically distinguished from each other in order to settle conceptually the 'protect' scenario. Nor did he deem it necessary to settle the difficulty of attributing responsibility for purposes of his RtR. The problem, it can be safely said, is that the legal separation of entities is an unavoidable aspect whenever discussing the RtR of business groups. Ruggie is mindful of its crippling effects, wrote explicitly on it, but did not crack it conceptually. Instead he chose a subtle strategy of avoidance (presented it as an obstacle to access to remedies relevant to Pillar 3 instead of an issue of corporate responsibility in Pillar 2) and postponement (legal professionals and national legal systems deal with this obstacle) in the context of his more general approach being principle-based (a foundational treatment with details to be spelled out later on) and not legalistic (no scheme for the attribution of liability is needed). In fairness, limited liability is a tough nut to crack, but remains inescapably relevant to future treatments of the RtR of large business groups and networks simply because "the corporation enjoys separate legal personhood [which is one of the] essential legal attributes of the corporate form of business organization".[210]

As a result there is a possibility that the 'respect' aspect of Ruggie's RtR appears mandatory, imperative under the 'do no harm' principle, while the 'protect' aspect remains aspirational as it is grounded in something else than do no harm.[211] That this aspirational element remains in Ruggie's RtR is remarkable given his principled rejection of the sweeping responsibilities proposed by the Draft Norms. The implications for the implementation of the RtR are particularly disturbing: when policy pronouncements endorsing Ruggie's RtR reach the ground, the RtR becomes atomised in the RtR of separated companies with no imperative on the core company to oversee and influence affiliates. One is pressed to admit then that such affirmations of responsibility can only

---

209   Further steps, *supra* note 78, paras. 105–106.
210   Stevelman, *supra* note 77, p. 836. Stevelman further wrote that "the limited liability of corporate shareholders is valorized as a major driver of wealth creation … after fifteen years of reflecting on cases in which the courts are called upon to pierce the corporate veil, I can find little depth of legal reasoning in them, beyond the policy goals of incentivizing capital formation and encouraging investment in the corporate form. In essence, the legal rule quite nakedly embraces a policy judgment that even tort creditors' claims will be subordinated to those goals. There appears to be no deeper intellectual coherence in the limited liability case law. The fact that corporate law privileges the goal of capital formation over the compensation of tort victims is certainly a topic of social relevance." *Ibid.*, pp. 842–843 (reference omitted).
211   Such uncertainties in Ruggie's treatment were pinpointed in the comments of the EU comments on the draft Guiding Principles. The EU referred to "areas where the Guiding Principles could be more precise …: Clarification of the concept of responsibility within a corporate group would be useful …" EU comments, *supra* note 25.

be read, when it comes to the 'protect' component of the RtR, as aspirational, hortatory statements from policymakers well aware of the legal realities in their domestic systems. That is indeed a modest and limited treatment of the responsibility of business groups. Without that imperative character, and despite Ruggie's stated purpose of leveraging key players on the global governance stage, core companies are likely to recede in the background of the chess board that Ruggie masterly arranged.

Ruggie's conceptualisation of the RtR gave them this opportunity. It weakens calls for core companies to assume their responsibility to act when affiliates misbehave. They may be brought back to the forefront in a more ad hoc manner and on a voluntary basis through multistakeholder, public-private governance arrangements. Ruggie drew attention to this and also promoted the concept of 'shared responsibility'. Examples and lessons from supply chains make the point of shared responsibility forcefully.[212]

### 8.4.2. Supply Chain Issues

Back in the mid-1990s the media uncovered sweatshop practices in factories producing for famous global brands such as the market-leader Nike.[213] A stream of similar stories continues to this day.[214] Civil society put pressure on buyer companies to accept responsibility for workers' rights throughout their supply chains, and not few companies have done so.[215] After 15 years, it is time to take stock and learn the lessons of what works effectively and efficiently and what does not.[216]

---

212  UNCTAD referred to the imperative of building capacity for compliance in supply chains that would require from the buyer companies a strategy of 'shared responsibility' as opposed to 'offloading responsibility' on the suppliers. United Nations Conference on Trade and Development (UNCTAD), *2011 World Investment Report* (United Nations, 2011), p. 117.

213  Referring to that moment in time, Ruggie observed that "[t]he issue of business and human rights burst into global public consciousness in the 1990s. Some of the early cases have acquired iconic status: Shell accused of complicity for standing by silently as the Nigerian military government executed a leader of community groups demonstrating against the company's environmental degradation of the Delta region; BP accused of being responsible for alleged acts of murder, disappearances, torture, rape, and forced displacement of communities by a Colombian army brigade protecting its installation; allegations of sweatshop conditions and child labor in Nike's Indonesian, and the GAP's Salvadorian, suppliers." J. G. Ruggie, *Next steps in business and human rights*, Remarks at Royal institute of international affairs, Chatham house, London, 22 May 2008, <www.reports-and-materials.org/Ruggie-speech-Chatham-House-22-May-2008.pdf>.

214  'Fashion chain Zara acts on Brazil sweatshop conditions', *BBC*, 18 august 2011, <www.bbc.co.uk/news/world-latin-america-14570564>. *Ripe with Abuse: Human Rights Conditions in South Africa's Fruit and Wine Industries*, Human Rights Watch, 23 August 2011, <www.hrw.org/reports/2011/08/23/ripe-abuse-0>.

215  For multistakeholder initiatives dedicated to labour standards in supply chains, *see* those of the Fair Labor Association, Social Accountability International, and Ethical Trading Initiative.

216  *See* the chapters by Lukas, and Skadegaard Thorsen and Andreasen in this volume.

At one of the seminars convened by the SRSG, "[p]articipants were unanimous that change has to be systemic, not piecemeal or one-off. They suggested that a 'long fix' – as opposed to a 'quick fix' – was required".[217] The elements of a 'long fix' were identified to include empowering workers, building the capacity of suppliers, changing buyer's policies and practices, and building the capacity of labour inspectorates.[218] On a likeminded tone, the trade union view has consistently been that

> [i]nstead of playing cat and mouse, these companies are starting to get to the root causes of problems and deliver more sustainable supply chains ... The current approach is simply not sustainable in the longer term. It needs to be replaced by a mature system of industrial relations based on social dialogue where representatives of management and workers become daily monitors of workplace situations.[219]

Sometimes the solution to rights violations in the value chain seems easier, at least conceptually. This is the case of goods that can be boycotted and prevented from reaching markets. The Kimberley Process – the public-private governance arrangement to prevent conflict diamonds from reaching international markets – is a well-known example. More recently, cotton harvested in Uzbekistan with the use of forced child labour is being subjected to a private boycott. The civil society group Responsible Sourcing Network was joined by large retailers such as Wal-mart and Macy's and by TNCs such as Nike and Liz Claiborne in a signed pledge to boycott Uzbek cotton. This group of 70 companies demands that the government stops using forced child labour to harvest its cotton crops.[220] Also a recent story featured a company, Danish-based Lundbeck, which decided to act to prevent its products from being used by third parties to infringe rights. The company took steps to prohibit its drugs from being used to execute convicts in the US. According to Lundbeck policy, "[p]urchasers will have to sign a form affirming the drug is for their own use and will not be used for capital punishment and that they will not re-distribute the drug without the company's approval".[221]

---

217  Summary of five multi-stakeholder consultations, *supra* note 146, para. 246.
218  *Ibid.*
219  R. Wilshaw, 'Social audits flawed as a way of driving sustainable change', *The Guardian*, 12 July 2011, <www.guardian.co.uk/sustainable-business/blog/social-audits-flawed-companies-developing-world>.
220  K. Kattalia, 'Retailers such as Nike and Macy's boycott cotton from Uzbekistan to protest child labor', *Daily News Writer*, 7 July 2011, <www.nydailynews.com/lifestyle/fashion/2011/07/07/2011-07-07_retailers_boycott_cotton_from_uzbekistan_to_protest_child_labor.html>.
221  'Virginia executes Jerry Jackson amid death-drug row', *BBC*, 19 august 2011, <www.bbc.co.uk/news/world-us-canada-14579136>. Reprieve, the London-based rights group that sought the ban, welcomed the news. "Lundbeck has proven that manufacturers can control the use and distribution of their drugs. Any company manufacturing execution drugs who refuses to take such steps will be directly complicit in executions ... Other pharmaceutical companies should now follow Lundbeck's example." A. Gabbatt and D. Batty, 'Danish firm Lundbeck to stop US jails using drug for lethal injections', *The Guardian*, 1 July 2011.

But often the solution to abuses in value chains is clearly broader than a single-minded emphasis on buyer responsibility and often requires multistakeholder governance arrangements at different levels.[222] One such example with potential to protect rights sustainably and effectively comes from Indonesia where labour unions, major supplier factories and key sportswear brands have agreed to guarantee freedom to form unions and bargain collectively.[223] The role of the buyer company remains essential to solve other difficult issues, such as that of worker remuneration. Recently the NGO ActionAid hailed British retailer Marks and Spencer as the first retailer to commit itself to ensuring living wages for suppliers' employees.[224] The company promised to "[i]mplement a process to ensure our clothing suppliers are able to pay workers a fair 'living' wage in the least developed countries we source from, starting with Bangladesh, India and Sri Lanka by 2015. We will achieve this by ensuring that the cost prices we pay to our suppliers are adequate to pay a fair living wage and by rolling out our ethical model factory programme."[225]

Another difficult area refers to sourcing raw materials from conflict zones. The OECD dedicated a detailed guidance document aimed at securing human rights in conflict-affected and high-risk areas where minerals are sourced from. Due diligence steps are identified to trace minerals, and prevent and mitigate risks of human rights abuses.[226] The OECD outlook is premised on the realisation that "governments, international organisations and companies can each draw on their respective competences and roles to contribute to ensuring that trade and investment in natural resources is beneficial to society at large".[227]

## 9. Conclusion

In June 2011, the group of states (the 'Core sponsors') drafting the resolution to be adopted by the Human Rights Council recalled the complex and deeply divisive history of CSR in the UN and appreciated the "incremental approach so successfully carved

---

222 *See* the chapter by Skadegaard Thorsen and Andreasen in this volume.

223 O.Tudor, 'Adidas, Nike and Puma sign up with unions on Indonesian textile worker rights', Blog, 7 June 2011. *See* fulltext of the signed Freedom of Association Protocol at <play-fair.org/media/wp-content/uploads/FOA-Protocol_English-translation_May-20112.pdf>.

224 ActionAid, *Tax responsibility – The business case for making tax a corporate responsibility issue*, 2011, p. 7, <www.actionaid.org.uk/doc_lib/tax_responsibility.pdf>.

225 Objective 17 (Ensure workforces and communities benefit in our supply chain). Marks & Spencer, *How we do business report*, 2010, p. 47, <plana.marksandspencer.com/media/pdf/planA-2010.pdf>.

226 The Guidance recommends companies to commit themselves and orient there due diligence towards the following goal: "Regarding serious abuses associated with the extraction, transport or trade of minerals, [w]hile sourcing from, or operating in, conflict-affected and high-risk areas, we will neither tolerate nor by any means profit from, contribute to, assist with or facilitate the commission." Annex II, *Model Supply Chain Policy*, OECD, *supra* note 106.

227 OECD, *supra* note 106, p. 7.

out by Professor Ruggie".²²⁸ In an interview around the same time, Ruggie declared that "[h]istory marches in small steps, but to lay the foundation of future developments is an important first step ... We now have a uniform platform; a uniform foundation on which to build going forward."²²⁹ Several key issues highlighted in this chapter were left in suspension because of a lack of consensus in the legal community (*i.e.* extraterritoriality), the issue appeared intractable (*i.e.* legal separation of entities) or the complexity was overwhelming (*i.e.* responsibilities of actors in financial markets). In such cases more daring treatments from the SRSG side would have run the risk of backfiring. There is little doubt that legal departments in companies and governments are able and ready to pick on controversial positions and question the rigour of the entire work.

Aiming to facilitate a process where cumulative progress can be achieved, Ruggie left it to the follow-up process in the UN and elsewhere to push rule-making further. Further clarifications of the principles Ruggie outlined will be needed. Frankental's thoughts are relevant for grasping the task lying ahead for the academia and human right law experts: he considered that "a key challenge for Amnesty International in reshaping its business and human rights work will be to integrate human rights into other disciplines that also seek to raise standards for companies".²³⁰ As for Ruggie, who will remain involved in the business and human rights movement, he looked back to his mandate and said: "Dealing with all rights; all states; all businesses, national and transnational, large and small; and getting all of that diversity into a simple and coherent Framework, with guidance on how it should be implemented, was both intellectually and politically challenging."²³¹

---

228   *Introduction of draft resolution L17: Human Rights and transnational corporations and other business enterprises*, 17th session of the Human Rights Council, 2011, <www.business-humanrights.org/media/documents/ruggie/statements-norway-uk-business-human-rights-16-jun-2011.pdf>.
229   U. Mast-Kirschning, 'States, companies must ensure human rights, UN expert says', Interview with John Ruggie, *Deutsche Welle*, 20 June 2011, <www.dw-world.de/dw/article/0,,15173983,00.html>.
230   P. Frankental, *The Reshaping of Amnesty International's Business and Human Rights Work*, Institute for Human Rights and Business, 18 May 2011, <www.ihrb.org/commentary/guest/amnesty_international_business_human_rights.html>.
231   Interview, *supra* note 26.

## Annex 1 Reports of the Special Representative of the Secretary-General on the issue of human rights and transnational corporations and other business enterprises, John Ruggie*

Interim Report of the Special Representative of the Secretary-General on the Issue of Human Rights and Transnational Corporations and Other Business Enterprises, E/CN.4/2006/97, 2006.

Business and Human Rights: Mapping International Standards of Responsibility and Accountability for Corporate Acts, A/HRC/4/035, 2007.

State responsibilities to regulate and adjudicate corporate activities under the United Nations core human rights treaties: an overview of treaty body commentaries, Addendum 1 to the Report, A/HRC/4/35/Add.1, 2007.

Corporate responsibility under international law and issues in extraterritorial regulation: summary of legal workshops, Addendum 2 to the Report, A/HRC/4/35/Add.2, 2007.

Human Rights Policies and Management Practices: Results from questionnaire surveys of Governments and Fortune Global 500 firms, Addendum 3 to the Report, A/HRC/4/35/Add.3, 2007.

Business recognition of human rights: Global patterns, regional and sectoral variations, Addendum 4 to the Report, A/HRC/4/35/Add.4, 2007.

Human rights impact assessments – resolving key methodological questions, Companion report, A/HRC/4/74, 2007.

Protect, Respect and Remedy: a Framework for Business and Human Rights, A/HRC/8/5, 2008.

Clarifying the Concepts of "Sphere of influence" and "Complicity", Companion report, A/HRC/8/16, 2008.

Summary of five multi-stakeholder consultations, Addendum 1 to the Report, A/HRC/8/5/Add.1, 2008.

Corporations and human rights: a survey of the scope and patterns of alleged corporate-related human rights abuse, Addendum 2 to the Report, A/HRC/8/5/Add.2, 2008.

Business and human rights: Towards operationalizing the "protect, respect and remedy" framework, A/HRC/11/13, 2009.

Business and Human Rights: Further steps toward the operationalization of the "protect, respect and remedy" framework, A/HRC/14/27, 2010.

Guiding Principles on Business and Human Rights: Implementing the United Nations "Protect, Respect and Remedy" Framework, A/HRC/17/31, 2011.

Piloting principles for effective company/stakeholder grievance mechanisms: A report of lessons learned, Addendum 1 to the Report, A/HRC/17/31/Add.1, 2011.

Human rights and corporate law: trends and observations from a crossnational study conducted by the Special Representative, Addendum 2 to the Report, A/HRC/17/31/Add.2, 2011.

Principles for responsible contracts: integrating the management of human rights risks into State-investor contract negotiations: guidance for negotiators, Addendum 3 to the Report, A/HRC/17/31/Add.3, 2011.

Business and human rights in conflict-affected regions: challenges and options towards State responses, Companion report, A/HRC/17/32, 2011.

---

\* **Note.** *See also* a comprehensive List of documents prepared by, and submitted to, the SRSG at <www.reports-and-materials.org/Ruggie-docs-list.pdf>.

## Annex 2 Resolutions of the Commission on Human Rights and Human Rights Committee relevant to the SRSG mandate

Commission on Human Rights, Responsibilities of transnational corporations and related business enterprises with regard to human rights, Decision 2004/116, 2004.

Commission on Human Rights, Human rights and transnational corporations and other business enterprises, Resolution 2005/69, 2005.

Human Rights Council, Mandate of the Special Representative of the Secretary-General on the issue of human rights and transnational corporations and other business enterprises, Resolution 8/7, 2008.

Human Rights Council, Human rights and transnational corporations and other business enterprises, A/HRC/17/L.17/Rev.1, 2011.

# 2   The Ruggie Rules: Applying Human Rights Law to Corporations

John H. Knox*

## 1.   Introduction

In 2005, when John Ruggie was appointed as the United Nations (UN) Special Representative of the Secretary-General (SRSG) on human rights and transnational corporations and other business enterprises, the application of human rights law to corporations was highly contested. Lines of battle had formed between human rights groups and corporations over many issues, including whether corporations have, or should have, direct obligations under human rights law. At stake was more than the rhetorical advantage advocates might obtain from being able to accuse corporations of legal as well as moral misconduct. Clarification of corporate responsibility could determine whether corporations are subject to legal remedies for violating human rights law, including in suits brought against them under the Alien Tort Statute (ATS), a US law that allows aliens to seek monetary damages for torts committed in violation of international law.[1]

This chapter examines the relationship between John Ruggie's work as the SRSG and the evolution of corporate obligations under human rights law. At the outset, two points should be emphasised. First, this focus does not include all aspects of Ruggie's mandate, which extended beyond legal issues. Second, Ruggie's ability to shape international law was severely limited. His mandate did not (and could not) authorise him to create new legal norms. Still, human rights law was intrinsic to the challenges he faced and to the solutions he proposed, and his work sheds light on several important legal questions.

The chapter first analyses Ruggie's response to the most fundamental legal issue presented to him: does the entire body of human rights law apply directly to corporations? Rejecting the approach taken by a group of UN experts two years earlier, Ruggie

---

\*   Professor of Law, Wake Forest University.
1   The Statute provides jurisdiction to US courts for "any civil action by an alien for a tort only, committed in violation of the law of nations or a treaty of the United States". 28 U.S.C. § 1350.

answered the question with an emphatic negative. International law supports his position; indeed, the opposite view is legally untenable. By itself, however, his restatement of existing law would not have quelled the controversy over the relationship of human rights law and corporations. But Ruggie did not stop there. He offered a new Framework and Guiding Principles that attempt (1) to elaborate the legal duties of states to protect against human rights abuses by regulating corporate conduct, and (2) to set out responsibilities for corporations that are not binding but that nevertheless provide a basis for monitoring and remediating corporate misconduct. Many chapters in this book critique the Guiding Principles from various points of view. Here, I look at their complicated relationship with human rights law, examining both how the Principles draw on existing law and whether they prepare the ground for the law to recognise direct corporate duties in the future.

Second, the chapter discusses three narrower issues: (a) Even if corporations are not bound by the body of human rights law, are they at least obliged to refrain from committing particularly heinous abuses that are defined as international crimes?; (b) When can corporations be complicit in *state* violations of human rights law?; and (c) Does the state duty to protect extend extraterritorially to actions by corporations outside the territory of their home state? International law does not yet provide a definitive answer to any of these questions. This chapter describes Ruggie's positions: (a) corporations may be liable for committing international crimes; (b) corporations can be complicit in a state violation if they knowledgeably assist in its commission, even if they did not intend the violation to occur; and (c) the state duty to protect does not extend extraterritorially, although states should nevertheless encourage corporations to respect human rights abroad. These positions will help to inform, although they will certainly not end, the ongoing debate over how international law should address corporate abuses of human rights.

## 2. The Application of Human Rights Law to Corporations: From Draft Norms to Guiding Principles

Governments hoped that John Ruggie would quiet the controversy over the application of human rights law to corporations in part by clarifying the existing law. To that end, the Human Rights Commission asked that, as part of his mandate, he describe the human rights norms that apply to corporations, both those that apply directly and those that apply indirectly through states' obligations to protect against corporate abuses.[2] One difficulty in carrying out this task was that in many respects the law was not settled. As Ruggie pointed out in his first report to the Commission, the standards were often not already there, waiting to be recorded and implemented, but were rather still in the process of being socially constructed. "Indeed," he noted, "the mandate itself inevitably is a modest intervention in that larger process".[3]

---

2   *See* Human Rights Commission Res. 2005/69, U.N. Doc. E/CN.4/2005/135 (2005), pp. 268–270, para. 1(a).

3   *Interim Report of the Special Representative of the Secretary-General on the Issue of Human Rights and Transnational Corporations and Other Business Enterprises*, U.N. Doc. E/

Even where the law seemed relatively clear, the effort to describe it was complicated by the recent proposal by another UN human rights body of the Draft Norms on the Responsibilities of Transnational Corporations and Other Business Enterprises with Regard to Human Rights.[4] The Sub-Commission on the Promotion and Protection of Human Rights, a group of nominally independent experts operating under the auspices of the Human Rights Commission, had proposed the Draft Norms to the Commission in 2003.[5] The Norms had contributed to the controversy over the relationship of corporations and human rights by suggesting that human rights law already did apply directly to corporations – a position welcomed by many human rights advocates and strongly opposed by many corporations. As Ruggie told the Commission in his first report, it was difficult to have a discussion about the application of human rights standards to corporations without reprising the earlier debates over the Norms, which had ended in stalemate between their proponents and their critics.[6]

At the outset of his mandate, then, Ruggie had to decide how he would address the Norms and, more broadly, the approach to corporate duties that they represented. As the first of the following sections explains, human rights law as a whole so clearly does not apply directly to corporations that he had little choice but to reject the Norms as a restatement of existing law. His real challenge, as the second section discusses, was to reach that conclusion without abandoning the application of human rights law to corporations entirely, thereby alienating those working to bring human rights to bear on corporate misconduct. In response, Ruggie proposed a Framework and Guiding Principles that draw on human rights law extensively but do not explicitly redirect it at corporations, as the Norms did.

## 2.1. The Draft Norms as a Restatement of Human Rights Law

The Sub-Commission's Draft Norms on the Responsibilities of Transnational Corporations and Other Business Enterprises are in the form of a human rights treaty that provides that virtually every human right gives rise to a wide range of duties on virtually every corporation. Paragraph 1 states: "Within their respective spheres of activity and influence, transnational corporations and other business enterprises have the obligation to promote, secure the fulfillment of, respect, ensure respect of and pro-

---

CN.4/2006/97 (2006), para. 54 (hereafter '2006 Interim Report').

4   Sub-Commission on the Promotion and Protection of Human Rights, *Norms on the Responsibilities of Transnational Corporations and Other Business Enterprises with Regard to Human Rights*, U.N. Doc. E/CN.4/Sub.2/2003/12/Rev. 2 (2003) (hereafter 'Draft Norms'). See also Sub-Commission on the Promotion and Protection of Human Rights, *Commentary on the Norms on the Responsibilities of Transnational Corporations and Other Business Enterprises with Regard to Human Rights*, U.N. Doc. E/CN.4/Sub.2/2003/38/Rev. 2 (2003); D. Weissbrodt and M. Kruger, 'Norms on the Responsibilities of Transnational Corporations and Other Business Enterprises with Regard to Human Rights', 97 *Am. J. Int'l L.* (2003) p. 901.

5   Sub-Commission Res. 2003/16, U.N. Doc. E/CN.4/Sub.2/2003/L.11, at p. 52 (2003).

6   2006 Interim Report, *supra* note 3, para. 55.

tect human rights recognized in international as well as national law."[7] Later provisions refer to slightly more specific corporate duties in relation to non-discrimination, international crimes, labour rights and other areas.[8]

Although the Draft Norms were written as if they set out binding obligations, as the product of a group of independent experts they could have no legal effect in themselves. Indeed, they could have no directly binding effect even if the Human Rights Commission had adopted them. Nevertheless, the Norms raised the possibility that they might shape the development of human rights law, either by serving as the basis for a later treaty or by providing a statement of the law around which interpretation and practice might coalesce. There were indications that the Sub-Commission intended the Norms to have the second effect: it described the Norms as reflecting current human rights legal standards applicable to corporations,[9] and it expressed its intention to monitor their implementation.[10]

The Norms were controversial not just because their proponents claimed that they restated existing international law. Many corporations undoubtedly opposed the Norms simply because they feared that a new set of international corporate standards would lead to greater scrutiny of corporate behaviour.[11] Nevertheless, the Norms' sweeping legal claims did provide their critics ammunition, because the claims had little support in the law. The Norms neither reflected the existing state of international human rights law nor justified the legal changes that would be necessary to give them life. Indeed, the proponents of the Norms sometimes seemed oblivious to the size of the revolution in international law that they were seeking to realise.

---

7  Draft Norms, *supra* note 4, para. 1. The Norms define "other business enterprise" to include "any business entity, regardless of the international or domestic nature of its activities" (para. 21).

8  *Ibid.*, paras. 2–9.

9  Sub-Commission Res. 2003/16, *supra* note 5, pmbl. ("the Norms, as explicated by the Commentary, ... reflect most of the current trends in the field of international law, and particularly international human rights law, with regard to the activities of transnational corporations and other business enterprises"). See also Weissbrodt & Kruger, *supra* note 4, p. 913 (describing the Norms as a "restatement of international legal principles applicable to companies").

10 Sub-Commission Res. 2003/16, *supra* note 5, paras. 5–7. By itself, monitoring of compliance with standards does not indicate whether the standards are legal (since non-legal standards may also be monitored), but it may help to promote the general practice necessary to support the requirements of customary international law. See L. C. Backer, 'Multinational Corporations, Transnational Law: the United Nations' Norms on the Responsibilities of Transnational Corporations as a Harbinger of Corporate Social Responsibility in International Law', 37 *Colum. Hum. Rts. L. Rev.* (2005) p. 287, at pp. 380–382 (suggesting that the Norms would affect customary international law through changing corporate behaviour directly, bypassing the need for formal state consent).

11 See D. Kinley and R. Chambers, 'The UN Human Rights Norms for Corporations: The Private Implications of Public International Law', 6 *Hum. Rts. L. Rev.* (2006) p. 447, at p. 491.

To begin with some basics: one of the major differences between human rights in moral and political rhetoric and human rights in the form of international law is the nature of the duty-holders. In morality and politics, human rights can give rise to duties on anyone and everyone. Human rights *law*, in contrast, places its obligations almost entirely on states. The two International Covenants, for example, the most important human rights treaties, make clear that the rights they set forth give rise to correlative duties on the part of the state parties to the Covenants.[12]

Of course, states are not the only threat to human rights. It has long been clear that human rights may be abused by non-state actors. Slavery, terrorism and violence against women are among the countless historical and modern examples. International law does not ignore the threats that private actors pose to the enjoyment of human rights. However, with very few exceptions, it does not directly impose duties on them to refrain from such abuses. Instead, it requires each state not only to *respect* human rights itself, but also to take steps to *protect* rights from interference by non-state actors. States are required not just to refrain from slavery, for instance, but also to bring about its "complete abolition" throughout their jurisdiction.[13]

Although the scope and nature of private duties under international law are still emerging, their general outline had become clear by the time John Ruggie began his work.[14] At the lowest level of involvement, international law may merely contemplate that states take action to protect human rights from abuse by private actors, without indicating what measures the states must take. For example, the International Covenant on Civil and Political Rights (ICCPR) requires each state party "to respect and to ensure to all individuals within its territory and subject to its jurisdiction the rights recognized in the present Covenant".[15] Scholars and human rights bodies have interpreted the phrase "to respect and to ensure" as requiring in the first instance that the state avoid violating the rights itself, and in the second that it take action to protect the right by making it safe from loss or interference, including as a result of private action.[16] The same interpretive conclusion has been reached with respect to other human

---

12   International Covenant on Civil and Political Rights (ICCPR), 16 December 1966, 999 *UNTS* 171, Articles 2 and 3; International Covenant on Economic, Social and Cultural Rights (ICESCR), 16 December 1966, 999 *UNTS* 3, Articles 2 and 3.

13   Slavery Convention, 25 September 1926, 60 *LNTS* 253, Article 2; ICCPR, *supra* note 12, Article 8. *See also* Abolition of Forced Labour Convention (ILO 105), 25 June 1957, 320 *UNTS* 291, Articles 1 and 2.

14   The following several paragraphs draw on a more detailed account of private duties under human rights law in J. H. Knox, 'Horizontal Human Rights Law', 102 *Am. J. Int'l L.* (2008) p. 1, at pp. 16–31. *See also* J. K. Cogan, 'The Regulatory Turn in International Law', 52 *Harv. Int'l L.J.* (2011) p. 321 (examining the rise of indirect private duties in international law generally); M. Hakimi, 'State Bystander Responsibility', 21 *Eur. J. Int'l L.* (2010) p. 341 (examining state duty to protect human rights).

15   ICCPR, *supra* note 12, Article 2(1).

16   Human Rights Committee, General Comment No. 31, *The Nature of the General Legal Obligation Imposed on States Parties to the Covenant*, U.N. Doc. CCPR/C/21/Rev.1/Add.13 (2004); S. Joseph, J. Schultz and M. Castan, *The International Covenant on Civil and Po-*

rights treaties, including regional agreements.⁷ The generally accepted view is that the obligation on states is one of conduct, not of result. In other words, states have to undertake due diligence to ensure that human rights are protected from interference.¹⁸ The level of due diligence required will vary from right to right and from case to case.

Without further specification of the state's duty to protect, the state has a great deal of discretion to decide for itself how to satisfy the duty. But international law often specifies the duty to protect a particular right in more detail, through international agreement¹⁹ or the gradual elaboration of duties by human rights bodies, including the UN treaty bodies and the regional human rights tribunals, as they construe general legal obligations. For example, the treaty body charged with overseeing the Convention on the Elimination of Discrimination Against Women stated in 1992 that the general obligation the Convention places on states to take appropriate measures to eliminate discrimination against women includes a duty to address gender-based violence by non-state actors, and recommended specific measures state parties should take to that end.²⁰ The General Assembly endorsed that interpretation the following year.²¹

---

litical Rights: Cases, Materials, and Commentary 24 (2000); M. Nowak, *U.N. Covenant on Civil and Political Rights: CCPR Commentary* 36–38 (1993).

17  See e.g. Committee on Economic, Social and Cultural Rights (CESCR), General Comment No. 12, *The Right to Adequate Food*, U.N. Doc. E/C.12/1999/5 (1999), para. 15 (interpreting the International Covenant on Economic, Social and Cultural Rights); *Z v. United Kingdom*, 34 Eur. H.R. Rep. 3 (2002), para. 73 (European Convention on Human Rights); *Commission Nationale de Droits d'Homme et des Libertes v. Chad*, Comm. No. 74/92, 2000 Afr. H.R.L. Rep. 66, 68 (1995), para. 20 (African Charter on Human and Peoples' Rights); *Velasquez Rodriguez v. Honduras*, Inter-Am. Ct. H.R. (ser. C) No. 4 (1988), para. 172 (American Convention on Human Rights).

18  General Comment No. 31, *supra* note 16, para. 8; *Velasquez Rodriguez*, ibid., para. 172; A. Reinisch, 'The Changing International Legal Framework for Dealing with Non-state Actors', in P. Alston (ed.), *Non-state Actors and Human Rights* (Oxford University Press, 2005) p. 37, at p. 79.

19  See e.g. Convention on the Elimination of All Forms of Racial Discrimination (CERD), 21 December, 1965, 660 *UNTS* 195, Article 5(f); Convention on the Elimination of All Forms of Discrimination Against Women (CEDAW), 18 December 1979, 1249 *UNTS* 13, Article 13(b); Convention Concerning the Prohibition and Immediate Action for the Elimination of the Worst Forms of Child Labour (ILO 182), 17 June 1999, 2133 *UNTS* 161.

20  Committee on the Elimination of Discrimination Against Women, General Recommendation No. 19, *Violence Against Women* (1992), U.N. Doc. A/47/38 (1992). The most active regional tribunal in the specification of indirect private duties is the European Court of Human Rights. For descriptions of its work in this area, *see* A. Clapham, *Human Rights Obligations of Non-state Actors* (Oxford University Press, 2006) pp. 349–420; A. Mowbray, *The Development of Positive Obligations Under the European Convention on Human Rights* (Hart Publishing, Oxford, 2004).

21  Declaration on the Elimination of Violence Against Women, General Assembly Res. 48/104 (1993). *See also* Report of the Special Rapporteur on Violence Against Women, *Integration of the Human Rights of Women and the Gender Perspective: Violence Against Women; The Due Diligence Standard as a Tool for the Elimination of Violence Against Women*, U.N. Doc. E/CN.4/2006/61 (2006) para. 29 (arguing that customary international

Of course, there is no bright line between *contemplation* and *specification* of private duties. Over time, private duties often tend to move from lesser to greater specification under international law, narrowing states' discretion as to how to impose such duties. All along this spectrum, international law addresses private actors only through the intermediate role of states, which retain the primary responsibility under international law. Very occasionally, however, international law *directly places* obligations on non-state actors. The most commonly accepted examples of such duties are imposed by international criminal law, and include the obligations not to commit genocide, war crimes and crimes against humanity.[22] The Genocide Convention, for example, does more than require states to prosecute those accused of genocide; it specifically provides that "genocide … is a crime under international law".[23]

Even with respect to these crimes, the enforcement of the duty to refrain from committing them is left predominantly to national governments. But international law can and sometimes does go further, by *enforcing* duties directly, *e.g.* through the International Criminal Court (ICC) and other international criminal tribunals. The International Criminal Court has jurisdiction over the three crimes listed above, but only under limited circumstances: to be admissible, a case must concern a crime that was committed on the territory or by a national of a party to the Rome Statute (or a non party that has accepted the Court's jurisdiction) and that is not being investigated or prosecuted by a state with jurisdiction.[24]

As the degree of involvement by international law increases, from indirect contemplation and specification of private duties to direct placement and enforcement, the number of duties at each stage decreases. International law *contemplates* more private duties than it *specifies*, and it specifies many more duties than it directly *places* and *enforces*. As a result, private duties under international law form a kind of pyramid, with the lowest levels of involvement much larger than the higher levels. It may not be immediately evident why this should be so. Why does human rights law not directly place and enforce more private duties? Conversely, why are private duties not all at the lowest level of the pyramid, to be applied according to the discretion of states?

The answer to the first question is that international law lacks the practical and political capacity to impose more than a small number of duties directly on private actors. Practically, international legal institutions could not reproduce the vast domestic resources devoted to regulating private invasions of interests denominated as human rights by international law. For example, domestic legal systems already reprehend and try to prevent and punish murder, a gross infringement of the right to life. It would

---

law now requires states "to prevent and respond to acts of violence against women with due diligence").

22   Although for historical reasons international criminal law and human rights law are often treated as distinct fields, there is a great deal of overlap between them. In essence, international criminal law establishes direct private duties that correlate to particular human rights, especially the right to life. *See* Knox, *supra* note 14, pp. 24 and 27–31.

23   Convention on the Prevention and Punishment of the Crime of Genocide, 9 December 1948, 78 *UNTS* 277, Article 1.

24   Rome Statute of the International Criminal Court, 17 July 1998, 2187 *UNTS* 90, Article 17.

make no sense for international bodies to take on this task. And, politically, neither national governments nor the vast majority of their citizens would support the expansion of the authority and resources of international institutions that would be necessary for them to protect all human rights from private interference.[25] At the same time, there are powerful reasons not to leave private violations of human rights completely to domestic law. In some cases, the nominally non-governmental actor may be acting as if it were a government and should be treated accordingly. Even when the actor is clearly acting in a private capacity, domestic governments may be unwilling or unable to prevent it from interfering with others' human rights. There is a need, then, for international human rights law to play a role.

Taken together, these cross-cutting pressures have resulted in a very strong presumption in the practice of states that almost all international legal duties on private actors will be mediated through domestic law: that placement and enforcement even of specific duties will usually be through domestic procedures, not international ones. To overcome this presumption, it is not enough that a violation be particularly heinous. International law expects states, rather than international institutions, to prosecute even such abhorrent international crimes as torture and slavery. To warrant direct intervention by international institutions, violations must be considered both of extraordinary international significance and extraordinarily ill-suited for domestic enforcement.

How do corporations fit in this pyramid of private duties? In some respects, quite easily. There is no difficulty in concluding that states have duties to regulate corporations, along with other private actors, to ensure the enjoyment of human rights. Some international agreements and human rights bodies specifically include legal as well as natural persons in setting out indirect duties. For example, the Convention on the Elimination of Discrimination Against Women requires its state parties "[t]o take all appropriate measures to eliminate discrimination against women by any person, *organization* or *enterprise*",[26] and the treaty body charged with monitoring the International Covenant on Economic, Social and Cultural Rights (ICESCR) has stated that states' obligation to protect the right to water requires them to prevent third parties, including "individuals, groups, *corporations* and other entities", from interfering with the right.[27] In many other cases, there is no basis for excluding corporations from

---

25 The preference for local resolution of human rights issues appears in many forms, including the requirement that claimants to human rights tribunals and quasi-tribunals first exhaust available local remedies. See e.g. Optional Protocol to the ICCPR, 16 December 1966, 999 *UNTS* 302, Article 2.

26 CEDAW, *supra* note 19, Article 2(3) (emphasis added). For equivalent language, *see* International Convention on the Rights of Persons with Disabilities, 13 December 2006, 46 *ILM* 443, Article 4(e).

27 CESCR, General Comment No. 15, *The Right to Water*, U.N. Doc. E/C.12/2002/11 (2002), para. 23 (emphasis added). For examples of similar statements, *see* Special Representative of the Secretary-General, *State responsibilities to regulate and adjudicate corporate activities under the United Nations core human rights treaties; an overview of treaty body commentaries*, U.N. Doc. A/HRC/4/35/Add. 1 (2007), paras. 18–38.

the scope of general legal obligations on states to protect against harm to human rights from private actors. It would be nonsensical, for example, to exclude corporations from the scope of the state duty to suppress slavery. In short, the private duties at the lower levels of the pyramid, from mere contemplation to more detailed specification of indirect duties, normally include corporations.

It is also clear that the highest level of the pyramid, duties enforced by international bodies, does not currently include corporations. Neither the International Criminal Court nor the criminal courts for Rwanda or the former Yugoslavia have jurisdiction to prosecute corporations. This absence does not exempt the human rights records of corporations from any oversight by international human rights bodies. In monitoring states' duties to protect against corporate and other private abuse of human rights, these bodies will necessarily examine cases in which corporate behaviour interferes with human rights.[28] But the primary legal focus will be on the direct duties of states under international law, not the indirect duties imposed on corporations.

The remaining question is whether corporations are subject to duties at the second-highest level of the pyramid – that is, duties that international law directly applies but does not necessarily enforce. That question can be divided in two: (a) does the entire body of human rights law apply directly to corporations?, and (b) if the answer to the first question is negative, are corporations nevertheless subject to the same direct duties as individuals – *i.e.* the duties not to commit international crimes such as genocide? This part of the chapter looks only at the first question, leaving the second question to the first section of part 3.

The short answer to the first question is No. There is no legal support for the proposition that the entire body of human rights law applies directly to corporations, any more than it applies directly to individuals or other non-state actors. Arguments that all human rights obligations apply directly to corporations (and other private actors) tend to overlook the distinction between direct and indirect duties. For example, it has been suggested that human rights treaties do not state which persons or entities have the duties that correspond to the rights, so the duties must apply to everyone.[29] This is simply incorrect. The International Covenants and later treaties make clear that their obligations apply directly to states, not to private actors.[30] There is no exception for corporations. Because the treaties are explicit on this point, proponents of direct duties

---

28 See e.g. *Report of the Special Rapporteur on the adverse effects of the movement and dumping of toxic and dangerous products and wastes on the enjoyment of human rights*, U.N. Doc. A/HRC/12/26 (2009) (reviewing the effects of the shipbreaking industry on human rights).

29 J. Paust, 'Human Rights Responsibilities of Private Corporations', 35 *Vand. J. Transnat'l L.* (2002) p. 801, at p. 810.

30 *E.g.* ICCPR, *supra* note 12, Article 2(1); ICESCR, *supra* note 12, Article 2(1); CERD, *supra* note 19, Article 2; CEDAW, *supra* note 19, Article 2; Convention on the Rights of the Child, 20 November 1989, 1577 *UNTS* 3, Article 2(1); European Convention for the Protection of Human Rights and Fundamental Freedoms, 4 November 1950, 213 *UNTS* 221, Article 1(1); American Convention on Human Rights, 22 November 1969, 1144 *UNTS* 123. The African regional human rights treaty does include some private duties, but those duties are converse (*i.e.* owed by the individual to the state), rather than correlative (owed by the

often look to customary international law, citing the General Assembly's proclamation of the Universal Declaration of Human Rights as "a common standard of achievement for all peoples and all nations, to the end that every individual and organ of society ... shall strive ... to promote respect for these rights and freedoms and by progressive measures ... to secure their universal and effective recognition and observance".[31] But the drafters of the Declaration did not intend this language to give rise to legal obligations on private actors. The drafters did not view the Declaration as legally binding at all, and they expected that legal duties corresponding to its rights would later be imposed, by treaty, on *states* – as the Covenants eventually did.[32] Although implementation of the Declaration is certainly relevant to customary international law, there is no evidence of a general custom directly applying the entire range of obligations under human rights law to private actors generally or to corporations specifically.[33]

As a result, the Sub-Commission's Draft Norms would have made a revolution in human rights law if they had been generally accepted. Instead, the government representatives on the Human Rights Commission declined to adopt them, stating that the Norms have "no legal standing" and instructing the Sub-Commission not to monitor them.[34] At the same time, the Commission kept the issue of human rights and corporations on its agenda. It requested the Office of the High Commissioner for Human Rights (OHCHR) to prepare a report on human rights standards relating to corporations,[35] and, after considering that report in 2005, it decided to request the appointment of the SRSG. By refusing to adopt the Norms, the Human Rights Commission threw cold water on the proposition that corporations, unlike other private actors, were directly subject to the entire range of duties set out by human rights law. But the Commission did not explicitly discard the idea, and many human rights groups urged Professor Ruggie to use the Draft Norms as the starting point for his work.[36] As a result, as Ruggie noted, the debates over the Norms threatened to "shadow" his mandate.[37]

---

individual in respect of other individuals' human rights). African Charter on Human and Peoples' Rights, 27 June 1981, 1520 *UNTS* 217. See Knox, *supra* note 14, pp. 14–18.

31    Universal Declaration of Human Rights, GA Res. 217A (III), U.N. Doc. A/810, at p. 71, pmbl.

32    See Knox, *supra* note 14, p. 30, note 133.

33    See J. Zerk, *Multinationals and Corporate Responsibility: Limitations and Opportunities in International Law* (Cambridge University Press, 2006) pp. 276–277. Some international instruments, notably the UN Global Compact and the OECD Guidelines for Multinational Enterprises, do call on corporations to respect human rights, but those instruments do not purport to be legally binding.

34    Human Rights Commission, Dec. 2004/116, U.N. Doc. E/CN.4/2004/127 (2004), pp. 332–333.

35    *Report of the United Nations High Commissioner on Human Rights on the responsibilities of transnational corporations and related business enterprises with regard to human rights*, U.N. Doc. E/CN.4/2005/91 (2005) (hereafter '2005 OHCHR report').

36    J. G. Ruggie, 'Business and Human Rights: The Evolving International Agenda', 101 *Am. J. Int'l L.* (2007) p. 819, at p. 822, note 17.

37    2006 Interim Report, *supra* note 3, para. 55.

To remove that shadow, Ruggie made clear in his very first report, in February 2006, that he rejected the Norms. Predictably, his primary criticism was that they lacked support in international law. Referring to their "exaggerated legal claims and conceptual ambiguities", he called them "engulfed by [their] own doctrinal excesses".[38] The next year, in his full response to the Human Rights Commission's request to map the existing human rights law relating to corporations, he stated that human rights instruments generally do not "currently impose direct legal responsibilities on corporations".[39] As this section explains, Ruggie was on solid ground in concluding that the Norms had no legal basis. Human rights law does not generally apply directly to private parties, and he could not credibly have argued otherwise. But rejecting the Norms presented the next problem: what should Ruggie propose in their stead?

## 2.2. Rejecting the Norms in Favour of ... What?

By itself, rejection of the Norms' attempt to apply human rights law directly to corporations could not end the controversy over corporations and human rights. Corporations had been implicated in terrible atrocities, and the demand that human rights standards be brought to bear on them would not disappear. Moreover, many proponents of direct duties for corporations understood quite well that the Norms were ahead of existing international law. They supported the Norms not as a restatement of current law, but rather as an effort to move international law in the direction of more direct duties on corporations. They could make a strong argument that relying on indirect corporate duties had proved to be grossly inadequate, since states routinely failed to comply with their duty to protect against corporate abuses.

One might ask why the legal status of the Norms (or other international standards for corporate responsibility) was worth disputing. Compliance with legal standards, especially *international* legal standards, and most especially international *human rights* legal standards, is often weak. Conversely, voluntary or "soft law" approaches to corporate social responsibility may change corporate behaviour, as the vast literature on such approaches suggests. Rather than waste energy fighting over whether standards are legal in some abstract sense, why not focus on making corporate codes and other non-legal standards, such as the Global Compact, more effective, thereby causing the changes in corporate conduct that purportedly binding legal standards should, but often do not, produce?[40]

---

38  Ibid., para. 59.
39  *Report of the Special Representative of the Secretary-General on the Issue of Human Rights and Transnational Corporations and Other Business Enterprises, John Ruggie: Business and Human Rights: Mapping International Standards of Responsibility and Accountability for Corporate Acts*, U.N. Doc. A/HRC/4/35 (2007), para. 44, (hereafter '2007 Mapping Report').
40  As Ruggie himself noted, in the course of describing multi-stakeholder initiatives such as the Kimberley Process Certification Scheme, as soft law approaches "strengthen their accountability mechanisms, they also begin to blur the lines between the strictly voluntary and mandatory spheres for participants." *Ibid.*, para. 61.

A full answer to this question would take another chapter, or book, but the abridged version is that proponents and opponents of legalisation of international corporate standards believe that the issue is worth the fight because they recognise that legalisation has real consequences.[41] Establishing that a norm is legal can change the "logic of appropriateness" that influences actors' behaviour. Governments, corporations and individuals may accept the norm as defining a value of their society or internalise it as part of the environment in which they act.[42] Of course, non-legal norms can affect this logic of appropriateness as well. But it is reasonable to believe that laws – at least, laws adopted through procedures that are widely accepted as legitimate – are more likely to exert this kind of effect.

Apart from potentially changing actors' views of appropriate behaviour, legal standards have instrumental consequences. They may trigger a stronger array of regulatory and remedial mechanisms than non-legal norms, making it more difficult for actors to avoid compliance.[43] This is obvious at the level of domestic law, but it is true at the international level as well. Human rights mechanisms, while weak, already exist to monitor and promote compliance with human rights norms, and they are guided by their understanding of human rights *law*. The United Nations treaty bodies and the regional tribunals established by human rights agreements apply *legal* standards. They regularly reject claims by individuals of human rights violations if the claims do not meet the legal requirements imposed by the agreement that they implement. These compliance mechanisms are very far from fully effective, but they do not apply at all to non-legal norms.

As the previous section explains, human rights law already does address *indirect* corporate duties pursuant to the state duty to protect. International mechanisms such as the treaty bodies and regional tribunals can therefore already speak to corporate abuses by examining states' compliance with their duty to protect against them. To some extent, the possibility of establishing direct corporate duties may be attractive because it could lead to increased attention from international bodies.[44] But the debate over the direct applicability of international human rights standards to corporations has been so intense in large part because of its implications for the availability of one legal mechanism, in particular: the US Alien Tort Statute. Beginning in the late 1990s,

---

41  See D. McBarnet, 'Corporate Social Responsibility Beyond Law, Through Law, for Law: the New Corporate Accountability', in D. McBarnet, A. Voiculescu and T. Campbell (eds.), *The New Corporate Accountability: Corporate Social Responsibility and the Law* (Cambridge University Press, 2007) p. 9, at pp. 25–27.

42  See M. Finnemore and K. Sikkink, 'International Norm Dynamics and Political Change', 52 *International Organization* (1998) p. 887, at p. 903. *See generally* J. G. March and J. P. Olsen, *Rediscovering Institutions: The Organizational Basis of Politics* (Free Press/Macmillan, 1989).

43  See R. Mares, 'Global Corporate Social Responsibility, Human Rights and Law: An Interactive Regulatory Perspective on the Voluntary-Mandatory Dichotomy', 1 *Transnat'l Legal Theory* (2010) p. 221, at pp. 238–239.

44  International Council on Human Rights Policy, *Beyond Voluntarism: Human Rights and the Developing Legal Obligations of Companies* (2002) p. 3.

plaintiffs have increasingly turned to the ATS as an avenue for suits against multinational corporations for human rights abuses. The ATS not only offers victims of human rights abuses the possibility of damages; under the US system of contingent attorneys' fees, the prospect of damage awards allows plaintiffs to hire law firms with the resources necessary to bring expensive, lengthy suits against corporations with massive resources. But the ATS may be available only for violations of *direct* duties under international law.[45]

This situation presented Ruggie with an extraordinarily difficult political calculus. To develop a consensus on how to bring human rights law to bear on corporations, Ruggie had to propose an alternative to the Norms that addressed the desire for a robust application of human rights law to corporations but did not alienate the governments whose cooperation would be necessary to make the proposal effective. In legal terms, the central issue was whether Ruggie could draw on human rights law to develop stronger standards for corporate behaviour without making claims (as the drafters of the Norms had) that exceeded the bounds of the law or threatened to develop it in ways that governments would not accept.

One possibility, which would have been popular with many human rights groups, was for Ruggie to take the position that even though the Norms were not an accurate reflection of the law as it currently exists, they should be viewed as the standard toward which the law should be striving, much as the Universal Declaration of Human Rights was an aspirational standard that became the basis for a legally binding set of obligations. Ruggie rejected this course of action. He criticised the Norms in terms that made it clear that he saw them as a poor model for the evolution of international law. He highlighted their "imprecision in allocating human rights responsibilities to States and corporations", pointing out that although corporations and states play very different roles in society, the Norms "articulate no actual principle for differentiating human rights responsibilities based on the respective social roles performed by States and corporations".[46] He expressed the concern that in the absence of such a principle, the allocation of responsibilities between states and corporations could turn on their respective capacities, "so that where States are unable or unwilling to act the job would be transferred to corporations".[47] The result, Ruggie feared, would be to undermine corporate autonomy, reduce "the discretionary space" of governments to decide for themselves how best to secure the fulfilment of the economic, social and cultural rights corporations may most influence, undermine efforts to make governments more

---

45 Although this is a widespread view, it may be mistaken. It is possible to read the language of the ATS, which refers to torts "committed in violation of the law of nations", as including tortious actions taken in violation of *indirect* as well as *direct* duties imposed by international law. Including indirect duties would not open the door to vast numbers of claims, because the Supreme Court has limited the scope of claims to those for violations of international legal norms with no less "definite content and acceptance among civilized nations than the historical paradigms [such as piracy] familiar when [the ATS] was enacted" in the late 18th century. *Sosa v. Alvarez-Machain*, 542 U.S. 692, 732 (2004).

46 2006 Interim Report, *supra* note 3, para. 66.

47 *Ibid.*, para. 68.

responsible to their own citizens, and lead to "endless strategic gaming and legal wrangling" between governments and businesses over their respective responsibilities.[48]

Ruggie could (and did) try to salvage a set of direct corporate duties by more clearly delineating the respective responsibilities of states and corporations. However, any attempt to make the duties legally binding would have faced other obstacles. Negotiating human rights instruments is notoriously difficult, even when governments start with a clear agenda. The International Covenants that codify the rights in the Universal Declaration were adopted 18 years after the Universal Declaration and took another decade to enter into force. Even non-binding declarations typically take many years to complete, often because they are seen as potential first drafts of binding treaties. The negotiation of the Declaration on the Rights of Indigenous Peoples, adopted by the General Assembly in 2007, lasted more than 20 years; the General Assembly adopted guidelines on the right to a remedy and reparation in 2006 that were the result of over a decade of work; and negotiation began in 1984 on a declaration on human rights defenders that was finally adopted only in 1998. Moreover, governments had already rejected the Draft Norms, the previous effort to induce them to negotiate an instrument on human rights and corporations. If Ruggie had introduced another draft of a legally binding agreement, or even a non-binding declaration, it seemed likely to meet the same fate, and the effort could distract from other initiatives with more immediate benefits.[49]

Rather than draft an aspirational instrument, therefore, Ruggie took a different approach. He proposed a new Framework for Business and Human Rights in 2008 as well as Guiding Principles to implement the Framework in 2011 that are avowedly consistent with the law *as it is* rather than the law as it might someday be.[50] As the following paragraphs explain, he based the Framework and Guiding Principles on human rights law where he could. Where that was impossible, he still drew on human rights law in creative ways that helped to give the Framework and Guiding Principles clarity, substance and weight.

The first principle of the Framework is the state duty to protect against human rights abuses by private actors, including corporations. Ruggie repeatedly emphasised in the strongest terms that this duty is a legal obligation imposed by existing human rights law.[51] Although in some respects the duty to protect reflects a relatively new understanding of the law, it has a strong legal pedigree and has been endorsed by human

---

48  Ibid.; see Ruggie, *supra* note 36, p. 826.
49  See J. Ruggie, 'Treaty Road Not Travelled', *Ethical Corporation* (6 May 2008) pp. 42–43.
50  Special Representative of the Secretary-General, *Protect, Respect and Remedy: a Framework for Business and Human Rights*, U.N. Doc. A/HRC/8/5 (2008), para. 9 (hereafter '2008 Framework Report'); Special Representative of the Secretary-General, *Guiding Principles on Business and Human Rights: Implementing the United Nations "Protect, Respect and Remedy' Framework*, U.N. Doc. A/HRC/17/31 (2011) (hereafter 'Guiding Principles').
51  E.g. 2007 Mapping Report, *supra* note 39, para. 18 ("In sum, the State duty to protect against non-State abuses is part of the very foundation of the international human rights regime. The duty requires States to play a key role in regulating and adjudicating abuse by business enterprises or risk breaching their international obligations").

rights bodies, instruments and scholars for years. Ruggie added a systematic elaboration of the duty in the context of corporate activity. He presented detailed reports on the jurisprudence of the UN treaty bodies interpreting the duty to protect in the context of corporate activity; he held a series of consultations with interested parties that built understanding of and support for the application of the duty to corporate conduct; and he translated the law, as informed by those consultations, into accessible Guiding Principles reflecting different aspects of the duty. In short, he helped to remove any remaining doubts that the duty to protect covers the activities of corporations, and he clarified how the duty operates. These are real achievements.

By themselves, however, they fell far short of what human rights advocates sought, which was the direct application of human rights law to corporations. In the second and third principles of his Framework, Ruggie tried to steer between the Scylla of overstating corporations' legal obligations and the Charybdis of excusing them from any obligations at all. The second principle brings his effort part of the way through the strait by stating that corporations have a "responsibility to respect" human rights law. By grounding this responsibility on *societal expectations* rather than human rights law,[52] Ruggie provided a less controversial basis for the responsibility, but at the potential cost of making it softer and more inchoate. He tried to address these weaknesses by drawing on human rights law.

First, he used human rights law to define the scope of the corporate responsibility to respect. He characterised the societal expectation on which the responsibility rests as being that corporations respect human rights *as they are set out in international law* – in particular, the major human rights and labour conventions.[53] As noted above, earlier international initiatives such as the UN Global Compact and the Organisation for Economic Co-operation and Development (OECD) Principles had already stated that corporations have a responsibility to respect human rights, as had the OHCHR report on corporations and human rights.[54] But defining the rights as those contained in specific legal instruments provides more certainty than simply using the idea of human rights as a general moral foundation for their application to corporations. Second, the third pillar of the Framework tries to make the responsibility to respect more substantive by stating that states must establish effective legal remedies for human rights abuses by corporations.[55] Ruggie repeatedly emphasised that human rights law requires states to do so, as part of their duty to protect.[56]

Ruggie also gave his "responsibility to respect" more substance and weight by providing more detail as to what it includes. The Norms had been criticised for failing to explain which human rights corporations should be obliged to respect, instead opt-

---

52    2008 Framework Report, *supra* note 50, para. 9.
53    Guiding Principles, *supra* note 50, para. 12.
54    2005 OHCHR Report, *supra* note 35, paras. 23, 30 and 41.
55    Guiding Principles, *supra* note 50, para. 25. The Guiding Principles also encourage corporations to establish operational-level grievance mechanisms (para. 29).
56    2008 Framework Report, *supra* note 50, para. 82; *Business and Human Rights: Towards Operationalizing the "Protect, Respect and Remedy" Framework*, U.N. Doc. A/HRC/11/13 (2009), para. 87; Guiding Principles, *supra* note 50, para. 25.

ing to say only that corporations should respect *all* of them. After examining the issue himself, Ruggie agreed that "there are few if any rights business cannot impact – or be perceived to impact – in some manner. Therefore, companies should consider all such rights."[57] Instead of limiting the number of rights relevant to corporations, Ruggie tried to define the responsibilities of corporations relative to the rights. His Guiding Principles generally construe the responsibility to respect as meaning that corporations should avoid infringing on rights themselves.[58] A duty to respect human rights is less controversial, and perhaps easier to implement, than duties to *protect* and *fulfil* rights, which treaty bodies have used to urge states to take a broad range of affirmative actions. But under Ruggie's approach, the responsibility to respect is not just negative; it also includes positive due diligence obligations on corporations to "address adverse human rights impacts with which they are involved", including by trying to prevent or mitigate impacts that are directly linked to their operations, products or services by their business relationships.[59] More specifically, it requires corporations to make high-level commitments to meet their human rights responsibilities, to carry out human rights impact assessments before beginning activities, to integrate human rights policies throughout their operations, and to monitor and audit their performance.[60]

Even as clarified in these respects, the responsibility to respect may still seem too vague to be of much concrete use. Human rights groups strongly criticised the Guiding Principles for not providing enough detail about corporations' and governments' responsibilities.[61] The Principles leave many difficult issues to be addressed in the course of translating the responsibility to respect into specific obligations in specific contexts, as Fiona Haines, Kate Macdonald and Samantha Balaton-Chrimes explain in their chapter in this book. However, as they note, Ruggie had real political constraints on defining the responsibility to respect further. In order to attract the political support necessary for his proposal to move beyond the stalemate that he inherited, he may have felt that it was necessary to underspecify some aspects of corporate responsibilities.[62] Along the same lines, his careful use of human rights law to support and inform his proposal should be seen as an effort to insulate it from political criticism. The stronger the legal supports for his proposal, the less controversy it would attract. In this respect, he was successful: the Human Rights Commission and its successor, the Human Rights Council, adopted their annual resolutions on his work by

---

57  2008 Framework Report, *supra* note 50, para. 52. This conclusion is debatable. As I have argued elsewhere, general transfer of human rights from the governmental to the corporate context raises issues of overinclusion, because not all rights are obviously applicable to corporations, and of underinclusion, since not all types of corporate misconduct clearly implicate human rights. Knox, *supra* note 14, pp. 41–42.
58  Guiding Principles, *supra* note 50, para. 11.
59  *Ibid.*, paras. 11 and 13.
60  *Ibid.*, paras. 15–20.
61  *Joint Civil Society Statement on the Draft Guiding Principles on Business and Human Rights* (31 January 2011), available at <www.fidh.org/Joint-Civil-Society-Statement-on-the-draft,9066>.
62  *Ibid.*

consensus, and in 2011, the last of the resolutions unanimously endorsed the Guiding Principles and appointed a five-person working group to promote their dissemination and implementation.[63]

His reliance on human rights law was more than a political strategy to obtain governmental acceptance. It also helped to establish a platform for further development of state and corporate obligations under human rights law and policy. Although that development may occur in many ways, it seems probable that human rights advocates will continue to press for a legally binding instrument setting out a broader array of duties on corporations.[64] Indeed, Amnesty International and other human rights groups urged the Council to instruct the new working group to analyse "gaps" in legal protection against corporate abuses in order to prepare the ground for such an instrument.[65] Ruggie himself, in his closing statement to the Council, suggested that instead of seeking to negotiate an instrument on the entire range of issues concerning corporations and human rights, governments should clarify the law on a much narrower and (presumably) less controversial set of issues, concerning the application to corporations of prohibitions on particularly gross human rights abuses, amounting to international crimes.[66]

The Council did not accept either of these suggestions, which suggests that most of its member governments remain uninterested in negotiating new legal norms in this area. Are the Guiding Principles likely to change this dynamic? In particular, does the "responsibility to respect" create an embryonic legal obligation on corporations, which will later develop into hard law? If so, Ruggie may have influenced the law in a more subtle manner than reframing existing standards or urging that they develop in a particular direction. Under the guise of rejecting direct duties for corporations, he may have written a rough draft of such duties, much as the drafters of the Norms sought to do.

In principle, the responsibility to respect could make the transition to hard law either through customary international law or through treaty. To bind corporations

---

63   Human Rights Council Res. 17/4, U.N. Doc. A/HRC/RES/17/4 (2011), paras. 1 and 6(a).

64   The instrument could also address other issues, such as the extraterritorial scope of states' duty to protect, an issue discussed below.

65   Amnesty International, *A Call for Action to Better Protect the Rights of Those Affected by Business-Related Human Rights Abuses* (14 June 2011), available at <www.amnesty.org/en/library/asset/IOR40/009/2011/en/55fab4a5-fb8a-4572-93f3-67581b2dca45/ior400092011en.html>; International Federation of Human Rights (FIDH), International Commission of Jurists (ICJ), Human Rights Watch (HRW), International Network for Economic, Social and Cultural Rights (ESCR-Net), Rights & Accountability in Development (RAID), *Joint Civil Society Statement on Business and Human Rights to the 17th Session of the UN Human Rights Council* (15 June 2011), available at <www.escr-net.org/actions_more/actions_more_show.htm?doc_id=1605781>.

66   J. G. Ruggie, *Presentation of Report to United Nations Human Rights Council* (30 May 2011), available at <www.business-humanrights.org/media/documents/ruggie-statement-to-un-human-rights-council-30-may-2011.pdf>. See also J. G. Ruggie, *Recommendations on Follow-up to the Mandate* (11 February 2011), available at <www.business-humanrights.org/media/documents/ruggie/ruggie-special-mandate-follow-up-11-feb-2011.pdf>.

directly as a matter of customary law, states would have to act consistently as if corporations were so bound, and states would have to do so on the basis of their understanding of their obligations under international law. One might imagine that implementation of the responsibility to respect might help to persuade governments and corporations to accept that corporations do have direct obligations under international law. But the mere implementation of the responsibility to respect as part of the Guiding Principles would not in itself constitute the necessary evidence of custom, because such implementation would be consistent with the view of the Principles that Ruggie has expressed: that is, that they follow from the state duty to protect (which is based on international law) and the corporate responsibility to respect (which is not). In other words, implementation of the Principles, without more, would be consistent with human rights law *as it already is*, and would not be evidence of a *change* in human rights law to make corporations directly obligated by it.

Nevertheless, implementation of the Principles might change the political climate in ways that remove obstacles to the legal recognition of direct corporate duties. The more comfortable governments (and corporations) become with using human rights standards to judge corporate conduct, the more willing they might be to accept applying these standards directly, rather than through the intermediate step of national implementation. One could even imagine that corporations might start to agitate for such obligations at the international level, in order to protect themselves from differing national standards.[67]

If the political environment changed, governments and corporations might prefer that such direct obligations take the form of a new human rights treaty, rather than rely on the possibly slow and uncertain development of customary international law. (The development of a treaty with general acceptance could, of course, also provide evidence of the development of customary law.) In addition to further elaborating the state duty to protect against corporate abuses of human rights, such a treaty could set out direct duties on corporations. Those duties might well resemble not only the Guiding Principles, but also the nominally discredited Norms. In that case, it might indeed be possible to conclude, as some scholars have already said, that: "The Norms are dead, long live the Norms."[68] In this scenario, Ruggie's rejection of the Norms would eventually come to be seen as one of the greatest "retreats in order to advance" in the history of international law.

On the other hand, it is also easy to imagine that if the Guiding Principles are effectively implemented, the desire for direct corporate duties might decrease. Greater specification of the state duty to protect and the corresponding regulation, monitoring and remediation of corporate conduct, if they do occur, will make corporations more accountable for their compliance with international legal norms without having

---

67  See Mares, *supra* note 43, pp. 255–264 (describing how experience with non-binding approaches to influencing corporate behavior may lead to corporate acceptance of, or even lobbying for, regulation).

68  D. Kinley, J. Nolan and N. Zeral, '"The Norms Are Dead! Long Live the Norms!" The Politics Behind the UN Human Rights Norms for Corporations', in McBarnet, Voiculescu and T. Campbell, *supra* note 41, p. 459.

to impose those obligations directly. Even a hypothetical corporate desire for more uniform standards could be addressed more feasibly through greater specification of state duties to protect. After all, the practical and political objections to adopting direct international legal obligations for private actors – the reasons why the top of the pyramid of private duties is thin – will continue to apply to the private duties of corporations as well. Ruggie's work does not overturn those reasons; it reinforces them. By emphasising the state as the primary duty-holder under international human rights law, by warning against the potential for games-playing with duties if corporations are assigned them directly, and by trying to establish a workable system for improving corporate human rights performance that does *not* involve wholesale application of direct duties on private actors, Ruggie's Framework and Guiding Principles seem likely to continue to be seen as an alternative to, rather than a prototype for, direct corporate legal obligations.[69]

## 3. The Relationship Between Ruggie's Mandate and Other Legal Issues

As part 2 of this chapter explains, human rights law as a whole does not apply directly to corporations, any more than it applies directly to other private actors. Other issues concerning the relationship between human rights law and corporate conduct are less clear, however. In his work as the SRSG, John Ruggie took positions on several of these issues, including the responsibility of corporations not to commit international crimes, the standard for corporate complicity in state violations of human rights, and the extraterritorial application of state duties to protect against corporate misconduct.

### 3.1. Are Corporations Bound Not to Commit International Crimes?

That the entire range of human rights obligations does not apply to corporations does not resolve whether corporations are subject to the relatively small number of duties that are placed directly on individuals. In terms of the pyramid of private rights, the question is whether the second-highest level of the pyramid, representing duties directly placed by international law, includes corporations to the same extent that it includes individuals. As noted above, these duties are defined primarily by international criminal law, and they include obligations not to commit genocide, war crimes and crimes against humanity.

This issue is surprisingly difficult to answer definitively. On the one hand, it is easy to imagine (or to recall) that legal as well as natural persons can commit human rights atrocities, and logic suggests that they should all be subject to the same international standards. It seems strange, even repulsive, to suppose that the international norm that prohibits natural persons from committing genocide has nothing to say

---

69    In that respect, it will be consistent with the development of private duties in other areas of international law, which are addressing private duties with greater specificity, but almost always through indirect rather than direct regulation. *See* Cogan, *supra* note 14.

about legal persons that participate in the same conduct.[70] On the other hand, the sources of international law that are generally cited for the existence of prohibitions on genocide and other international crimes do not explicitly refer to corporations, and some important sources limit their coverage to individuals. The Rome Statute establishing the International Criminal Court, for example, which provides for prosecutions (under certain conditions) of genocide, war crimes and crimes against humanity, limits the jurisdiction of the Court to "natural persons",[71] as do the instruments establishing the jurisdiction of the international criminal courts for Rwanda and the former Yugoslavia.[72] In this respect, they follow the precedent of the war crimes trials after the Second World War, none of which prosecuted corporations.[73]

However, the exclusion of legal persons from the jurisdiction of international criminal courts does not necessarily resolve the issue. As part 2 of this chapter explains, there is a distinction between international *enforcement* and *placement* of private duties. There is no doubt that international law does not currently enforce duties not to commit international crimes against corporations, but that does not foreclose the possibility that international law nevertheless prohibits corporations from taking certain actions defined as international crimes. International law is an immature legal system whose enforcement mechanisms often lag behind its legislation. International criminal law prohibited genocide and other actions long before standing international courts were established to try those accused.[74] Even now, the courts that have been created do not have jurisdiction over every individual accused of committing the crimes. That a particular person does not fall within the jurisdiction of one of the courts therefore does not mean that the person did not commit an international crime. Similarly, the decision to exclude corporations from the jurisdiction of international courts does not necessarily exclude them from otherwise applicable prohibitions on their conduct.

The difficulty, again, is that the usual sources of such prohibitions do not refer explicitly to corporations. The Genocide Convention, for example, states that "[p]ersons committing genocide … shall be punished, whether they are constitutionally respon-

---

70  See *Kiobel* v. *Royal Dutch Petroleum Co.*, 621 F.3d 111, 157 (2d Cir. 2010) (Leval, J., concurring in judgment).

71  Rome Statute, *supra* note 24, Article 25(1).

72  Security Council Res. 827, U.N. Doc. S/RES/827 (1993); Security Council Res. 955, U.N. Doc. S/RES/955 (1994).

73  The two military charters for trials of war criminals appear to contemplate only prosecutions of individuals. Agreement for the Prosecution and Punishment of the Major War Criminals of the European Axis, 8 August 1945, 82 *UNTS* 279, Article 6; Charter of the International Military Tribunal for the Far East, 19 January 1946, Article 5. Historical evidence indicates that the Nuremberg prosecutors considered bringing actions against corporations under Control Council Law No. 10, which has somewhat broader language than the charters, although it, too, does not explicitly provide jurisdiction over corporations. In the event, no such prosecutions were attempted. See J. A. Bush, 'The Prehistory of Corporations and Conspiracy in International Criminal Law: What Nuremberg Really Said', 109 *Colum. L. Rev.* (2009) p. 1094, at pp. 1098 and 1149–1160.

74  To take one example, the Genocide Convention was adopted in 1948, 50 years before states agreed to create the International Criminal Court.

sible rulers, public officials or private individuals".[75] While it is possible to read the references to "persons" here and elsewhere in the Convention to include legal persons, the examples provided (rulers, officials, private individuals) make that interpretation harder to reach. More generally, international crimes have roots in customary international law, a field whose scope and sources lend themselves to dispute. To take one example: The Nuremberg tribunal hearing the case against executives of I.G. Farben, which worked closely with the Nazi regime, referred to Farben, not just the executives, as having violated international law.[76] Should this reference be treated as an authoritative statement of the scope of customary international law, or is the more important indication of the law the fact that the trial was of the executives, not the corporation? Scholars and judges disagree.[77]

Whether corporations have any direct duties under international law might seem to be of only academic interest as long as they are not subject to the jurisdiction of international criminal courts. But even in the absence of an international court able to enforce prohibitions on corporate criminal conduct, direct duties might trigger other legal mechanisms. The monitoring procedures under the purview of the Human Rights Council, for example, might be employed directly against corporations if they are subject to direct obligations. The US Alien Tort Statute might be available for suits against corporations if they can be shown to commit a tortious violation of international law, as part 2 explains. And the recognition of direct corporate duties under international law might help to prepare the way for stronger international enforcement, such as an amendment to the Rome Statute to expand its jurisdiction to include corporations.[78]

In his work as the SRSG, John Ruggie contributed to the debate over the applicability of international criminal standards to corporations by emphasising that the strong trend is to subject corporations to the standards. His first report states that while human rights instruments do not generally impose duties directly on corpora-

---

75  Genocide Convention, *supra* note 23, Article IV.

76  VIII *Trials of War Criminals Before the Nuernberg Military Tribunals* (1952) pp. 1132–1133 and 1140.

77  *Cf.* S. R. Ratner, 'Corporations and Human Rights: A Theory of Legal Responsibility', 111 *Yale L.J.* (2001) p. 443, at pp. 477–478, *and Doe VIII* v. *Exxon Mobil Corporation*, __ F.3d __, 2011 WL 2652384 (D.C. Cir. 2011), p. 74 (citing *Farben* as support for direct corporate duties under customary law), *with Brief of* Amicus Curiae *Professor James Crawford in Support of Conditional Cross-Petitioner*, p. 9, on petition for a writ of *certiorari* in *Presbyterian Church of Sudan* v. *Talisman Energy Inc., and Kiobel*, 621 F.3d at 134–136 (majority opinion) (emphasising that the tribunal did not have jurisdiction over corporations). *See also Flomo* v. *Firestone Natural Rubber Co.*, 643 F.3d 1013, 1017 (7th Cir. 2011); *Doe VIII* v. *Exxon Mobil*, in this footnote, p. 75 (pointing to Allies' decision at the end of World War II to break up German corporations that had aided the Nazi regime as evidence that the corporations were viewed as having violated customary international law).

78  France proposed such an extension during the negotiation of the Rome Statute, but it was not adopted. *See* Andrew Clapham, 'The Question of Jurisdiction Under International Criminal Law over Legal Persons: Lessons Learned from the Rome Conference on an International Criminal Court', in M. T. Kamminga and S. Zia-Zarifi (eds.), *Liability of Multinational Corporations Under International Law* (Kluwer Law International, 2000) p. 139.

tions, "emerging practice and expert opinion increasingly do suggest that corporations may be held liable for committing, or for complicity in, the most heinous human rights violations amounting to international crimes, including genocide, slavery, human trafficking, forced labor, torture, and some crimes against humanity".[79] His second report notes that the Rome Statute does not extend the jurisdiction of the ICC to corporations, but attributes that failure to "differences in national approaches", and states that "just as the absence of an international accountability mechanism did not preclude individual responsibility for international crimes in the past, it does not preclude the emergence of corporate responsibility today".[80] The report concludes that although corporate criminal responsibility "continues to evolve", there is already "observable evidence of its existence".[81]

In support of this position, Ruggie pointed to two factors of particular importance in shaping the development of direct corporate duties.[82] One is the growth of corporate responsibility for abuses of international law under domestic legal systems. He cited research by the Norwegian Institute of Applied Social Science (Fafo), which surveyed 16 countries to determine the remedies they provide in their domestic laws for grave breaches of international law by corporations.[83] Of the 16 countries, nine have fully incorporated the three crimes in the Rome Statute into their domestic laws, two others were in the process of doing so, and the remaining five all have legislation incorporating at least one of the crimes.[84] Because most of these countries provide for criminal liability of corporations as well as individuals, the effect is to subject corporations to domestic legal remedies for violation of international crimes.

Ruggie also emphasised the burgeoning US jurisprudence under the ATS, which has been informed by "the expansion and refinement of individual responsibility" by the international criminal courts.[85] Courts construing the ATS have recognised that international law directly prohibits individuals from taking certain actions, including genocide and war crimes, and have found that such actions constitute torts in violation of the law of nations, within the meaning of the Statute.[86] Since the late 1990s, they have extended this reasoning to cases seeking damages from corporations for human rights

---

79  2006 Interim Report, *supra* note 3, para. 61.
80  2007 Mapping Report, *supra* note 39, para. 21.
81  Ibid., para. 33.
82  Ibid., para. 22.
83  A. Ramasastry and R. C. Thompson, *Commerce, Crime and Conflict: Legal Remedies for Private Sector Liability for Grave Breaches of International Law* (2006), available at <www.fafo.no/pub/rapp/536/536.pdf>.
84  Ibid., p. 15. The countries studied that provide for criminal corporate liability of some kind include Argentina, Canada, France, India, Indonesia, Japan, South Africa, the United Kingdom and the United States. *Ibid.*, p. 13.
85  2007 Mapping Report, *supra* note 39, paras. 22–23; see 2006 Interim Report, *supra* note 3, para. 62.
86  See e.g. Kadic v. Karadzic, 70 F.3d 232 (2d Cir. 1995).

abuses. Although only a few of the cases have resulted in payments by the defendants, many more remain pending.[87]

Ruggie's observations about corporate liability for actions defined as international crimes may have helped forge the political consensus around his Framework and Principles. His statements that international prohibitions on genocide and other grave human rights offenses do apply to corporations offset, to some degree, his rejection of the Draft Norms' position that all human rights obligations apply directly to corporations. Apart from this potential political effect, how accurate are Ruggie's views, and what influence are they likely to have on the development of the law?

The trends Ruggie described do not provide conclusive evidence that customary international law already binds corporations not to commit actions defined as international crimes, such as genocide and war crimes. The incorporation of penalties for such actions in the domestic law of some countries, as surveyed by the Fafo study, does not, by itself, show either the consistent practice or the *opinio juris* necessary to evidence customary international law. When Ruggie published his description of ATS jurisprudence, the US decisions generally assumed that corporations could be liable on the same grounds as individuals,[88] but since then the issue has given rise to intense disagreement between US courts, with some denying and some defending the principle of corporate liability.[89] Even if the Supreme Court resolves the question as far as the ATS is concerned,[90] any interpretations the Court makes of international

---

87  For a description of a settlement, *see* I. Wuerth, '*Wiwa v. Shell*: The $15.5 Million Settlement', 13 *ASIL Insights* (2009) p. 14. The pending cases include *Sarei v. Rio Tinto, PLC*, 625 F.3d 561 (9th Cir. 2010) (alleging that Rio Tinto committed war crimes and crimes against humanity in the course of mining operations on Bougainville in Papua New Guinea); *Abdullahi v. Pfizer, Inc.*, 562 F.3d 163 (2d Cir. 2009) (alleging that Pfizer carried out medical tests on Nigerian children without their consent); *In re South African Apartheid Litigation*, 617 F.Supp.2d 228 (S.D.N.Y. 2009) (alleging violations by many companies in connection with the apartheid regime in South Africa).

88  Decisions assuming that the ATS may reach corporate conduct without examining the issue separately from other types of non-state conduct include *Doe v. Unocal Corp.*, 395 F.3d 932 (9th Cir. 2002), vacated, 395 F.3d 978 (9th Cir. 2003); *Wiwa v. Royal Dutch Shell Petroleum Co.*, 226 F.3d 88 (2d Cir. 2000).

89  Decisions holding that corporations may be liable include *Flomo*, 643 F.3d at 1017-21; *Doe VIII v. Exxon Mobil*, supra note 77; *Sinaltrainal v. Coca-Cola Co.*, 578 F.2d 1252, 1263 (11th Cir. 2009); *Al-Quraishi v. Nakhla*, 728 F. Supp. 2d 702, 753 (D. Md. 2010); *In re XE Services Alien Tort Litigation*, 665 F. Supp. 2d 569, 588 (E.D. Va. 2009). Decisions denying such liability include *Kiobel*, 621 F.3d at 111; *Doe v. Nestle, S.A.*, 748 F.Supp.2d 1057, 1143–1144 (C.D. Cal. 2010). To complicate matters, the issue of corporate liability under the ATS does not necessarily turn on whether corporations are directly liable under international law, both because courts could interpret the ATS to include indirect as well as direct duties, *see supra* note 45, and because some courts have based corporate liability under the statute on their reading of US law rather than international law. See e.g. *Doe VIII v. Exxon Mobil*, supra note 77, at p. 84 ("domestic law, *i.e.*, federal common law, supplies the source of law on the question of corporate liability").

90  In June 2011, the plaintiffs in *Kiobel*, one of the decisions denying corporate liability, requested the Supreme Court to review the decision. Petition for Writ of *Certiorari*,

law could have only persuasive effect outside the United States. But Ruggie was careful not to overstate the importance of the Fafo study or of the interpretations of international law by ATS courts. He merely pointed out that national courts were already able to impose criminal and civil liability on corporations for violations of international criminal standards, which is clearly true.

One might think that Ruggie's position arrived in good time to affect the outcome of the ATS debate. It is difficult to discern a clear influence, however. Although many briefs in ATS cases have referred to his work, they have often cited him incorrectly, as indicating that corporations do not have any direct obligations at all, on the basis of his statement in the 2007 Mapping Report that the international human rights instruments reviewed there do not impose direct legal responsibilities on corporations.[91] One lower court has also made this mistake.[92] On the other hand, one of the appellate courts that found corporate liability under the ATS cited Ruggie correctly, as pointing out the extension of responsibility for international crimes to corporations under domestic law, including through the ATS.[93]

In any event, asking whether Ruggie's work will influence legal interpretations by domestic courts is probably the wrong way to evaluate his impact. Ruggie did not present his views as definitive scholarly conclusions on the current state of corporate direct duties under international criminal law. Rather than affecting the development of law directly, through making a legal argument, Ruggie's description of the trend toward greater potential corporate liability seems more likely to have the aim and effect of raising awareness of the *practical* consequences of this trend. Although the status of direct corporate responsibility under international law (and ATS jurisprudence) remains unclear, there is no doubt that the developments Ruggie outlines are, as he put it, "creating an expanding web of potential corporate liability for international crimes, imposed through national courts".[94]

Although he draws legal conclusions from this observation, his larger point is that corporations should be aware of the potential legal costs of behaviour that could lead to accusations that they have violated these standards. If the US Supreme Court eventually rejects corporate liability under the ATS, then one high-profile avenue of corporate accountability will disappear. But Ruggie's reports demonstrate that the ATS is far

---

available at <harvardhumanrights.files.wordpress.com/2011/06/kiobel-petition-for-writ-final-6-6-2011.pdf>.

91   E.g. *Presbyterian Church of Sudan* v. *Talisman Energy, Inc.*, 2010 WL 2568101, on petition for a writ of *certiorari* from the Supreme Court to the US Court of Appeals for the Second Circuit (2010) (brief of *amicus curiae* Professor James Crawford); *Presbyterian Church of Sudan* v. *Talisman Energy Inc.*, on petition for writ of *certiorari* (2010) (brief of *amicus curiae* Professor Malcolm N. Shaw); *Sarei* v. *Rio Tinto PLC*, 2009 WL 6023779 (9th Cir. 2009) (motion for leave to file *amicus curiae* brief of international law professors); *Balintulo* v. *Daimler AG*, 2009 WL 7768620 (2d Cir. 2009) (letter brief of *amici curiae* international law professors).

92   *Doe* v. *Nestle*, 748 F.Supp.2d at 1141.

93   *Doe VIII* v. *ExxonMobil*, *supra* note 77, p. 23.

94   2007 Mapping Report, *supra* note 39, para. 22.

from the only potential source of grave consequences for corporations if they violate international standards for heinous human rights abuses such as genocide and crimes against humanity. Apart from the potential for civil liability based on other domestic laws, corporations are increasingly likely to find themselves subject to criminal prosecution for such actions in domestic courts around the world. His warning is designed to convince corporations that they need to take these international standards more seriously.

At the same time, this emphasis on the practical consequences of corporate liability under domestic law may turn out to affect not only corporate behaviour, but also the long-term evolution of international law on this issue. His statements that the law is moving in this direction, and in particular his publicisation of the Fafo study showing that many countries already provide for domestic responsibility for infringements of international criminal law, may help to provide evidence of the gradual accretion of practice relevant to customary international law. Moreover, a greater understanding by states of the widespread responsibility of corporations for such crimes in the context of domestic legal systems might prepare the ground for an eventual amendment to the Rome Statute to expand the jurisdiction of the International Criminal Court to include corporations.

### 3.2. *Corporate Complicity in State Human Rights Violations*

Another outstanding issue concerns the potential responsibility of corporations that are implicated in state actions. States can be responsible for violations of international law when they are acting through or with corporations, but under what circumstances can corporations be responsible when they are acting for or with states? Again, this issue has come into focus in the context of litigation against corporations under the US Alien Tort Statute. There, the debate has centred on whether the international standard for aiding and abetting an international crime requires a *mens rea* of knowledge of the principal action, or of intent to assist it.[95]

As the SRSG, Professor Ruggie came out firmly on behalf of the lower standard of knowledge alone. In a detailed report on complicity, Ruggie reviewed the applicable jurisprudence of the international criminal tribunals and concluded, without qualification, that the cases "have required that the accused know the criminal intentions of the principal perpetrator, and that their own acts provide substantial assistance to the commission of the crime", but not that "the individual share the same criminal intent as the principal, or even desire that the crime occur".[96] He cited decisions of the international criminal courts for Rwanda and the former Yugoslavia, as well as by

---

[95] *See generally* D. Cassel, 'Corporate Aiding and Abetting of Human Rights Violations: Confusion in the Courts', 6 *Nw. J. Int'l Human Rts.* (2008) p. 304; C. Keitner, 'Conceptualizing Complicity in Alien Tort Cases', 60 *Hastings L.J.* (2008) p. 61.

[96] Special Representative of the Secretary-General on the Issue of Human Rights and Transnational Corporations and Other Business Enterprises, *Clarifying the Concepts of "Sphere of Influence" and "Complicity"*, U.N. Doc. A/HRC/8/16 (2008) para. 42.

the Nuremberg tribunals, all of which construed customary international law on this issue.[97]

Ruggie's position seems well-supported by the relevant law. Still, the apparent clarity of the law is somewhat muddied by the language of the Rome Statute, which states that a person shall be criminally liable within the jurisdiction of the International Criminal Court "if that person ... [f]or the *purpose* of facilitating the commission of such a crime, aids, abets or otherwise assists in its commission or its attempted commission".[98] Although the ICC has not confirmed that this provision requires a finding of intent, it has influenced ATS litigation. In 2009, in *Presbyterian Church of Sudan v. Talisman Energy, Inc.*, the Second Circuit Court of Appeals relied on it in holding that the international standard for aiding and abetting requires intent rather than knowledge.[99] The Court acknowledged that other international criminal courts have employed the less stringent standard. Nevertheless, it decided that the Rome Statute showed that the knowledge standard does not command universal acceptance, which it believed that US jurisprudence requires in order for a norm to be treated as customary international law.[100]

The importance of the *Talisman* decision to the evolution of international law should not be overstated. Subsequent *amicus* briefs filed by legal experts have strongly criticised the decision as misconstruing the Nuremberg precedents and disregarding other provisions of the Rome Statute that suggest that knowledge may also be an acceptable *mens rea*.[101] Most important, *Talisman* does not take into account that the Rome Statute can impose a stricter standard than that of customary international law without thereby changing customary international law.[102] On the basis of these arguments, the next appellate court to consider the question, the D.C. Circuit, rejected *Talisman* in favour of the knowledge standard.[103]

These decisions provide another opportunity to examine the relationship of Ruggie's work to the development of the law. The *Talisman* plaintiffs, as well as the *am-*

---

97   Ibid., paras. 42–44.
98   Rome Statute, *supra* note 24, Article 25(3)(c) (emphasis added).
99   *Presbyterian Church of Sudan v. Talisman Energy, Inc.*, 582 F.3d 244 (2d Cir. 2009), *cert. denied*, 131 S. Ct. 79, 122 (2010). The *Talisman* court largely adopted a concurring opinion in an earlier case. See *Khulumani v. Barclay National Bank Ltd.*, 504 F.3d 254, 275–277 (2d Cir. 2007) (Katzmann, J., concurring).
100  *Talisman*, 582 F.3d at 259. See *Flores v. Southern Peru Copper Co.*, 414 F.3d 233, 248 (2d Cir. 2003) ("[I]n order for a principle to become part of customary international law, States must universally abide by it").
101  E.g., Brief of *Amicus Curiae* International Commission of Jurists, at 15–16, *Presbyterian Church of Sudan v. Talisman Energy, Inc.*, on petition for a writ of *certiorari* from the Supreme Court to the US Court of Appeals for the Second Circuit (2010) (citing Rome Statute, *supra* note 24, Articles 25(3)(d) and 30).
102  Brief of *Amicus Curiae* International Law Professors, at 17–20, *Presbyterian Church of Sudan v. Talisman Energy, Inc.*, on petition for a writ of *certiorari* from the Supreme Court to the US Court of Appeals for the Second Circuit, 2010 WL 1787371 (2010).
103  *Doe VIII v. ExxonMobil*, *supra* note 77, p. 11.

*icus* legal scholars, cited Ruggie in their briefs to the Supreme Court asking it to hear their appeal from the decision. They were able to draw not only on his general reports on corporate complicity, but also his criticisms of the *Talisman* decision in particular.[104] In a speech shortly after the decision, Ruggie did not pull punches. He not only called the intent standard adopted by *Talisman* "against the weight of international opinion", he said that its outcome was "absurd" and pointed out that "as long as an I.G. Farben intended only to make money, not to exterminate Jews, [the intent standard] would make it permissible for such a company to keep supplying a government with massive amounts of Zyklon B poison gas knowing precisely what it is used for".[105] He said that the decision "demonstrates, if further demonstration were needed, ... that we are far from a systemic solution to ensuring access to judicial remedy for individuals and communities affected by corporate-related abuse".[106]

The Supreme Court refused to hear the appeal from the *Talisman* decision and, although the D.C. Circuit did adopt the "knowledge" test, it did not rely on Ruggie's views. As stated in the previous section, however, examining his effect on any one case is not the best way to assess Ruggie's impact on the development of international law and policy. That impact, if it is felt, will take place over many years and in combination with many other factors. In this respect, *Talisman* illustrates a particular type of contribution that can be made by independent experts appointed to high-profile positions within the UN human rights system. Although they do not have the power to change the law, they can use their visibility to draw attention to specific developments and praise or criticise them in light of the applicable law as they construe it. Although their opinions have less weight than tribunals, they are freer than tribunals to act quickly and on their own initiative. Through their responses to specific situations, they may influence others' behaviour and views of the law and, eventually, the law itself.

With occasional exceptions, such as his remarks on *Talisman,* Ruggie only rarely exercised this power. Rather than respond to individual cases, he usually concentrated on developing an overall approach to corporations and human rights. Now that the Human Rights Council has endorsed the Guiding Principles, the five-person working group appointed by the Council to promote them will likely devote more attention to examining their application to particular situations, continuing to try to bend the future development of the law in the directions that Ruggie has outlined.

---

104 Petition for *Certiorari*, at 17, note 25, *Presbyterian Church of Sudan* v. *Talisman Energy, Inc.*, 2010 WL 1602093 (2010); Brief of *Amicus Curiae* International Law Professors, *supra* note 102, at 23–24.

105 J. G. Ruggie, *Remarks for ICJ Access to Justice Workshop* (29 October 2009), available at <198.170.85.29/Ruggie-remarks-ICJ-Access-to-Justice-workshop-Johannesburg-29-30-Oct-2009.pdf>.

106 *Ibid.*

## 3.3. The Extraterritorial Scope of States' Duty to Protect Against Corporate Abuses of Human Rights

As part 2 explains, international human rights law indisputably imposes a duty on states to protect against private abuses of human rights, including by corporations. Several aspects of the duty to protect remain unclear, however, including the degree to which the duty applies extraterritorially. Many of the corporations accused of the worst human rights abuses have committed such abuses in developing countries with ineffective legal systems. When the host country is unable or unwilling to comply with its duty to protect, do other states have an obligation to protect against these abuses?

The issue is usually not whether other states have the legal authority to exercise regulatory jurisdiction. While territory is the most important basis for jurisdiction,[107] international law recognises other bases, of which nationality is the clearest and least contested.[108] Although corporate nationality can sometimes be difficult to establish,[109] most multinational corporations are identifiably based in countries that have effective legal systems. The key question is therefore not whether the home state (or any other state with a non-territorial basis for jurisdiction) *may* regulate corporations to prevent human rights abuses abroad, but whether human rights law *requires* it to do so.

Professor Ruggie examined this issue early in his mandate, holding expert consultations and conducting a thorough review of the commentaries of the treaty bodies charged with overseeing compliance with the major United Nations human rights agreements.[110] He concluded that the treaty bodies' guidance "suggests that the treaties do not require States to exercise extraterritorial jurisdiction over business abuse".[111] He stressed that the treaties do not *prohibit* states from doing so, and noted that "there is increasing encouragement at the international level, including from the treaty bodies, for home States to take regulatory action to prevent abuse by their companies overseas".[112]

---

107 *Report of the International Bar Association Task Force on Extraterritorial Jurisdiction* (2008) p. 11; *Restatement (Third) of Foreign Relations Law of the United States* (1987), § 402, comment b.

108 *Ibid.*, § 402(2); R. Jennings and A. Watts (eds.), *Oppenheim's International Law*, 9th ed. (1992) § 138.

109 Subsidiaries and supply chains raise complications. See O. de Schutter, *Extraterritorial Jurisdiction as a Tool for Improving the Human Rights Accountability of Transnational Corporations* (2006) pp. 29–45, available at <198.170.85.29/Olivier-de-Schutter-report-for-SRSG-re-extraterritorial-jurisdiction-Dec-2006.pdf>.

110 *See State Responsibilities to Regulate and Adjudicate Corporate Activities Under the United Nations Core Human Rights Treaties: An Overview of Treaty Body Commentaries*, U.N. Doc. A/HRC/4/35/Add.1 (2007), paras. 81–92; *Corporate Responsibility Under International Law and Issues in Extraterritorial Regulation: Summary of Legal Workshops*, U.N. Doc. A/HRC/4/35/Add. 2 (2007).

111 2007 Mapping Report, *supra* note 39, para. 15.

112 2008 Framework Report, *supra* note 50, para. 19.

Ruggie's conclusion that the duty to protect does not extend extraterritorially is certainly defensible, and it is not without scholarly support.[113] Nevertheless, it attracted strong criticism, especially from human rights groups.[114] In particular, it can be criticised for paying insufficient attention to the differences in the language of human rights treaties on this point. Some treaties, like the International Covenant on Civil and Political Rights, include explicit jurisdictional limits.[115] The ICCPR requires each of its parties "to respect and to ensure to all individuals *within its territory and subject to its jurisdiction* the rights recognized in the present Covenant".[116] Under the most commonly accepted interpretation of this language,[117] a state's obligations extend extraterritorially only to those who are "subject to its jurisdiction", which has been construed as meaning within its "effective control".[118] Other agreements, however, such as the Genocide Convention, include no jurisdictional limit, which suggests that none should be implied.[119] Finally, some include language that arguably extends their duties extraterritorially. The most important agreement in this category is the International Covenant on Economic, Social and Cultural Rights, which requires each of its parties "to take steps, individually *and through international assistance and co-operation*, especially economic and technical, to the maximum of its available resources, with a view to achieving progressively the full realization of the rights recognized in the present Covenant by all appropriate means".[120]

Although this language is arguably ambiguous, the Committee on Economic, Social and Cultural Rights, the body charged with overseeing compliance with the

---

113  *E.g.* de Schutter, *supra* note 109, pp. 18–19; Zerk, *supra* note 33, p. 91.

114  *E.g.* January 2011 Joint Civil Society Statement, *supra* note 61.

115  Besides the ICCPR, *see* European Convention, *supra* note 30, Article 1; American Convention, *supra* note 30, Article 1(1).

116  ICCPR, *supra* note 12, Article 2(1) (emphasis added).

117  The word "and" might suggest that a state owes duties only to individuals who are both within its territory and subject to its jurisdiction. *See* M. J. Dennis, 'Application of Human Rights Treaties Extraterritorially in Times of Armed Conflict and Military Occupation', 99 *Am. J. Int'l L.* (2005) p. 119, at pp. 122–125. The dominant interpretation, however, has been that the language should be read disjunctively, to require each party to respect and ensure the rights of those within its territory and those subject to its jurisdiction. *See Legal Consequences of the Construction of a Wall in the Occupied Palestinian Territory*, Advisory Opinion, 2004 I.C.J. 136, (July 9), para. 111; T. Buergenthal, 'To Respect and to Ensure: State Obligations and Permissible Derogations', in L. Henkin (ed.), *The International Bill of Rights* (Columbia University Press, 1981) p. 72, at p. 74; T. Meron, 'Extraterritoriality of Human Rights Treaties', 89 *Am J. Int'l L.* (1995) p. 78, at p. 79.

118  General Comment No. 31, *supra* note 16, para. 10. *See Legal Consequences of the Construction of a Wall*, *ibid.*, para. 111; D. McGoldrick, 'Extraterritorial Application of the International Covenant on Civil and Political Rights', in F. Coomans and M. T. Kamminga (eds.), *Extraterritorial Application of Human Rights Treaties* (Intersentia, 2004) p. 41, at pp. 63–65.

119  *See Application of the Convention on the Prevention and Punishment of the Crime of Genocide (Bosnia-Herzegovina v. Yugoslavia)*, 1996 ICJ Rep. 595, 616 (July 11).

120  ICESCR, *supra* note 12, Article 2(1) (emphasis added).

ICESCR, has long interpreted it as giving rise to extraterritorial obligations.[121] Since 1999, almost every one of its general comments on particular rights, including the rights to food, health, water, work, social security, and to take part in cultural life, includes a section on such obligations.[122] Although many of its statements have to do with duties to assist developing countries to meet their obligations, some speak directly to the extraterritorial application of the duty to protect. In particular, the Committee has stated that parties to the ICESCR should protect the rights to health, to water and to social security by taking steps to influence those within their jurisdiction to respect the rights "in other countries".[123] More specifically, it has indicated that the ICESCR parties should take steps "to prevent their own citizens *and companies* from violating the right to water of individuals and communities in other countries".[124]

Ruggie took the position that through statements such as these, the Committee (and other treaty bodies) merely "seem to be encouraging States to pay greater attention to preventing corporate violations abroad".[125] Although it is possible that the Committee's occasional use of the term "should" in connection with states' duty to protect against extraterritorial abuses indicates that it does not view its statements as describing binding obligations, that interpretation is undercut by the placement of the statements in a section of the general comments entitled "international obligations", and by the use of language better suited for describing binding legal duties.[126] The

---

121  CESCR General Comment No. 3, *The Nature of States Parties Obligations* (1990) para. 14 ("[I]nternational cooperation for development and thus for the realization of economic, social and cultural rights is an obligation of all States. It is particularly incumbent upon those States which are in a position to assist others in this regard").

122  General Comment No. 12, *supra* note 17, paras. 36–38; General Comment No. 14, *The Right to the Highest Attainable Standard of Health*, U.N. Doc. E/C.12/2000/4 (2000), paras. 38–42; General Comment No. 15, *supra* note 27, paras. 30–36; General Comment No. 17, *The right of everyone to benefit from the protection of the moral and material interests resulting from any scientific, literary or artistic production of which he or she is the author*, U.N. Doc. E/C.12/GC/17 (2006), paras. 36–38; General Comment No. 18, *The Right to Work*, U.N. Doc. E/C.12/GC/18 (2006), paras. 29–30; General Comment No. 19, *The Right to Social Security*, U.N. Doc. E/C.12/GC/19 (2008), paras. 52–58; General Comment No. 21, *Right of Everyone to Take Part in Cultural Life*, U.N. Doc. E/C.12/GC/21 (2009), paras. 56–59.

123  General Comment No. 14, *ibid., para.* 39; General Comment No. 15, *supra* note 27, para. 33; General Comment No. 19, *ibid.*, para. 54.

124  General Comment No. 15, *supra* note 27, para. 33 (emphasis added). *See also* General Comment No. 19, *supra* note 122, para. 54 (states "should extraterritorially protect the right to social security by preventing their own citizens and national entities from violating this right in other countries").

125  2007 Mapping Report, *supra* note 39, para. 15, note 9.

126  *E.g.* General Comment No. 14, *supra* note 122, para. 39 ("*To comply with their international obligations* in relation to article 12, *States parties have to* respect the enjoyment of the right to health in other countries, and to prevent third parties from violating the right in other countries, if they are able to influence these third parties by way of legal or political means, in accordance with the Charter of the United Nations and applicable international law") (emphasis added).

Office of the High Commissioner for Human Rights has characterised the Committee's views, without caveat, as identifying several types of "extraterritorial obligations", including "*legal obligations* to … [t]ake measures to prevent third parties (e.g. private companies) over which they hold influence from interfering with the enjoyment of human rights in other countries."[127]

Of course, Ruggie was entitled to disagree with the Committee on this point, or to note that all states do not accept its position. The Committee's views are not legally binding, and developed countries have long disputed that they have extraterritorial obligations under the ICESCR, especially obligations to provide financial assistance.[128] But, in that case, it would have been more accurate to characterise the interpretations of the ICESCR consistently as disputed or unsettled, rather than indicating that the Covenant includes no binding extraterritorial obligations to protect.[129]

Moreover, even as he rejected the notion that current law imposes extraterritorial duties to protect, Ruggie could have done more to acknowledge the movement toward greater recognition of such duties. A report prepared for the SRSG by Olivier de Schutter, for example, agrees that the current state of the law does not clearly recognise extraterritorial duties to protect, but goes on to state: "This classical view may be changing, however, especially as far as economic and social rights are concerned. There is a growing recognition that the fact of the interdependency of States should lead to impose an extended understanding of State obligations, or an obligation on all States to act jointly in face of collective action problems faced by the international community of States."[130] Apart from the statements by the Committee on Economic, Social and Cultural Rights, this trend is apparent in the work of many different human rights bodies, including other treaty bodies,[131] the Office of the High Commissioner for

---

127 *Report of the Office of the United Nations High Commissioner for Human Rights on the Relationship Between Climate Change and Human Rights*, U.N. Doc. A/HRC/10/61 (2009), paras. 86 and 99 (emphasis added).

128 *See* M. Craven, 'The Violence of Dispossession: Extra-Territoriality and Economic, Social, and Cultural Rights', in M. A. Baderin and R. McCorquodale (eds.), *Economic, Social and Cultural Rights in Action* (Oxford University Press, 2007) p. 71, at p. 77.

129 Ruggie did describe the law as unsettled in some of his reports, *e.g.* 2008 Framework Report, *supra* note 50, para. 19; 2009 Operationalizing Report, *supra* note 56, para. 15. But, at the same time, he described the treaty bodies as suggesting that states are not required to regulate corporations extraterritorially.

130 De Schutter, *supra* note 109, at 19.

131 *See e.g.* M. Wabwile, 'Re-Examining States' External Obligations to Implement Economic and Social Rights of Children', 22 *Can. J.L. & Juris.* (2009) p. 407, at pp. 425–428 (arguing that states' reports to the Committee on the Rights of the Child suggests growing acceptance of extraterritorial obligations).

Human Rights,[132] and special rapporteurs working under the auspices of the Human Rights Council.[133]

Despite his narrow view of the legal obligations, Ruggie also contributed to that trend, by urging states to do more to prevent "their" corporations from abusing human rights abroad. His 2010 report to the Council states:

> Legitimate issues are at stake and they are unlikely to be resolved fully anytime soon. However, the scale of the current impasse must and can be reduced. To take the most pressing case, what message do States wish to send victims of corporate-related abuse in conflict affected areas? Sorry? Work it out yourselves? Or that States will make greater efforts to ensure that companies based in, or conducting transactions through, their jurisdictions do not commit or contribute to such abuses, and to help remedy them when they do occur? Surely the latter is preferable.[134]

The commentary to the Guiding Principles underscores that "[t]here are strong policy reasons for home States to set out clearly the expectations that businesses respect human rights abroad, especially where the State itself is involved in or supports those businesses".[135] And in his 2011 proposal that the Council follow up his mandate by, *inter alia,* working toward a legal instrument on the application to corporations of prohibitions on gross human rights violations, Ruggie suggested that the effort should particularly consider states' extraterritorial jurisdiction over corporations operating in conflict zones.[136] The Council did not accept this suggestion.

In assessing Ruggie's position on this issue, it is again important to consider the political constraints that he faced. The Council's refusal even to adopt his limited proposal to begin a process of clarifying extraterritorial duties in conflict zones illustrates the difficulty of finding a consensus here. Developed countries have generally opposed extraterritorial human rights obligations, and developing countries may not always like the idea, either, in the context of a duty to protect (as opposed to a duty to assist). Olivier de Schutter states that, "in general, it may be anticipated that control by the home States of the activities of transnational corporations will be resented as a

---

132  See OHCHR Report on the Relationship Between Climate Change and Human Rights, *supra* note 127, paras. 84–87 and 99 (describing duty of international cooperation in relation to climate change).

133  See e.g. J. B.de Mesquita, P. Hunt and R. Khosla, 'The Human Rights Responsibility of International Assistance and Cooperation in Health', in M. Gibney and S. Skogly (eds.), *Universal Human Rights and Extraterritorial Obligations* (University of Pennsylvania Press, 2010) p. 104 (describing the views of the special rapporteur on the right to health).

134  Special Representative of the Secretary-General, *Business and Human Rights: Further Steps Toward the Operationalization of the "Protect, Respect and Remedy" Framework*, U.N. Doc. A/HRC/14/27 (2010), para. 47.

135  Guiding Principles, *supra* note 50, p. 7. The Commentary also reiterates that "[a]t present States are not generally required" to regulate the extraterritorial activities of businesses domiciled in their territory".

136  Ruggie, *Recommendations on Follow-up to the Mandate, supra* note 66, pp. 4–5.

limitation to the sovereign right of the territorial States concerned to regulate activities occurring on their territory, or as betraying a distrust of the ability of those States to effectively protect their own populations from the activities of foreign corporations".[137] If Ruggie believed that stronger statements of legal obligation would have been opposed from both richer and poorer countries, then he may have felt that he could go no further than emphasising, as he did, that states have the authority to regulate the extraterritorial conduct of their companies and that they should exercise that authority more often. As so often in international law, legal changes in this regard may follow changes in the practice of states, rather than *vice versa*.

## 4. Conclusion

The debate over the application of human rights law to corporations has never questioned that corporations can have enormous effects on the enjoyment of human rights or that they have been involved in massive human rights abuses. The difficulty has been to convert that understanding into workable legal standards. For many years, efforts at the United Nations to develop an effective approach either stayed at a level of abstract generality or devolved into fruitless debates. The appointment of John Ruggie was something of a high-stakes gamble that he could do what had not been done: bring some consensus out of this contested field. Over the course of his six-year mandate, he did not resolve every issue. Some questions remain unsettled, such as whether states have a duty to regulate the extraterritorial conduct of their corporations. On other issues, his views may not be accepted or implemented by all of the interested parties. Corporate abuses of human rights will undoubtedly continue.

But, after all, Ruggie was not given the impossible task of ending all disputes over the application of human rights standards to corporations, far less of ending all corporate infringements on human rights. His mandate was initially to clarify the standards of corporate responsibility with regard to human rights, then to develop an approach to those standards that could command general support, and finally to make operational the framework principles of corporate responsibility that he had developed. To a remarkable degree, that is exactly what he did. He took the legal framework that was emerging for private actors and carefully extended it to include corporations. He developed Guiding Principles on business and human rights that elaborate how this framework applies to corporations and include feasible, concrete ways to implement it. Most important, he built a consensus among governments, corporations and (to a significant degree) advocacy groups around the basic elements of his approach. In light of the challenges he faced, those achievements must count as a great success.

---

137   De Schutter, *supra* note 109, p. 21.

# 3  The Development of the 'UN Framework': A Pragmatic Process Towards a Pragmatic Output

Karin Buhmann*

## 1. Introduction

Prodded in part by the resolutions that created his first mandate (2005–2008) and extended it for a second term (2008–2011), the Special Representative of the Secretary-General (SRSG) has adopted a broad consultative process, including not only those governmental, intergovernmental and non-governmental actors who are conventionally consulted in international law-making on human rights and related 'global concerns', but also the private sector, that is, private non-state actors that are prospective duty-bearers. Due to the state-centrist structure of international law and politics, the private sector has previously been excluded from international law-making, at least formally. The Guiding Principles that are the main topic of this book were developed as an 'operationalisation' of the *Protect, Respect, Remedy* report presented by SRSG John Ruggie in 2008.

This chapter discusses the development of the SRSG's 'UN Framework', focusing on the consultative approach adopted during the SRSG's 2005–2008 mandate and the difference to the development of the UN Norms on the Responsibilities of Transnational Corporations and other Business Enterprises with regard to Human Rights ('the Norms') and the reception that the Norms met in the Commission on Human Rights. The chapter considers the process leading to the UN Framework and the 'unanimous welcoming' that the Framework was given by the Human Rights Council. Discussion of the substantive contents and qualities of the UN Framework and the Guiding Principles or their possible status as soft or hard international law is beyond the focus of the chapter.

---

\*   Associate Professor of Law, Institute of Food and Resource Economics, University of Copenhagen.

The course of the mandate that led to the UN Framework has been described by the SRSG as "principled pragmatism".[1] For a UN human rights special procedure, the SRSG process was unusual in its approach to stakeholder consultation. Consulting with stakeholders is not by itself unusual for a human rights special procedure. But consulting with prospective duty-holders that do not have direct access to the conventional process of international law-making is. Under international law, states are both primary duty-holders and by default participants in the law-making process. Companies, by contrast, are neither typical duty-holders under international law, nor typically involved in international law-making.

Much as the prospective duty-holding role for companies is an effect of the general corporate social responsibility (CSR) paradigm, the SRSG's approach did set the process apart from previous UN efforts to develop business responsibilities for human rights. This chapter argues that although the UN Framework is not as comprehensive or detailed as some might like, its significance is in simply having become accepted by the Human Rights Council and having been prepared through a process that allowed diverging interests to be presented, tested and addressed in the process. Acceptance by the Human Rights Council does not make for formal international law by itself, but it paves the way for further efforts that may eventually reach the UN General Assembly for formal adoption. By being accepted by the Human Rights Council, the UN Framework paved the way for what has become the Guiding Principles. That may in turn lead to further detailed guidance on human rights responsibilities for the business sector, both through the work of UN human rights bodies and perhaps through formal international hard or soft law.

The perspective taken in this chapter is that the broad consultative process provided the UN Framework with an element of process legitimacy that led to output effectiveness in terms of the broad acceptance of the Framework. This provided the normative as well as politically accepted background for the Guiding Principles.

## 2. The Background for the 'UN Framework': Windy Course Towards UN Regulation of Business Social and Human Rights Responsibilities

Defining human rights duties for multinational enterprises (or as these are generally referred to in UN contexts, 'transnational companies' (TNCs)) has been on the agenda of international organisations for decades. The results have been varied, but so far have at most led to relatively open-ended recommendations rather than specific obligations. The first major attempt by the UN to formulate a code of conduct for transnational corporations was initiated in the 1970s by the Commission on Transnational Corporations.[2]

---

1 Interim report of the Special Representative of the Secretary-General on the issue of human rights and transnational corporations and other business enterprises, UN Doc. E/CN.4/2006/97, 22 February 2006, *see especially* section B.
2 Established by the Economic and Social Council under resolution 1913 (LVII), 5 December 1974.

The text of the UN Draft Code of Conduct on Transnational Corporations,[3] finalised during the late 1980s, contained duties for TNCs to respect host countries' development goals, observe their domestic law, respect fundamental human rights, and observe consumer and environmental protection objectives. The UN Code project was abandoned, however, partly due to opposition and divergence of investment related interests among certain governments.

From the mid-1990s attention to companies' adverse impact on human rights resurfaced within the UN. In 1998 a working group under the UN Sub-Commission on the Promotion and Protection of Human Rights (hereinafter the Sub-Commission), itself established under the UN Human Rights Commission, began work to draft a document setting out human rights obligations for companies. Under the title (draft) Norms on Human Rights Responsibilities of Transnational Corporations and other Business Enterprises[4] the draft Norms were adopted by the Sub-Commission on 13 August 2003. The Sub-Commission recommended that the draft Norms be referred to the UN Human Rights Commission for adoption. The Commission considered the draft Norms at its 60th session in 2004 and deferred further discussion on the Norms to its 61st session in 2005. The Commission requested the Office of the High Commissioner for Human Rights (OHCHR) to make a report on the scope and legal status of existing initiatives and standards relating to the human rights responsibilities of corporations in the meantime.[5] In a decision adopted at its 60th session, the Commission stated that the draft Norms "as a draft proposal" have no legal standing.[6]

At its session in 2005, the Commission adopted the resolution that led to the appointment of the SRSG. The Commission did not deal further with the Norms. Thus, prior to the Human Rights Council's 'unanimous welcoming' of the UN Framework in 2008, efforts undertaken within the UN to define human rights duties for business had not yielded much.

Some efforts within other international organisations to define human rights duties for companies have been more successful. In the 1970s, the International Labour Organization (ILO) and the Organisation for Economic Co-operation and Development (OECD), whose members are mainly wealthy industrialised states, adopted soft law instruments setting out certain recommendations for TNCs. Originally, references to human rights were limited. Both the 1976 OECD Guidelines for Multinational Corporations and the 1977 ILO Tripartite Declaration of Principles concerning Multinational Enterprises and Social Policy were revised in 2000 to include more detailed reference to human rights.

The ILO Tripartite Declaration was intended to realign TNCs' activities with host state policy objectives and workers' interests. The Tripartite Declaration seeks to en-

---

3   *Draft Code of Conduct on Transnational Corporations*, last version of the proposed Draft Code: UN Doc. E/1990/94, 12 June 1990.
4   *Norms on the Responsibilities of Transnational Corporations and Other Business Enterprises with regard to Human Rights 2003*, UN Doc. E/CN.4/Sub.2/2003/12/Rev.2.
5   Human Rights Commission, *Decision 2004/116*, UN Doc. E/CN.4/2004/L.73/Rev.1, 16 April 2004.
6   Ibid.

gage TNCs in complying with ILO social policy conventions and recommendations even where the host state is not bound by or does not enforce these. The ILO Tripartite Declaration of Principles concerning Multinational Enterprises and Social Policy were revised in 2000 to incorporate the fundamental principles and rights at work and again in 2006 to update references to other ILO instruments.[7]

The OECD Guidelines were drafted with the intention of providing a degree of home state guidance for TNCs incorporated in OECD member states. The background for the Guidelines was the concern among industrialised states (*i.e.* OECD member states) that political or other interference by TNCs in developing host states might lead those states to impose restrictions on the rights of foreign investors. The 2000 revision included a call for corporations to "respect the human rights of those affected by their activities", to "contribute to the effective elimination of child labour", and to "end forced or compulsory labour in their operations". The revision also extended the applicability of the Guidelines to worldwide activities of OECD based multinational enterprises and a recommendation to encourage compliance with the Guidelines through the supply chain.[8] A revision adopted in May 2011[9] expands the human rights provisions but does not alter the soft character of the Guidelines with regard to companies.

Both instruments are relatively weak: The OECD Guidelines address themselves only indirectly to companies. The Guidelines may be recommended by states to TNCs hosted within their jurisdiction. The Guidelines are not legally enforceable, and although the National Contact Points (NCP) complaints handling mechanism established with the 2000 revision was innovative, it has not yet proven to be very effective. As a declaration, the ILO Tripartite Declaration has neither the strength of an ILO convention, nor of an ILO recommendation, in terms of the obligations that ILO member states have undertaken under the ILO Constitution to present such instruments to their national authorities with a view to adoption.

At the time when work on the draft Norms was initiated, several other reports or notes by other members of the Sub-Commission that drafted the Norms addressed the issue of business and human rights.[10] Some general comments from treaty bodies under UN human rights treaties as well as case law or reports from some regional

---

[7] ILO Tripartite Declaration of Principles concerning Multinational Enterprises and Social Policy, <www.ilo.org/public/english/employment/multi/download/english.pdf>.

[8] OECD Guidelines for Multinational Enterprises, <www.olis.oecd.org/olis/2000doc.nsf/LinkTo/NT00002F06/$FILE/JT00115758.PDF>.

[9] OECD, *OECD Guidelines for Multinational Enterprises: Update 2011*, Doc. C(2011)59, 3 May 2011.

[10] E. Asbjørn, *Corporations, states and human rights: A note on responsibilities and procedures for implementation and compliance*, Sub-Commission on the Promotion and Protection of Human Rights, UN Doc. E/DN.4/Sub.2/2001/WG.2/WP.2; G. El-Hajdi, *The realization of economic, social and cultural rights: The question of transnational corporations*, Sub-Commission on the Promotion and Protection of Human Rights, UN Doc. E/DN.4/Sub.2/2001/WG.2/WP.3.

human rights instruments have also addressed the issue.[11] In terms of actually defining human rights duties for companies, results however have been limited to efforts to reach agreement on the Code of Conduct for TNCs, or the draft UN Norms, both of which failed to be approved in the political and international law-making organs within the UN system (the General Assembly and the Human Rights Council, which has a preparatory role).

From a human rights perspective the organisation's limited success in defining human rights obligations for companies may well be considered disconcerting. That is particularly so if one takes into account the impact on human rights that TNCs have come to have since the UN Charter and the Universal Declaration were adopted in the 1940s. Both are based on the conventional state-centrist conception of international law and its subjects and were developed at a time when few were able to imagine the economic, political and transnational expansion of corporate power that came to take place during the second half of the 20th century. Most particularly, the UN's limited success in regulating companies' conduct is disconcerting in view of limited willingness of some nation states to enforce applicable law to companies within their territories, let alone for home states of large TNCs – most of which are concentrated in the rich global north – to extend application of their law to 'their' companies when those act outside the territory of the home state.

The story of the draft UN Norms was not just one among other regulatory efforts that were launched but became stalled within the UN law-making system. The debate that surrounded the Norms not only within but particularly outside the UN since their adoption by the Sub-Commission and the decision by the Commission on Human Rights to avoid specific reference to the Norms in the mandate of the SRSG is also indicative of the high stakes that were associated with the Norms. Without a formal place in the state-centrist composition of the Human Rights Commission and its Sub-Commission and working group, companies took to lobbying states to protect their interests. Whether justified or not, companies and their organisations felt excluded. The debate became heated to the extent that the Norms project came to be characterised metaphorically as a 'train wreck',[12] indicating that a good idea has become entangled in so many converging views that it was close to dying.

Indeed, setting out human rights duties for companies, which from a legal perspective may appear a relatively simple exercise, presents high stakes for states and companies, as well as for international organisations with particular mandates but

---

11  See further SRSG, *Background paper: Mapping States parties' responsibilities to regulate and adjudicate corporate activities under seven of the United Nations' Core Human Rights Treaties: Main trends and issues for further consideration*, prepared for meeting between the SRSG on Human Rights and Business and Treaty Bodies, 19 June 2007; SRSG, *Report of the Special Representative of the Secretary-General on the issue of human rights and transnational corporations and other business enterprises: Addendum: State responsibilities to regulate and adjudicate corporate activities under the United Nations core human rights treaties: an overview of treaty body commentaries*, UN Doc. A/HRC/4/35/Add.1,13 February 2007.

12  SRSG, *Remarks*, Bamberg, Germany, 14 June 2006.

with law-making structures based on states' consent. Much is also at stake for individual human beings and the civil society organisations that have taken it upon themselves to argue and defend the rights and interests of individuals.

## 3. Legitimacy of Process for Output Effectiveness

Legitimacy has a number of connotations and sub-connotations. In democratic societies, laws (statutes) are assumed to be legitimate because they are produced through a parliamentary process that allows for participation through representatives and subsequent (political) accountability. As mirrored in the assumption that laws resulting from a democratic parliamentary process are legitimate, the law-making process, however, must itself be perceived to be legitimate. A legitimacy perspective, which has gained recognition in recent years as *throughput* legitimacy, connects input legitimacy and output legitimacy through emphasis on the procedural quality of the law-making process. Throughput legitimacy refers to a process that allows input to feed into output through transparency, procedures that ensure wide representation, and options for deliberation.

Legal theory typically focuses on output effectiveness in terms of a rule's effectiveness to provide compliance and deliver the effects that it was intended for. Professor Thomas M. Franck has defined legitimacy in the international law context as

> a property of a rule or rule-making institution which itself exerts a pull towards compliance on those addressed normatively because those addressed believe that the rule or institution has come into being and operates in accordance with generally accepted principles of right process.[13]

Franck's definition is tailored to state-centrist international law. Even so, some points are of particular interest in the context of regulating companies. Franck emphasises that legitimacy "exerts a pull to compliance which is powered by the quality of the rule or of the rule-making institution and not by coercive authority. It exerts a claim to compliance in the voluntarist mode."[14] Due to the general absence of coercive institutions at international level, intergovernmental regulation of CSR normativity addressing companies also needs to rely on a pull to compliance based on non-coercive measures. Assuming that legitimacy can promote compliance, legitimacy is an important factor in making companies follow CSR norms developed at the international level. For a rule to promote compliance, it also needs to come into existence, and therefore to be accepted by the formal institutions or procedures required for its existence to be acknowledged. Thus, a law-making process needs not only to deliver rules with a 'compliance-pull', but also to be of such character that the outputs – rules – that they produce are accepted as the result of the process. Throughput legitimacy is an

---

13   T. M. Franck, *The power of legitimacy among nations* (Oxford University Press, Oxford, 1990) p. 24.
14   Ibid., p. 26.

important factor in establishing the conditions for such acceptance, that is, for what is referred to in this chapter as output effectiveness.

Legitimacy is understood in this article with particular emphasis on throughput legitimacy, that is, the procedural quality of a law-making process as an important factor for the delivery and acceptance of the output. Options for those for whom rules are made to participate and provide input through a form of deliberation with broad access to debate interests and concerns adds a qualitative dimension to the assumption that law-making processes are legitimate, if and to the extent that they formally represent the interests of those for whom they make rules. Emphasis on duty-bearers in this section and the remainder of the chapter is made for delimitation reasons and does not indicate lack of concern with rights-holders (be they states or individuals, including victims).

Studies of non-binding international instruments suggest that compliance is contingent on the degree to which the procedure for developing the norms is perceived as legitimate in terms of reflecting the concerns and interests of stakeholders.[15] This ties in with the connection between deliberation and acceptance of the output. Consider comments made by a United Nations body in 1990 in the context of drafting a UN (draft) Code of Conduct for multinational corporations: "[T]he effectiveness of an international instrument does not necessarily depend on its legal form. The pertinent question is: does the instrument effectively influence the decision makers – governmental or corporate – in applying the prescribed standards? The answer to this question will depend not so much on the legal characteristics of the instrument as on the extent to which its provisions are acceptable to Member States, transnational states, trade unions and other relevant groups."[16]

Professor Dinah Shelton has emphasised that the perception of a rule being a result of a process perceived as legitimate is a condition for a rule's 'compliance pull':

> The language of law, especially written language, most precisely communicates expectations and produces reliance, despite available ambiguities and gaps. It exercises a pull toward compliance by its very nature. Its enhanced value and the more serious consequences of non-conformity lead to the generally accepted notion that fundamental fairness requires some identification of what is meant by 'law', some degree of transparency and understanding of the authoritative means for creating binding norms and the relative importance among them. *A law perceived as legitimate and fair is more likely to be observed.*[17]

The issue of legitimacy and effectiveness presents a particular challenge in the context of super-national regulation of business impact on society. Effectiveness of rules in-

---

15   E. B.Weiss, 'Conclusions: Understanding compliance with soft law', in D. Shelton (ed.) *Commitment and compliance: The role of non-binding norms in the international legal system* (Oxford University Press, Oxford, 2000) pp. 542–543.
16   *Transnational corporations, services and the Uruguay Round*, UN Doc. ST/CTC/103.
17   D. Shelton, 'International law and "Relative Normativity"', in M. D. Evans (ed.), *International law* (Oxford University Press, Oxford, 2003 ) p. 161 (emphasis added).

tended to be implemented within systems with weak legal enforcement institutions is highly contingent on duty-holders accepting the regulating instruments as a source of law that leads them to compliance. In the human rights and business context, this is highly relevant for companies' acceptance of rule-making at the super-national level seeking to establish norms of conduct for transnational and other companies. This makes the question of what it takes for such rule-making to be legitimate in terms of process leading to an output that will be accepted and complied with highly acute in relation to intergovernmental regulation of business responsibilities for human rights.

That point has been addressed by Lambooy in a broader CSR context as a question of "whether a regulation is effective in the sense that the underlying goals, the ideals and the basic reasons for the introduction of the regulations are *accepted by the addressees (and others)*".[18] Lambooy notes that "adequate involvement of any stakeholders directly affected by a certain regulation" is one way to address legitimacy of a regulatory process, but inclusion of all relevant actors presents a challenge especially to regulatory processes that involve non-state actors.[19]

Research on the development of environmental regulation at the intergovernmental level shows that in the absence of formal access to the law-making process at the international stage, corporations use political and economic power to assert considerable influence on decisions of states in relation to CSR issues.[20] Such strong non-state actor influence challenges the legitimacy of the resulting decisions. These may appear as state decisions but in effect may be heavily imprinted by one particular type of non-state actors through a non-democratic process of access to the informal decision-making process.

As companies do not have access to UN law-making processes and as business organisations with Economic and Social Council (ECOSOC) consultative status (including the International Chamber of Commerce – ICC) have only limited access to participation compared to states, companies may resort to informal lobbying of states in order to promote and protect their interests to the extent that they perceive draft instruments as opposing those interests. Of course, human rights organisations are in principle subjected to similar conditions as business organisations. In practice, some organisations such as Amnesty International and other organisations with a human rights mandate that have consultative status under ECOSOC have considerable experience in UN law-making on human rights, whereas most companies and business organisations have only recently begun to consider human rights as having direct relevance to their operations.

---

18  T. Lambooy, 'Private regulation: indispensable for responsible corporate conduct in a globalizing world?', in *Law & Globalisation* (Bocconi School of Law and VDM Publishing, Saarbrucken, 2009) p. 116.

19  *Ibid.*, pp. 117–118.

20  M. A. Hajer, *The Politics of Environmental Discourse: Ecological Modernization and the Policy Process* (Clarendon Press, Oxford, 1995); A. Kolk, 'Multinational enterprises and international climate policy', in B. Arts, M. Noortmann and B. Reinalda (eds.), *Non-state actors in international relations* (Ashgate, Hants, 2001/2003) pp. 211–225.

The difference between the interests presented by human rights organisations and business organisations differ on a crucial point: Human rights organisations represent victims, that is, rights-holders. Business organisations represent prospective duty-bearers. That point is not made to say that one of those interests is more legitimate than the other, but to indicate the difference in interests at stake in the emerging discourse on human rights responsibilities for business and its emerging institutionalisation through UN efforts such as the mandate of the SRSG, compared to most previous international law-making.

The discourse on human rights and business differs from conventional international law discourse by its focus on non-state actors as duty-bearers. The human rights and business discourse does not in any way deny that victims remain also typically non-state actors, but it shifts or at least widens the duty-bearing role from states to also encompass companies. Thus, interests represented by civil society organisations widen from those of victims, typically represented by human rights non-governmental organisations (NGOs) and similar organisations, to also encompass those of companies. The widening of prospective duty-bearers entails a shift from the situation where states as primary duty-bearers under international law enjoyed access to the law-making process by default, to a situation where companies as prospective duty-bearers do not enjoy such access.

Until the late 1990s, business interest with international law-making on human rights was limited because human rights were generally discussed from the perspective of state obligations. Partly spurred by the general CSR debate, some companies engaged actively in considering their impact on human rights. Others, by contrast, saw the emerging discourse on business responsibilities for human rights as potentially limiting the freedom of enterprise and engaged in the discourse to seek to ward off an institutionalisation of human rights responsibilities for business.

As noted by various legal theorists in the national law-making context, involvement in law-making makes for acceptance by those subjected to the resulting norms.[21] From the legitimacy perspective, the implication is that participation provides for input legitimacy, which in turn provides for output legitimacy and in turn acceptance and – hopefully – respect. As noted, given the limited enforcement powers of the international legal system, duty-holders' acceptance of norms of conduct is crucial for effectiveness. Thus, as duty-holding personality at the international level expands from states to companies, a pragmatic approach may recognise that underlying connection between legitimacy, participation and acceptance by actively involving companies.

The SRSG's consultation of companies is at a different level of participation than that granted by international law to states. It is not participation in terms of formal law-making (which rests with the UN General Assembly) but invites companies into the technical room of practical negotiations. It recognises the interests of companies

---

21   Such points have been made, for example, by Jürgen Habermas (J. Habermas, *Between facts and norms: Contributions to a discourse theory of law and democracy* (Polity Press/Blackwell, Cambridge, 1996) and Gunther Teubner in his theory on reflexive law (*cf.* K. Buhmann, 'Integrating human rights in emerging regulation of Corporate Social Responsibility: The EU case', 7:2 *International Journal of Law in Context*.

as prospective duty-holders, and does so by inviting them into meetings and consultations with other stakeholders, including those representing victims. It does not change the formal status of states as international law-makers, but it involves both right-holding interests and prospective duty-holding non-state actors at the negotiations that fed into the output that was presented to the Human Rights Council. This is a pragmatic take on formal international law-making and its limitations on participation.

Over the past decades, some international law scholars concerned with companies' impact on society have argued that companies should be integrated in international law-making on company conduct. Those arguments implicitly recognise that there is a difference between representing rights-holders and representing duty-holders. Already in 1964, in his study on the changing character of international law, Professor Wolfgang Friedman argued in favour of the inclusion of the business sector in international law-making intended to have implications for companies.[22] In 1983 Professor Jonathan I. Charney made a similar argument.[23] At a time when the development within intergovernmental forums of international codes of conduct for TNCs was in its relative infancy, Charney commented that the development of such rules with little or no direct participation of TNC participation was detrimental to the effectiveness as well as the implementation of the codes. Charney held that because TNCs represent major independent powers of influence, failure to include them in negotiations under UN or other intergovernmental auspices to produce norms for TNCs' behaviour would result in rules that do not accurately reflect the realities of TNC interest and power. This could result in TNC resistance to implementation, should the international community try to convert the soft codes into binding international or national law, or in other words: TNC resistance towards to compliance, and to being subjected to rules developed without their participation. Failure to allow direct TNC participation in the development of potential international law pertaining to their interests would mean that the proposed codes "do not resolve the underlying political and economic issues, they merely convert them into *legal* issues".[24]

Charney held that direct involvement in the norm making process facilitates communication within the international legal system regarding interests, needs and conditions of stakeholders and those subjected to rules, and commitment to the system. Greater participation of TNCs might in fact strengthen the system of international law by recognising the increasing power of TNCs and reducing protection of business interests through lobbying states. TNCs need not be given full international personality. Rather, they should be awarded limited procedural rights to enable them to participate through formal and informal avenues in the development and enforcement of international law-making relevant to their interests. That might be comple-

---

22  W. Friedmann, *The changing structure of international law* (Stevens & Sons, London, 1964).
23  J. I. Charney, 'Transnational Corporations and developing public international law', 32 *Duke Law Journal* (1983) pp. 748–788.
24  Ibid., p. 754.

mented with awarding TNCs limited substantive rights and duties in recognition of their role in specific substantive areas of public international law.[25]

Partly based on observations of how companies and international organisations cooperate in network-like structures, Professor Sol Picciotto has emphasised that in an era of increasingly technical, fragmented and transnational law-making, there is a need to provide for legitimacy of debate and decision-making of regulatory networks and other multi-level governance regulatory structures.[26] Picciotto has called for extended use of public-private regulation, such as framework conventions that may allow governments or intergovernmental organisations a certain say in terms of substance and to set minimum standards, while leaving private non-state actors the freedom to self-regulate within the set framework and to define higher standards for themselves.[27]

Scholars have sought to conceptualise the emergence of new actors and new concerns through new legal theories encompassing elements from other social sciences. Under labels such as 'new governance'[28] and 'global administrative law' (GAL),[29] the gist of arguments made by these scholars and theories is that there is a need for more extensive and formal recognition and integration of non-state actors and their contributions in new forms of law and modes of regulation that are observably emerging. In his capacity as a political science academic, John Ruggie has suggested that non-state actors be included in regulatory processes to address needs that result from globalisation and reflect the increased power and social significance of non-state actors.[30] GAL recognises that companies (among other non-state or even state actors without formal law-making mandates) already in practice engage in law-making and production of rules at the transnational or 'global' level through a number of networks or technically specialised structures.[31] GAL takes this observation as a point of departure for transparency, participation and accountability requirements of such processes. Other authors, on the other hand, have indicated concern with the role of business organisations as regulators because they lack formal law-making legitimacy.[32]

---

25  Ibid., pp. 775–780.
26  S. Picciotto, 'Regulatory networks and multi-level governance', in O. Dilling et al. (eds.), Responsible Business: Self-governance and law in transnational economic transactions (Hart, Oxford, 2008) pp. 315–341.
27  S. Picciotto, 'Rights, responsibilities and regulation of international business', 42:1 Columbia Journal of Transnational Law (2003) p. 150.
28  For example, D. M. Trubek and L. G. Trubek, 'New Governance and Legal Regulation: Complementarity, Rivalry or Transformation', 13 Columbia Journal of European Law (2006) pp. 1–26.
29  For example, B. Kingsbury et al., 'The Emergence of global administrative law', 68:3 Law and Contemporary Problems (2005) pp. 15–61.
30  J. G. Ruggie, 'Reconstituting the global public domain – issues, actors and practices', 10:4 European Journal of International Relations (2004) pp. 499–531.
31  Kingsbury, supra note 29.
32  R. B. Reich, Supercapitalism: The transformation of business, democracy and everyday life (Knopf, New York, 2007); V. Haufler, A public role for the private sector: Industry self-reg-

The following sub-section will consider legitimacy from the process perspective, with a particular emphasis on the impact of legitimacy of process for the acceptance of an output. Process legitimacy is therefore significant for output effectiveness.

## 4. The Output Effectiveness Lesson of the Norms Process

As noted, the Norms were drafted by a working group and submitted to the UN Commission on Human Rights.[33] The initial aim was to formulate a code of conduct for corporations.[34] Gradually this developed into the much more ambitious aim of formulating an authoritative instrument that might develop into legally binding norms.[35] The term 'Norms' was adopted by the working group in early 2002.[36] The Norms' draftsman has referred to them as "amount[ing] to more than aspirational statements of desired conduct", "[going] beyond the voluntary guidelines found in the UN Global Compact, the ILO Tripartite Declaration, and the OECD Guidelines for Multinational Enterprises."[37] The Norms were contested for a number of reasons, including substantive ones. Substantive matters related to the Norms have been addressed at some length by legal scholars[38] and by the SRSG in his 2006 ('interim') report.[39] In contradistinction, this section will address only the process aspects related to the development and consultation on the Norms and the legitimacy and effectiveness aspects of that process.

The drafting process engaged some other societal actors beyond the drafting group. This was especially the case for the last part of the drafting process. At the first meetings of the working group, members of the group and experts of the Sub-

---

ulation in a global economy (Carnegie Endowment for International Peace, Washington D.C., 2001).

33  The Sub-Commission was a subsidiary body of the UN Commission on Human Rights, comprising 26 experts.
34  *Report of the sessional working group on the working methods and activities of transnational corporations*, 1st session, UN Doc. E/CN.4/Sub.2/1999/9.
35  *Report of the sessional working group on the working methods and activities of transnational corporations*, 2nd session, UN Doc. E/CN.4/Sub.2/2000/12; 3rd session, UN Doc. E/CN.4/Sub.2/2001/9; 4th session, UN Doc. E/CN.4/Sub.2/2002/13; *see also* D. Weissbrodt and M. Kruger, 'Norms on the Responsibilities of Transnational Corporations and Other Business Enterprises with Regard to Human Rights', 97:4 *American Journal of International Law* (2003) pp. 901–922.
36  *Report of the sessional working group on the working methods and activities of transnational corporations*, 4th session, UN Doc. E/CN.4/Sub.2/2002/13, para. 14.
37  Weissbrodt and Kruger, *supra* note 35, p. 913; *cf.* D. Weissbrodt, 'UN perspectives on "Business and humanitarian and human rights obligations"', *ASIL Proceedings: Proceedings of the 100th annual meeting* (Washington DC, March 29–April 1 2006) pp. 135–139.
38  *For example*, D. Kinley and R. Chambers, 'The UN Human Rights Norms for Corporations: The Private Implications of Public International Law', 6 *Human Rights Law Review* (2006) p. 447.
39  *Supra* note 1.

Commission commented that "[t]he working group should explore ways to bring the various constituencies together, in order to develop a widely accepted and effective set of standards which would address the human rights responsibilities of TNCs and the States in which they operate."[40] It appears that NGOs were considered an integral part of these constituencies from the outset, whereas TNCs and other business enterprises were not seen in quite the same way. While the working group "intend[ed] to consider developing a code of conduct for TNCs based on the [elaboration of business relevant] human rights standards" and felt that "[s]uch a code would attempt to involve in a constructive manner the relevant business community and NGOs", the working group member who volunteered to prepare the code of conduct would do so "in cooperation with NGOs having expertise on the subject".[41]

An invitation to submit relevant background materials to the working group at its next session was extended to "NGOs and other interested parties"[42] but not explicitly to the business community. This was repeated at the second and third sessions of the working group.[43] Initially, the sessions of the working group included opportunities for experts and representatives of United Nations specialised agencies, non-governmental organisations and civil society to make comments to the working group reports and debates. Later, TNCs and other business enterprises and other interested parties including labour unions were also invited to submit their views and recommendations.[44] Two public meetings were held during the fourth session of the working group,[45] and multi-stakeholder consultations in the later stages of the Norms preparation process included, *inter alia*, the International Business Leaders Forum and the World Business Council for Sustainable Development.[46] Some business representatives, however, did not perceive the process to be sufficiently inclusive. They felt that business was not given a sufficient say in the process or involved at a sufficiently early stage.[47]

---

40   *Supra* note 34, para. 25.
41   *Ibid.*, para. 32.
42   *Ibid.*, para. 35.
43   E/CN.4/Sub.2/2000/12, *supra* note 35, para. 61; *supra* note 34, para. 62, *cf.* para. 51 second-last sentence.
44   Weissbrodt and Kruger, *supra* note 35; E/CN.4/Sub.2/2002/13, *supra* note 35, para. 36.
45   *Supra* note 35 (E/CN.4/Sub.2/2000/12, E/CN.4/Sub.2/2001/9; E/CN.4/Sub.2/2002/13, para. 3).
46   D. Kinley, J. Nolan and N. Zerial, 'The politics of corporate social responsibility: Reflections on the United Nations Human Rights Norms for Corporations', *Company and Securities Law Journal* (2007) pp. 35–42; *see also* the discussion in J. Nolan, 'The United Nation's compact with business: hindering or helping the protection of human rights?', 24 *University of Queensland Law Journal* (2005) pp. 445–466.
47   B. Hearne, 'Proposed UN Norms on human rights: Is business opposition justified?', *Ethical Corporation* (22 March 2004), *but cf.* Kinly, Nolan and Zerial, *ibid.*, p. 40; L. C. Backer, 'Multinational Corporations, transnational law: The United Nations' Norms on the Responsibilities of Transnational Corporations as a harbinger of Corporate Social Responsibilty in international law', 37 *Columbia Human Rights Law Review* (Winter 2006) pp. 321–327.

Reports from the Sessional Working Group indicate that international organisations, states and NGOs had been consulted relatively extensively during the drafting process. Those reports and other documents suggest that businesses, mainly through their representative organisations, were only consulted late and not to a very considerable extent.[48]

A number of TNCs, such as Shell and Novo Nordisk, and business organisations, such as CSR Europe and the World Business Council on Sustainable Development, had a history of addressing CSR. Many of those appreciated UN initiatives such as the UN Global Compact and the draft Norms as helpful towards clarifying societal expectations of business. However, towards the end of the Norms process, a relatively small number of umbrella organisations for industry and employers entered the stage with arguments that strongly opposed the draft Norms. The International Chamber for Commerce, the International Organisation of Employers (IOE) and the United States Council for International Business (USCIB) argued that the draft Norms were counterproductive to the UN's efforts to make companies support and observe human rights through their participation in the Global Compact. Spokespeople for the organisations further held that the draft Norms were problematic in terms of the role and powers that they assumed business to have *vis-à-vis* states in relation to the respect and protection of human rights. Statements presented to substantiate arguments against the draft Norms referred to limited legal authority of businesses and legal guarantees in national law. They argued that the draft Norms were an effort to shift obligations from states to corporations, and that the draft Norms were a re-write of international law in this respect.[49] Some arguments against the draft Norms noted that insufficient human rights implementation at the national level was the cause for business related human rights problems.[50] Spokespeople for business organisations opposed to the Norms characterised the Norms process as starting from a pre-determined outcome. Presenting a somewhat simplified construction of the implications of the draft Norms, they held that establishing human rights responsibilities for business and human rights could lead to absurdities. It was argued that the draft Norms would make companies responsible for governmental violations of freedom of expression or religion and that a company's payment of taxes could lead to it being complicit in states' human rights violations.[51] More broadly, business perception of being excluded from the Norms process (whether justified or not) became a significant factor behind the sector's widespread opposition to the Norms and their influence on state reactions at the UN Commission on Human Rights debate in 2004.

---

48   Weissbrodt and Kruger, *supra* note 35; Hearne, *ibid.*

49   A. Warhurst and K. Cooper in association with Amnesty International, *The 'UN Human Rights Norms for Business'*, Maplecroft, United Kingdom, 26 July 2004: 16 with references; B. Hearne, 'Analysis: Proposed UN Norms on human rights shelved in favor of more study', *Ethical Corporation* (3 May 2004).

50   Joint views of ICC and the IOE on the draft "Norms on the Responsibilities of Transnational Corporations and Other Business Enterprises with regard to Human Rights" submitted to the United Nations Commission on Human Rights, 24 November 2003.

51   Hearne, *supra* note 49.

Human Rights NGOs, on the other hand, generally argued a need to integrate human rights in a globalisation process, which they perceived to be dominated by economic concerns. They hoped to preserve the draft Norms as the foundation of such efforts, and sought to counter the argument made by business that the draft Norms were trying to shift government responsibilities to business. Amnesty International voiced concerns and interests held by many other civil society organisations. For example, Amnesty International argued that business arguments had ignored aspects of the Norms, such as companies only being expected to do what lies within their sphere of influence and not taking on the role of governments. Amnesty argued that the adverse social effects of the economic power and impact of businesses must be countered through human rights standards and accountability of an enforceable character. Amnesty held that such standards should be internationally adopted because the activities of business go beyond the regulatory capacities of any one national system.[52]

Some governments also opposed the idea of the Norms and other forms of UN regulation of business responsibilities for human rights on lines related to those argued by ICC, IOE and USCIB. Hesitation towards the draft Norms was also expressed by governments normally favouring international human rights regulation and concerned with human rights conditions in supplier states. For example, comments on the draft Norms made in late 2004 to the Human Rights Commission by the government of Australia opposed a mandatory approach. Referring broadly to corporate social responsibilities, the statement avoids direct mention of human rights and bases its argument on an alleged principle that CSR guidelines should be voluntary. It argued that the Norms represented a major shift away from voluntary adherence and that the need for such a shift had not been demonstrated.[53]

Official governmental statements preceding the Commission's 2005 resolution on the SRSG mandate[54] are indicative of the diversity of states' interests and their impact on the construction of business social responsibilities, particularly with regard to human rights. That resolution was presented by a group of governments in an effort to salvage the basic ideas behind UN efforts to regulate business responsibilities for human rights, and keep the work under the Commission on the issue. The resolution omitted specific reference to the draft Norms and instead set out details for the mandate for a human rights special procedure to carry forth such work. The resolution was sponsored by 38 states,[55] representing most continents, although the majority of states

---

52 Amnesty International, *2005 UN Commission on Human Rights: The UN's chief guardian of human rights?* (1 January 2005); Hearne, *supra* note 47.
53 Quoted in Kinley, Nolan and Zerial, *supra* note 46, p. 40, *see* Nolan, *supra* note 46, endnote 27.
54 Commission on Human Rights, *Human rights and transnational corporations and other business enterprises*, UN Doc. E/CN.4./2005/L.87, 15 April 2005.
55 Argentina, Austria, Belgium, Canada, Chile, Croatia, Cyprus, Czech Republic, Denmark, Estonia, Ethiopia, Finland, France, Germany, Greece, Guatemala, Hungary, India, Ireland, Italy, Latvia, Lithuania, Luxembourg, Malta, Mexico, Netherlands, Nigeria, Norway, Poland, Portugal, Romania, Russian Federation, Slovakia, Slovenia, Spain, Sweden, Switzerland and United Kingdom of Great Britain and Northern Ireland.

were from Europe. The resolution was adopted by the Commission by a roll-call vote of 49 in favour to three against, with one abstention.[56]

Comments from the representatives of the United States and South Africa, two of the three states that voted against the resolution, underscore the lingering discursive struggle among Commission members and the states they represented on the appropriateness and need of public let alone international regulation of business responsibilities for human rights.

The explanation of the no-vote by the United States opened with a presentation of US national law regulation of company conduct and argued the benefits that business present to society, including to development and human rights. It characterised the resolution as treating business "as potential problems rather than the overwhelming positive forces for economic development and human rights that they are".[57] It argued that "the anti-business agenda pursued by many in this organization over the years has held back the economic and social advancement of developing countries" and that legal regulation of companies in relation to human rights would be detrimental to development. It concluded that the US government would vote against a resolution that would entail legal regulation of companies.[58]

In complete contrast to the approach of the United States, the South African representative sought in vain to have the resolution amended to include a specific reference to the draft Norms, and explained that it voted against the resolution because it made no reference to the Norms.[59]

The process concerns that troubled some organisations may have added to other objections that companies had to the Norms, such as the extent of business responsibility or the Norms being insufficiently clear in distinguishing between governments' duties and companies' responsibilities. Some private sector organisations' perception of the draft Norms as more 'binding' or closer to a final hard law instrument than they actually were may have further added to this. A combination of legal and political concerns such as these are likely to arise in efforts to define responsibilities and rules

---

56  The result of the vote was as follows: *In favour*: Argentina, Armenia, Bhutan, Brazil, Canada, China, Congo, Costa Rica, Cuba, Dominican Republic, Ecuador, Egypt, Eritrea, Ethiopia, Finland, France, Gabon, Germany, Guatemala, Guinea, Honduras, Hungary, India, Indonesia, Ireland, Italy, Japan, Kenya, Malaysia, Mauritania, Mexico, Nepal, Netherlands, Nigeria, Pakistan, Paraguay, Peru, Qatar, Republic of Korea, Romania, Russian Federation, Saudi Arabia, Sri Lanka, Sudan, Swaziland, Togo, Ukraine, United Kingdom and Zimbabwe. *Against* (3): Australia, South Africa and United States. *Abstention* (1): Burkina Faso.

57  United States, *Explanation of no-vote, Commission on Human Rights, Item 17: Transnational Corporations*, April 20, 2005 (on file with author).

58  Ibid.

59  United Nations, *Press Release: Commission requests Secretary-General to appoint Special Representative on Transnational Corporations* (Commission on Human Rights, 20 April 2005); *see also* Amnesty International, *2005 UN Commission on Human Rights: Amnesty International welcomes new UN mechanism on Business and Human Rights*. Public statement, 21 April 2005. Detailed explanation of the South-African statements and explanation of the no-vote has not been available to this author.

of conduct under international law, just as they often arise in national law-making setting rules of conduct for non-state actors. This underscores the significance that throughput legitimacy – including transparency and wide representation and debate of interests through deliberation – may have for the acceptance of responsibilities or duties and specific rules of conduct. This element of the Norms process underscores the challenges that the establishment of rules of conduct for business through the international law-making system may meet, simply because of the state-centrist construction of the system.

Technically nothing prevents the creation of obligations under international law for non-state actors that are corporations. Obligations for legal persons have been created through treaty-law in relation to environmental protection of the sea. As argued by Philip Alston, wider corporate obligations under international law have been held back by a combination of traditionalist thinking among international lawyers and strong corporate lobbying.[60] The history of the Norms, however, also suggests that part of the failure was at least due in part to a legitimacy deficit due to lack of business participation in the process. That history and the lessons it taught appear to have played a considerable part in the process that led to the UN Framework becoming accepted by the Human Rights Council in 2008.

## 5. The Development of the UN Framework: The Process Towards the Output

In setting out the mandate for the SRSG in 2005, the Commission on Human Rights did not limit itself to setting out the issues to be addressed by the mandate holder. It also set out the method through which the mandate holder was intended to develop his recommendations. The inclusion of a request to the mandate holder "to consult on an ongoing basis with all stakeholders" and the resolution's listing of not only states and intergovernmental organisations but also "transnational corporations and other business enterprises, and civil society, including employers' organizations, workers' organisations, indigenous and other affected communities and non-governmental organizations"[61] indicates that inclusion of a wide group of stakeholders was hoped to be a way towards an output that could be widely accepted. The wide stakeholder orientation suggests a concern with legitimacy as a precondition for effectiveness of the output in terms of acceptance.

The individual who was appointed as SRSG was neither a newcomer to the UN system, nor to the debate on corporate social responsibilities. John Ruggie had served as Assistant Secretary-General and had worked with (then) UN Secretary-General Kofi Annan to set up the UN Global Compact.

Upon being appointed as SRSG in July 2005, John Ruggie adopted a method of consultations and working with stakeholders, ranging from civil society and business organisations to specialists in various topics, especially those of legal character includ-

---

60 P. Alston, 'The 'Not-a-Cat' Syndrome', in P. Alston (ed.), *Non-State Actors and Human Rights* (Oxford University Press, New York, 2005) p. 21.
61 Commission on Human Rights, *supra* note 54, paras. 2, 3 and 5.

ing 'complicity' and 'sphere of influence'.[62] He also announced a plan to conduct a survey of business policies and practices with regard to human rights, in collaboration with business organisations including IOE and ICC, and to expand the debate into developing countries. The SRSG welcomed contributions from human rights groups and others to develop an understanding of dilemmas concerning business in relation to human rights through case studies.[63]

Throughout his mandate, but particularly during the second year, the SRSG conducted consultations with states, NGOs, international business organisations, individual companies, international labour organisations, the UN and other international agencies, and legal experts. Multi-stakeholder consultations were held in Africa (Johannesburg), Asia (Bangkok) and Latin America (Columbia). At the end of the three-year term, the SRSG and his team had convened 16 multi-stakeholder consultations in addition to sector-specific or topical consultations and conducted more than two dozen research projects, some with the assistance of global law firms and other legal experts, NGOs, international institutions, academics and other individuals.[64]

Based on what he referred to as "principled pragmatism", the SRSG "took as a premise" that the objective of the mandate was to strengthen the promotion and protection of the human rights in relation to transnational corporations and other business enterprises but that governments bear principal responsibility for human rights.[65] Referring to his understanding of the resolution establishing the mandate that the Commission intended for his work to be "primarily evidence based",[66] the SRSG stated at an early stage during his first mandate term[67] and on several later occasions that he wished to avoid doctrinal debates.

In essence, the SRSG's method of work comprised wide consultation with civil society in many parts of the world, business and business organisations, governments and intergovernmental organisations, collaboration with academics and other experts including UN human rights treaty bodies, and annual presentations of a report to the Human Rights Council. The gradual development of findings and recommendations was made in a way that allowed stakeholders the possibility to make comments. That approach therefore also allowed the SRSG the opportunity to test ideas and proposals, and integrate them into later stages of the process and its written outputs (reports).

---

62  A list of meetings and consultations conducted by the SRSG is available at the SRSG Portal of the Business & Human Rights resource site at <www.business-humanrights.org/SpecialRepPortal/Home/Consultationsmeetingsworkshops>.

63  J. G. Ruggie, *Opening remarks* (Wilton Park conference on Business & Human Rights, 10–12 October 2005).

64  *Protect, respect and remedy: A framework for business and human rights*, Report of the Special Representative of the Secretary-General on the issue of human rights and transnational corporations and other business enterprises, John Ruggie, UN Doc. A/HRC/8/5 (2008), para. 4.

65  *Supra* note 1, para. 7.

66  *Ibid.*

67  Commission on Human Rights, *supra* note 54.

One particularly interesting example of the SRSG's approach was his invitation in December 2005 to the IOE to develop guidelines for companies to deal with dilemma situations encountered in 'weak governance zones'. In undertaking this work, the IOE would liaise with its members and other business organisations, including the ICC and the Business and Industry Advisory Committee (BIAC) of the OECD.[68] Recall that the IOE and ICC had been strongly opposed to the draft UN Norms. Engaging them in work on human rights dilemmas in weak governance zones might look like letting the fox into the henhouse. As it turned out, the move resulted in a change in stances within those organisations and probably in the support among them and their members of the work and recommendations of the SRSG, and a reference to international human rights law as a fall-back position for companies working in areas where national law is lacking.[69]

The SRSG invited and enabled business participants to learn about societal needs and expectations harboured by a large range of stakeholders from different parts of the world, and to reflect upon their impact on society and gain ground for self-regulation. The SRSG combined consultation with a discursive strategy that enabled acceptance by various stakeholders of the solutions offered.[70] This led to a process of developing the *Protect, Respect, Remedy* Framework that provided sufficiently broad support for the Framework to be 'unanimously welcomed' by the UN Human Rights Council. In view of past experience, particularly of the draft UN Norms and the debates in the Commission on Human Rights, it seems fair to assume that the inclusive consultative process helped the Framework pass in the Human Rights Council in 2008. The key is both that the Framework had been tested in front of various actors, including prospective duty-holders (companies), and that it had been effectively if informally approved by key interest groups, ranging from business to civil society to academics. Without the process that allowed key stakeholders to obtain a sense of participation and making their views and concerns felt, those without direct access to the Human Rights Council – that is, particularly companies – might have resorted to informal influence-seeking, such as lobbying of states and application of media strategies seeking to construct a negative image among formal decision makers of those aspects of the SRSG's output that could be adverse to business interests and economic freedom.

---

68 *Announcement by John Ruggie, Special Representative of the UN Secretary-General on business & human rights, regarding initiative by International Organization of Employers* (21 December 2005).

69 IOE, ICC, BIAC, *Business and human rights: The role of business in weak governance zones: Business proposals for effective ways of addressing dilemma situations in weak governance zones* (Geneva, December 2006).

70 See further K. Buhmann, 'CSR fra kollektive forventninger til individuel regulering: En diskursanalytisk inspireret sammenligning af CSR-regulering gennem FN og EU', in S. Schaumburg-Muller and J. Vedsted Hansen (eds.), *Ret, individ og kollektiv* (DJOEF Publications, Copenhagen, 2011).

Although it does not provide detailed guidance for companies on how they should deal with particular human rights, the UN Framework itself is sufficiently normative[71] to provide some basis for business self-regulation. It makes clear that all human rights have relevance to companies for the purpose of avoiding abuse; and it sets out basic elements of a human rights due diligence that may be applied by companies.

The mandate for the 2008–2011 term[72] specifically asked the SRSG to continue the consultative approach that he had adopted during the 2005–2008 mandate. The significance of this should not be overlooked. The Council's recognition of the SRSG's approach to conducting a process that may lead to international soft or hard law, and its invitation to the SRSG to continue working along those lines, extends beyond the 2008–2001 SRSG term. It indicates acknowledgement that broad consultation with those to be subjected to rules is an effective way towards a hopefully effective output.

The Guiding Principles were developed through a process that built on the experience of the first SRSG term, adding innovative usage of the internet to solicit input and comments from general society.[73] Although by some measures the 2008–2011 SRSG process was perhaps on an overall scale less innovative and broadly consultative in that it followed a path now already established, it proved to be ground-breaking too. It delivered an output that describes responsibilities for states and companies on business-related human rights abuse, and which compared to the UN Framework is closer to conventional international law language and pretensions ('Principles' and no hesitation in referring to the 2011 Report as normative, contrary to linguistic usage of 'policy' employed to refer to the UN Framework at its publication in 2008).

## 6. Conclusion and Perspectives

This chapter has considered the process leading to the 'welcoming' that the UN 'Protect, Respect, Remedy' Framework received at the Human Rights Council upon its presentation in 2008. The UN Framework was a major feat within international endeavours to protect human rights at a time when globalisation and the economic and political clout of TNCs were putting conventional international law under pressure. The UN Framework should be assessed on the backdrop of what was politically possible. The SRSG's 2005–2008 process delivered in terms of pushing the boundaries of what could actually be achieved through a pragmatically inclusive approach. It delivered a normative document whose importance is in simply having come into existence through

---

71 For a competing assessment in relation to a particular type of private sector actors, *see* chapter by Sullivan and Hachez in this volume.

72 *Mandate of the Special Representative of the Secretary-General on the issue of human rights and transnational corporations and other business enterprises* (Human Rights Council Resolution 8/7, June 2008).

73 Direct correspondence between stakeholders and the SRSG through electronic communication, usage of the SRSG Portal of the Business and Human Rights Resource Centre (<www.business-humanrights.org/SpecialRepPortal/Home>), and the SRSG 'BASESwiki' (<baseswiki.org/en/Main_Page>).

navigating the informal as well as formal political obstacles that sunk previous UN attempts at regulating companies with regard to social responsibility.

The UN Framework was groundbreaking in becoming accepted by the UN Human Rights Council, a political body representing states, on the background of a process that expanded consultation to include non-state actors not only as rights-holders or their spokes-groups (NGOs), but as duty-holders. An assessment of the ambitions, contents and qualities of the UN Framework should take into account the events and efforts that preceded it, particularly the antagonistic politicisation of the issue of human rights responsibilities for business that had marked the closure of the UN Human Rights Commission's debate on the draft Norms. A comparison with the UN Norms process suggests that the broadly consultative approach and inclusive process played a part in effectively delivering and legitimising the UN Framework. The acceptance of the Framework in 2008 created the foundation for further work to refine business responsibilities for business, starting with the Guiding Principles in 2011.

The pragmatic approach adopted by the SRSG was unusual in an intergovernmental context but was useful for the development of a normative framework that was accepted by business, civil society and governments. The consultative approach adopted by the SRSG allowed the types of discursive struggles that caused the demise of the draft UN Norms to be undertaken in relatively open forums during the mandate, allowing for a degree of deliberation on interests and their justification. The broad acceptance of the Framework is all the more noteworthy because the UN Framework, despite its official label as a 'conceptual and policy framework', is in fact quite normative, both in terms of the state duty to protect and the corporate responsibility to respect. That normative character has become more specific with Human Rights Council's endorsement of the Guiding Principles in June 2011.

From a normative human rights perspective, both the UN Framework and the Guiding Principles could be more ambitious. However, placing more ambitious normative details in the Framework rather than focusing on the process and a broadly acceptable normative outcome might have put the output into jeopardy, simply creating a repetition of the fate of the UN Norms. The SRSG process is an example of a politically pragmatic process towards a legally pragmatic output. With the Human Rights Council's endorsement of the Guiding Principles, legal work on normative details has a politically accepted foundation. Time will show whether the Guiding Principles will deliver the compliance 'pull' that will make them effective beyond simply coming into existence. However, without the UN Framework and the pragmatic process that led to its 'unanimous welcome' by the Human Rights Council in 2008, the Guiding Principles would most likely not even had had the opportunity to demonstrate that compliance pull.

# 4 Contextualising the Business Responsibility to Respect: How Much Is Lost in Translation?

Fiona Haines,* Kate Macdonald**
and Samantha Balaton-Chrimes***

## 1. Introduction

As the work of the UN Special Representative of the Secretary-General (SRSG) for business and human rights moves towards its conclusion in mid-2011, the 'responsibility to respect' principles have received widespread endorsement from businesses, non-governmental organisations (NGOs) and governments. The corporate responsibility to respect is based on an account of 'negative' responsibility, namely the imperative that business should 'at least do no harm'.[1] There has been broad-based support for this proposition that business should respect (but not necessarily protect or promote) internationally recognised human rights.

The Protect-Respect-Remedy Framework articulates non-negotiable goals, but endorses flexible means for achieving these goals. The SRSG's final report states clearly that "the responsibility to respect human rights applies fully and equally to all business enterprises".[2] But the report also acknowledges that the translation of these general

---

\*   Associate Professor, School of Social and Political Sciences, University of Melbourne.
\*\*  Lecturer, School of Social and Political Sciences, University of Melbourne.
\*\*\* PhD Candidate, School of Political and Social Inquiry, Monash University.
1   Deployment of such a positive/negative distinction by the UN Special Representative's 'responsibility to respect' Framework is explicit in 'Promotion and Protection of All Human Rights, Civil, Political, Economic, Social and Cultural Rights, Including the Right to Development; Protect, Respect and Remedy: A Framework for Business and Human Rights', in *Report of the Special Representative of the Secretary General on the issue of human rights and transnational corporations and other business enterprises, John Ruggie* (Human Rights Council, 2008), p. 9: "To respect rights essentially means not to infringe on the rights of others – put simply, to do no harm."
2   *Report of the Special Representative of the Secretary General on the Issue of Human Rights and Transnational Corporations and Other Business Enterprises, John Ruggie: Guiding Principles on Business and Human Rights: Implementing the United Nations "Protect, Respect and Remedy" Framework* (Human Rights Council, 2011), p. 21.

principles into specific obligations governing business activity will need to differ according to context and that "[w]hen it comes to means for implementation ... one size does not fit all".[3] What is needed is flexibility – the capacity to take account of particular circumstances to ensure that all businesses, irrespective of circumstance, can fulfil their responsibility to respect human rights.

However, close scrutiny needs to be paid to how this flexibility is manifest both in code development and implementation. Clearly, there are benefits to a flexible approach. Flexibility can help ensure that demands placed on businesses are both reasonable and feasible given prevailing conditions. This in turn can strengthen both the legitimacy and enforceability of regulatory standards governing business activity. However, the practical task of translating general standards into varying local contexts is complex and contested, especially when dealing with business responsibilities for indirect forms of harm. These contests mean that flexibility can undermine the achievement of human rights. As we have discussed in more detail elsewhere,[4] human rights abuses often result from business interaction with other actors and institutions in their external environment. Varying contextual environments therefore have an important bearing on defining the specific obligations required of businesses to avoid *indirect* harm. There is significant room for disagreement regarding which business obligations are both reasonable and feasible to demand in any particular locale. In diverse arenas, and under conditions of uncertainty and political contestation, there is a risk that flexibility can result in a 'watering down' of general principles to the lowest common denominator.

The central goal of this chapter is to understand why and under what conditions this loss or watering down is likely to arise, and how regulatory standards for business and human rights might be designed to enable the responsibility to respect principle to be applied in context-sensitive ways, without losing regulatory force. The complex and politically contested reasons why overarching regulatory principles can get 'lost in translation' when applied in practice have important implications for understanding how the corporate responsibility to respect can be meaningfully implemented across widely varying regulatory contexts. This chapter takes an important first step in unpicking how watering down occurs, though much analytical work remains to be done.

Our empirical analysis draws its insights from multiple, intersecting academic literatures. In section 2 below we tease out the various contributions from political

---

3   Ibid., p. 5.
4   S. Balaton-Chrimes, F. Haines and K. Macdonald, 'Holding the Invisible Hand to Account? Beyond Individual Corporate Responsibility for Human Rights', in *Australian Political Science Association* (Melbourne, 2010); K. Macdonald, 'Re-Thinking "Spheres of Responsibility": Business, Human Rights and Institutional Action', 99:4 *Journal of Business Ethics* (2011).

science,[5] regulatory[6] and aspects of postcolonial[7] literatures that can provide a nuanced appreciation of context, and through which the moral and practical ambiguities underlying the demand for sensitivity to context are drawn out. Caution is required, however, since whilst these literatures can communicate with one another, they also inhabit separate spheres so that terms and conversations within each sphere may appear similar, but can also carry specific meanings that are not easily translated between settings.[8]

Translation of business responsibilities from principle to practice involves at least two steps. The first step is from internationally recognised human rights to guidelines or standards detailing corresponding business responsibilities. The second is the translation of the principles as found in the guidelines into everyday practice. The SRSG's Framework account of a business responsibility to respect all internationally recognised human rights involves the first kind of translation from rights to responsibilities.[9] Likewise, private regulatory standards for business and human rights involve translation of this kind. Although most private regulatory codes do not address the full range of internationally recognised human rights, their goal is to translate those rights they do target into regulatory standards that codify corresponding business obligations.

The SRSG's final report explicitly recognises the important ways in which principles of business responsibility are institutionalised through a diverse range of private regulatory codes aimed at improving business practice, involving: "commitments undertaken by industry bodies, multi-stakeholder and other collaborative initiatives,

---

5   P. Alston (ed.), *Non State Actors and Human Rights* (Oxford University Press, Oxford, 2005); S. Kobrin, 'Private Political Authority and Public Responsibility: Transnational Politics, Transnational Firms, and Human Rights', 19:3 *Business Ethics Quarterly* (2009).

6   *See e.g.* N. Gunningham and P. Grabosky, *Smart Regulation: Designing Environmental Policy* (Clarendon Press, Oxford,1998); I. Ayres and J. Braithwaite, *Responsive Regulation: Transcending the Deregulation Debate* (Oxford University Press, New York, 1992); C. Parker, *The Open Corporation: Effective Self-Regulation and Democracy* (Cambridge University Press, Cambridge, 2002), N. Gunningham and R. Johnstone, *Regulating Workplace Safety: System and Sanctions* (Oxford University Press, New York, 1999).

7   A. Anghie, 'The Evolution of International Law: Colonial and Postcolonial Realities', 27:5 *Third World Quarterly* (2006); A. Anghie, *Imperialism, Sovereignty, and the Making of International Law*, Cambridge Studies in International and Comparative Law: 37 (Cambridge University Press, Cambridge, New York, 2004).

8   A specific example is the use of the term 'continuous improvement' in the regulatory literature (*see for example* Gunningham and Johnstone, *supra* note 6, pp. 41-44) which requires companies to improve specific standards over time as technology and work processes develop. This is quite different from the term 'progressive realisation', which is used in international law and human rights literatures to refer to the process where a business is understood as non-compliant with a particular standard but with an understanding that it will reach the required standard over time. Yet, these terms are sometimes used interchangeably.

9   The difficulties involved in this translation from rights to responsibilities are discussed in the chapters by Knox and Mares in this volume, among others.

through codes of conduct, performance standards, global framework agreements between trade unions and transnational corporations, and similar undertakings".[10] These codes address a wide range of issues, including labour rights standards, occupational health and safety (OHS), social services and infrastructure, environmental protection, cultural and indigenous rights and 'fair' terms of market exchange. Once business responsibilities have been codified at the level of general guidelines and/or more specific regulatory standards, these duties then need a further phase of translation, in order to shape everyday decision-making and local practices of transnational businesses. This is the second step in the translation of principle into practice, and that on which this chapter focuses.

Our empirical analysis is based on data relating to the content and the implementation of existing private regulatory systems that govern the impact of transnational business enterprises on social and labour dimensions of human rights. The widespread and established nature of these systems makes them suitable objects of investigation for exploring how general principles regarding a business responsibility to respect are being translated into varying local contexts.

To analyse code content (section 3), we conducted a detailed coding analysis of 33 existing private standards systems relating specifically to business responsibilities for human rights, including labour rights (see Appendix 1). We focused on codes centred on human rights which had a significant international profile and market penetration.[11] We excluded codes that specialised in only one area of regulation (*e.g.* OHS or unions), or that operated only at the level of single companies.

Analysis of the codes was complemented by research into their interpretation and implementation on the ground in the tea sector in India, outlined below in section 4. This enabled us to examine whether the provision of context-sensitive flexibilities within regulatory codes operated to strengthen the contribution of regulatory codes to human rights compliance, or allowed businesses to water down or avoid their responsibilities. To examine implementation, we undertook field based research on two major regulatory standard systems, identified as among the most extensively developed with regard to context-sensitive provisions: Fairtrade Labelling Organisation (FLO) and Rainforest Alliance.

As we explain, the extent to which context-sensitive flexibilities within regulatory codes operated to strengthen or dilute their effectiveness in enhancing human rights

---

10   *Supra* note 2, p. 26.

11   In selecting regulatory codes to analyse, we have aimed to analyse the whole relevant 'population', as we conceptualise it, though given the plurality and heterogeneity of these standards, it is difficult to draw clear conceptual or empirical boundaries around our 'population'. To help resolve conceptual ambiguities about how to define human rights standards in the context of MNCs, we conceptualised our population as including any standards that addressed three or more categories of internationally recognised human rights. To address the lack of consistent information from private standards organisations about numbers of accredited firms, we drew on other academic and grey literature, as well as discussions with staff from some private standards organisations and other experts in the field to identify the most influential and widely adopted standards.

realisation depended both on the way flexibilities were formulated in code content (explored in section 3), and dynamics of code interpretation and implementation (section 4).

## 2. Context-Sensitive Standards and the Elusive Art of Translation: Exploring the Relevant Debates

Debates about the merits of applying general norms to diverse social and institutional contexts are familiar to both regulatory and human rights scholars. Further, the substance of their respective debates lies along similar continua with those arguing for universal norms (or regulatory goals) at one end and those arguing for different norms or regulatory goals to apply in different contexts at the other. Between these two poles lie arguments from those who promote flexibility in the means utilised to achieve regulatory goals or requisite standards, but view the required standards themselves as non-negotiable – at least in the medium to long term.[12] Yet, at the same time universal application of norms – albeit with flexible means – raises concerns about 'imperialism', and fears that contemporary dynamics of 'soft' legal transplant may be yet another expression of colonial power relations.

Political demands from activists and some (often Western) governments for a non-negotiable set of human rights norms that apply to business comprise a significant element of this literature.[13] Despite this demand, there remains significant uncertainty about what strategies would enable human rights principles to be adapted sensitively to varying contexts. Further, when *indirect* harms flowing from business practice are taken into account, sensitivity to context is critical in understanding the specific ways business interacts with the community, shapes community development and affects economic sustainability.[14] Yet there is currently little detailed understanding of how varying social and institutional contexts affect the capacities of different actors to discharge responsibilities for human rights.

The regulatory literature contains analogous debates (and uncertainties). For a substantial portion of this literature, the regulatory goals in question are assumed to be both necessary and non-negotiable. Safe workplaces or an unpolluted environment, for example, are understood as fundamental indicators of effective regulatory regimes. Debate is centred instead on the most effective means for achieving compliance, and how the context and the character of the particular regulated enterprise itself (*e.g.* its size, the orientation of its organisational 'culture,' position in the contracting hi-

---

12  Gunningham and Johnstone, *supra* note 6; Ayres and Braithwaite, *supra* note 6; J. Braithwaite, *Regulatory Capitalism: How It Works, Ideas for Making It Work Better* (Edward Elgar, Cheltenham, 2008), M. K. Sparrow, *The Regulatory Craft: Controlling Risks, Solving Problems and Managing Compliance* (Brookings Institution Press, Washington DC, 2000).

13  For an overview *see* P. Utting, 'Rethinking Business Regulation: From Self-Regulation to Social Control', in *UNRISD Technology Business and Society Programme Paper Number 15* (UNRISD, Geneva, 2005).

14  Balaton-Chrimes, Haines and Macdonald, *supra* note 4; Macdonald, *supra* note 4.

erarchy and so on) affect compliance capacity. Views differ regarding the value (or otherwise) of prescriptive rules,[15] process standards[16] or various iterations of enforced self regulation or 'meta' regulation.[17] The comparative regulatory literature takes this a step further to explore the way regulatory strategies in one economic, political and cultural context may be inappropriate and ineffective in another.[18] Direct imposition of a particular regulatory approach from an alien economic and political context has been argued to act as a legal "irritant" contributing to ongoing entrenchment of disadvantage.[19]

The international reach of private regulatory codes and their cross-national enforceability also resonates with elements within the postcolonial literature. For some, international laws, regulations, codes and standards are argued to continue the colonial 'civilising mission'.[20] This perspective can alert us to the moral complexities surrounding private regulation. It cautions actors (particularly liberal activists from the West and North) to be wary of advancing another form of colonial imperialism, albeit this time through promotion of a (private) regulatory regime aimed at protecting human rights. This is difficult territory since such moral sensibility sits uncomfortably with demands for the realisation of absolute standards. Further, engendering what might be termed 'postcolonial guilt' in fair-trade regimes also may provide leverage for local actors to invoke existing economic and other constraints[21] to push for retention of an (oppressive) status quo.

Each of these literatures draws attention to the importance of human rights (or regulatory aims) in *general* terms, but suggests very real challenges to meaningful and practical translation of the general to specific goals on the ground. The political science literature highlights the political and social contestation surrounding the translation; the post-colonial literature highlights the moral complexity; while the regulatory literature engages with the practical challenges confronting goals of effective enforcement. Together, these literatures prompt us to evaluate how principles can be both accepted as legitimate *and* result in improved human rights outcomes.

The SRSG Framework inhabits a 'middle ground', a place recognisable from the debates above: one where the goals are non-negotiable but means to achieve those goals can be flexible. The SRSG's Framework is clear about the universal applicability of core

---

15  For a discussion *see* J. Black, *Rules and Regulators* (Clarendon Press, Oxford, 1997).

16  C. Coglianese and D. Lazer, 'Management-Based Regulation: Prescribing Private Management to Achieve Public Goals', 37:4 *Law and Society Review* (2003); Gunningham and Johnstone, *supra* note 6.

17  Ayres and Braithwaite, *supra* note 6; Parker, *supra* note 6.

18  *See generally* the essays in D. Nelken and J. Feest (eds.), *Adapting Legal Cultures*, Oñati International Series in Law and Society (Hart, Oxford, 2001).

19  *See* G. Teubner, 'Legal Irritants: Good Faith in British Law or How Unifying Law Ends up in New Divergences', 61:1 *The Modern Law Review* (1998).

20  Anghie, *supra* note 7; *see also* F. Haines, *Globalization and Regulatory Character: Regulatory Reform after the Kader Toy Factory Fire*, ed. D. Nelken, Advances in Criminology (Ashgate, Dartmouth, 2005).

21  Constraints that clearly may be shaped by the demands made by global business networks.

regulatory goals, stating that "all business enterprises have the same responsibility to respect human rights wherever they operate".[22] However, the need to adjust interpretations of business responsibility to local contexts is also explicitly recognised at various points throughout the SRSG's final report.[23] The report suggests that the means through which a business enterprise meets its responsibility to respect human rights will vary depending on both internal characteristics of different business enterprises, and features of the external context.

Both internal firm level characteristics and external contextual issues are addressed in the Framework. With regard to *internal* firm characteristics, the size of a given firm as well as the extent to which it operates individually or as part of a corporate group are identified as relevant variables. Discussion of *external* context, too, contains some specificity. There are various references to the need for any given business to take into account "the nature and context of its operations",[24] variations in "operational context", and variations across economic sectors in considering what specific practices the responsibility to respect principle demands.[25] Moreover, the SRSG has stated clearly that "business enterprises may be involved with adverse human rights impacts" not only as a result of their own activities, but also "as a result of their business relationships with other parties",[26] so that the business responsibility to respect extends to cases in which businesses "contribute to abuse through the relationships connected to their activities, such as with business partners, suppliers, state agencies and other non state actors".[27] The report goes further here to discuss the degree of leverage that businesses can exercise over other actors in their external environment.[28]

In places, the SRSG's final report goes further still, detailing examples of what businesses should (and should not) do to be compliant with the responsibility to respect principle. In relation to interactions with governments, for example, it is stated

---

22   *Supra* note 2, p. 21.

23   *For example*: "[T]he Guiding Principles are not intended as a tool kit, simply to be taken off the shelf and plugged in. While the Principles themselves are universally applicable, the means by which they are realised will reflect the fact that we live in a world of 192 United Nations Member States, 80,000 transnational enterprises, 10 times as many subsidiaries and countless millions of national firms." See *ibid.*, p. 5.

24   *Ibid.*, p. 16.

25   *Ibid.*, p. 14.

26   *Ibid.*, p. 14.

27   *Supra* note 1. The SRSG's final report gives further clues regarding which external actors businesses have responsibilities towards, with particular emphasis placed on business partners. Explanatory notes to p. 14 indicate that "[f]or the purpose of these Guiding Principles a business enterprise's ... 'business relationships' are understood to include relationships with business partners, entities in its value chain, and any other non-State or State entity directly linked to its business operations, products or services".

28   Among the factors that will enter into the determination of the appropriate action in such situations are the enterprise's leverage over the entity concerned, how crucial the relationship is to the enterprise, the severity of the abuse, and whether terminating the relationship with the entity itself would have adverse human rights consequences. *Supra* note 2, p. 19.

that "[b]usiness enterprises should not undermine States' abilities to meet their own human rights obligations, including by actions that might weaken the integrity of judicial processes".[29] More broadly, it is suggested that "[l]everage may be increased by, for example, offering capacity building or other incentives to the related entity, or collaborating with other actors".[30]

Nonetheless, there remains significant room for interpretation of how companies are obliged to behave. There is no doubt that the SRSG takes the need for context-sensitivity seriously, but what this means in practice remains ambiguous. While a range of useful illustrative examples of contextual variation are offered, clear principles or procedural guidelines for determining how responsibilities should be adapted to contexts in which businesses confront varying capacities and constraints remain elusive.[31]

## 3. Code Content – Translating Principles into Rules

In light of such ambiguity, how, then, are business obligations for human rights currently being codified? Our analysis of private regulatory codes can help us understand how adaptation of general principles to varying contexts is currently being approached, and whether such ambiguity has demonstrable consequences in terms of either strengthening or weakening regulatory outcomes. In the analysis below, we identify the most common methods whereby regulatory standards are made sensitive to context. The most important of these is some form of progressive realisation provision within a particular code. In some cases progressive realisation is codified directly, via acknowledgement that demanding immediate fulfilment of regulatory goals is not feasible and/or reasonable, together with specification of some means of indicating what progress towards regulatory goals is expected over a given timeframe. In other cases, the principle of progressive realisation is codified by spelling out specific obligations businesses should undertake in the presence of barriers to full compliance.

### 3.1. Direct Codification of Progressive Realisation

Direct codification of the principle of progressive realisation is a common means through which existing private regulatory standards try to deal with the mediating influence of social conditions and constraints across varying local contexts. Progressive realisation provisions explicitly recognise that there may be constraints internal and/

---

29   Ibid., p. 13.
30   Ibid., p. 18.
31   The final report is not completely silent in relation to procedural approaches to resolving ambiguities around contextual operationalisation. Repeatedly throughout the report there is reference to the need to draw on consultation and expertise to resolve such matters, for example: "In assessing how best to respond, [businesses] will often be well advised to draw on not only expertise and cross-functional consultation within the enterprise, but also to consult externally with credible, independent experts, including from governments, civil society, national human rights institutions and relevant multi-stakeholder initiatives" (ibid., p. 21).

or external to the firm that prevent full and immediate compliance. Firms may find that their efforts to avoid participation in harmful social practices are undermined by regulatory, market or wider social constraints. Such constraints might result from government policy, such as constraints on union rights and freedoms; from market competition; or from pervasive social norms, such as entrenched patterns of employment discrimination against minority groups.

Progressive realisation provisions provide flexibilities to enable compliance over time, whilst seeking to define the reasonable limits of business responsibility for ongoing processes of change.[32] For example, private standard-setting schemes such as FLO or Rainforest Alliance have developed separate minimum and 'progress' standards, laying out defined timelines over which processes of capacity building and organisational change can be undertaken to help overcome both internal and external constraints.

Provisions of this kind were quite widespread in our data, though by no means standard practice. Eighteen of the 38 codes we analysed included provisions for progressive realisation in some form, though the principle was implemented in quite different ways. Fixed timeframes could be specified, such as with FLO where six-year audit cycles demanded compliance with increasing numbers of standards. In some cases, such as Rainforest Alliance, a cumulative or points system operated allowing companies to fall short on some standards that they found particularly difficult, so long as they compensated in other areas.

These progressive realisation provisions can operate either to extend or delimit business responsibility. On the one hand they can let business 'off the hook', enabling businesses to repeatedly refuse to address the hardest categories of issues, such as union capacity and freedom in highly politicised environments. On the other hand, some progressive realisation provisions made it clear that constraints were no excuse for non-compliance in the longer term; those standards demanding full compliance with *all* provisions required over a fixed and auditable timeframe would fall into this category. In this latter case, however, at the end of this specified timeframe the progressive realisation provisions effectively come to an end, leaving the standards open to the charge of contextual insensitivity over the medium term.

Despite these sometimes extensive provisions for progressive realisation, the practical demands they impose on business remain ambiguous. In particular, they are weakened by the absence of clear statements of principle about the kinds of costs and risks businesses can reasonably be asked to incur in contributing to progressive realisation of challenging principles, how costs and risks vary depending on the different capacities of different firms, and over what timeframes it is therefore reasonable to expect fulfilment of human rights outcomes of different kinds to be achieved. Further, statements about what processes businesses should put in place to resolve these questions lacked clarity.

---

32    R. Locke, F. Qin and A. Brause, 'Does Monitoring Improve Labor Standards?: Lessons from Nike', *MIT Sloan Research Paper No. 4612-06* (2006).

### 3.2. Codifying Specific Obligations Designed to Build Capacity for Compliance

Most existing codes recognise the risk that businesses may invoke progressive realisation provisions continually thereby failing to build their capacity for full compliance in the longer term. To address this risk, codes can require that some form of internal system be put in place to manage progression to full compliance. For example, the ISO26000 draft standards require businesses to develop a "plan for addressing some social responsibility issues in the short term and some over a period of time [that] should be realistic and should take into account the capabilities of the organization, the resources available and the priority of the issues".[33] The particular content of these kinds of provisions varies depending on the outcomes being pursued, and the nature of the constraints that are expected to be confronted.

Internal management systems also were commonly required to build capacity in avoiding business contribution to human rights harm. Thirty-three out of 38 standards have process standard requirements of some kind. Thirteen codes specifically codify business responsibilities for carrying out formal human rights risk assessments. For example, such issues were codified within the International Finance Corporation's (IFC) Performance Standards and the Organisation for Economic Co-operation and Development's (OECD) Guidelines on Multinational Enterprises (MNEs).

In other cases, standards specified directly how businesses should conduct their relationships (especially with sub-contractors in supply chains). The most common example here was standards requiring businesses to carry out due diligence to identify important sources of indirect harm arising from their supply chain or other business partnerships. Twenty-four of the 38 standards we analysed included requirements for due diligence of this kind. However, emphasis remained on obligations to *identify* risks, with little articulation of actions required to confront risks.

The nature of the relationship between businesses and governments was also addressed by some codes. While such provisions were less common, 8 of the 38 codes included standards relating to payment of taxes, lobbying, avoidance of bribery and corruption, and so on. The Global Compact cites 'contribution to the public debate' as one of the ways in which companies can support and respect human rights. Similarly, the OECD Guidelines on MNEs emphasise the importance of government policy frameworks in supporting human rights compliance, and acknowledge that businesses should not undermine institutional and policy conditions favourable to human rights compliance. For example, its principles suggest that companies should "[r]efrain from seeking or accepting exemptions not contemplated in the statutory or regulatory framework related to environmental, health, safety, labour, taxation, financial incentives, or other issues";[34] "[c]ontribute to the development of environmentally meaningful and economically efficient public policy, for example, by means of partnerships or

---

33  International Organization for Standardization, *Guidance on social responsibility ISO 26000* (December 2008, draft), section 7.4.3.
34  OECD Guidelines for Multinational Enterprises 2011, Principle A5, General Policies, p. 17.

initiatives that will enhance environmental awareness and protection";[35] and "[a]bstain from any improper involvement in local political activities".[36]

Similarly, the Global Reporting Initiative aims to "focus attention on the impacts organizations have on the communities in which they operate, and disclos[e] how the risks that may arise from interactions with other social institutions are managed and mediated. In particular, information is sought on the risks associated with bribery and corruption [and] undue influence in public policy-making …".[37] In a small number of private codes businesses have also committed to transparent disclosure of lobbying positions or receipt of government assistance as part of their corporate social responsibility programmes.[38]

Broader, almost quasi-governmental responsibilities were specified in a number of codes that encapsulated the ethic of progressive realisation. For example, 26 out of the 38 standards specified that business should contribute in varying ways to social services and infrastructure within their local communities. These typically involved obligations to provide or facilitate housing, educational or health facilities, or to maintain these to a certain level.

Responsibilities to facilitate or provide employment opportunities for wider community members were also present. However, in the context of high levels of poverty, poor education and health provision, and so on, most standards did not require that businesses provide social services and infrastructure at a level that might be considered fully compliant with social and economic rights. Rather, the principle governing these obligations was for business to make some ongoing contribution to maintaining these conditions, but within the constraints of local context. In other words, these business obligations seem (implicitly) to be interpreted as contributing to longer term processes of progressive rights realisation, in interaction with the roles and obligations of other local actors.

These provisions can strengthen the contribution of regulatory codes to human rights realisation in so far as they require business to take on some responsibility for broader social problems. But they can also weaken regulatory effectiveness if their demands on business overstretch what companies are sustainably capable of delivering, and/or ask businesses to take on roles that are not appropriate to their particular status as business-oriented organs of society.[39] Excessive obligations regarding provision of social infrastructure around farms could contribute to hollowing out state provision – reinforcing problematic forms of dependency and reproducing paternalistic relationships between farm owners and agricultural workers. Further, strategies of defiance or creative compliance can develop around regulatory demands considered illegitimate.

---

35   Ibid., Principle 8, Environment, p. 42.
36   Ibid., Principle 15, General Policies, p. 18.
37   Global Reporting Initiative, *Sustainability Reporting Guidelines G3*, 2006, p. 33.
38   It should, however, be noted that there remains an important qualitative distinction between disclosure and guarantee of sound practices.
39   The SRSG's final report emphasises that the Framework is grounded on an affirmation of the view of business enterprises as "specialised organs of society performing specialised functions". *See supra* note 2, p. 6.

Yet, if the standards are not sufficiently demanding, they risk a ritualistic approach to progressive realisation where existing practice that falls well below regulatory goals is legitimised instead.

The principle of progressive realisation remains important as a means of adapting business responsibilities to varying contexts, and thereby helping to minimise problems of empty symbolism and ritualism when standards are infeasible, or problems of perceived illegitimacy when standards are perceived to be unreasonably demanding. Yet, within the majority of the codes there remains a striking absence of a clear principled account of how to assess reasonable burdens and timeframes appropriate to particular capacities and constraints. Without this specificity, internal management systems and due diligence procedures can fail to build sufficient capacity to engender full compliance. The codes, important as they are, leave the possibility for little meaningful change to occur on the ground.

## 4. The Interpretation and Implementation of Codes – Translating Rules into Behaviour

In the presence of persistent ambiguities both within the SRSG's responsibility to respect Framework, and existing private regulatory codes for business and human rights, how then are these standards being implemented on the ground within regulated sectors? Based on our analysis of code interpretation and implementation in the Indian tea sector, we analyse both how context-responsive provisions are working to strengthen the purposes of the regulatory schemes (that is, to help ensure appropriate business contributions to the protection of human rights), and how they are being used to water down the business contribution to human rights realisation. Overall, these ambiguities within codes were resolved in very *ad hoc* ways. Whether the inclusion of contextual flexibilities strengthened or weakened standards depended on the informal dynamics of negotiation between standard setting organisations, auditors and producers at the local level regarding appropriate standard interpretation and implementation.

Our analysis focused on two schemes: Fairtrade Labelling Organisation and Rainforest Alliance. FLO operates across multiple sectors (mainly but not exclusively agriculture), and authors and manages several different sets of standards that focus on a range of commodities, and are adapted for different production arrangements: small producers, hired labour and contract labour. Our analysis focuses on the hired labour standards that apply to tea plantations in India.[40] FLO certified businesses are audited by FLO-CERT, an independent auditing body. Like FLO, Rainforest Alliance authors and manages standards that are applied in a number of agricultural sectors across many different countries. Rainforest Alliance only works with one standard – the Sustainable Agriculture Network (SAN) standard – though this encompasses several addendums and interpretation guidelines adapted to different commodities

---

40  Tea in India is also produced, to a lesser extent, on small farms; however very few of these are organised into cooperatives, and there is only one cooperative certified to the FLO Small Producers Organisation (Tea) standard.

and production countries. We focus on the generic SAN standard as it applies to the Indian tea sector.[41]

Both FLO and Rainforest Alliance have fairly extensive provisions addressing how to adapt business obligations to varying regulatory contexts. Both include extensive provisions for progressive realisation; require businesses to contribute in some way to ensuring worker access to adequate forms of social services and infrastructure where government provision is not forthcoming; and incorporate modest obligations for remediation when business obligations have not been met. For example, Rainforest Alliance standards require buyers to provide some training and technical assistance to producers lacking capacity. FLO also offers some programmes to assist producers with compliance in cases of demonstrated need.

The tea sector in India was an appropriate case study for a number of reasons. Despite the presence of law and regulation to curb abuse of human rights, tea workers in India have suffered considerably from the establishment of the first plantations by the British in the colonial era to the present. The Plantation Labour Act 1949 stipulates a range of social services that must be supplied by plantations for workers, such as housing, education and medical care. Yet the standard of these services usually remains low.[42] Legislative provisions at the state level prescribe a minimum wage for workers; nevertheless, the plantation workers' minimum wage is lower than the minimum wage for non-plantation workers. Further, minimum wages on plantations vary between states: wages in the North-East Indian states of Assam and West Bengal are half the level of those in South Indian states of Kerala and Tamil Nadu. The dramatic fall in the price of tea in the early 2000s has increased the economic pressure on plantations and small farmers, increasing hardship for workers. Recent crises such as these compound society-wide challenges of a caste system and the historically embedded 'social system' of plantations.[43]

Our field research was based in Tamil Nadu, and to a lesser extent Kerala, with some business and NGO interviews in Chennai, Bangalore and Kolkata. Overall, we interviewed 92 individuals from 51 organisations across the Indian tea sector. These included interviews with estate workers, smallholders, representatives of unions and other activist organisations, lawyers, estate managers, trading companies, government regulators, industry bodies, auditors, and representatives of standard setting schemes.

---

41  At the time of research, Rainforest Alliance was in the process of developing interpretation guidelines for tea in India, in consultation with businesses and environmental NGOs in the country.

42  A. Morser, 'A Bitter Cup: The Exploitation of Tea Workers in India and Kenya Supplying British Supermarkets', (War on Want, London, 2010); S. Van der wal, 'Sustainability Issues in the Tea Sector: A Comparative Analysis of Six Leading Producing Countries', (SOMO, Amsterdam, 2008); S. Goddard, 'Tea Break: Crisis Brewing in India', (ActionAid UK, London, 2005); J. Neilson and B. Pritchard, *Value Chain Struggles: Institutions and Governance in the Plantation Districts of South India* (Blackwell, Oxford, 2008).

43  S. K. Bhowmik, 'The Plantation as a Social System', 15 *Economic and Political Weekly* (1980); Neilson and Pritchard, *supra* note 40.

In the analysis below, we focus on implementation of provisions for progressive realisation of standards, as the most important form in which private standards facilitate responsiveness of obligations to regulatory context. In the tea sector in India, progressive realisation provisions apply within both the Rainforest Alliance and FLO standards. Several such regulatory standards were singled out by tea producers we spoke with as being particularly problematic. These were standards governing: minimum or living wages; provision of social infrastructure for plantation workers; and environmental protection of certain kinds. We documented widespread resistance among producers to acceptance of and compliance with these standards. Because these resistance strategies we observed are of potentially broad relevance it is useful to outline them in some detail.

### 4.1. Elements of Resistance Strategies

Resistance strategies were built on several inter-related (somewhat inconsistent) claims made by local businesses. First, interviewees would conspicuously affirm businesses' commitment to the general regulatory principles founded on a universal commitment to realising human rights. At the same time, businesses would then question the specific regulatory standards through which these recognised rights were being translated into auditable obligations.

The discrediting of standards occurred in two somewhat contradictory ways. First, some businesses claimed that local regulations made these international demands redundant, arguing that existing state and local regulatory obligations were sufficiently effective in protecting universal human rights-based standards. Producers argued that the general principles of rights protection codified within private regulatory standards were already being implemented by virtue of local regulatory systems. Most producers affirmed the strength of existing national regulations and their equal or in some cases superior rigour to that of international standards. For example, the President of a major Planters' Association asserted that:

The enforcement of the [Plantations] Act is very foolproof – everything is there – everything is being implemented by the Inspector of Plantations. They are empowered with all necessary powers to prosecute management, even to criminally prosecute management. ... The following of Acts is compulsory – it doesn't matter if it is difficult, you have no answer to that – just because you are finding it difficult doesn't mean it can be ignored – you have to follow the Act and follow the Legislation.[44]

At the same time, though, it was argued that specific FLO or Rainforest Alliance standards were unrealistic and/or inappropriate to the local context. External constraints were commonly invoked to show the infeasibility of implementing these standards. Despite putting a strong case for the redundancy of international regulatory codes early in his interview, for example, the President of the Planters' Association later argued: "[C]ertain provisions are impractical, creating problems for citizens, even law abiding citizens." Both government and international standards were open to challenge. The President continued: "Whenever any difficulties are faced by management

---

44  Interview with author, 7 July 2010.

or employers in implementing certain provisions we will take up the case with government, saying that we can't implement it, and that we are facing difficulties."[45]

Wage levels were a particular issue here. On this important and politically charged issue, resistance involved two distinct elements. First, the distinction between legal minimum wages and 'living wages' – the latter concept being given formal expression in regulatory standards such as those of FLO – was not acknowledged by local actors. Within local debates about wages, discussion shifted immediately from living wages to the Indian state and the local politics of setting minimum wages. Discussion of what is or should comprise a living wage in the Indian context was conspicuous by its absence.

With the focus of debate thus narrowed, arguments about the infeasibility of increasing legal minimum wages within the local context were invoked. Government-defined minimum wage setting has been deeply politicised in the Indian tea sector. The local trade publication the *Planters' Chronicle* documents the extensive debate concerning wages. While on the one hand businesses publicly affirm the general principle of protecting minimum wages, there is significant debate regarding how this principle should be interpreted and implemented. One editorial in the *Planters' Chronicle* claims that the "plantation industry is strangulated by the promulgation of a politically engineered minimum wage without taking into consideration the capacity of the plantation sector to pay it", going on to argue that the definition of minimum wages must consider prevailing market conditions.[46]

Specific environmental standards – specifically buffer zones around plantations – were also targets for criticism. The claim that "the aim of this [environmental requirement] is to make production unsustainable; to make business unsustainable" was expressed at a Rainforest Alliance local stakeholder forum that included 20 or so tea plantation managers held in Ooty (a major tea growing district of Tamil Nadu).[47] Again, the importance of local standards was emphasised:

> The purpose of the standard is to come up with local standards relevant to how we do things here – to develop local indicators. These are global standards and they are not taking that into account.

Various elements at play here comprised a strategy that might be considered a 'judo move', which can wrestle realisation of human rights to the ground. First, criticism was pre-empted through claims that rights were already being realised through the application of local law. Secondly, the superiority of local law as a means of regulating local practice was bolstered by de-legitimating 'foreign' or 'international' demands as (a) insensitive and (b) likely to result in pushing business to the brink of insolvency under prevailing economic conditions. The claims of redundancy on the one hand, and contextual inappropriateness on the other, sit in some tension with one another. However, they share in common assumptions about the superior legitimacy and authority of locally authored regulatory standards. Both claims assume that locally au-

---

45   Ibid.
46   *Planters' Chronicle*, July 2008, p. 3.
47   16 July 2010.

thored standards are able to respond to context more effectively than international standards, since they can better understand and accommodate contextual capacities and constraints. This 'judo move' was facilitated by a postcolonial sensibility in which 'outsiders' are reluctant to challenge established local practice.

### 4.2. The 'Judo Move' in Action

Debate around standards regulating business contributions to the provision of social infrastructure illustrate how this resistance strategy was deployed. Relatively minor issues were invoked as a means of questioning the authority and overall credibility of the standards' authorship and local relevance. For example, at the Rainforest Alliance event we attended in Ooty,[48] one plantation manager commented that the national standards in the Plantation Labour Act (PLA) were generally higher than the Rainforest Alliance standards in regard to provision of housing, but that the Rainforest Alliance standards included reference to the provision of heating, furniture and so on for plantation labourers – provisions that are not in the PLA. One planter read out from the standard a provision demanding heating for cold climates, and everyone laughed. Much laughter was also generated by the issue of the requirement for sufficient supplies of toilet paper, leading to a relatively uncontested conclusion that this provision should be removed, since it was irrelevant in the local context. This discussion set a tone whereby the difficulty of adapting general standards to local contexts was generally acknowledged within the room, putting the international standard setters – who were all too aware of their own deficiencies in understanding local context (and yet clearly committed to the principle of responding to it) – on the back foot.

Yet, discussion then moved quickly onto more controversial issues, such as OHS regulations prohibiting women from applying chemicals. Several plantation managers at the forum stated that local practices allowed all workers to apply chemicals at certain times. Further, the viability of local production practices, where women dominate the labour force, required that this be permitted to continue. Someone asked: "What if there are no other labourers to do it – what do you do, close down the plantation?" The Rainforest Alliance representative stayed firm on this point, arguing: "It is difficult for us to dilute the standards on these things" but affirmed that individual farms could choose not to comply on this issue and simply receive fewer points on the scheme's progressive compliance metric. The representative continued: "[So] you can take the non-conformity, though I know that's not a satisfying solution."

Invoking the existence of context-specific constraints in these ways operated as a further means of resisting the implementation of international standards. Contested interpretations of the balance between business capacity to make changes on the one hand, and external constraints that they cannot control on the other, played a central role in determining how these dynamics were resolved. Universal principles sitting behind the standards were not questioned (or glossed over in the case of living wages), yet the demands for sensitivity to local context in interpreting general principles upset

---

48   16 July 2010.

automatic translation of general principles into specific obligations on business, creating spaces within which implementation could be resisted.

In other cases, reference to the 'imperialist' nature of the codes' international authorship was even more explicit. For example, an article in the *Planters' Chronicle*, dealing with international certifying agencies (such as Fairtrade and Rainforest Alliance), asserted:

> The certifying agencies as such are institutions that are capitalising on the poverty of the farmers and the guilt of conspicuous consumption of the highly affluent in the western world ... As far as India is concerned it has much better labour protective legislation than the US, China and many of the European Countries ... Does it mean that there are no unethical practices in the developed countries? Does it also mean that those who are not certified in the developing countries are following unethical practices? Does it not imply such an inference? If so it is a clear case of defamation and the certifying agencies should be made to pay compensation to all other producers who are following the laws of the land and providing the required welfare measures to their workers.[49]

In this way, the legitimacy of the authorship of the international standards was widely questioned, enabling resistance of specific demands placed on businesses, without the universal applicability of the overarching human rights norms being called into question.

## 4.3. *Lost in Translation?*

Counter strategies able to be employed by representatives of standards bodies are also important to consider. Lack of specificity and interpersonal dynamics are important to understand here. Lack of specificity in the codes, discussed above, made counter-arguments by these representatives difficult to mount. In practice, it was often extremely challenging to specify the reasonable limits of business responsibility for institutional change. It was unclear under what conditions existing constraints should count as 'indemnities' from responsibility (on the grounds that 'ought implies can'), or under what conditions businesses could instead reasonably be required to engage in processes of capacity building and institutional change.

Interpersonal dynamics were also important. Resistance strategies deployed by business were strengthened by the anxiety of international standard setting representatives not to impose themselves 'imperialistically' in situations they did not fully understand. The 'judo move' described above was capable of invoking feelings of 'postcolonial guilt' in local standard setting bodies. For example, one staff member from Rainforest Alliance who we interviewed commented:

> We want to be sensitive; we don't want to throw our weight around in an area like this that we don't really understand – we defer to the collective bargaining agreement on labour issues. There are vocal and strong trade unions here – we can't start getting involved in

---

49   *Planters' Chronicle*, February 2009, p. 29.

> things like negotiating wages – you could get bogged down in a quagmire with all those kinds of things ... You can get mired in that stuff – we are just a small team here. We know our limits and want to stay focused on action.[50]

In another case, core staff of one standard setting organisation explicitly rejected the notion that international standard setting bodies could operate as legitimate forums for settling sector wide issues such as wages and overtime. One FLO staff member argued:

> There's nothing I can do about it because it's all something that government is involved in ... [T]here are unions that are involved in it, tea management is involved in it. It's not just one tea management, one union and one estate. The entire tea sector is involved. In fact currently the wage decision is under dispute with the High Court – the tribunal award has been disputed by the tea management and the case is going in the High Court. ...There is no role for anybody in fact, no role for anybody from fair trade I think, because the law of the land does take its own course.[51]

Overall, then, contestation and resistance surrounding the definition and interpretation of standards played an important role in shaping dynamics of code implementation, influencing what degree of compliance can realistically be expected to result from private regulatory standards. When considering whether the inclusion of contextual flexibilities strengthens or weakens private standards systems, it may well be important to consider not only formal provisions within code content, but also the informal dynamics through which interpretation and implementation is negotiated between businesses, standard setting organisations and other stakeholders.

## 5. Conclusions: Implications for the Business Responsibility to Respect and Refining the Art of Translation

The SRSG's Framework clearly recognises the value of human rights responsibilities of business being adapted to accommodate the varying social and institutional environments in which transnational businesses operate. Similar principles of contextual-responsiveness are embodied within the multiple private regulatory codes that currently exist to regulate the human rights impacts of transnational business activity. However, in the absence of clear principles and procedures to regulate the translation of general principles into varying contexts, the context-specific human rights obligations of transnational business remain deeply ambiguous. The under-specification of business obligations provides an opening to allow some businesses to resist their human rights obligations at various stages of the regulatory process, in particular during processes of interpretation and implementation of codified regulatory standards. Further, resistance strategies are enhanced when the legitimacy of the codes' authorship is widely questioned.

---

50  16 July 2011.
51  19 July 2010.

As a result, there is a persistent risk that regulatory efficacy will be 'lost in translation', as contestation over the definition of specific business responsibilities is resolved in inconsistent and *ad hoc* ways. Yet the potential benefits of context-responsiveness in implementation means that it is not possible to simply read across codes and judge which are responding to context in ways that strengthen regulatory effectiveness, and which operate to allow companies off the hook.

What, then, does our analysis suggest for how the SRSG's responsibility to respect principles might be operationalised in context-responsive ways that strengthen rather than weaken the regulatory purposes of the responsibility to respect Framework? First, these regulatory systems require clearer substantive principles to regulate how relevant contextually-variant capacities, burdens and constraints are to be identified and weighed.[52] This is a significant challenge and will require robust collaboration and negotiation between code setting bodies and relevant industries. Ultimately, however, codes need to make more explicit which aspects of local context are to be taken into account in operationalising standards of progressive realisation.[53]

A first step is the clarification of procedures that can establish these substantive principles. Yet clear processes for resolving contestation around standard interpretation are absent from many existing regulatory schemes. Clearer procedures through which contestation about context specific interpretations of regulatory principles can be resolved in particular cases are important, as highlighted by Melish and Meidinger's chapter in this volume. There are examples of leadership on this issue. Some private regulatory initiatives have established quite extensive processes of producer consultation in particular locations, for example via formal regional bodies in the case of FLO, or via more *ad hoc* yet regular consultative forums in the case of Rainforest Alliance. These offer at least some means of informal deliberation through which negotiations around interpretation of standards can occur.

Moreover, the result of these deliberations needs to be shared to develop greater clarity around what can, and cannot, be expected through the certification process. Such consultation can provide an important basis for pushing back against the 'judo move' we described above. Working from areas of agreement (specifically agreement on commitment to human rights) can help build common understanding of how to realise these rights. This process is more than just talk. It can provide a forum to share

---

52  We have elaborated elsewhere normative principles that could provide some basis for clarifying some of the ambiguities discussed above. *See for example* Macdonald, *supra* note 4.

53  One possible short-cut to this end that has been used in some existing cases is to benchmark progressive realisation obligations against businesses identified as the best in a particular location or region. One informative example in this respect is the ILO's WISE program, discussed in F. Haines, *The Paradox of Regulation: What Regulation Can Achieve and What It Cannot* (Edward Elgar, Cheltenham, 2011) pp. 164–166. In other cases, wage rates and/or requirements regarding provision of social infrastructure have been audited with reference to local or regional standards. *See for example* discussion of the Starbucks Cafe Practices programme in K. Macdonald, 'Globalising Justice within Coffee Supply Chains? Fair Trade, Starbucks and the Transformation of Supply Chain Governance', 25:7 *Third World Quarterly: Special Issue on 'Beyond CSR? Business, Poverty and Social Justice'* (2007).

concrete examples – from industry, workers and from standard setting bodies – of how resource constrained businesses in developing contexts can meet human rights standards in an effective but cost-conscious way. This in turn may help reduce resistance to the external imposition of international standards based on perceptions of these standards as new expressions of a colonial project. Building processes of setting and implementing private regulatory standards that enable greater influence for businesses, farmers and workers in producing countries could take the force out of at least some of these resistance strategies, and increase the capacity of private international standard setters to push back against such resistance.

It is no coincidence that the kinds of issues we are highlighting here go to the heart of the most political aspects of the institutional arrangements through which regulatory standards are managed. The contestation and resistance documented above highlight the deeply political character of these kinds of private regulatory standards, which press businesses to accept potentially burdensome responsibilities for supporting public regulatory goals. Not only can these responsibilities be costly in terms of resources and time, but they can require companies to go well beyond local norms (for example in paying living not minimum wages), and to give up significant forms of control, subjecting themselves in quite intrusive ways to interventions by affected stakeholders. It is not surprising then that businesses may seek to resist and limit such obligations where possible.

Given this, our conclusions highlight not only what is missing from existing approaches, but also one of the most serious obstacles to promoting regulatory processes of this kind: that is, the need to confront deeply political problems of entrenched power relations, conflicting interests, and competing claims of legitimacy. One of the most politically appealing features of the responsibility to respect Framework is almost certainly the modest character of the demands that it places on powerful businesses and governments. This follows as much from what is *underspecified* within the Framework as the substance of what the Framework clarifies. By advocating clearer business responsibilities for realising human rights, the Framework at least affirms the values and purposes of those seeking deeper social transformation. But by leaving key details of such obligations underspecified, the Framework's formulation ensures that it does not pose any serious challenges to existing distributions of social power and resources.

In this sense, the SRSG's responsibility to respect Framework is perhaps giving greater weight than is usually recognised to context of a rather different kind: the context of the prevailing *political* environment. The SRSG's Framework needs to survive in this international political environment if it is to have the opportunity go to work as a framework of transnational business regulation. While current ambiguities regarding the distribution of regulatory burdens may mean that much is lost in translation from the perspective of regulatory efficacy, such ambiguities may play an important role in enabling the regulatory standards to survive within an inhospitable political environment. This is a trade-off that both regulatory and human rights scholars would do well to take more seriously.

## Appendix 1: Standards analysed in coding

1. 4C Code of Conduct and related docs
2. Business Social Compliance Initiative Code of Conduct
3. Electronic Industry Code of Conduct
4. Equator Principles
5. Ethical Tea Partnership
6. Ethical Trading Initiative
7. Fairtrade Labelling Organisation – Generic Hired Labour, Generic Contract Production, Generic Small Producer, Generic Trade
8. Fair Wear Foundation Code of Labor Practices
9. FLA Workplace Code of Conduct
10. Flower Label Program International Code of Conduct
11. Forestry Stewardship Council Principles and Criteria
12. Global Social Compliance Programme
13. International Council on Mining and Metals Sustainability Framework 10 Principles
14. ICTI CARE Process: International Toy Industry's Ethical Manufacturing Programme
15. ILO Tripartite Declaration of Principles Concerning Multinational Enterprises and Social Policy
16. International Finance Corporation's Performance Standards on Social and Environmental Sustainability
17. OECD Guidelines for Multinational Enterprises
18. Rainforest Alliance Sustainable Agriculture Standard, including Addendum and Local Interpretation Guidelines
19. SA8000
20. UTZ Certified 'Good Inside' Coffee, Coca, Tea Farms, Tea Factories
21. Worker Rights Consortium / United Students Against Sweatshops
22. World Fair Trade Organization 10 Principles of Fair Trade
23. Worldwide Responsible Accredited Production (WRAP)
24. Principles and Criteria for Sustainable Palm Oil
25. Monash Castan Centre & International Business Leaders Forum 'Human Rights Translated'
26. IFC Performance Standards Guidelines
27. FLA Guide to Best practice in hiring, termination, disciplinary procedures and resolving grievances
28. Global Compact
29. Flower Label Program Guidelines for the socially and environmentally responsible production of cut flowers, ferns, plants and foliage
30. SA8000 Guidelines
31. Principles for Global Corporate Responsibility: Bench Marks for Measuring Business Performance
32. International Confederation of Free Trade Unions Code of Labour Practice
33. Voluntary Principles on Security and Human Rights

ISO 26000 was still in draft form at the time of writing, and though investigated was not included in the full coding.

# 5 Remodelling Responsible Supply Chain Management: The Corporate Responsibility to Respect Human Rights in Supply Chain Relationships

Sune Skadegaard Thorsen* and Signe Andreasen**

## 1. Introduction

Sustainable or responsible supply chain management (RSCM) emerged in the 1990s as an important part of the corporate social responsibility (CSR)[1] discourse. The latter discourse has evolved considerably over the last few decades. Most importantly, the United Nations Special Representative of the Secretary-General on Human Rights and Transnational Corporations[2] and other Business Enterprises (SRSG), Professor John Ruggie, presented in 2008 a framework (hereinafter, the UN Framework) for addressing the core international principles of social sustainability.[3] In March 2011, the United Nations Guiding Principles on Business and Human Rights (hereinafter, the UNGPs) were submitted by the SRSG as a proposal to make the Framework more operational for the primary actors, states and corporations.[4] Similar to the UN Framework in June 2008 the UNGPs were unanimously endorsed by the UN Human Rights Council in June 2011. The UNGPs outline expectations for corporations on how to take respon-

---

\* CEO & Senior Partner, GLOBAL CSR. For more information on GLOBAL CSR visit <www.global-csr.com>.
\*\* CSR Advisor, GLOBAL CSR.
1 CSR is used as the generic term in this chapter as synonymous to terms like corporate sustainability, corporate responsibility and corporate citizenship. CSR is defined as: *The responsibility business enterprises have to ensure that they contribute, while not being a barrier to, international principles for social, environmental and economic sustainable development.*
2 The term 'corporation' is used in this chapter as covering all forms of business enterprises.
3 J. Ruggie, *Promotion and protection of all human rights, civil, political, economic, social and cultural rights, including the right to development*, Human Rights Council, Eighth session, Agenda item 3, 2008.
4 J. Ruggie, *Guiding Principles on business and human rights: implementing the United Nations 'Protect, Respect and Remedy' framework*, Human Rights Council, Seventeenth session, Agenda item 3, 2011.

sibility for human rights, expectations for the policy commitment, the due diligence process and access to remedy. The due diligence process is designed to enable corporations to identify, prevent and mitigate adverse human rights impacts. The process includes adverse human rights impacts in business relationships, including suppliers.

In June 2010 the SRSG published a discussion paper on the corporate responsibility to respect in supply chains on the request of the Organisation for Economic Co-operation and Development (OECD) and in conjunction with the work on the recent update of the OECD Guidelines for Multinational Companies.[5] The OECD paper represents the most elaborate discussion by the SRSG on the issue of RSCM to date and thus constitutes, together with the UNGPs, the point of departure of this chapter.

A statement from the SRSG on RSCM, such as the OECD paper, was awaited. Corporations have been investing in RSCM for more than a decade without authoritative guidance on how to go about the issue. The result has been a mushrooming of approaches and initiatives on how to practice RSCM; a concept with many synonymous names: *i.e.* ethical purchasing, responsible procurement and sustainable supply chain management, just to name a few. What constitutes 'good' or 'best practice' RSCM is yet up for discussion. The recent statements from the SRSG are therefore much needed and welcomed.

However, while the SRSG's OECD paper and the UNGPs do take us a step further in defining corporations' responsibilities in RSCM, they do not provide full guidance on how to make RSCM fully operational in relation to human rights. In short, the OECD paper and the UNGPs lack information and subsequent guidance on two levels. Firstly, there is a gap at the operational level since concrete guidelines on the issue are still needed. Secondly, it would appear that obvious gaps at the conceptual level of existing approaches to RSCM remain largely unchallenged.

This chapter questions the viability of such existing approaches to RSCM. In doing so it is argued that the RSCM approach applied by the SRSG seems to remain within current RSCM paradigms. These approaches were to a large extent developed in an ad hoc manner focusing on immediate risks rather than attending to sustainability objectives. In other words, neither the OECD paper nor the UNGPs manage to explicate the full consequences of the UN Framework in relation to RSCM. Consequentially, they appear to fall short of challenging existing approaches conceptually, and may – on the contrary – be interpreted as reinforcing current approaches to RSCM.

In addition to addressing RSCM in light of the SRSG's work, this chapter seeks to describe such conceptual challenges.

Research undertaken by GLOBAL CSR and the Copenhagen Business School (CBS) and partly financed by the Danish Ministry of Foreign Affairs provides the empirical and analytical foundation for this description.[6] This research combined four

---

5   J. Ruggie, *The corporate responsibility to respect human Rights in supply chains*, 10th OECD Roundtable on Corporate Responsibility Discussion Paper (30 June 2010).

6   See <um.dk/en/danida-en/activities/business/partnerships/b2b-programme/news/news displaypage/?newsid=f45f3efc-4e1f-43a9-a919-00bbb89c39b6>. The approaches and ideas were developed in close collaboration with Prof. Soeren Jeppesen, Copenhagen Business School, and Ron Nielsen, Senior Director, International Centre for Business Innovation

sets of data: 1) primary data collection from 16 major international buyer companies (Danish and non-Danish) selected as so-called 'critical cases' (being front-runner companies); 2) primary data from 27 randomly selected suppliers (incl. small and medium enterprises – SMEs) and suppliers' associations from field studies in two countries (Kenya and Bangladesh); 3) primary data from seven organisations, associations and individuals working in the field; and 4) secondary data gathered through three desk studies. The secondary data includes a review of the international literature on Codes of Conduct, a review of the international literature on SMEs & Codes/CSR and finally a web study of the content of the Codes of Conduct of 38 international buyer companies, industry associations and multi-stakeholder initiatives.[7] The three reviews have each provided a synthesis of existing material and knowledge.[8]

The study suggests that existing approaches to RSCM suffer from considerable shortcomings in terms of social sustainability and may indeed create barriers to sustainable economic development. GLOBAL CSR proposes a new model to address RSCM in a sustainable manner as a natural 'next step' and also in line with the SRSG's Framework. We call the suggested model: 'Responsible Supply Chain Management 3.0'. RSCM 3.0 represents a long-term solution for establishing a sustainable approach to RSCM. Therefore, at the outset of integrating the RSCM 3.0 approach, RSCM 3.0 should be understood as a supplement to current RSCM approaches.

Whereas this chapter builds on findings from the study as well as existing literature, it is important to note that the ideas presented below are informed by practice rather than theoretical speculation. The points made in this chapter are to a large extent inspired by 15 years of advising international corporations and governments on how to practice CSR and RSCM.

## 2. RSCM Today – What Corporations Currently Do

RSCM primarily emerged as a corporate response to human rights risks appearing in suppliers' operations: sweat shops, child labour, forced labour, safety and health neglect and similar violations. Lack of effective human rights governance in the home state of suppliers combined with stakeholders putting pressure on buyers to meet expectations from *e.g.* customers, the media, employees and investors paved the way for RSCM as we observe it practised by large corporations today.[9] Carter and Easton re-

---

and Sustainability (ICBIS). Special thanks to research group members Signe Andreasen, Elise Lind Jacobsen, Mireille Jacobsen and Ernesto Luna Madrid.

7   Refer to Annex 1 in this chapter.
8   For detailed information on methodology *see* S. Skadegaard Thorsen and S. Jeppesen, *Changing Course – a study into responsible supply chain management*, Annex Volume (Copenhagen Business School and Global CSR for the Danish Foreign Ministry, 2011) p. 9.
9   S. Barrientos, 'Globalisation and Ethical Trade: Assessing the implications for development', 12 *Journal of International Development* (2000) pp. 560 *et seq.*; C. Schmitz-Hoffmann, 'Mainstreaming of Standards and Standards for the Mainstream – Experiences of Standard Initiatives in Public-Private Partnerships and Multi-Stakeholder Approaches', in M. Huniche and E. Rahbek Pedersen (eds.), *Corporate Citizenships in Developing Coun-*

cently emphasised the importance and durability of RSCM as a concept stating that "sustainability is ... [a] license to do business in the twenty-first century".[10]

Current approaches to RSCM can roughly be divided into two main groups, denominated 1st and 2nd generation approaches (hereinafter referred to as 'RSCM 1.0' and 'RSCM 2.0', respectively). RSCM 1.0 is currently the most widespread approach to RSCM. This approach involves a corporation developing a Code of Conduct (hereinafter 'Code') to outline the general demands that its suppliers are expected to meet. The Code will often be referenced in contract provisions creating legal obligations that the standards are upheld at the supplier level.[11] To ensure compliance with the Code, a buyer corporation will often monitor and audit its suppliers. Regular visits at suppliers' premises by corporation employees trained to assess suppliers' performance against Code requirements have become common practice. In addition, corporations increasingly require external auditing by independent third-party CSR auditors.[12] Despite variations in implementation, RSCM 1.0 approaches all have the effect that suppliers are met with a range of demands and controlled with regard to their adherence to them.[13]

RSCM 2.0 constitutes an attempt to address some of the pitfalls of the RSCM 1.0 approach. In RSCM 2.0, corporations use a shared Code rather than their individual Codes, *e.g.* a Code for an entire industry or a Code established through a multi-

---

tries – New Partnership Perspectives (Copenhagen Business School Press, Copenhagen, 2006) pp. 215 *et seq.*; M. Andersen and T. Skjoett-Larsen, 'Corporate Social Responsibility in global supply chains', 14:2 *Supply Chain Management: An International Journal* (2009) p. 77; R. Jenkins, 'Corporate Codes of Conduct – Self-regulation in a Global Economy', *Technology, Business and Society, Programme*, Paper No. 2, United Nations Research Institute for Social Development, 2001, p. 7; R. Jenkins, R. Pearson and G. Seyfang, *Corporate Responsibility and Labour Rights : Codes of Conduct in the Global Economy* (Earthscan Publications, 2002) pp. 1 *et seq.*

10   C. R. Carter and L. P. Easton, 'Sustainable supply chain management: evolution and future directions', 41:1 *International Journal of Physical Distribution & Logistics Management* (2011) p. 59.

11   Ruggie, *supra* note 6, p. 2.

12   GLOBAL CSR participates in the advisory group to AIM Progress, the fast moving consumer goods brand organisation's RSCM project. The first three years focused on creating a mechanism for mutual recognition of audits; *see more* at <www.aim.be/responsible_sourcing.htm>.

13   R. Locke, F. Qin and A. Brause, *Does Monitoring Improve Labor Standards? Lessons from Nike*, Working Paper No. 4612-06, MIT, July 2006, pp. 3 *et seq.*; D. O'Rourke, 'Multi-Stakeholder Regulation: Privatizing or Socializing Global Labor Standards?', 34:5 *World Development* (2006) pp. 901 *et seq.*; F. Ciliberti, P. Pontrandolfo and B. Scozzi, 'Investigating corporate social responsibility in supply chains: a SME perspective', 16 *Journal of Cleaner Production* (2008) p. 1580; N. Egels-Zandén, 'Suppliers' compliance with MNCs' codes of conduct: Behind the scenes at Chinese toy supplier', 75 *Journal of Business Ethics* (2007) pp. 3 *et seq.*

stakeholder process thereby achieving economies of scale[14] [15]. Examples of RSCM 2.0 approaches can be found in the Electronic Industry Citizenship Coalition, Business Social Compliance Initiative, Ethical Trading Initiative, Social Accountability 8000, ILO's Better Work initiative, and Fair Labour Association. In addition to creating and using common Codes, many RSCM 2.0 initiatives are shifting focus from solely monitoring compliance to developing supplier capacity; most notable is the Business for Social Responsibility 'Beyond Monitoring' initiative. Often, a shared 'clearing house' is established to manage monitoring or certification of suppliers and accreditation of auditors. While achieving obvious advantages, such as economies of scale, corporations joining RSCM 2.0 initiatives may lose the ability to address criticism adequately since they lose both control and knowledge of the practices of specific suppliers in relation to CSR.

Practicing RSCM 1.0 or 2.0 are not mutually exclusive. Quite a number of corporations join industry- or multi-stakeholder initiatives, while enforcing their own Code and approach in relations to suppliers simultaneously. Thus, grouping all the work corporations currently undertake on RSCM into the two categories RSCM 1.0 and 2.0 inevitably holds the risk of losing nuances and complexity. However, the use of the denominations makes it easier to point out some general limitations and challenges facing the way corporations currently practice RSCM; the approaches implied in the work of the SRSG.

When corporations first started practising RSCM, their efforts were welcomed and supported even by their worst critics: the non-governmental organisations (NGOs).[16] The efforts of corporations that were beginning to practice RSCM 1.0 and 2.0 were considered best practice and as such it is difficult to criticise the background and intent of the RSCM field. However, one might argue that the positive impact of RSCM initially was taken for granted.[17] The initial optimism is very understandable: how can integrating concerns for *e.g.* human rights in your supplier relations be criticised? As years have passed, researchers, suppliers, NGOs and corporations themselves are increasingly voicing concerns about the appropriateness and sustainability of current RSCM approaches. A somewhat disturbing question is now being raised: what if practising RSCM (as seen today) is in fact not responsible?

## 3. The SRSG and RSCM – Missing Pieces of the Puzzle

In the following, discussions on some of the challenges to the SRSG's approach to RSCM and how these relate to the way corporations currently practice RSCM will be presented. At the end of the section, the authors argue that there is a need to view the topic of RSCM from a different angle. Current approaches, including those implied

---

14   M. Blowfield, 'Reasons to be Cheerful? What we know about CSR's impact', 28:4 *Third World Quaterly* (2007) p. 691.
15   Note that some multi-stakeholder initiatives do not entail Codes.
16   L. Compa, 'Trade unions, NGO's, and corporate codes of conduct', 14:1-2 *Development in Practice* (2004) pp. 211 *et seq*.
17   Blowfield, *supra* note 15, p. 686.

with the statements of the SRSG, are inadequate in contributing to sustainable development.

### 3.1. Bringing Back State Governance

The SRSG framework of 2008 was unanimously approved by the United Nations Human Rights Council and gained support from all major business associations, NGOs and governments. The first two pillars of this adopted framework underline that (1) states have a *duty to protect* against human rights violations from business, and (2) corporations have a distinct *responsibility to respect* human rights. The SRSG points to the fact that the two pillars are interrelated and both needed in addressing the development of human rights challenges emerging from business activities.[18]

Placed in the SRSG's framework, both RSCM 1.0 and 2.0 respond to corporate challenges with suppliers by establishing pillar two responses: pillar one – 'state duty to protect' – is not addressed directly. To some extent, the SRSG's latest work on supply chain issues as presented in the OECD paper and the UNGPs appears to imply, and thereby enforce, the focus on the corporate responsibility to respect (pillar two). In the OECD paper, engaging local or central government to try to minimise adverse human rights impacts is mentioned. However, it is included as one out of seven suggestions on how corporations should try to increase leverage towards suppliers having discovered adverse human rights impacts by such suppliers. Thus, addressing state practices, or lack of practices, is not implied as a primary or preferred suggestion to deal with supply chain issues in the deliberations of the SRSG. In other words, the interrelatedness of the first and second pillar of the framework seems to be demoted. The primary focus is on what corporations can and should do on their own.

The current neglect of integrating the state duty to protect into the way corporations practice RSCM provides interesting food for thought. The fact that lack of state governance is the core reason for undertaking RSCM in the first place[19] appears to be disregarded by practitioners as well as scholars. From a sustainability perspective it seems questionable to leave the state out of the equation in RSCM, especially keeping the importance, if not primacy, of pillar one in mind. That pillar one to a large extent has been disregarded in current RSCM approaches might be due to the fact that bringing in the state is difficult in the short-term. Corporations have found it necessary to act on their own, as an immediate response to lack of state governance in home countries of their suppliers. However, as short-term approaches become more and more common, they tend to sediment themselves as 'the way to do things'. The short-termism of the immediate responses therefore becomes an obstacle for working towards a more sustainable model that brings back state governance.

---

18   Ruggie, *supra* note 4, pp. 4 *et seq.*
19   R. Locke, M. Amengual and A. Mangla, *Virtue out of Necessity?: Compliance, Commitment and the Improvement of Labor Conditions in Global Supply Chains*, MIT Sloan Working Paper No. 4719-08, 2008 (updated March 2009), p. 3.

A limited body of research has questioned whether established models of RSCM favour sustainable development.[20] Some scholars have accused current RSCM efforts of eroding, or even worse substituting, attempts by governments and unions to protect workers. From this point of view, RSCM, as it is practiced today, is viewed as a privatisation of human rights including workers' rights. Critics emphasise how RSCM at one point in time can render governmental regulation superfluous and legitimise its absence.[21] Corporate practices such as Codes, monitoring and auditing procedures build a parallel and private system of governance to traditional state governance. Such private governance systems are exerted with increased rigour where lack of state governance on human rights, environmental protection and anticorruption is most profound, often in economic developing countries. If no or very little state governance exists, this is an understandable response by corporations; however, problems occur if their actions undermine the development of well-functioning state governance systems. Corporations that appreciate the task of improving human rights standards in supply chains should be welcomed to do this, if there was agreement on the positive impact of current RSCM practices. However, this is far from the case. The presumed impact of RSCM will be elaborated further below.

### 3.2. RSCM – The Impacts So Far

In the OECD paper the SRSG stresses how the use of Codes or contract provisions can be a useful step towards RSCM, but also how it in itself is an insufficient instrument in meeting the corporate responsibility to respect.[22] Previous research indicates that the introduction of Codes in supply chains may not have had the intended positive impacts. Permanently employed male workers experience some improvements, mainly in the area of 'outcome rights' (*e.g.* living wages, working hours, safety and health). However, improvements are limited in the area of 'process- or enabling rights' (*e.g.* freedom of association and collective bargaining). Current efforts appear to fail in reaching the most disadvantaged groups of workers such as migrant workers, women, casual workers and workers employed by third-party labour contractors. Improvements furthermore reach first tier suppliers only.[23] When assessing the actual impact on the ground, improvements may be found; nevertheless, they tend to be temporary – limited to the buyer-supplier's existing relationship – or even momentarily – while the monitoring or audit session is taking place.[24] In general, international literature on the subject

---

20 Blowfield, *supra* note 15; M. Prieto-Carron *et al.*, 'Critical perspectives on CSR and development: what we know, what we don't know, and what we need to know', 82:5 *International Affair* (2006) p. 982.

21 Jenkins, Pearson and Seyfang, *supra* note 10, p. 5; Compa, *supra* note 17, pp. 212 *et seq.*; Jenkins, *supra* note 10, pp. 29 *et seq.*; Prieto-Carron, *ibid.*, p. 986.

22 Ruggie, *supra* note 6, p. 2.

23 S. Barrientos and S. Smith, *Report on the ETI Impact Assessment 2006: The ETI Code of Labour Practice – Do Workers Really Benefit?*, Institute of Development Studies, University of Sussex, 2007.

24 Egels-Zandén, *supra* note 14.

highlights difficulties attached to measuring impact, which partly results in limited knowledge on the actual impact of RSCM.[25]

Current RCSM efforts are further criticised for their limited scope. RSCM is practised by an increasing number of corporations; however, it is much more common in some industries compared to others.[26] This 'industrial bias' transforms into a 'geographical bias' since clothes, shoes, toys and selected foods, which are industries where RSCM is quite common, are produced in certain countries. Codes are almost exclusively implemented in international value chains by large multinational corporations sourcing all over the world. Hence, workers in non-export oriented industries will not meet any improvements through current RSCM efforts.[27]

### 3.3.    Code Mania Times Three

It is arguably problematic that current approaches might not have the desired positive effects or extensive reach as described in the above. But even worse, current RSCM approaches may actually prove to have a negative impact. The concept of 'Code mania' implies how suppliers are met with a multitude of Codes; in the worst cases, one or more per customer or buyer that purchases goods from them.[28] Suppliers interviewed in the study, referenced in the introduction of this chapter, substantiate that suppliers are indeed met with numerous Codes from buyers. They do, however, not necessarily see the Codes themselves as a problem. Codes are usually very similar in content, covering the same basic requirements (*e.g.* core labour rights) described in broad terms. However, suppliers point to the fact that challenges appear during implementation of the Codes, where detailed subsets of requirements in relation to various items in the Codes differ considerably. These differences put significant pressure on suppliers

---

25   D. O'Rourke, 'Monitoring the monitors: A Critique of Pricewaterhousecoopers (PWC) Labor Monitoring',. *Corporate Responsibility and Ethical Trade: Codes of Conduct in the Global Economy* (2000); P. Lund-Thomsen, 'The Global Sourcing and Codes of Conduct Debate: Five myths and Five recommendations', 39:6 *Development and Change* (2008) p. 1013; O'Rourke, *supra* note 14, p. 902.

26   Lund-Thomsen, *supra* note 26, p.1006; Jenkins, *supra* note 10, pp. 19 *et seq.*; Barrientos, *supra* note 10, pp. 566 *et seq.*

27   Jenkins, *supra* note 10, pp. 26 *et seq.*; D. Vogel, 'Private Global Business Regulation', 11*Annual Review of Political Science* (2008) pp. 269, 274; Barrientos, *supra* note 10, p. 566; Schmitz-Hoffmann, *supra* note 10, p. 220; Lund-Thomsen, *supra* note 26, p. 1006; M. Emmelhainz, 'The apparel industry response to sweatshop concerns: A review and analysis of codes of conducts', *The Journal of Supply Chain Management: A Global Review of Purchasing and Supply* (1999) p. 52.

28   R. Welford and S. Frost, 'Corporate Social Responsibility in Asian Supply Chains', 13 *Corporate Social Responsibility and Environmental Management* (2006) p. 169; P. Raynard and M. Forstater, *Corporate Social Responsibility: Implications for Small and Medium Enterprises in Developing Countries*, UNIDO's Small and Medium Enterprises Branch and the World Summit on Sustainable Development, 2002; World Bank, *Strengthening Implementation of Corporate Social Responsibility in Global Supply Chains*, The World Bank, 2003; Locke, Qin and Brause, *supra* note 14, p. 5.

in order for them to comply, thereby draining suppliers of both financial and human resources.[29]

The way in which suppliers experience the situation of Code mania can be grouped into three main categories. Firstly, suppliers describe the problems connected with complying with multiple Codes and auditing or monitoring procedures simultaneously. Secondly, suppliers mention how the demands in the implementation manuals in connection to the Codes can directly contradict each other, making it impossible to comply with all Codes. Lastly, suppliers draw attention to how differences in the level of compliance demanded by the buying corporations have consequences for their market access, making some buyers unapproachable. These suppliers describe RSCM as yet another technical trade barrier complicating export to buyers in developed countries.[30]

### 3.4. *Challenges in Traditional RSCM Practices*

Another unintended consequence of RSCM stems from buyers' traditional procurement practices. Buyers have for years been managing their supply chains through a set of traditional procurement criteria relating to price, delivery time, flexibility in meeting orders, financial stability and quality. Compliance with new CSR criteria on human rights, including labour rights, the environment and anti-corruption, are increasingly required from suppliers via Codes. However, these new CSR criteria do not always correspond well to traditional supply chain management criteria. The imposition of buyers' additional CSR requirements to their traditional supply chain management entails that suppliers have to comply with criteria from both practices simultaneously: CSR criteria on the one hand and traditional procurement criteria on the other.

However, the two practices sometimes present opposing demands, creating a situation of cross-pressure for suppliers. Buyers tell them to *e.g.* implement high CSR standards while at the same time asking for lower prices and shorter delivery terms. As an example, the supplier needs to manage shorter delivery terms without the use of overtime labour, or ensure minimum wages while competing on lower prices.[31] These cross-pressures have severe implications for suppliers' ability to comply and thus become a daily dilemma when making difficult business decisions. Hence, buyers' conflicting demands, arising from the 'additionality' of CSR requirements, put pressure on suppliers from two sides, and thereby considerably reduce the manoeuvring space for supplier corporations.[32]

---

29  Schmitz-Hoffmann, *supra* note 10, p. 224; Vogel, *supra* note 28, p. 273; Jenkins, *supra* note 10, p. 17; BSR Education Fund, *Suppliers' Perspectives on Greening the Supply Chain*, Business for Social Responsibility, 2001, p. 23.
30  Schmitz-Hoffmann, *supra* note 10, p. 224; Vogel, *supra* note 28, p. 273.
31  Insight Investment and Acona, *Buying your way into trouble – the challenge of responsible supply chain management*, 2004, p. 23; Welford and Frost, *supra* note 29, p. 174; BSR Education Fund, *supra* note 30, p. 16.
32  BSR Education Fund, *supra* note 30, pp. 5 and 23; Barrientos, *supra* note, p. 566; Skadegaard Thorsen and Jeppesen, *supra* note 9, pp. 20 *et seq.*

## 3.5. Ex Ante *and* Ex Post *RSCM*

The SRSG's OECD paper constitutes a substantial contribution to what is expected from corporations after having identified adverse human rights impacts in their business relations; *i.e. ex post* responses. *Ex post* responses have to some extent been absent in RSCM discussions. Focus has been on setting standards and demanding continuous improvements and not so much on what to do if violations were discovered. In the OECD paper, John Ruggie provides a detailed decision matrix for corporations to apply when a human rights violation by a supplier is detected. The proposed responses are ambitious. Roughly, if the buyer corporation does not have leverage to change harmful practices of a supplier, it should do its utmost to obtain such leverage.

An example from the Danish context highlights the challenges connected to applying the SRSG's proposed responses in case of suppliers in violation.[33] Recently, a large Danish retail corporation named COOP announced in their 2010 CSR Report that only 11.2 per cent of their suppliers in the Far East were deemed 'satisfactory' or were in the category of 'continuous improvement needed' as a result of COOP's auditing, while the rest were non-compliant with COOP's Code. Since COOP identified specific adverse human rights impacts, COOP would be expected to follow the basic expectations of the UNGPs. If COOP were to implement the SRSG's OECD paper in its business practices, it would have to take appropriate action, taking its dependency and its leverage towards the given supplier into consideration in each of the instances where suppliers failed with regard to compliance: *i.e.* in relation to 88.8 per cent of its suppliers. Acknowledging that the 'appropriate action' might not be cumbersome in each case, having to assess each of the non-compliant suppliers in order to determine what would be the appropriate action is challenging alone. While constituting a daunting task for a medium-sized Danish retail corporation, presumably, it would be an even more challenging task for some of the world's largest corporations dealing with tens of thousands of suppliers.

Little concrete guidance is given in the OECD paper on what the expectations are for corporations in relation to identifying and detecting possible adverse human right impacts *ex ante*, or, in other words, what are the concrete expectations placed on companies to identify potential and actual adverse human rights impacts either connected to their own actions towards suppliers or solely by the independent actions from suppliers. From the UNGPs we learn that corporations are advised to 'conduct due diligence' and 'identify risks' in all relations, but very little advice is given on how corporations should actually carry out these actions towards their relations.

While it was not possible in the UNGPs for the SRSG to provide detailed guidance on CSR in each business area, the fact still remains that this is information that corporations are currently lacking. Corporations thus ask how they are to identify appropriate measures. What *ex ante* actions constitute adequate due diligence and risk assessment? From the COOP example one may anticipate that the rather extensive expectations to *ex post* actions described in the OECD paper will discourage buyer

---

33  <www.coop.dk/ansvarlighedsrapport2010/etisk_handel/4-5_leverandoerer.html> (3 June 2011).

corporations from identifying concrete harmful impacts in the first place; as the saying goes: "out of sight, out of mind". One answer can be that buyers altogether stop assessing concrete adverse impacts from suppliers and start assessing the existence of supplier systems that are aligned with the UNGPs. However, these questions are currently not answered in the SRSG's statements. Also, the SRSG did not – in his reports – address the possible challenges to sustainable development from existing *ex ante* RSCM activities.

### 3.6. *Adverse Impacts on which Human Rights?*

During the World Conference on Human Rights in Vienna in 1993, the United Nations declared that: "All human rights are universal, indivisible and interdependent and interrelated. The international community must treat human rights globally in a fair and equal manner, on the same footing, and with the same emphasis."[34] In addition, the SRSG's Framework for Human Rights and Business adopted in June 2008 states that all business sectors in all regions of the world can potentially affect virtually all human rights contained in the International Bill of Human Rights.[35] The SRSG reemphasises this in Principle 12 of the 2011 UNGPs. Adequate risk management by corporations therefore implies that all human rights are included, also in their approach to RSCM. According to the UNGPs, prioritisation of some human rights while discarding others could result in inadequate handling of adverse human rights impacts and thus inadequate RSCM.

A review of 38 supplier Codes of Conduct carried out as part of the above-mentioned study revealed that current Codes from perceived front-runner buyer corporations as well as RSCM 2.0 initiatives include only a few basic human rights, typically the four core ILO labour rights and an additional four labour rights, with no buyer corporation or initiative having explicitly included all human rights in their Code (refer to Table 1 below).[36] [37] This finding is similar to previous research on the content of Codes of Conduct.[38]

Table 1 – Human rights mentioned in the Codes of Conduct

| Human right | Generation 1.0 Codes (%) | Generation 2.0 Codes (%) | % of total Codes mentioning the right |
|---|---|---|---|
| Prohibition against slavery, **Forced- or compulsory labour** | 100 | 100 | 100 |

---

34 <www.unhchr.ch/huridocda/huridoca.nsf/%28symbol%29/a.conf.157.23.en> (20 May 2011).
35 Ruggie, *supra* note 4, p. 4.
36 Skadegaard Thorsen and Jeppesen, *supra* note 9, pp. 23 *et seq.*
37 Refer to Annex 1 in this chapter for a listing of the reviewed Codes of Conduct.
38 Jenkins, *supra* note 10, p. 22; Emmelhainz, *supra* note 28, pp. 54 *et seq.*

| Human right | Generation 1.0 Codes (%) | Generation 2.0 Codes (%) | % of total Codes mentioning the right |
|---|---|---|---|
| The right to a family life (marriage, **maternity** and children) + prohibition of **exploitative child labour** | 100 | 100 | 100 |
| The rights of the **child** | 100 | 100 | 100 |
| **Non-discrimination** | 100 | 100 | 100 |
| The equal rights of **men and women** | 100 | 100 | 100 |
| The right to form and join **trade unions** and the right to strike | 96 | 100 | 97 |
| **Freedom of association**, including right to form and join trade unions | 93 | 100 | 95 |
| Right to a **living wage**, The right to **safe and healthy working conditions**, The right to **rest**, leisure and holidays | 86 | 100 | 89 |
| The right to **health** | 82 | 100 | 87 |
| Prohibition against **torture, inhumane and degrading treatment** | 75 | 100 | 82 |
| The right to **education** | 46 | 70 | 53 |
| The right to **adequate food**, fair distribution of food, the right to **clothing** and the right to **housing** | 18 | 50 | 26 |
| The right to **privacy** | 11 | 40 | 18 |
| Minority rights to **culture, religious practice and language** | 14 | 20 | 16 |
| The right of **peaceful assembly** | 18 | 10 | 16 |
| The right to **work** | 4 | 30 | 11 |
| The right to **hold opinions, freedom of expression, freedom of information** | 14 | 0 | 11 |

Note: The table shows the human rights mentioned in more than 10 per cent of the Codes. The 'equal rights of men and women' is an anomaly in comparison with the other rights, as it is almost exclusively mentioned implicitly, e.g. as references to gender issues etc. N=38.

In the study, buyer corporations further disclosed that they seek enforcement of the human rights that they included in their Codes with different emphasis depending on the given right. Apparently corporations prioritise between the rights from the International Bill of Human Rights when they formulate their Codes. Such selection contrasts the above-mentioned UN Vienna Declaration. The SRSG underlines both in the UN Framework and the UNGPs that corporations may have adverse impacts on all human rights; a prioritisation in the foundational documents that form the basis for assessments (or due diligence) limiting the scope to a handful of rights thus leads to inadequate risk management and does not live up to the expectations expressed in the UNGPs.

### 3.7. Tiresome Tiers

In the OECD paper, the SRSG also provides for guidelines to address adverse human rights impacts with suppliers beyond the first tier. Enforcing contractual obligations with suppliers that the corporation does not directly engage with can be challenging as a corporation's leverage decreases when moving deeper into the upstream value chain. However, the SRSG stresses that corporations do have a responsibility towards suppliers beyond first tier and should therefore perform due diligence including a general risk assessment *vis-à-vis* these relations. Ensuring that sub-suppliers themselves practise due diligence and maintain appropriate standards evidently decreases the risks for buyer corporations.

In reality, few corporations practice RSCM beyond their first tier of suppliers.[39] The reasons for not including, engaging with and monitoring sub-suppliers are many. Six different, though related, reasons are mentioned by the buyer corporations in the abovementioned study:

a) No contractual control or influence over sub-supplier (no leverage)
b) Very difficult to extract relevant information from the sub-suppliers
c) Lack of capacity to deal with sub-suppliers
d) Resistance from first tier suppliers
e) Difficulty tracing raw materials down the supply chain
f) Lack of resources

Nevertheless, nearly half (43 percent) of RSCM 1.0 Codes analysed included a paragraph claiming that the sub-suppliers were covered by the Codes. In effect the buyer corporations merely 'request' that first tier suppliers ensure that their suppliers in turn comply with the Code. Of examined RSCM 2.0 Codes, approximately a third (30 per cent) includes similar paragraphs on sub-suppliers.[40]

Due to the reasons mentioned above, actual risk management in the full upstream value chain including sub suppliers, their suppliers and so on would appear to be extremely challenging, if not impossible. International literature, albeit limited on the subject, highlights that the impacts of Codes are very limited, if at all traceable,

---

39  Andersen and Skjoett-Larsen, *supra* note 10, p. 83; Jenkins, *supra* note 10.
40  Skadegaard Thorsen and Jeppesen, *supra* note 9, p. 104.

among sub-suppliers.[41] Interestingly, many of the buyer corporations participating in the study foresee that moving beyond the first tier will be 'the next major issue to address' in RSCM. However, existing approaches cannot adequately meet this challenge, which underlines the importance of providing alternative approaches that can handle the RSCM risks in an increasingly constructive and sustainable manner. Extending present RSCM 1.0 and 2.0 practices may aggravate and scale up the challenges if all human rights are to be part of future RSCM approaches in accordance with the UN Framework and the UNGPs. A different approach to RSCM thus appears to be needed.

### 3.8. *RSCM 2.0 – Improvement but no Solution*

RSCM 2.0 provides some advantages when compared to RSCM 1.0. Firstly, the problem of Code mania is, in theory, reduced as suppliers primarily have to comply with a single Code and its monitoring requirements. Secondly, buyer corporations can obtain economies of scale by sharing the costs and experiences of monitoring and auditing suppliers, making RSCM more cost-effective. Thirdly, the increased focus on capacity development in many RSCM 2.0 initiatives, rather than strict "pass or fail" audits, has better potential to contribute to sustainable development.

However, in reality, many suppliers still experience being subject to several RSCM 1.0 and RSCM 2.0 Codes simultaneously. Since the Codes themselves do not differ much, the challenges for suppliers primarily relate to differences in monitoring or audit schemes, and in this respect RSCM 2.0 schemes may often be far more elaborate than RSCM 1.0 requirements. Also, RSCM 2.0 carries a challenge to corporate risk management. RSCM 2.0 often becomes an arm's-length exercise where the buyer corporation criticised for its supplier's misconduct cannot answer the media or NGOs adequately, since it does not have direct interaction, information about or experience on these issues. The loss of control connected to RSCM 2.0 leads many companies to continue their own RSCM practises alongside a RSCM 2.0 engagement. The study earlier alluded to thus illustrated that RSCM 2.0 Codes also appear to contribute significantly to Code mania as buyers often join RSCM 2.0 initiatives as a supplement, and not an alternative, to their existing RSCM 1.0 efforts.[42]

### 3.9. *Paradigm Shift Ahead*

The SRSG has over the years made immense contributions in conceptualising CSR in relation to social sustainability, and more recently also in making the concepts operational for corporations. While the SRSGs recommendations on business and human rights may be perceived by corporations as very ambitious, his work relating to RSCM appears to emerge from what corporations are already doing. There is no doubt that the SRSG has raised the bar for what constitutes adequate RSCM, but little has been done to address some of the obvious limitations of the existing approaches to RSCM,

---

41  S. Barrientos and S. Smith, 'Do workers benefit from Ethical Trade? Assessing codes of labor practice in global production systems', 28:4 *Third World Quarterly* (2007) pp. 713–729.
42  Skadegaard Thorsen and Jeppesen, *supra* note 9, pp. 16 *et seq.*

and the SRSG appears to not have addressed such issues by linking his pillars. The OECD paper and the UNGPs appear to remain within the same paradigms, which are characteristic of current RSCM actions. As illustrated above, such paradigms have thus far been unable to prove their worth when it comes to sustainable and scalable systemic impacts. Nevertheless, the paradigms have displayed convincing staying power, possibly because of the structural changes required, if to be changed: *i.e.* corporate inertia. Against this backdrop, the authors will in the following section present an alternative RSCM model.

## 4. Change of Course – RSCM 3.0

In the following, RSCM 3.0 is introduced as a possible response to the challenges and limitations identified in relation to RSCM 1.0 and 2.0 as they are practiced today; approaches that appear supported by the UNGPs and supporting statements by the SRSG. RSCM 3.0 represents a long-term solution for establishing a sustainable approach to RSCM. Therefore, at the outset of integrating the RSCM 3.0 approach, RSCM 3.0 should be understood as a supplement to current RSCM approaches. With time, RSCM 3.0 can, however, become an alternative to RSCM 1.0 and 2.0 and by that constitute an actual paradigm shift. Elements of the RSCM 3.0 approach can be found in the existing Ghana Business Code Initiative.[43] However, the Ghana Business Code project does not go all the way in placing the state at the centre of its model. The basic characteristics of RSCM 3.0 are described below; subsequently possible limitations to RSCM 3.0 will be discussed.

### 4.1. Concept and Main Characteristics of RSCM 3.0

RSCM 3.0 represents a markedly different approach to RSCM in comparison to current approaches. Both RSCM 1.0 and 2.0 have a vertical value chain focus on the relationship between individual buyers and suppliers. The same approach to RSCM is implied in the statements from the SRSG.

RSCM 3.0 is detached from vertical value chains as it has an alternative focus on improving the standards on human rights, hereunder labour rights, the environment and anti-corruption within delimited geographical zones. Taking a geographical approach immediately answers some of the main limitations to current approaches, namely limitations in terms of scope and coverage. All human rights will be addressed in compliance with existing international obligations. Furthermore, all corporations are included within a specific zone. The industry, degree of export orientation or place in the global value chain of a given corporation within the zone would be unimportant as these would automatically be included in the zone. These main characteristics make RSCM an approach with a much wider scope and coverage compared to existing approaches.

---

43 <www.ghanabusinesscode.com/_index.php?page=8cf04a9734132302f96da8e113e80ce5_&cid=1> (1 June 2011).

The vision of RSCM 3.0 is to build 'CSR risk free sourcing and investment zones'. These are envisioned as geographical areas from which buyer corporations can source or corporations invest without a notable risk that suppliers are involved in violations of internationally agreed standards derived from the UN Global Compact principles.[44] Evidently, since violations occur in all countries in the world and within all sectors, violations will also occur in 'risk free' zones; however, these will not occur systematically and they will be addressed by the authorities. *De facto*, many buyer corporations already operate within 'risk free' zones, *i.e.* in countries or areas where they do not raise demands, undertake monitoring or auditing, but simply rely on the fact that effective implementation of laws and regulation addressing the Code requirements are in place. CSR risk free zones would thus have to demonstrate effective mechanisms to address violations in relation to the UN Global Compact principles.

A key difference between RSCM 1.0, 2.0 and RSCM 3.0 is the inclusion of the state or local authorities as crucial partners in the latter approach. The inclusion of the state acknowledges the first pillar of the UN SRSG's framework on business and human rights: the state duty to protect from human rights violations. Similarly, international requirements rest on states in relation to environmental protection and eradication of corruption. Thus, RSCM 3.0 combines the SRSG's framework concerning the state's duty to *protect* against human rights abuses by third parties, and the corporate responsibility to *respect*.[45] The RSCM 3.0 approach thus abstains from developing competing parallel structures to the traditional state-society contract and, instead, seeks to motivate and enable the state to carry out its international obligations and to effectively enforce its regulation. Adequate legislation ensuring that international obligations are adhered to is already in place in most countries, also in economic developing countries; implementation, however, is often lacking. The importance attached to the state duty in RSCM 3.0 is in line with suggestions for ways forward referenced in current literature. Locke *et al.* for instance state that "developing country government authorities ... could gain the capacity and the legitimacy to exercise their rightful duty and enforce their own laws".[46]

Many governments in economic developing countries do not have the resources to build capacity in order to adequately enforce regulation in accordance with international principles. Establishment of 'CSR risk free sourcing and investment zones' requires the development of local public capacity in order to carry out necessary control, monitoring and business development tasks. In addition, to ensure compliance with local regulations in accordance with international principles, such capacity development activity can be combined with developing and enhancing the local authorities' skills to develop local business' (and thus suppliers') capacity to improve performances, similar to the capacity development that buyers increasingly appear to engage in today.

RSCM 3.0 introduces a partnership approach where the creation of partnerships between international buyers and local government bodies are central. When apply-

---

44   <www.unglobalcompact.org/> (3 June 2011).
45   Ruggie, *supra* note 4.
46   Locke, Qin and Brause, *supra* note 14, p. 38.

ing the model in economic developing countries a third partner becomes important, namely development cooperation agencies (DCAs). DCAs become facilitators of the process, but only by invitation from the local authorities. Depending on existing governance structures, local exporting corporations (suppliers), labour- and employers' associations, civil society, and other stakeholders would also be involved in a RSCM 3.0 model – in line with current recommendations.[47]

Buyers, as well as DCAs, have important roles to play in the realisation of RSCM 3.0. Buyer corporations have a good opportunity to create leverage with local state authorities since their willingness to source from, or invest in, a specific geographical area has great economic impact locally. The idea of buyers using their leverage to make a change is reflected in the OECD paper where the option is mentioned as one of more options for corporations who wish to increase their leverage when seeking to prevent human rights violations. The SRSG argues that a corporation's leverage, amongst others, has to do with "the ability of the enterprise to engage local or central government in requiring improved human rights performance by the supply chain entity through implementation of regulations, monitoring, sanctions, etc.".[48] If local governments succeed in establishing a 'CSR risk free sourcing and investment zone', the ability of the local business environment to sell goods and to attract investments will increase. Buyer corporations' role in RSCM 3.0 is primarily to motivate local authorities to commit to and plan for the establishment of a 'CSR risk free sourcing and investment zone'.

Once the ownership of the project is created with the authorities, DCAs may engage to finance, partly or in full, the needed capacity development activities and provide for technical assistance. DCAs have decades of interest, technical expertise and experience in collaborating on such projects. The capacity development component of RSCM 3.0 thus feeds directly into existing approaches of many DCAs. A group of buyer corporations with considerable economic interests in a specific location that create motivation and local ownership combined with the expertise and support from DCAs may enable local authorities to establish a 'CSR risk free sourcing and investment zone' within a specific locality or even within a country.[49]

### 4.2. *Implementation and Transition*

The terms RSCM Generation 1.0, 2.0 and 3.0 might lead readers to expect that the three approaches function stepwise. However, corporations do not have to start by practicing RSCM 1.0, then upgrading to RSCM 2.0, and so forth. However, shifting from RSCM 1.0 and 2.0 to RSCM 3.0 may pose some challenges; established corporate management systems and professionals taking care of the systems may be expected to resist changes.

Change will not be made overnight. In order to keep up risk management in relation to suppliers' conduct, it should be expected that buyers will engage in a long-term

---

47  Lund-Thomsen, *supra* note 26, p. 1016; Compa, *supra* note 17; BSR Education Fund, *supra* note 32, pp. 20 *et seq.*
48  Ruggie, *supra* note 6, p. 3.
49  State, region, city or even an export processing zone.

transition where traditional RSCM approaches continuously are being implemented, maybe altered to answer some of the challenges, and only gradually phased out, while capacities in relation to RSCM 3.0 are being built. Hence, in the outset of integrating the RSCM 3.0 approach, RSCM 3.0 will only act as a supplement to RSCM 1.0 and RSCM 2.0, which will then eventually be phased out. Thus, RSCM 1.0, 2.0 and 3.0 may unfold simultaneously with a given corporation.

Scholars have argued that one of the main obstacles as regards impact of current RSCM efforts is lack of compliance incentives for suppliers.[50] A remodelled approach should thus include a business case not only for buyers – but for all actors involved in creating RSCM 3.0. By creating a regulatory race to the top,[51] local authorities as well as local suppliers within a zone will benefit from the attraction of international buyers looking for CSR risk free sourcing and investment. Improved incentive structures might help ease and accelerate the period of transition and implementation of RSCM 3.0.

### 4.3.    Possible Limitations to RSCM 3.0 and Future Research

Notwithstanding, there are several challenges accompanying the implementation of a RSCM 3.0 approach. Challenges range from the reform of embedded systems of corruption and political instability in some emerging economies to resistance by CSR professionals enforcing current established systems that at a glance appear more directly to support corporate risk management. However, in connection to the latter, Blowfield stresses that the field of CSR including RSCM has not been a static entity. Rather, "there are clear signs of learning both in terms of how to implement CSR and in what issues can or should be considered".[52] There is therefore no reason to believe that professionals will outward resist a gradual reform of RSCM efforts.

The above-mentioned study in itself raised important considerations with regards to developing a new approach to RSCM. A stakeholder who was interviewed for the study emphasised that "the government is not fulfilling its basic obligations at the moment. There are problems with infrastructure, electricity, communication etc … As long as these basic services are not in place, how can we expect the government to take on another responsibility?"[53] This statement highlights the crucial importance of the capacity development of local governments, especially when establishing the concept in economic developing countries. Without the intervention of buyers and the support from DCAs, it will not be realistic for such governments to live up to their duties and ensure enforcement. However, if a local government commits to a project and receives sufficient support to establish and maintain a 'CSR risk free sourcing and investment zone', it is possible that the necessary capacity will be built and developed over a few years. In areas of poor state governance or in conflict-torn areas, capacity development

---

50    Welford and Frost, *supra* note 29, p. 174.
51    Vogel, *supra* note 28, p. 273.
52    Blowfield, *supra* note 15, p. 691; Vogel, *ibid.*, p. 269.
53    Skadegaard Thorsen and Jeppesen, *supra* note 9, p. 42.

may take 20 or more years. It all depends on the local context and existing governance structures, which varies significantly amongst countries and even states, regions and municipalities.

A second concern is that RSCM 3.0 will become geographically skewed creating 'islands of good practice in an ocean of abuse'. However, this concern actually reflects the bias created by existing RSCM approaches. The extent to which buyer corporations practice RSCM today varies greatly from industry to industry and thereby also from country to country. The corporate responsibility to respect is, however, not restricted to some industries or countries – it is universal. Moreover, the SRSG reminds us that all sectors in all regions of the world face human rights challenges. That being said, the fact that RSCM is more widespread in some industries, and thereby in some countries, can be seen as an opportunity. Enabling such 'burdened' countries to become the first in enjoying the benefits of a RSCM 3.0 model can motivate other locations to move forward as well.

A final concern is the issue of corruption within governmental bodies. There is a general fear that inclusion of governmental agencies, in the enforcement of international standards, will create more room for corruption, ultimately hurting the suppliers. Most large corporations and DCAs have vast experiences working with anti-corruption in collaboration with governments in economic developing countries. Some stakeholders interviewed for the study emphasised that corruption should not become an excuse to abstain from involving local governments in a new approach: " [I]t is the citizens of a country and the private sector that can mobilise a change in corruption. Because the private sector actually rules the government; they are the ones that are funding money to the government and they can make those decisions if they want to. So there has to be a buy-in of the private sector, they have to lobby and advocate with the government."[54] This comment stresses the importance of the leverage that buyer corporations have *vis-à-vis* the local governments. If buyers as well as suppliers see an advantage in changing to a RSCM 3.0 model, then it is likely that governments too will be motivated to participate in the initiative. But most importantly, RSCM 3.0 is built on the universal principles referenced by the UN Global Compact; anti-corruption will be one of the basic requirements for establishing a 'CSR risk free sourcing and investment zone' (refer to UN Global Compact Principle 10).[55] Thus, effective implementation of anti-corruption regulation will be part and parcel of the basic requirements and certification for the zones to be established.

In previous research there has been a tendency to focus on *whether* corporations are practicing RSCM and not on *how* they are doing it and *what* the outcome or impacts on the ground of RSCM initiatives are. The above chapter, however, stresses that there is a need to distinguish between output and outcome or impacts when it comes to RSCM. The sheer fact that a corporation practices RSCM does not necessarily entail improvements or contributions to sustainable development for those that

---

54　Ibid., p. 43.
55　Global Compact Principle 10: Businesses should work against corruption in all its forms, including extortion and bribery, <www.unglobalcompact.org/AboutTheGC/TheTenPrinciples/principle10.html> (22 June 2011).

the initiatives are meant to benefit. Seemingly, there is a need for further research on the *outcome or impacts on the ground* of RSCM. Furthermore, there is a major lack of knowledge on how RSCM is received amongst suppliers and sub-suppliers as well as on the long-term impact of RSCM on suppliers in economic developing countries. Consequently, there continues to be a need to explore whether current approaches to responsible supply chain management are in fact responsible.

While there is still room for improvement on account of research on the contribution to sustainable development of RSCM, the above chapter indicates quite clearly that the positive impact of RSCM should not be presupposed. Practitioners, as well as scholars, need to question current approaches and look for sustainable, supplementary and with time alternative models of RSCM.

## 5. Conclusions

The SRSG, Professor John Ruggie, has without a doubt brought clarity to the field of RSCM and taken a step in the right direction when it comes to sustainability. By drafting concrete guidelines on the subject, the SRSG has made the corporate responsibility to respect in the supply chain explicit and tangible.

While the guidelines are meant as an operationalisation of the SRSG's 2008 Framework, they do not, however, thoroughly manage to develop more concrete guidelines on RSCM that can be of direct applicability for today's corporations. At the same time, the SRSG's statements on RSCM, in the guidelines as well as in the OECD paper, appear to remain within existing paradigms of RSCM. Thereby, the SRSG risks reinforcing approaches that might not be sustainable in a long-term perspective or even have a positive short-term impact. By decreasing the role of the state into only one out of seven ways for a corporation to increase its leverage towards suppliers, the SRSG neglects the importance he initially gave pillar one, namely 'the state duty to protect'. Re-establishing the indivisibility of the three pillars from the SRSG's 2008 Framework in relation to RSCM would take us a long way in finding sustainable solutions to the challenges facing current approaches to RSCM. This is made possible via RSCM 3.0, which represents a marked shift from current approaches to RSCM in its reinstatement of the state duty to protect.

RSCM 3.0 has the potential to provide corporations with a long-term and sustainable solution to CSR risk management in relation to suppliers' conduct. The approach answers key challenges of the RSCM 1.0 and 2.0 approaches identified above. Firstly, RSCM 3.0 has the potential to end Code mania with time. Supplier companies will have to comply with the law and possibly additional regulation reflecting the international standards, instead of a multitude of individual Codes. Secondly, the geographical focus of RSCM 3.0 answers the challenge that all corporations face, that they are expected by stakeholders as well as the SRSG to address all tiers of suppliers in their efforts to ensure compliance with basic standards. Finally, it is expected that government ownership of RSCM 3.0 will have a larger and lasting impact compared to current practices. Evidence pointing in this direction can be found in some developed economies, where governments, in collaboration with associations and the business sector, have taken it upon themselves to ensure respect for, *e.g.*, workers rights.

However, it will be a continuous task to evaluate and ensure the impact of a RSCM 3.0 model on workers and other stakeholders. Here the vast experience of DCAs on measuring impact and development will be of great value.

## Annex 1 – Codes of Conduct reviewed

| RSCM 1.0 (Danish) | | RSCM 2.0 | |
|---|---|---|---|
| 1 | Bestseller | 29 | Ghana Business Code |
| 2 | Carlsberg | 30 | Ethical Trading Initiative |
| 3 | Danfoss | 31 | SA 8000 |
| 4 | Coloplast | 32 | Fair Labour Association |
| 5 | Egmont | 33 | International code of conduct for the production of cut flowers |
| 6 | JYSK | 34 | WIETA |
| 7 | Maersk | 35 | Fashion Institute NICE program |
| 8 | NKT | 36 | BSCI (IC Companys) |
| 9 | Toms | 37 | Pharmaceutical Industry Principles for Responsible Supply Chain Management (Novartis) |
| 10 | Hartmann | 38 | Electronic Industry Code (HP) |
| 11 | LEGO | | |
| 12 | VELUX | | |
| 13 | DONG | | |
| 14 | Kohberg | | |
| RSCM 1.0 (Non Danish) | | | |
| 15 | Nestlé | | |
| 16 | GAP | | |
| 17 | Telenor | | |
| 18 | GE | | |
| 19 | The Coca Cola Company | | |
| 20 | Ikea | | |
| 21 | Wal-mart | | |
| 22 | H&M | | |
| 23 | Anglo American | | |
| 24 | American Eagle | | |
| 25 | Ericsson | | |
| 26 | Nike | | |
| 27 | HSBC Holdings | | |
| 28 | UN supplier Code | | |

# 6  Human Rights in the Supply Chain: Influence and Accountability

Karin Lukas*

## 1.  Introduction

The supply chain is a particularly unclear area regarding the human rights responsibilities of companies. It is characterised by complex relationships and power structures that tend to blur the scope of human rights responsibilities. Issues such as the sphere of influence of lead firms (mainly transnational corporations), cost pressures on suppliers, and legal and institutional frameworks influencing these actors play a major role.

Several concepts have been introduced to capture these complexities in the human rights context. One is the concept of the sphere of influence, a term developed *e.g.* by the Office of the High Commissioner for Human Rights (OHCHR) and the United Nations Global Compact (UNGC). Another is the concept of due diligence, which has been introduced by the UN Special Representative John Ruggie into the human rights and business debate. Both concepts seek to assess the human rights responsibilities of companies in this regard.

In the following sections, these two approaches will be analysed in the context of the supply chain and problematic issues of the Ruggie Framework – both on the levels of concept and implementation – will be addressed. A short overview of current corporate initiatives (corporate responsibility to respect human rights, RtR) and legal regimes (state duty to protect human rights) attempting to secure human rights in the supply chain demonstrate that the implementation of the Ruggie Framework cannot on its own provide adequate human rights protection in such situations. I argue that a more extensive international legal framework of human rights protection that is capable of safeguarding human rights in trans-border multi-actor settings of global production and outsourcing is required.

---

\*  Senior Legal Researcher at the Ludwig Boltzmann Institute of Human Rights, Vienna, Austria.

## 2. The Human Rights Responsibilities of Companies in the Supply Chain

### 2.1. The Concept of the Sphere of Influence in the Supply Chain

The sphere of influence is a term introduced by OHCHR and UNGC into the human rights discourse. Nowhere is it authoritatively defined. According to OHCHR/UNGC, the sphere of influence "will tend to include the individuals to whom the company has a certain political, contractual, economic or geographic proximity".[1] The sphere of influence of a company cannot be exactly defined in general terms on the basis of international human rights standards. It needs to be determined on a case-by-case basis, *e.g.* in the course of a baseline study or a social impact assessment.

According to OHCHR/UNGC, the following criteria are relevant to determine the sphere of influence of a company:
- size
- strategic influence
- the human rights issue concerned
- proximity to (potential) victims and perpetrators of human rights violations
- operational influence
- area of operation

The concept of the sphere of influence has been widely used by companies in reference to their human rights responsibilities. Other organisations have utilised it as an integral element of their tools[2] and analyses[3] in this regard. The majority of transnational corporations (TNCs) that consider themselves to act socially responsible have elaborated in greater detail on what they consider to be their sphere of influence in relation to their suppliers. The following examples can be seen as representative of the majority of policy statements on the company sphere of influence regarding the supply chain.

The energy corporation E.ON UK stipulates the following specific provisions for suppliers:

> We aim to implement our Responsible Procurement Policy throughout our supply chain, within our sphere of influence. We also expect that our suppliers encourage and work with their own suppliers to ensure that they also meet the principles of the UN Global

---

1 OHCHR/UNGC, *Embedding Human Rights in Business Practice* (2005) p. 18.
2 *See* the Human Rights and Business Learning Tool of the UN Global Compact, the Guideline SR 26000 on Social Responsibility, and the Vienna Human Rights Matrix of BIM/HRCV.
3 *See for example* S. Wood, 'In Defence of the Sphere of Influence', (2010), <ssrn.com/abstract=1607438>; the International Commission of Jurists (ICJ) refers to the concept as useful but also requiring further clarifications in assessing human rights responsibility. ICJ identifies proximity to the human rights violation as the main determinant of human rights responsibility (ICJ, *Corporate Complicity and Legal Accountability* (2008), Vol. 1, p. 24).

Compact. All business partners and suppliers to E.ON will as a minimum requirement comply both with the principles laid out in the Responsible Procurement Policy and the applicable laws in the countries in which they operate. E.ON has identified three areas it believes to be key to securing a high level of CSR within the supply chain. These are:
1. Respect the Human Rights and secure appropriate working conditions of employees.
2. Minimise environmental impact.
3. Maintain high standards of ethics and business integrity.[4]

The textile corporation H&M stresses direct influence and assigns priorities in terms of human rights protection:

> [W]e look at the complete cycle of our operations, from how our suppliers produce the products we sell to the customers' experience of using them. We focus on areas where we can make the most difference and that are within our sphere of influence, and partner with others to help address those where our direct influence is less.[5]

The electronics corporation Hewlett Packard focuses on first tier suppliers:

> HP requires all our suppliers in our supply chain to follow the Electronic Industry Code of Conduct ... which states that HP suppliers must conduct their worldwide operations in a socially and environmentally responsible manner. We expect suppliers to integrate environmental, occupational health and safety, and human rights and labor policies into their business and decision-making processes. HP has made significant progress with our first tier suppliers conforming to the EICC. To date, HP has focused on our first tier suppliers, where we think we have the most influence. ... HP is limited on how many suppliers, beyond our first tier, we can engage with directly. It is the responsibility of our first tier suppliers to require the EICC to be followed by their suppliers, and so on.[6]

These examples show that companies accept the wider field of the sphere of influence but assign priorities in areas where they can have most impact, for example with first tier suppliers. Generally speaking, the sphere of influence determines the scope of responsibilities: the more influence, the stronger the responsibilities. A TNC's sphere of influence is strongest with its employees, in whatever setting. In addition, a TNC exerts a certain influence over other business partners, especially over its suppliers. The following diagram[7] shows the layers of influence of a TNC:

---

4   E.ON UK Responsible Procurement Policy – Supplier Code of Conduct,<www.eon-uk.com/about/procurement.aspx>, accessed July 2008.
5   H&M CSR Report 2007:1.
6   HP response to makeITfair questionnaire, 2009.
7   BIM/HRCV, Vienna Human Rights Matrix, Explanatory Notes (2008), p. 6. In this context, the term contractors used in the diagram includes suppliers.

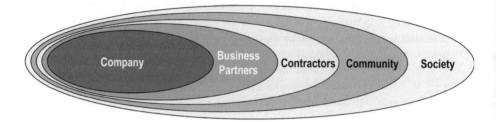

A company exerts a certain influence over other business partners, especially its suppliers and contractors. According to the authors of the Vienna Human Rights Matrix, the company has the responsibility to develop an adequate supply chain management, including monitoring of human rights compliance of suppliers.[8] According to the International Commission of Jurists, "the further down the supply chain, the less knowledge the company will have, or be expected to have, about the practices of its suppliers and often the less impact its conduct will have on the conduct of the supplier."[9] Conversely, the closer the supplier is to the company in the network, the greater the company's accountability for human rights violations of the supplier. Besides the proximity aspect, the relevance of the buyer for the supplier is important as well. If the company is only the buyer of a supplier, its influence is usually higher, and thus its responsibility is greater.[10]

The main difference to the concept of due diligence is that the sphere of influence can be seen as a fluid concept, a concept of parameters, that has to be applied on a case-by-case basis. It presents the power lines of responsibility, showing the core and the periphery of responsibility, but cannot give more in-depth answers to this question if not applied to a concrete situation.[11] Some of these parameters are reflected in John Ruggie's discussion paper on the corporate RtR in the supply chain[12] as indicators of leverage. These parameters mentioned by Ruggie are, among others, direct control or a contractual obligation.

### 2.2. The Concept of Due Diligence in the Supply Chain

John Ruggie views the sphere of influence as "a useful metaphor" but notes that it "conflates two very different meanings of influence: one is impact, where the company's activities or relationships are causing human rights harm; the other is whatever leverage a company may have over actors that are causing harm. The first falls squarely within

---

8    Ibid., p. 36.
9    ICJ, *supra* note 3, p. 30.
10   Ibid.; *see also* section 2.3 of this chapter.
11   K. Lukas, *The Protection of Labour Rights in Global Production Networks* (forthcoming).
12   J. Ruggie, *The Corporate Responsibility to Respect Human Rights in Supply Chains*, 10th OECD Round Table Discussion on Corporate Responsibility, Discussion Paper, 10 June 2010, <www.oecd.org/document/43/0,3343,en_2649_34889_45356907_1_1_1_1,00.html>, accessed 4 September 2010.

the responsibility to respect; the second may only do so in particular circumstances."[13] In the Ruggie Framework, the sphere of influence is replaced by due diligence, which according to Ruggie is – as an established legal principle – more clearly defined. Similar to the German term *"Sorgfaltspflicht"*, due diligence can be defined as "diligence reasonably expected from, and ordinarily exercised by, a person who seeks to satisfy a legal requirement or to discharge an obligation".[14] Regarding the responsibility to act diligently, Ruggie identified several factors that have to be considered by a company in order to determine its responsibility:

- country and local context of the business activity
- impacts of the company's activity within that context as a producer, buyer, employer, etc.
- whether and how the company might contribute to abuse the relationships connected to its activities[15]

Ruggie also refers to a company's role and size, and gives the following example:

> [A] bank's human rights due diligence for a project loan will differ in some respects from that of the company operating the project. Nevertheless, banks do have human rights due diligence requirements in this context, and human rights risks related to the projects are also risks to the banks' liability, returns and reputation. Beyond banks lies an even more complex array of lenders, investors, and asset managers. Precisely how their respective due diligence differs requires further clarity.[16]

This again relates to the question of proximity. A company which has the role of a lender, for example regarding an infrastructure project, will have a weaker influence on the supplier than a company operating in an infrastructure project that the supplier is a contractor of. This issue is not further dealt with in later reports of the Special Representative, but it is highly relevant in the context of the supply chain because the role and size of a company are key determinants in supply chain settings. For example, the purchasing decisions of transnational corporations have immense consequences on the ability of their suppliers to provide fair wages or sufficient working hours (see further below in this section).

According to Ruggie, "[c]ompanies do not control some of these factors, but that is no reason to ignore them. Businesses routinely employ due diligence to assess exposure to risks beyond their control and develop mitigation strategies for them." Turning to the supply chain, Ruggie notes:

---

13   J. Ruggie, *Protect, Respect and Remedy: A Framework for Business and Human Rights*, 7 April 2008, p. 19.
14   *Black's Law Dictionary 2006*; J. Ruggie, *Business and human rights: Towards operationalizing the "protect, respect and remedy" framework*, 22 April 2009, p. 18.
15   Ruggie, *supra* note 13, p. 17.
16   *Ibid.*, p. 18.

It is often overlooked that suppliers are also companies, subject to the same responsibility to respect human rights as any other business. The challenge for buyers is to ensure they are not complicit in violations by their suppliers. How far down the supply chain a buyer's responsibility extends depends on what a proper due diligence process reveals about prevailing country and sector conditions, and about potential business partners and their sourcing practices. A growing number of global buyers are finding it necessary to engage in human rights capacity-building with suppliers in order to sustain the relationship.[17]

It is certainly true that suppliers are bound by law to adhere to labour rights standards as much as the TNC which buys from them. However, the challenge lies in making them comply with these responsibilities. On a practical level, it is hardly possible to expose suppliers to the same public scrutiny and pressure as TNCs to ensure human rights compliance, as expressed for example in national labour law.

In the aforementioned discussion paper of June 2010, Ruggie addresses due diligence in the supply chain in more detail.[18] He rightly rejects approaches that attempt to limit corporate responsibility based on the level of trade and argues that such numerical thresholds are arbitrary when applied across different sectors and sizes, and risk encouraging companies to remain below the threshold that would make them responsible.[19] In assessing responsibility, two categories are identified:
- a company contributes to the human rights violation by its own actions or omissions
- a company is implicated only by the link to the goods or services it procures

In the first case, RtR requires that the company takes appropriate steps "to address these contributions". In the second category, a further distinction is made:
- whether the company considers the supplier crucial to its business
- whether the company has leverage over the supplier

According to Ruggie, a *crucial supplier* is one that provides an essential product or service for which no other reasonable alternative source exists. *Leverage* may entail one or more of the following factors: direct control over the supplier; contractual obligations between the company and the supplier; the importance ("proportion of business") of the company for the supplier; the ability of the company to "incentivise" the supplier to be human rights compliant (capacity-building assistance, reputational advantage); the ability of the company to engage other companies working with the supplier to influence its human rights performance; and the ability of the company to engage the government to require improved human rights performance of the supplier.[20]

How do the two factors – leverage and the crucial supplier – combine to shape human rights compatible business decision-making according to Ruggie? If the supplier

---

17   Ibid., para. 75.
18   Ruggie, *supra* note 12.
19   Ibid., p. 2.
20   Ibid., p. 3.

is crucial and can be influenced by the company, the company should use its leverage to mitigate the human rights violation. If the use of leverage proves unsuccessful, leverage is less than it was estimated to be; then the company should increase its leverage, for example by offering capacity-building, or work together with other companies and/or government. If this is unsuccessful, the company will need to take steps to end the relationship or will have to demonstrate that it has done everything reasonably possible to mitigate the abuses and will need to be prepared to face the consequences for maintaining the relationship. In case the supplier is not crucial but the company has leverage, it should use this leverage; if unsuccessful, it can be expected to end the relationship. In case none of the two criteria are met, the company can be expected to end the relationship.[21] This approach applies to existing supply chain relationships. As for the decision whether to enter into a new relationship, this should only be done if the company comes to the conclusion that it can mitigate the abuse.

According to Ruggie, knowledge of human rights abuses beyond the first tier suppliers can be more difficult. In this situation, companies should apply due diligence on a broader level by taking the following steps. First, the identification of general areas of risk of serious human rights abuse in the supply chain, for example because of the region, the product, or its materials. Ruggie then recommends to mitigate such risks by seeking to ensure that suppliers are acting diligently and follow appropriate standards. After a general risk assessment, the company should identify specific suppliers that are abusing human rights and take decisions as outlined earlier.

These steps are in principle stringent and pragmatic, quite the "Ruggie brand". However, some inconsistencies should be pointed out. Ruggie uses the wording "mitigating human rights abuse", which is much weaker than for example the notion "ending the human rights violation". This seems to indicate that corporate human rights responsibility stops at mitigating, and not at ending a human rights violation. One wonders what the reason for this cautionary approach might have been. The document does not provide any explanation. This approach is however questionable: if a company knows of a human rights violation of a supplier, and, to use the Ruggie criteria, the supplier is both a crucial company and the company has leverage on the supplier, why cannot it be expected to use that leverage to end the human rights violation? In particular in case of a "serious" human rights violation (on the term "serious" see below) it is difficult to argue that a company's responsibility is reduced to "risk mitigation". The Ruggie Framework does not provide an argument that would justify to draw the line at mitigation only.

Secondly, Ruggie introduces the term of a "serious" human rights abuse when describing the identification of general areas of risk. One wonders why this due diligence step has been limited in such a way. Again, this raises the definitional problem of the seriousness of a human rights abuse. What is the threshold in such cases? Is the term "serious human rights abuse" comparable to "grave human rights violations" according to Article 7 of the Rome Statute of the International Criminal Court?[22] This seems

---

21    For an illustration of these steps (decision-matrix) *see ibid.*, p. 5.
22    Article 7 includes the following definition: "any of the following acts when committed as part of a widespread or systematic attack directed against any civilian population, with

unlikely given the human rights violations referred to in the Statute, as the threshold would be an immensely high one. The paper provides no explanation for this distinction. In the author's view, an assessment of general areas of risk would be important regardless of the severity of the human rights violation.

In Ruggie's last report, *Guiding Principles on Business and Human Rights: Implementing the United Nations "Protect, Respect and Remedy" framework*, another term has been introduced: that of "severe impacts". The term "severe" is used in several guidelines. According to Guideline 14, severity is determined by "scale, scope and irremediable character". In Guideline 17(b), due diligence will vary according to, *inter alia*, "the risk of severe human rights impacts". Guideline 19 (appropriate action to prevent and mitigate human rights abuse) states that "the more severe the abuse, the more quickly the enterprise will need to see change before it takes a decision on whether it should end the relationship. In any case, for as long as the abuse continues and the enterprise remains in the relationship, it should be able to demonstrate its own ongoing efforts to mitigate the impact and be prepared to accept any consequences – reputational, financial or legal – of the continuing connection."[23] Guideline 21 foresees specific formal reporting requirements in such cases, and Guideline 24 recommends to "prioritize action" in view of severe human rights impacts. Thus, Ruggie does not provide examples of severe human rights impacts. The only more specific criterion is that of irremediability. The other recommendations refer to proposed action to the company in such cases and give no further indication of what constitutes a "severe human rights impact".

The issue of leverage is also a crucial one. It seems to clandestinely re-introduce the concept of the sphere of influence because what is, in practical application, the difference between using leverage and exercising influence as determined by the sphere of influence? The concept of due diligence must take recourse to the sphere of influence when determining leverage for a specific company in a specific situation. It is a concept to assess what a company can do to support human rights or end a human rights violation of an actor with regard to a certain power proximity and relationship of influence. The concept needs to be applied to a concrete situation. For example, a company which

---

knowledge of the attack, these are: murder; extermination; enslavement; deportation or forcible transfer of population; imprisonment or other severe deprivation of physical liberty in violation of fundamental rules of international law; torture; rape, sexual slavery, enforced prostitution, forced pregnancy, enforced sterilization, or any other form of sexual violence of comparable gravity; persecution against any identifiable group or collectivity on political, racial, national, ethnic, cultural, religious, gender, or other grounds that are universally recognized as impermissible under international law, in connection with any act referred to in this paragraph; enforced disappearance of persons; the crime of apartheid; other inhumane acts of a similar character intentionally causing great suffering, or serious injury to body or to mental or physical health". Rome Statute of the International Criminal Court, A/CONF.183/9 of 17 July 1998.

23  Report of the Special Representative of the Secretary-General on the issue of human rights and transnational corporations and other business enterprises, J. Ruggie, *Guiding Principles on Business and Human Rights: Implementing the United Nations "Protect, Respect and Remedy" Framework*, A/HRC/17/31, 21 March 2011, para. 19 (commentary).

detects a human rights violation of one of its suppliers will only have leverage according to its sphere of influence: Does it have the strategic and operational influence to end the human rights violation? What is the company's proximity to the human rights violation? Is the human rights violation caused by a first tier supplier – and therefore a direct contractor – of the company? What is the nature of the human rights violation? Is it for example a violation of the International Labour Organization core labour standards,[24] which are widely accepted minimum standards, and will at least with regard to reputation harm the company? What is the company's area of operation? Is it a big buyer in the apparel industry, a sector which is known for, in particular, labour rights problems in the supply chain? Ideally, an influential company will already have used its influence to establish a monitoring and capacity-building system that prevents the human rights violation.[25] Thus, in the author's opinion, both concepts are complementary and need each other in real world decision-making.

In the Guiding Principles, most of the analysis of the 2010 Ruggie discussion paper is included, such as the issue of leverage. However, the Guiding Principles do not clarify the problematic issues identified in the discussion paper; it merely reiterates some of the issues and analyses of the discussion paper, such as the aforementioned problem of "severe impacts". Thus, on the level of conception, quite a number of questions remain unanswered.

Regarding the practical application of due diligence by corporate actors, the following section will review company initiatives that seek to protect and monitor human rights in the supply chain. The focus will be on corporate Codes of Conduct, which quite a number of TNCs have developed in response to public pressure following allegations of human rights violations of their suppliers and which can be seen as key instruments to observe human rights compliance in the supply chain.[26]

## 2.3. *Corporate Self-Regulation as Due Diligence in the Supply Chain*

In response to public pressure concerning human rights violations in the supply chain, a multitude of Codes of Conduct at the sectoral and company level committed to, *inter alia*, human rights compliance, have been created.[27] As there are no generally accepted

---

24   *See* the ILO Declaration on the fundamental principles and rights at work (1998), which stipulates the following standards as fundamental: freedom of association and the effective recognition of the right to collective bargaining; the elimination of all forms of forced or compulsory labour; the abolition of child labour; and the elimination of discrimination in employment and occupation, <www.ilo.org/public/english/standards/relm/ilc/ilc86/com-dtxt.htm>, accessed 9 June 2011.

25   For details *see* next section.

26   *See for example* the allegations of labour rights violations of suppliers of Nike in Southeast Asia and the subsequent establishment of Nike's corporate social responsibility strategy, details at <www.nikebiz.com/responsibility/>.

27   The number of companies that have created Codes of Conduct are still comparatively small. According to Bernstein and Greenwald, who analysed data of 2,508 TNCs, only 28 per cent have a supplier policy, and 15 per cent have established a specific labour rights

standards or model codes to comply with, a wide variety of Codes of Conduct with different levels of standards and protection have been developed.[28]

Most Codes of Conduct include at least some of the ILO core labour standards as the bottom line of labour rights protection and a reference to the Universal Declaration of Human Rights. Very few explicitly refer to the International Covenant on Economic, Social and Cultural Rights. Thus, the integration of human rights standards is uneven across TNC Codes, and the above-mentioned standards can be found in all variations, which makes it very difficult to compare the human rights performance of TNCs in relation to their supply chains. Therefore, a main limitation of Codes of Conduct is that they do not follow a uniform set of standards with regard to human rights as each Code of Conduct covers different standards depending on the sectoral and company actors and their interest.

Besides the different content of Codes of Conduct, the actual implementation and monitoring of these Codes of Conduct are key challenges. In this regard, one of the major problems in the area of Codes of Conduct implementation has been to ensure compliance with Codes of Conduct at all levels of the supply chain. The common instrument to secure compliance is through audits that are either conducted internally by the company or through external organisations. The development of Codes of Conduct to improve working conditions in the supply chain has brought improvements in some areas but also shows several limitations when it comes to effectively securing human rights.[29] A growing body of literature[30] highlights the following issues:

- inefficiencies in multiple audits for the same supplier by each buyer
- widespread false evidence and double-book-keeping by suppliers
- limited capabilities of third party and in-house auditors to understand and detect violations, particularly of freedom of association
- a focus on policing and finding flaws, rather than on advising and fixing problems
- limited scope for reaching sub-contractors and the more vulnerable casual and home-based workers

---

code for suppliers. 6 per cent monitor suppliers or set labour rights improvement targets, and only 7 per cent provide for enforcement procedures; A. Bernstein and C. Greenwald, *Benchmarking Corporate Policies on Labor and Human Rights in Global Supply Chains* (2008) p. 4.

28   *See for example* OECD, *Codes of Corporate Conduct: Expanded Review of their Contents* (2001); R. Jenkins, R. Pearson and G. Seyfang, *Corporate Responsibility and Labour Rights: Codes of Conduct in the Global Economy* (Earthscan, 2002); World Bank, *Company Codes of Conduct and International Standards: An Analytical Comparison* (2003); G. Standing, 'Decent Workplaces, Self-Regulation and CSR: From Puff to Stuff?', *DESA Working Paper* No. 62 (2007).

29   *See* the chapter by Skaadegaard Thorsen and Andreason in this volume.

30   OECD-ILO, *Annual Report of the OECD Guidelines for Multinational Enterprises – Employment and Industrial Relation* (2008) p. 230; Standing, *supra* note 28; Mamic, *Implementing Codes of Conduct* (ILO, 2004); R. Mares, 'The Limits of Supply Chain Responsibility: A Critical Analysis of Corporate Responsibility Instruments', 79 *Nordic Journal of International Law* (2010) pp. 193–244.

- internal misalignment within firms between social responsibility and economic imperatives
- lack of engagement with public labour inspections and other efforts to improve governance and compliance over the long term

Some of these issues are inherently linked to the complexities of and power relations in the supply chain. Audits are so far mostly concerned with health and safety issues, paying less attention to wages, overtime or trade union rights, which are critical to improve overall working conditions. Improvements such as better lighting, ventilation or ergonomic chairs relate to process upgrading as they also increase productivity by a more '"efficient" use of the "human resource". In contrast to such "win-win" situations, issues that are in conflict with the prevailing business logic (*e.g.* living wage, working time, trade union rights) remain contested. Respecting those rights would entail restrictions with regard to flexibility and prices (and accordingly wages) paid.[31] Thus, it is essential that TNCs assess the impact of their purchasing decisions and sourcing policies on suppliers. In this context, the International Commission of Jurists gives the following example: if a company is the sole buyer of a supplier and can dictate such a product price and high speed of delivery that the supplier has to use forced labour, it can be said that the company enabled, exacerbated or facilitated the harm suffered by the workers.[32] Deadlines that are too tight and will lead to overtime of suppliers' workers, and pricing pressures that make suppliers cut production costs, including wages, will be likely amount to non-adherence to human rights responsibilities.

Moreover, if lead firms are not able to reach and influence their suppliers in their supply chain in terms of control and capacity-building, the consequence must be to reduce the supply chain to a level where such influence can still be exerted. Thus, it should be the responsibility of the TNC to have influence on and control over the supply chain in order to be able to secure human rights. Some buyers, such as Nike, have made efforts to streamline suppliers in order to gain greater influence and control in the supply chain.

There is also a lack of coherence at the buyers' level since the persons in charge of Codes of Conduct and corporate social responsibility (CSR) and the ones in charge of production and price negotiations are generally not the same and their agendas tend not to be complementary. Hence, apparel suppliers are confronted on the one hand with tight price and delivery time demands as well as last minute changes to orders from the clients' sourcing department and on the other hand with demands from the CSR department that usually does not have the power to reward the supplier for investments and improvements in working conditions (*e.g.* via higher prices or more stable contractual relationships).[33] The Guiding Principles reflect this problem by highlighting the need for "effective integration" by *e.g.* appropriate company level response and oversight mechanisms (see Guiding Principle 19).

---

31   L. Plank, C. Staritz and K. Lukas, *Labour Rights in Global Production Networks* (Wien, 2009) p. 40, <www.arbeiterkammer.at/bilder/d103/LabourRights.pdf>.
32   ICJ, *supra* note 3, p. 30.
33   *Ibid.*; *also* Lukas, *supra* note 11.

Moreover, it has been extremely difficult for TNCs to monitor the whole supply chain, for a number of reasons: the complexity of the chain, and, linked to that, the lack of influence of the lead firm to monitor all actors in the chain; competitive market environments; industrial processes ("fast-fashion") that give a low price and short lead times preference over decent working conditions; the inadequate integration of working conditions into purchasing decisions; and lack of supplier and workers' ownership over the process.

Some efforts have been made to provide positive incentives for suppliers with good working conditions and capacity-building for suppliers who need to improve their human rights records.[34] A few of the more pro-active TNCs have adopted the "Beyond Monitoring" approach.[35] Having experienced the limited effectiveness of supply chain control through audits, because impacts were not sustainable and isolated incidences instead of root causes were addressed, companies such as Nike turned to capacity-building of and dialogue with suppliers rather than top-down control to ensure compliance.[36] Some have also identified the inclusion of workers in the compliance procedure as a critical criterion for success.[37]

Regarding the integration of human rights (mostly the issue of working conditions) into purchasing decisions, some positive changes have taken place. For example, the Levi Strauss & Company's Code of Conduct team reports on sourcing practices as well, and Hewlett-Packard has established a cross-functional supply chain team that includes sourcing and social and environmental compliance groups. HP's procurement management process includes social and environmental responsibility components in the supply chain. Nike has created a cross-functional overtime task force to analyse the impact of design and other market and product processes on working time.[38] As this is a recent and ongoing process, its impact cannot be assessed yet.

Parallel to this development, the question still remains whether Codes of Conduct can be made legally binding and enforceable in the supply chain. As regards enforceable compliance with Codes of Conduct, quite a number of TNCs have integrated parts or refer to the entire Code of Conduct in contracts with their suppliers. As an integral element of the supplier contract and thus of a contractual obligation of civil law, these provisions can be enforced in civil courts. A few companies such as Nike have a

---

34 *See for example* Business for Social Responsibility, *Shared Mindset and Supplier Ownership: A Beyond Monitoring Trends Report* (2008).

35 S. Barrientos and S. Smith, *The ETI Code of Labour Practice: Do workers really benefit?* (Ethical Trading Initiative, 2006) and Business for Social Responsibility, *Beyond Monitoring: A New Vision for Sustainable Supply Chains* (2007).

36 R. Locke, F. Quin and A. Brause, *Does Monitoring Improve Labour Standards? Lessons from Nike* (2006), <www.hks.harvard.edu/m-rcbg/CSRI/publications/workingpaper_24_locke.pdf>; *see also* Nike, *Evolving beyond monitoring*, <www.nikebiz.com/crreport/content/workers-and-factories/3-1-3-evolving-beyond-monitoring.php?cat=overview>, accessed 10 March 2010.

37 *See for example* Barrientos and Smith, *supra* note 35, p. 59 and Business for Social Responsibility, *supra* note 35, pp. 5 *et seq.*

38 Business for Social Responsibility, *supra* note 35, p. 7.

gradual sanction system for such situations. In case of violations of labour rights, the supplier gets the opportunity to remedy the situation. If no compliance occurs within a given timeframe, the contract will be terminated. Only in cases of very severe human rights violations (such as the systematic use of child labour) will a termination be immediate.[39]

However, this contractual obligation cannot be extended to third parties but is only enforceable between the two parties of the contract. Thus, it is a binding mechanism for first tier suppliers, but not for suppliers further down the chain. However, it would be feasible to include an obligation for the first-tier suppliers to subcontract only to suppliers who will adhere to the labour standards as stipulated in the Code of Conduct. In this context, the Code of Conduct would be part of the contract between the first- and second-tier supplier and would be enforceable between these two suppliers. Questions of controlling compliance with the labour rights standards stipulated in the contract still remain. Nevertheless, so far, this is the only way of giving binding effect to human rights in company Codes of Conduct.

In conclusion, this evidence shows that company Codes of Conduct have had – to some extent – a positive impact on the protection of some human rights in the supply chain, but they are less effective than hoped for. The patchy nature of improvements suggests that the "business case" is at least equally important as the "social case". Thus, Codes of Conduct must be seen as only one, and certainly not the most encouraging, avenue to human rights protection in the supply chain.

## 3. The Human Rights Responsibilities of States in the Supply Chain

As a different avenue, some states have enacted legislation that addresses questions of liability in the supply chain. Previous state regulation has lost effectiveness to secure human rights in the new environment of global production due to the transnational dimension of supply chains that require cross-territorial cooperation between state authorities as well as the complexity of and asymmetric power relations in these chains. Given the rise of and the frequency of human rights violations in such subcontracting relationships, national liability regimes have emerged in effort to protect human rights in these settings. These regimes can be seen as "pioneer legislation" in order to effectively apply the state duty to protect human rights in supply chains. Although they are so far limited to two sectors (construction and clothing) they could be applied to other sectors with complex supply chain relationships.

### 3.1. Legislation on the State Duty to Protect Human Rights in the Supply Chain

In the construction sector, so-called "chain liability regimes" have been enacted that allow for holding all elements of the chain liable for the entire debt of the subcontractor regardless of the degree of fault or responsibility. The objective of this approach is to hold the person with the more promising financial resources liable for "essen-

---

39  Nike, *supra* note 36.

tial debts" such as wages and social security contributions. So far, only a handful of European Union member states have such national liability systems, which are applicable to the construction sector only: Austria,[40] Belgium, Finland, France, Germany, Italy, the Netherlands and Spain. As an example of a non-European country, Australia has enacted similar provisions.[41]

The existing liability regimes have delivered some positive results in securing labour rights while also – according to some employers' associations and trade unions – providing a level playing field for companies operating fairly. Still, this kind of legislation only covers employment relationships within one country's territory but not employment relationships that span over different countries, which is the norm in most global production settings, and it is limited to the construction sector.[42]

In principle, this type of legislation could be extended to all sectors where complex chain relationships serve as an "incentive" to commit human rights violations. The construction sector has been a focal point of such issues,[43] and state initiatives have also been motivated by the capture of taxes and other contributions (for example social security contributions). Insolvencies are much less prevalent in other sectors, which might have been a key factor to establish such legislation. However, this cannot be seen as an impediment *per se* to enact similar legislation in other sectors.

The example of Australia shows that legislation on the human rights compliance of suppliers via buyers can be realised in other sectors as well. After unsuccessful attempts to increase the protection of workers through voluntary company codes of conduct, legislation[44] was enacted to oblige retailers – who have a dominant position in the Australian clothing industry – to provide state authorities and trade unions with full information on contracting arrangements with suppliers, including identities and

---

40    Law Nr. 91/2008, Haftung bei Beauftragung zur Erbringung von Bauleistungen. For a detailed analysis of the Austrian legislation *see* B. Bartos and P. Maska, Generalunternehmerhaftung. AuftraggeberInnen-Haftungsgesetz, § 67a – 67d und § 112a ASVG, <www.wkw.at/docextern/sgewerbe/oeffentlichkeitsarbeit/navigationspunkt_service/Generalunternehmerhaftung_Neu.pdf>, accessed October 2009.

41    I. Nossar *et al.*, 'Regulating Supply-Chains To Address the Occupational Health and Safety Problems Associated with Precarious Employment: The Case of Home-Based Clothing Workers in Australia', 17 *Australian Journal of Labour Law* (2004) p. 137.

42    Regarding considerations to extend such a liability regime to all EU member states *see* Lukas, *supra* note 11.

43    According to Huwerzijl and Peters, "[c]ompanies at a lower level in the value chain – with the exception of specialised subcontractors with highly technical or other sophisticated activities – are not in a position to act on an equal footing with the main contractor. An imbalance of power in the lower parts of the chain can lead to questionable contracts that define the market transactions between the different levels". Huwerzijl and Peters, *Liability in subcontracting processes in the European construction sector* (European Foundation for the Improvement of Living and Working Conditions, 2008) p. 8, <www.eurofound.europa.eu/pubdocs/2008/94/en/1/EF0894EN.pdf>.

44    Industrial Relations (Ethical Clothing Trades) Act 2001, New South Wales, Outworkers Improved Protection Act 2003, Victoria.

locations of all parties supplying for the retailers.[45] These information requirements enable the retailer to know where the products have been made and under which conditions. This includes the contractual obligation of the supplier to allow regulatory authorities access to all production sites without prior notification. The regime also introduced a commercial remedy mechanism that foresees commercial sanctions for "persistent breaches" of certain employment standards (non-payment of wage, health and safety regulations). Similar to European chain liability legislations, workers (in particular home workers) are entitled to claim unpaid entitlements toward any contractor within the chain, up to the principal manufacturer him- or herself.

These systems have the precondition that the key players must be located within the relevant jurisdiction where the legislation has been enacted. However, global production often involves a TNC based in a "developed" country and supplier firms in "developing" or "transition" countries. Policy-makers in some developing countries see low wages and weak labour rights regulation as "competitive advantages" in such settings. Thus, the majority of host states where suppliers are situated balance their interest with regard to employment and exports with their interest to protect human rights.[46] An accountability gap becomes evident where host states are unable or unwilling to protect human rights on their territory in the context of global competition and asymmetric power relationships in global production arrangements. This problem points at an issue of wider consequence.

### 3.2. An International Legal Framework to Protect Human Rights in the Supply Chain

In view of the above, it would be necessary to go beyond corporate due diligence considerations, which rely on the willingness of companies to adhere to human rights, and envisage a more binding framework of corporate accountability. Besides improving existing legal instruments to protect human rights in the supply chain, an international legal framework that can hold corporations accountable for human rights violations in global production networks, such as an international convention on combating human rights violations by transnational corporations, is needed to complement this patchwork of current initiatives.[47]

---

45  Nossar *et al.*, *supra* note 41, p. 14.
46  Lukas, Plank and Staritz, *supra* note 31, p. 48.
47  John Ruggie expressed a number of reservations to this idea, *e.g.* that treaty negotiations run the risk of settling on a "lowest common denominator" agreement that is far below the high standards that current voluntary agreements achieve and that such a treaty could be difficult to enforce (Global Governance Watch, *John Ruggie Wary of Corporate Human Rights Standards Treaty*, excerpt of interview, 19 May 2008, available at <www.globalgovernancewatch.org/spotlight_on_sovereignty/john-ruggie-wary-of-corporate-human-rights-standards-treaty>, accessed 7 July 2011. The first difficulty could be met by the "advanced groups of states" approach as outlined later in this chapter. Although such a treaty is likely to face enforcement problems, the Ruggie Framework faces implementation problems along similar lines as companies must be willing to implement the Framework, which is likely to encompass only a minority of companies.

Two proposals have been made here: an international convention for states that only binds companies on their territory, or a convention that is adopted by states and corporations alike.[48] Although a direct accountability of non-state actors, which would be the case in the second option, is still underdeveloped in international law, it is not excluded.[49] For example, companies can already be made liable for environmental damages on the international level.[50] In this regard, it has been highlighted that initially the consent of all UN member states is not necessarily required but that a group of like-minded states may take the first essential steps toward such a convention. This has been the case for the Ottawa Convention on the Prohibition of Landmines or the preparation process for the establishment of the International Criminal Court.[51] This convention should be complemented by an international court of human rights[52] that would adjudicate complaints once national avenues have been exhausted or are seen as ineffective to bring about justice for TNCs' human rights violations.

Although it will take time to reach the political consent for such a structure, the pressure from public interest groups, including trade unions, critical consumers and non-governmental organisations is rising and court cases seeking to hold TNCs accountable for labour rights violations are increasing. For example, in April 2010, the TNC Lidl was brought to court when it was alleged that Lidl misleadingly advertised labour rights compliance of its clothing suppliers in Bangladesh.[53]

---

48   K. Lukas and F.-J. Hutter, *Menschenrechte und Wirtschaft* [Human Rights and Business] (NWV, 2009) pp. 211 *et seq.*

49   A. Reinisch, 'The Changing International Legal Framework for Dealing with Non-State Actors', in P. Alston, *Non-State Actors and Human Rights* (Oxford University Press, 2005) p. 82.

50   For example, the Convention of the Law of the Sea provides for international liability of companies for environmental maritime damages, see Lukas and Hutter, *supra* note 48, p. 154.

51   J. Martens, 'Prekärer Pragmatismus: Die Arbeit des UN-Sonderbeauftragten für Wirtschaft und Menschenrechte' [Precarious Pragmatism: The Work of the UN Special Representative on Business and Human Rights], *Journal for Human Rights* (ZfMR, 2009).

52   Extensive research and concrete proposals have been made in this regard, *see* J. Kozma, M. Nowak and M. Scheinin, *A World Court of Human Rights. Consolidated Statute and Commentary* (2010).

53   In a first reaction, Lidl withdrew its advertisements in this matter. See ECCHR, *Lidl muss Werbung zurückziehen* [Lidl must withdraw advertisement], <www.ecchr.de/lidl-klage/articles/lidl-muss-werbung-zurueckziehen.620.html> and Saage-Maaß and von Gall, 'Fairer Wettbewerb weltweit! Am Beispiel Lidl' [Fair competition worldwide! The example of Lidl], *Gegenblende* (July/August 2010), <www.gegenblende.de/04-2010/++co++362c1648-8dc6-11df-7fa7-001ec9b03e44/#unionlab>, accessed 5 May 2011. A similar case in the US was settled in 2003. In the case *Kasky* v. *Nike* [12 Cal 4th 939 (SCt Cal 2002)], the plaintiff alleged that Nike had made false and misleading claims regarding its labour practices. However, the Court confirmed the lower court's decision that Nike was protected by the US Constitution's First Amendment guarantee of free speech. The US Supreme Court [123 SCt 2554 (SCt US 2003)] dismissed the case on procedural grounds. A few months after the Supreme Court decision the parties agreed to settle the case.

## 4. Conclusions

The protection of human rights in the supply chain is still full of gaps and difficulties. Power asymmetries, competitive pressures and related industry dynamics – mainly shaped by lead firms, which usually are TNCs – exert considerable pressure on suppliers to meet tight production deadlines and produce at low costs, which can be detrimental to the compliance with human rights.

The Ruggie Framework certainly provides very useful elements and analyses to address some of these issues, such as the rejection of merely numerical or threshold approaches to human rights responsibility or the emphasis on company measures to ensure the integration of human rights considerations, such as oversight mechanisms. But the Framework also contains several inconsistencies, which have been highlighted in this chapter. In particular, the distinction between leverage as an element of the RtR and the sphere of influence does not seem to be as clear-cut as the Ruggie Framework presents it. In a concrete human rights situation, the parameters of the sphere of influence are needed to determine actual leverage. In practical application, the two concepts are complementary. Other concept-related issues include unclear terminology ("severe" or "serious" human rights impact) and the particular limitations of RtR (*e.g.* the terminology "mitigating" human rights abuse).

In contrast to previous UN initiatives, notably the development of the "UN Draft Norms",[54] the Ruggie Framework is pragmatically limited and therefore does not include steps towards binding international TNC regulation. However, current state and corporate practice shows that the existing legal regimes and company initiatives fail to provide adequate human rights protection in the supply chain. Current state legislation covering cross-border supply chain situations is scarce and limited to a few specific sectors. It can hardly be seen as more than a patchwork of human rights protection measures. These systems also have the precondition that the key players must be located within the relevant jurisdiction where the legislation has been enacted. In global production settings, this is not often the case. In addition, the majority of host states where suppliers are situated balance their interest with regard to employment and exports with their interest to protect human rights. An "accountability gap" becomes evident where host states are unable or unwilling to protect human rights on their territory in the context of global competition.

Company initiatives also face a number of problems. For example, the possibility to reach sub-contractors further down the chain and the more vulnerable group of casual and home-based workers has so far been very limited. Some of these problems are inherently linked to the complexities of and power relations in the supply chain.

---

54   Sub-Commission on the Protection and Promotion of Human Rights, *Norms on the responsibilities of transnational corporations and other enterprises with regard to human rights*, E/CN.4/Sub.2/2003/12/Rev.2 of 26 August 2003. Instead of endorsing the Draft Norms, states agreed to nominate a Special Representative on the human rights responsibilities of transnational corporations and other business enterprises; John Ruggie was nominated. On the mandate *see* Commission on Human Rights, *Human Rights and transnational corporations and other business enterprises*, E/CN.4/2005/L.87 of 15 April 2005.

However, other limitations are due to conflicting interests and objectives of social responsibility and economic considerations. Improved working conditions such as better lighting or ventilation also increase productivity. In contrast to such "win-win" situations, human rights that are in conflict with the prevailing business logic (such as decent wage, working time, trade union rights) remain contested. Some human rights cannot be easily aligned with economic interests. This conflict is a major weakness of a voluntary approach such as Ruggie's. The Ruggie approach of "principled pragmatism" cannot fully address the "accountability gap", which is particularly prevalent in supply chain settings as many suppliers and buyers without brand names have little incentive to implement voluntary frameworks. Thus, the Ruggie Framework should not – and maybe will not – be the last step on the road to corporate accountability in the supply chain.

# 7  Responsibility to Respect: Why the Core Company Should Act When Affiliates Infringe Human Rights

Radu Mares*

## 1. Introduction

This chapter discusses the treatment that Professor Ruggie's Guiding Principles offer for the responsibility to respect human rights (RtR) as applied to core companies whose affiliates' operations infringe human rights. The issue is about a core company's responsibility to act to address abuses that occur towards the periphery of its group or network. The fairness of globalisation is often questioned with examples from industries where business enterprises are structured along buyer-supplier, parent-subsidiary and joint venture arrangements. Export-oriented labour-intensive industries and extractive industries are cases in point. The concern here is that the RtR raises difficult issues when applied to a business group or network as opposed to a single business entity.

Ruggie clearly entertains a responsibility for core companies. What remains rather unclear, however, is why the core company should have a responsibility to act when it did not *contribute* through its own decisions in any way to those abuses, but was merely *associated*, by virtue of its business relationships, with its affiliates. This scenario is clearly distinguishable from that of core companies taking decisions that have rippling effects on affiliates and thus have a role in the abuses;[1] this scenario is less problematic and is not covered in this chapter. These two situations – contribution or mere association – where a core company's RtR may be brought up in the discussion are very different and require, it is submitted, a more critical treatment than they received in the Ruggie reports.

The situations that give concern here are easy to exemplify: a buyer company purchases goods from a supplier, which independent of any decisions of the buyer, uses

---

\*   Senior researcher, Raoul Wallenberg Institute of Human Rights and Humanitarian law, Lund, Sweden.
1   Ruggie referred to 'brand-induced problems', such as flexible production, fast turnaround, surge orders, changed orders and so on. J. G. Ruggie, *Remarks Delivered at Forum on Corporate Social Responsibility*, Bamberg, Germany, 14 June 2006.

child and forced labour; a parent company has a subsidiary overseas, which independent of any decisions of the parent, destroys the livelihood of local populations through pollution and repressive practices, alone or in complicity with local entities. In these situations none of the core company's decisions contributes to the abuses perpetrated by affiliates against right holders overseas. Are these buyer and parent companies absolved of any responsibility in face of their affiliate's misconduct? If not, on what conceptual foundation would a core company's responsibility to act be based? So this chapter asks questions such as: Why does a core company have to act where it apparently did not contribute to its affiliates' harmful impacts? Why would an omission to act be blameworthy? These are foundational questions that precede any discussion of due diligence; in other words whether a responsibility exists precedes discussions about how that responsibility could and should be discharged. The appropriateness of Ruggie's due diligence recommendations is not challenged.

Ruggie's Guiding Principles are critically reviewed in section 2 for how they deal with the issue of a core company's responsibility to act. Section 3 seeks inspiration in tort jurisprudence[2] in an attempt to justify a responsibility to act and thus reinforce Ruggie's foundational work on the RtR. Section 4 identifies some outstanding issues related to the RtR that could benefit from further research and attention in the post-Ruggie period.

## 2. Ruggie's Treatment of RtR as Applied to Core Companies

### 2.1. *Coverage of Core Companies*

Ruggie consistently addresses the RtR to "business enterprises, both transnational and others, regardless of their size, sector, location, ownership and structure".[3] This is general enough to cover all types of business enterprises including core companies, but does Ruggie account explicitly for core companies? He clearly does and more specifically in all three Pillars of his Framework. Thus in Pillar 1, dealing with a state's duty to protect human rights, Ruggie lays down as a foundational principle that "States should set out clearly the expectation that all business enterprises domiciled in their territory and/or jurisdiction respect human rights throughout their operations".[4] The

---

2   Ferrari noted that "[t]he definitions of tort, unerlaubte Handlung, délit, and fatto illecito, seem to differ greatly from one another in different legal systems. Nonetheless, there are certain requirements in all legal systems without which no right to claim damages exists. Without (1) an intentional or negligent act (or omission) which (2) causes (3) damages, no tortious liability results, i.e., no obligation to compensate for damages arises." F. Ferrari, 'Comparative Remarks on Liability for One's Own Acts', 15 *Loyola of Los Angeles International and Comparative Law Journal* (June 1993) p. 813 (references omitted).

3   *Guiding Principles on Business and Human Rights: Implementing the United Nations "Protect, Respect and Remedy" Framework*, Report of the Special Representative of the Secretary-General on the issue of human rights and transnational corporations and other business enterprises, John Ruggie, A/HRC/17/31, 21 March 2011, (hereinafter Guiding Principles), p. 6.

4   Ibid., para. I.A.2.

Commentary exemplifies with "domestic measures with extraterritorial implications [such as] requirements on 'parent' companies to report on the global operations of the entire enterprise".[5] Home countries are thus invited to address the core companies headquartered in their jurisdictions, and their international operations.

Furthermore, Pillar 2, dealing with the corporate responsibility to respect human rights, refers to "adverse human rights impacts either through their own activities or as a result of their business relationships with other parties".[6] For further clarity, "'business relationships' are understood to include relationships with business partners, entities in its value chain, and any other non-State or State entity directly linked to its business operations, products or services".[7] Abuses occurring in affiliate operations are thus clearly relevant in defining a core company's RtR.

Finally, in Pillar 3, which is dedicated to remedies, Ruggie is mindful of "legal, practical and other relevant barriers that could lead to a denial of access to remedy".[8] Among the potential legal barriers lies "the way in which legal responsibility is attributed among members of a corporate group under domestic criminal and civil laws facilitates the avoidance of appropriate accountability".[9] In his previous reports, Ruggie expanded on issues of legal separation of entities and limited liability, most often in relation to judicial remedy discussions.[10]

So the special case of core companies is clearly acknowledged in Ruggie's reports. So are two different situations where their responsibility might be invoked; indeed, core companies at the top of business groups or at the centre of business networks can be related to abuses in different ways depending on whether a contribution to harm was made or not. According to Ruggie, the core companies are expected to:

(a) Avoid causing or *contributing to adverse human rights impacts through their own activities*, and address such impacts when they occur;

---

5  *Ibid.*, Commentary on para. I.A.2.
6  *Ibid.*, Commentary on para. II.A.13.
7  *Ibid.*, Commentary on para. II.A.13.
8  *Ibid.*, para. III.B.26.
9  *Ibid.*, Commentary on para. III.B.26.
10 Ruggie wrote in 2008: "[T]he legal framework regulating transnational corporations operates much as it did long before the recent wave of globalization. A parent company and its subsidiaries continue to be construed as distinct legal entities. Therefore, the parent company is generally not liable for wrongs committed by a subsidiary, even where it is the sole shareholder, unless the subsidiary is under such close operational control by the parent that it can be seen as its mere agent. Furthermore, despite the transformative changes in the global economic landscape generated by offshore sourcing, purchasing goods and services even from sole suppliers remains an unrelated party transaction. Factors such as these make it exceedingly difficult to hold the extended enterprise accountable for human rights harm." *Protect, Respect and Remedy: A Framework for Business and Human Rights*, Report of the Special Representative of the Secretary-General on the issue of human rights and transnational corporations and other business enterprises, A/HRC/8/5, 2008, para. 13.

(b) Seek to prevent or mitigate adverse human rights impacts that are directly linked to their operations, products or services by their business relationships, *even if they have not contributed to those impacts*.[11]

So Ruggie draws an important distinction between contributing to affiliate's misconduct and merely being associated with a misbehaving affiliate. What are the consequences that flow from this distinction?

### 2.2. Spectre of Overreaching

So there can be responsibility for affiliate misconduct. That can be very demanding for business enterprises with presence in dozens of countries and counting their affiliates in the hundreds or thousands. As the core company has a responsibility to act when affiliates' operations infringe human rights, the spectre of overreaching begins to loom over the RtR. Ruggie deals with the problem in different ways. One is prioritising the most *severe impacts*.[12] Thus, "business enterprises should first seek to prevent and mitigate those that are most severe or where delayed response would make them irremediable".[13]

Another way is to emphasise due diligence; the nature of the RtR is to act reasonably, with care. Ruggie further highlights the flexibility and context-specificity of due diligence measures. More or less advanced due diligence measures, requiring commensurate resources, might suffice depending on many factors: "The responsibility of business enterprises to respect human rights applies to all enterprises regardless of their size, sector, operational context, ownership and structure. Nevertheless, the *scale and complexity of the means* through which enterprises meet that responsibility may vary according to these factors and with the severity of the enterprise's adverse human rights impacts".[14] Furthermore on business groups, he remarks that "the means through which a business enterprise meets its responsibility to respect human rights may also vary depending on whether, and the extent to which, it conducts business through a corporate group or individually".[15]

Finally, the buyer company is not expected to provide *remediation* regarding its suppliers' misbehaviour. The Commentary explains: "Where adverse impacts have occurred that the business enterprise has not caused or contributed to, but which are directly linked to its operations, products or services by a business relationship, the responsibility to respect human rights does not require that the enterprise itself provide for remediation, though it may take a role in doing so."[16] Only where the company has

---

11   *Guiding Principles*, *supra* note 3, para. II.A.13. (emphasis added).
12   See *Ibid.*, Commentary on para. II.A.14, for a definition of 'severity'.
13   *Ibid.*, para. II.A.24.
14   *Ibid.*, para. II.A.14 (emphasis added).
15   *Ibid.*, Commentary on para. II.A.14. This rather cryptic passage can be read in conjunction with the leverage discussion in the Commentary on para. II.B.19.
16   *Ibid.*, Commentary on para. II.B.22.

contributed to adverse impacts should it "provide for or cooperate in their remediation through legitimate processes".[17] If Ruggie does not call for remediation, he still calls on buyers to prevent or mitigate potential impacts as part of their RtR.[18]

So far Ruggie affirmed a core company's responsibility to act to address affiliate misdeeds. Also the separation of entities principle has been acknowledged as a business and legal reality. He also drew some limitations on the RtR, correct ones, but nonetheless limitations that inherently cannot answer the foundational question: why does a core company have to act where it apparently did not contribute to its affiliates' harmful impacts? Given that the separation principle can destroy the very foundation of a core company's responsibility to act, how does Ruggie square this principle with his RtR?

## 2.3. *Elephant in the Room: The Separation of Entities Norm*

Affiliates, from a legal perspective and a management of legal risks angle, are separate entities, and liability for misconduct remains localised with the affiliate. Only if the legal separation privilege is abused – the affiliate becoming an *alter ego* due to the core company controlling and dictating the affiliate's decisions[19] – will the limited liability benefit be lifted and the core company become liable for an affiliate's misdeeds.[20] The bottom-line is that sceptical core companies will ask: why are we held responsible for what third parties do when we did not contribute through our conduct to the harm inflicted?

Ruggie is too realistic to rely on the enterprise liability doctrine, which would overrule limited liability altogether. He does not advance this theory. Actually he deliberately does not advance *any* theory; one searches in vain for a principled treatment or guidance on how to allocate responsibility within corporate groups and networks. He deems it unnecessary for purposes of RtR. What Ruggie does is to skilfully relegate

---

17 *Ibid.*, para. II.B.22.
18 "Potential impacts should be addressed through prevention or mitigation, while actual impacts – those that have already occurred – should be a subject for remediation (Principle 22)." *Ibid.*, Commentary on para. II.B.17.
19 The ISO 26000 Guidance refers to control as "ability to dictate the decisions and activities of another party". It affirms responsibility "for the impacts of decisions and activities over which it has formal and/or de facto control (de facto control refers to situation where one organization has the ability to dictate the decisions and activities of another party, even where it does not have the legal or formal authority to do so)". ISO, *Guidance on Social Responsibility, ISO 26000*, 2010, para. 5.2.3.
20 If not for its abuse by the core company, the legal separation of entities principle can be lifted for reasons of public policy. These public policies respond to national priorities that seem not to be necessarily present in the vast majority of international CSR cases. The 'enterprise liability' doctrine is exceptionally employed in some areas of law – tax, environmental, disclosure laws – but in tort law limited liability remains the rule: "In relation to tort liability enterprise analysis has made virtually no impact." P. Muchlinski, 'Limited liability and multinational enterprises: a case for reform?', 34 *Cambridge Journal of Economics* (2010) p. 920.

legal separation as an issue of remedies, as a barrier to judicial remedies, discussed in Pillar 3.[21] Limited liability is thus downplayed as one among other barriers to remedies that should be lowered and dealt with in light of national legal specificities. In this way Ruggie effectively banishes legal separation from his concept of corporate responsibility elaborated in Pillar 2. He buries it in Pillar 3.

Does it matter that Ruggie places the separation of entities (legal) principle in Pillar 3 instead of Pillar 2? It would not really if the foundation for the core company's RtR was elaborated in a principled fashion and taking fully into account the separation principle. This treatment cannot be found in Ruggie's reports. Instead, Ruggie advances a RtR which is applicable to all companies, by drawing on soft law and societal expectations.[22] When applied to the specific situation of core companies, this foundation proves at a closer analysis truly weak: it rests on a raw societal norm placed on a collision course with the separation of entities principle.[23]

### 2.4. Verdict –Pluses and Deficiencies in Ruggie's Treatment

Ruggie can be commended for the broad reach of his RtR. He has made it clear that a core company is responsible for its decisions that are the single cause or, most often, one of the causes of abuses occurring in affiliate operations. A company that contributed to harm breaches the RtR. The fact that such abuse took place in the operations of a legally separated entity such as suppliers is not decisive; in other words, the legal separation of entities does not derail the RtR. The core company will remain responsible for the impacts of its own decisions rippling through its enterprise. Such a company will appear complicit in abuse. Furthermore, Ruggie protects the RtR from the danger of overreaching through several limitations: severe impacts are prioritised, the due diligence steps are reasonable and take into account the context, and no remediation is expected from buyer companies.

Also praiseworthy is the clear affirmation that not only 'contribution' but also 'association' may trigger due diligence; it is important to cover both of these types of conduct of a core company. On the foundation of why core companies have to act when affiliates infringe rights without contribution from the core company, Ruggie fails to persuade.[24] 'Contributing' to harm is rather different from being 'associated' with the

---

21 *Guiding Principles, supra* note 3, Commentary on para. III.B.26.
22 *Business and human rights: Towards operationalizing the "protect, respect and remedy" framework*, Report of the Special Representative of the Secretary-General on the issue of human rights and transnational corporations and other business enterprises, A/HRC/11/13, 22 April 2009, paras. 46–47.
23 In another article I analysed Ruggie's reports looking for the building blocks that support the RtR: soft law as the authoritative policy pronouncements of states, a social norm reflecting societal expectations, and the complicity jurisprudence and discourse. See section III in R. Mares, 'A gap in the corporate responsibility to respect human rights', 36 *Monash University Law Review* (2011).
24 Wood considered that "for all his emphasis on due diligence and complicity, Professor Ruggie is ultimately unclear about what kind and degree of connection to third-party hu-

affiliate and this changes the RtR equation significantly. In the latter case the separation principle weighs much more heavily: its very purpose is to keep associated but separately incorporated entities under the law separate for purposes of liability.

The culpable conduct of the core company is not pinpointed conceptually and the limited liability norm is not treated as a structural feature of business groups raising challenges for the RtR, but as a feature of legal systems hindering access to judicial remedies. This is an ambiguous treatment of the separation principle that is problematic as it diverts attention from a key problem. The conflict herein between the RtR and the separation principle is real. A treatment combining silence and 'pillar playing' can only fail to persuade a critical reader anchored in legal and business realities.[25] Ruggie's RtR concept for core companies is ingenious but ultimately unpersuasive.

My concern with Ruggie's treatment is that his RtR, despite being nominally applicable to multinational companies, will succumb to the pressure of the separation of entities principle and become atomised into a collection of RtR of each entity in the business group or network. Yes, the decisions of core companies rippling through affiliate operations will be covered by the RtR.[26] But, to the extent that core companies leave affiliates to operate autonomously (under a general, strategic mandate of making profits without further direction or operational interference), the core companies are off the hook because the separation principle will defeat the non-conceptual affirmation of RtR that Ruggie makes. The core company's responsibility to act needs to be justified more carefully.[27]

Overall I would prefer to deem Ruggie's treatment as 'incomplete'. The RtR of core companies should not be discarded because Ruggie's is not flawed but has to be refined

---

man rights violations is sufficient to engage corporate responsibility". S. Wood, *In Defence of the Sphere of Influence: Why the WGSR should Not Follow Professor Ruggie's Advice on Defining the Scope of Social Responsibility*, 7 May 2010, <ssrn.com/abstract=1607438>.

25   A report commissioned by the SRSG report noted that "[s]ome form of 'separate legal personality' and 'limited liability' exist in all of the 39 jurisdictions" surveyed and concluded that "[m]ost of the surveyed jurisdictions have similar approaches to the concepts of separate legal personality and limited liability – it is rare for the 'corporate veil' to be pierced". *Human rights and corporate law: trends and observations from a crossnational study conducted by the Special Representative*, Addendum 2 to the Report, A/HRC/17/31/Add.2, 2011, paras. 31 and 49.

26   This is consistent with current tort laws. For example, British courts dealt with the claims that mercury-poisoned South African workers raised against a UK-based parent company. The claimants alleged the parent's culpable conduct consisting of negligent design, transfer, set-up, operation, supervision and monitoring of intrinsically hazardous process. *Sithole v. Thor Chemicals Holdings Ltd.*, [1999] EWCA (Civ) 706 (Eng.)

27   Why this emphasis on justification? The Guiding Principles have already been endorsed unanimously by states in the Human Rights Council. Is this not enough legitimacy, authority and justification for the RtR? Arguably not if such 'soft law' or policy pronouncements of the HRC are in conflict with established cornerstones of business law, such as the separation of entities principle. Because such international soft law could not trump long lasting national hard law, soft law would be relegated to mere 'aspirations' and possibly discarded altogether in practice.

and strengthened. The coming sections aim to reinforce the foundation under Ruggie's RtR by pinpointing the culpable conduct of the core company and using jurisprudential insights to build an RtR argument in the 'shadow of law.' This conceptual treatment could render the foundation of RtR clearer and more legitimate, and make it able to handle better attacks from sceptics mindful of the separation of entities principle.

## 3. Building Support for the RtR

The aim of this section is to introduce key characterisations that can sustain a core company's responsibility to act. What is the culpable conduct of core companies? What is special about human rights in less developed countries? What is the nature of the resulting responsibility? Insights from negligence jurisprudence will be offered with reference to certain provisions from the American Law Institute's (ALI) Restatement of Torts[28] and the Alien Tort Claims Act (ATCA) litigation in the US.

### 3.1. Culpable Conduct of the Core Company

In his treatment of the separation of entities principle, Ruggie rightly wishes to avoid offering an easy escape to companies: the mere thing an evasive company would have to do is to set up a legally separated subsidiary or write an outsourcing contract. If constrained by limited liability, the RtR would be defeated easily through legal formalities with the result of localising responsibility with some affiliates. As shown above, Ruggie's way out of this conundrum was to banish limited liability from Pillar 2 and account for it as a barrier to judicial remedies in Pillar 3. But, especially when 'association' rather than 'contribution' to harm is the imputed blameworthy conduct, it would be short-sighted to think about the separation of entities principle simply as a legal obstacle; it is more properly understood as a legal, economic and social norm.[29]

A more coherent treatment, though unavoidably more complex, which in the context of the Special Representative of the Secretary General mandate would not be an asset, would rightly begin by focusing on potential abuses of the legal separation principle. After that, Ruggie could have put the spotlight on the key moment when the core company attempts to shed responsibility for its association with the subsidiary. This key moment is not the decision to set up the subsidiary, but the *decision of the core company to grant autonomy to the subsidiary.* Notably, imputing the conduct of the autonomous subsidiary to its parent is way more difficult than in the situation of the subsidiary that remains under the strategic and especially the operational control of the parent. In the latter case, autonomy is by definition diminished or even extinguished altogether. In such a case, based on current 'lifting the corporate veil' or negligent control legal doctrines, victims could already without controversy go directly after the parent company. The parent's wrongful conduct is clear and consists in

---

28   American Law Institute, *Restatement (Second) of Torts* (1965), (hereinafter Restatement of Torts)

29   Mares, *supra* note 23.

dictating decisions to the subsidiary and thus clearly causing or contributing to harm through its own actions.

Such intrusive conduct on the side of the parent company is not present when a subsidiary is autonomous. Still it is clear why such an autonomy-granting decision is problematic from a human rights angle: the core company sets up a separated entity in a dangerous environment (poorly governed developing country) and lets it loose with a certain mandate (profit-making) without any checks and oversight over subsidiary activities. Such an autonomy-granting decision creates risks for right holders overseas. It is for this decision that the core company should be held responsible under a due diligence standard. As a result, a duly diligent company would be free to set up subsidiaries but should retain some responsibility for initial structuring and on-going oversight.

What about other affiliates, such as contractors? Ruggie covers them with the term 'relationships'. Again the obstacle is in the separation principle, only that this time the buyer company cannot be accused that it abuses the limited liability norm by setting up legally separated entities, such as subsidiaries; the buyer merely outsources to pre-existing entities, the contractors and suppliers. What could be the culpable decision here?

The key decision of the buyer is not that of outsourcing *per se*, but *outsourcing to a risky contractor*, a contractor that poses foreseeable risks of human rights abuse. While outsourcing in itself is legitimate, the decision to outsource to irresponsible contractors without vetting and oversight procedures is problematic. Notably, tort jurisprudence already has remarkable provisions in this area, to be discussed below, which Ruggie unfortunately does not exploit to establish a responsibility of buyer companies to act.

This boils down to saying that a core company's responsibility to act does not result naturally from a broad responsibility to respect, that is, 'to do no harm';[30] it is additional to that and needs to be justified separately. A public comment sent to Ruggie after the Draft Guiding Principles were unveiled in late 2010 makes this point rather clear when discussing the parent-subsidiary relationship. It happens that the Guiding Principles ended up being lapidary on the separation of entities principle, while the Draft version offered more insight into how Ruggie attempted to deal with business groups.[31] In his comment on the Draft Principles, Muchlinsky, an authority in the field of corporate groups, wrote: "I am a little baffled why a subjective approach is taken to the identification of the group. It opens the way for a purely subjective definition of which entities are in the group or not and allows individual directors to allocate human rights responsibility in the group as they see fit … I think it is much easier to

---

30   *Protect, Respect and Remedy, supra* note 10, para. 24.

31   The Commentary on Principle 12 stated: "A corporate group may consider itself to be a single business enterprise, in which case the responsibility to respect human rights attaches to the group as a whole and encompasses both the corporate parent and its subsidiaries and affiliates. Alternatively, entities in a corporate group may consider themselves distinct business enterprises, in which case the responsibility to respect attaches to them individually and extends to their relationships with other entities – both within the group and beyond – that are connected to their activities." *Draft Guiding Principles*, Commentary on Principle 12, 2010.

say that all entities in the group have a responsibility to respect human rights and that *parent and holding companies have a responsibility to oversee* that their subsidiaries respect human rights ..."[32]

But the responsibility to oversee needs to be justified. As suggested herein, it helps whether this additional responsibility of core companies can be justified by identifying a culpable decision of the core company itself. Even more, it would be preferable to characterise the core company's conduct as a commission rather than omission and thus strengthen the foundation further.

### 3.2. Conduct by Commission

One of my aims has been to find a way to deal with the passivity of core companies in face of affiliate abuses. Pinpointing and reframing the core company's culpable conduct is a key move in the effort to attribute responsibility not for what third parties do, but for what the actor did when it entered into a business relationship that raised peculiar risks of harm. The parent company acted when it set up the subsidiary and then left it to its own devices in an environment riddled with risks of human rights abuses; the buyer company acted when it decided to outsource production without checking the human rights practices of its suppliers and to keep the relationship going when notices of abuse were provided.

It is important to reframe, if possible, inactions into actions. Culpability for omissions is always more problematic. As it was noted, "the prohibition of omissions is far more intrusive upon the individuals' autonomy and freedom than is the prohibition of acts, which is why the systematic imposition of (criminal or civil) liability for failures to act is to be resisted".[33]

This reframing is not unknown to tort jurisprudence. Thus Fletcher wrote that as the law of negligence evolved, "the failure to exercise due care – an omission – came to be seen as part of affirmative risks to others – the risks of driving, of medical care, of handling weapons, of manufacturing goods. In the context of these larger activities, the *omission is but an epicycle on the arc of risk generated by the affirmative conduct.* The omission becomes a minor part of the actor's assertive conduct ... *The fault was not the passivity of an omission, but the affirmative wrong of creating an unreasonable risk.*"[34] McCarthy wrote about the "conversion of omissions into actions, by simply taking a broader view of the activity".[35]

---

[32] P. Muchlinski, *Comments on the Draft Guiding Principles for Business and Human Rights*, January 2011, (emphasis added).

[33] The Law Commission (UK), *Participating in Crime*, (LAW COM No 305), 2007, para. 3.26, <www.justice.gov.uk/lawcommission/docs/lc305_Participating_in_Crime_report.pdf>.

[34] G. P. Fletcher, 'The Fault of Not Knowing', 3 *Theoretical Inquiries in Law* (July 2002) p. 265 (emphasis added).

[35] F. B. McCarthy, 'Crimes of Omission in Pennsylvania', 68 *Temple Law Review* (Summer 1995) p. 633.

A rather analogous situation is what Deakin discussed in the context of an employer's liability for the intentional torts of employees.[36] Customarily, the employer is not liable for the intentional wrongdoings of its employees. But in *Lister* v. *Hesley Hall* (2001), Lord Clyde was concerned that "it becomes inappropriate to concentrate too closely on the particular act complained of" and therefore the intentional wrong can be seen as one aspect of a larger pattern of conduct.[37] This being said, it should not be overlooked that when such reframing of omission into commission is performed, issues of proximity, remoteness and causality reassert themselves vigorously to limit potential liability. Therefore one needs to tread cautiously and see this as a reminder that we are still in the realm of exception from the no-liability-for-omissions rule. The foundation for a responsibility to act needs to be reinforced further.

The core company's responsibility to act needs to be further strengthened and limited to be legitimate. Not all misconduct of any affiliate should attract a responsibility to act from the core company. Only some risks of harm will be relevant. They have to do with the vulnerability of right holders in less developed countries. Noteworthy is that it will be a special type of vulnerability.

### 3.3. *Vulnerability of Stakeholders*

Vulnerability is a key concept in justifying a responsibility to act imposed on the core company. Some illustrations are in order. For local communities, setting up extractive operations on their land or in their neighbourhood can spell disaster. Dispossession of land, often without proper compensation;[38] abuses by security forces against restless local populations; pollution that affects access to food, water, health and livelihoods; and unmitigated effects of migration inflows that typically trigger higher prices, put pressure on infrastructure, increase transmittable diseases and criminality are among the usual risks for local communities, especially where regulatory gaps loom wide.[39] For indigenous people, with their special needs to have their way of life and culture preserved, the risks are obvious and well documented.[40]

Moving further to other sectors, such as in labour-intensive industries where production has been outsourced, the risks that employees encounter are well documented: child labour, discriminatory practices, union busting, and more broadly 'sweatshop' working conditions characterised by low pay, long hours, poor health and safety pro-

---

36  S. Deakin, 'Enterprise-Risk: The Juridical Nature of the Firm Revisited', 32 *Industrial Law Journal* (June 2003) p. 97.
37  Quoted in *ibid*. To keep liability for such torts within reasonable limits, courts devised the 'test of sufficient connection'. *Ibid*.
38  R. Mares, 'Corporate responsibility and compliance with the law: land, dispossession and aftermath at Newmont's Ahafo project in Ghana', *Business and Society Review* (2011).
39  Extractive Industries Review, *Striking a Better Balance*, World Bank, 2004; UNCTAD, *World Investment Report 2007: Transnational Corporations, Extractive Industries and Development*, 2007.
40  *Report of the Special Rapporteur on the situation of human rights and fundamental freedoms of indigenous people*, Rodolfo Stavenhagen, E/CN.4/2003/90, p. 2.

tections, and intimidation and abuse of all kinds. These practices are almost standard in factories where laws are weak, labour inspectors rare, and unions repressed.

The result is that right holders are in a state of vulnerability. To be clear, such vulnerability does not have to do with *poverty*, which is pervasive in less developed countries and exists even in developed countries where pockets of poverty persist. Neither does this refer to being vulnerable to *harm from business operations*; all residents in both developed and less developed countries are exposed to harm when industrial processes go wrong. It has to do with the *absence of effective remedies*. This is a specific type of vulnerability: that of being vulnerable to having no remedies when risks materialise. Such vulnerability comes precisely from regulatory gaps and the ineffective remedies right holders have at their disposal. These are the 'governance gaps' that Ruggie refers to in his writings. So the situation creating problems for the core company is not the risk of harm but the risk of *unremedied* harm in affiliate operations. Where right holders systematically lack institutional channels to contest human rights abuses and poor working conditions, this is disabling and highly problematic from a human rights perspective.

I propose that the issue of remedies is crucial for definitions of vulnerability. Were remedies at national level effective, a core company's action would be redundant. However where those remedies are ineffective, the responsibility of core companies becomes essential. So the interaction between responsibility to act (Pillar 2) and access to remedies (Pillar 3) is a substantive one, not a procedural one:[41] the very existence of a core company's responsibility to act depends on the state of remedies practically available to right holders.

Now I turn to jurisprudence for further insights on when vulnerability and risks trigger a responsibility to act. The American Law Institute's Restatement of Torts will be used as illustration. Certain characterisations relevant to RtR as applied to core companies can be gleaned from tort jurisprudence in relation to elements such as foreseeability of harms, 'peculiar' risks, non-delegable duties, obligation of careful selection of contractors and obligation to take special precautions.

### 3.4. *Foreseeability of Risk of Harm in Affiliate Activities*

Previously I pinpointed the culpable conduct of the core company: the autonomy-granting decision after a subsidiary was set up, respectively the outsourcing to a contractor, with disregard to the risks of abuse posed in weakly governed host countries. Risks of abuse are foreseeable in both cases. The Restatement of Torts has a broad

---

41  The relationship between Pillars 2 and 3 was discussed by Catá Backer in 2009: "For the moment it is not clear whether the Third Pillar is merely the dependent on the substantive elaborations of the First and Second Pillars, or whether the Third Pillar serves as an independent source of substantive standards. It would seem that the later approach is more in keeping with the work of the SRSG. But the temptation to reduce the Third Pillar to a set of mechanics is still strong." L. Catá Backer, 'On the Evolution of the United Nations' "Protect-Respect-Remedy" Project: The State, the Corporation and Human Rights in a Global Governance Context', 9:1 *Santa Clara J. int'l Law* (2010).

clause applicable to both settings discussed herein. Namely, section 302, which talks about an actor's negligent conduct where it involves an unreasonable risk of harm to another through the foreseeable action of a third person.[42] This provision covers the negligent or intentional misconduct of the third party.

The Comment on section 302 explains the negligence in a situation "[w]here the actor has *brought into contact or association* with the other a person whom the actor knows or should know to be peculiarly likely to commit intentional misconduct, under circumstances which afford a peculiar opportunity or temptation for such misconduct".[43] This description seems tailor-made for large infrastructure projects such as those in the extractive industry, especially in greenfield projects. There a parent company commences mining operations that are bound to bring in contact the local communities with new and potentially irresponsible actors, such as security forces, corrupt officials, abusive contractors, and the parent's own autonomous subsidiary. A positive find of minerals brings in all these actors that can and have committed human rights abuses against local communities.

One can argue that, by taking the decision to develop a mine (or more generally a large infrastructure project), the core company abroad brought local communities in contact with actors that were not present there before mining operations commenced. For this reason, the mining company has a responsibility to act and address risks presented by its subsidiary and its local partners. The undeniable fact is that setting up a mining operation does create risks of harm for local communities, risks that are more likely and severe when the legal frameworks are weak. A responsibility to act should be recognised to cover those parent companies based overseas that fail to influence their subsidiaries, which *directly*[44] or *indirectly through its partners* infringed with impunity the rights of local communities.

The idea that harm is foreseeable is present in the case of contracting as well.[45] If the core company does not select diligently a competent contractor, harm is likely to follow. Following the Restatement's section 411, the tort idea of 'proper selection' holds the hiring party liable for harm to third persons for "failure to exercise reasonable

---

42   "A negligent act or omission may be one which involves an unreasonable risk of harm to another through either (a) the continuous operation of a force started or continued by the act or omission, or (b) the *foreseeable action of* the other, *a third person*, an animal, or a force of nature." Section 302, *Restatement of Torts, supra* note 28.

43   *Ibid.*, Section 302, Comment (emphasis added).

44   Leigh Day & Co, *Shell accepts responsibility for oil spill in Nigeria*, 3 August 2011, <www.leighday.co.uk/news/news-archive-2011/shell-accepts-responsibility-for-oil-spill-in>.

45   Previously I presented the foreseeable risk of harm when the company brought right holders into contact with perpetrators. This seems to work much better for contractors that harm *non-employees*, such as local communities harmed by security contractors. They were brought into contact by the company. But one cannot argue that the buyer brought the supplier and its *employees* into contact, as they were already employed before the order was placed. So employees are not properly covered by this reasoning of bringing in contact under Section 302. Instead they are covered by the specific provisions on contracting such as sections 411 and 413 below.

care to employ a competent and careful contractor".⁴⁶ The Restatement explains that the "words 'competent and careful contractor' denote a contractor who possesses the knowledge, skill, experience, and available equipment which a reasonable man would realize that a contractor must have in order to do the work which he is employed to do without creating unreasonable risk of injury to others, and who also possesses the personal characteristics which are equally necessary".⁴⁷

So an employer can be held liable for the actions of an independent contractor if the employer was negligent in hiring or retaining that contractor, if the employer knew, or should have known with reasonable care, that the contractor was reckless or incompetent. Calvert Hanson mentions a US case that concerned

> an inexperienced independent contractor hired to dispose of pressurized cylinders containing hazardous chemicals. The Virginia Supreme Court concluded that there was "no conflict in the evidence of [the hiring party's] failure to investigate" and that "there can be no doubt that [the independent contractor's] incompetence was the ultimate cause of the losses claimed in this case." In this case, the failure to thoroughly investigate the contractor coupled with the hiring of the untrained contractor was the cause of the harm, thus providing the requisite linkage.⁴⁸

Another case involved a company that had an "aggressive indifference to the fitness of its vendor", indifference that could have resulted in liability under a negligent selection theory.⁴⁹

This clause on negligent selection covers foreseeable risks in general. Should 'peculiar' risks arise, not only does an obligation of 'proper selection' apply but also an additional obligation to 'take special precautions'. Section 413 of the Restatement indicates that special precautions are called for when an independent contractor poses a peculiar risk of harm; the employer might be liable if these precautions are not taken.⁵⁰ The Commentary further explains that

---

46   "An employer is subject to liability for physical harm to third persons caused by his failure to exercise reasonable care to employ a competent and careful contractor (a) to do work which will involve a risk of physical harm unless it is skillfully and carefully done, or (b) to perform any duty which the employer owes to third persons." Section 411, *Restatement of Torts, supra* note 28.

47   *Ibid.*, Section 411, Comment a.

48   L. S. Calvert Hanson, 'Employers Beware! Negligence in the Selection of an Independent Contractor Can Subject You to Legal Liability', 5 *University of Miami Business Law Journal* (Spring 1995) p. 129 (references omitted).

49   *Ibid.*

50   The fulltext reads: "One who employs an independent contractor to do work which the employer should recognize as likely to create, during its progress, a *peculiar unreasonable risk of physical harm* to others unless *special precautions* are taken, is subject to liability for physical harm caused to them by the absence of such precautions if the employer (a) fails to *provide in the contract* that the contractor shall take such precautions, or (b) fails to exercise reasonable care to *provide in some other manner* for the taking of such precautions." Section 413, *Restatement of Torts, supra* note 28.

[t]his Section is concerned with special risks, peculiar to the work to be done, and arising out of its character, or out of the place where it is to be done, against which a reasonable man would recognize the necessity of taking special precautions ... "Peculiar" does not mean that the risk must be one which is abnormal to the type of work done, or that it must be an abnormally great risk ... The court stated that peculiar risk did not imply an abnormal risk, but rather, a recognizable danger arising from the work itself which has gone untended. Whether the work involved created a peculiar risk was a question of fact.[51]

In tort it seems that 'peculiar' risks arise out of 'inherently dangerous' activities.[52] In many corporate social responsibility (CSR) cases it would be too much of a stretch to consider risks of unremedied harm as 'peculiar'. But given the strong normativity of human rights and the absence of remedies, which in classical tort are available through tort litigation, I would argue that risks of unremedied harm are a special category of 'peculiar-light' risks that require some special precautions to be taken, some responsibility to act. This characterisation of risks of unremedied harm as 'peculiar' risks is not decisive as we can always default on 'foreseeable risks'; but the characterisation can further strengthen the legitimacy of a responsibility to act and covers not only initial selection but some on-going oversight of the supplier as well.

Noteworthy, ATCA cases often refer to the tort of negligence. In *Doe* v. *Unocal* (Burma), the broad argument was that "Unocal owed a duty to plaintiffs to exercise due care in conducting its international ventures".[53] Plaintiffs argued various doctrines, including negligence, negligent hiring, negligent supervision,[54] and negligent infliction of emotional distress. In *Doe* v. *Exxon* (Indonesia), the plaintiffs alleged that the "[d]efendants failed to exercise reasonable care in selecting, hiring, retaining and contracting" with the military and police forces; the defendants knew or reasonably should have known that the military and police forces would violate rights.[55] The judge dealt at length with issues of negligence in selection.[56] In *Roe* v. *Bridgestone* (Liberia),

---

51   Ibid., Section 416, Comment b (refers to and makes applicable Section 413).
52   Activities deemed to be inherently dangerous are the construction of reservoirs, handling of vicious animals, work involving electric wires, blasting, the production of firework exhibitions, and crop dusting. U. Gasser, *Responsibility for human rights violations, acts or omissions, within the 'sphere of influence' of companies*, The Berkman Center for Internet & Society at Harvard Law School, Research Publication No. 2007-12, 2007.
53   *Doe* v. *Unocal*, <upload.wikimedia.org/wikipedia/commons/b/b0/Doe_v_Unocal_Plaintiffs_Complaint_and_conformed_face_sheet.pdf>.
54   While negligent selection covers *independent contractors*, negligent supervision covers *agents* that the company controls and instructs. Independent contractors and agents are very different categories; the former conducts its enterprise independently as it fulfils the contract with the buyer, while the latter conducts its activities under the control and instructions of the principal. Therefore the principal has a duty of supervision, which the employer of the contractor does not.
55   *Doe* v. *Exxon* (original complaint), 11 June 2001, para. 112, <www.iradvocates.org/exxon-complaint.pdf>.
56   L. F. Oberdorfer (United States District Judge), *Memorandum & Opinion, John Doe I, et al.*, v. *Exxon Mobil Corporation, et al.*, Civil Action No. 01-1357 (LFO), United States Dis-

the plaintiffs argued, under Californian law, that the defendants were negligent and reckless because they knew that the plaintiffs were subjected to forced labour and, because they failed to exercise reasonable care to prevent these harms, they increased the risk of injury to the plaintiffs. The plaintiffs also claimed that the defendants were negligent in hiring and supervision, which was a major cause of the conditions allowing forced labour on the plantation.[57] In *Doe v. Chiquita Brands International* (Columbia), the plaintiffs invoked the company's negligent infliction of emotional distress as well as negligence, negligent hiring, and negligence *per se*.[58]

Surprisingly though, and despite numerous ATCA complaints invoking negligence law, CSR writings seeking to justify corporate responsibilities have appealed predominantly to complicity jurisprudence rather than negligence. The CSR discourse is overwhelmingly coated in complicity and 'aiding and abetting' terminology rather than negligence. This is justifiable when the core company 'contributed' to harm, but hardly so when the core company was merely being passive and 'associated' through normal business relationship with its affiliate.[59]

It should be remembered that this discussion of the buyer-contractor relation covers situations where the buyer did *not* impose stringent contractual requirements that forced the supplier into corner-cutting and labour rights abuses;[60] then the buyer's responsibility would have followed directly. Here the contract is assumed as in line with industry practices and thus apparently fair. Does this mean the buyer has no further responsibility to act? Does a *fair contract* mean that the buyer has a *fair relationship*

---

trict Court for the District of Columbia, 27 August 2008, <ecf.dcd.uscourts.gov/cgi-bin/show_public_doc?2001cv1357-365>.

57  *Plaintiffs' memorandum of points and authorities in opposition to Defendants' motion to dismiss*, 20 March 2006, <www.iradvocates.org/Opposition%20to%20Motion%20to%20Dismiss040306.pdf>.

58  *Doe v. Chiquita Brands International*, 18 July 2007, pp. 27-29, <www.earthrights.org/sites/default/files/legal/cbi-final-complaint-signed.pdf>.

59  Among the exceptions is a study that took note of responsibility of the employer for the acts of the independent contractor: "In certain cases, the concept of negligence may impute to business entities a minimum duty to avoid harming others in an unreasonable fashion ... For example, if a company hires members of another state's military forces for security purposes but fails to take sufficient measures to prevent them from torturing civilians in the course of providing "security," it is conceivable that the company's failure to implement protective measures could result in a determination of negligence, and that it would be required by a court to compensate the harmed individuals." International Peace Academy and FAFO AIS, *Business and International Crimes: Assessing the Liability of Business Entities for Grave Violations of International Law*, Executive Summary, 2004, p. 21.

60  In the *Wal-Mart* case the plaintiffs alleged that the company "knowingly impose[d] time and price requirements in its supplier agreement that necessarily result[ed] in abysmal conditions in Plaintiffs' factories". S. Meyerzon Nagiel, 'An Overlooked Gateway to Victim Compensation: How States Can Provide a Forum for Human Rights Claims', *Columbia Journal of Transnational Law* (2007). In the *Bridgestone (Liberia)* case, plaintiffs alleged that the buyer breaches its RtR by setting unfair contractual terms, <www.iradvocates.org/Firestone%20Complaint%20Final1105.pdf>.

with the suppliers' employees and other right holders? Writing a fair outsourcing contract is necessary but not sufficient to make the buyer's conduct legitimate; the buyer company can appear negligent unless it engages in careful selection and takes further precautions against risks elevated to 'peculiar risk' status. Buyers cannot claim no responsibility to act in regard to the abusive practices of suppliers. It is blameworthy to disregard foreseeable and peculiar risks to workers arising out of the process through which the buyer's goods are made.

### 3.5. Evolution of Law

The analysis so far deliberately rejected a view that such risks of unremedied harm in affiliate operations is normal, routine risks of business activity that fall exclusively within the responsibility of the affiliate. While the rule of non-liability applies and will not be abandoned, jurisprudence has amassed quite a number of exceptions to this rule. Here we want to note this remarkable evolution of tort jurisprudence and put RtR discussions into perspective. The limited liability principle does not operate in a social vacuum and does not offer a blanket protection to core companies.

The legal rule was explained in the Restatement of Torts: "[S]ince the employer has no power of control over the manner in which the work is to be done by the contractor, it is to be regarded as the contractor's own enterprise, and he, rather than the employer, is the proper party to be charged with the responsibility of preventing the risk, and bearing and distributing it …".[61] As Pearce noted, "the rationale behind this rule is that an independent contractor, by definition, does not fall under the control of an employer. While the employer and independent contractor agree on the task to be completed, the independent contractor has *control of its own work* and the *manner in which it performs* the work".[62]

Interestingly though, as the Restatement points out, the law has progressed via the recognition of a large number of exceptions to the general rule. These exceptions are so numerous now and have so far "eroded the 'general rule,' that it can now be said to be 'general' only in the sense that it is applied where no good reason is found for departing from it".[63] The reasons, that is, policy reasons in developed countries, why tort law looks beyond independent contractors are quite clear. One has to do with the fact that such contractors are simply individuals that may not be *solvent*, and thus not in a position to satisfy tort judgments against them because they are not in business anymore. Also the employer might have a possibility of *effective loss distribution* in ways that might not always be feasible for the independent contractor.[64] Another reason is

---

61  Section 409, Comment b, *Restatement of Torts*, supra note 28.
62  J. A. Pearce II, 'The Dangerous Intersection of Independent Contractor Law and the Immigration Reform and Control Act: The Impact of the Wal-Mart Settlement', 10 *Lewis & Clark Law Review* (Fall 2006) p. 597 (references omitted) (emphasis added).
63  Section 409, Comment b, *Restatement of Torts*, supra note 28.
64  E. Adjin-Tettey, 'Accountability of Public Authorities through Contextualized Determinations of Vicarious Liability and Non-Delegable Duties', 57 *University of New Brunswick Law Journal* (2007) p. 46.

that tort aims to "provide a timely and effective remedy for victims who do not have to worry about the *identity of the contractor*".[65] Finally, other policy factors play a role in anchoring such duties, as McLachlin explained: "the *reasonable expectation of vulnerable parties* in protective relationships" and "the *practical difficulties* that such persons might experience in trying to obtain compensation from independent contractors".[66]

The above reference to vulnerability resonates well with the present CSR argument, although vulnerability in protective relationships covers narrower situations such as that of children in foster homes. In CSR situations, the vulnerability resulting from risks of unremedied harms is different, but still they both have in common the need to account for special circumstances that those who suffer the harm find themselves in. Proponents of the RtR can take note of the evolution of tort law in this area where those harmed by outsourced operations were deemed vulnerable enough to obtain recourse against the contractor's employer. Law has proved highly dynamic, singled out blameworthy conduct and legitimised claims against entities' outsourcing activities despite the separation of entities principle. Also in relation to vulnerability, jurisprudence offers us another useful categorisation: that of non-delegable duties.

### 3.6. Responsibility to Act as Non-Delegable Duty to Maintain Safety

The notion of non-delegability has been articulated in tort jurisprudence to cover situations of vulnerability. Adjin-Tettey deems it a "unique pragmatic approach in response to the special vulnerability of potential victims … There does not appear to be a closed category of protective relationships for which non-delegable duties arise. This seems to be a flexible approach deployed for justice in particular cases where to do otherwise would effectively leave plaintiffs without a remedy".[67]

This explicit emphasis on vulnerability and lack of remedy invites us to characterise the core company's responsibility to act as a responsibility to maintain safety and a non-delegable duty. At its core, the non-delegability doctrine implies that outsourcing operations does not result automatically in outsourcing responsibility for the safety of activities. The Restatement explains that "[t]he words 'non-delegable duty' do not imply that there are duties which cannot be discharged by appointing others to perform them. They describe duties the performance of which can properly be delegated to another person, but subject to the condition that liability follows if the person to whom the performance is delegated acts improperly with respect to it."[68] Thus "it is the liability resulting from the nondelegable duty's violation, not the performance of the duty, that is nondelegable".[69]

---

65   Ibid.
66   Quoted in *ibid*. (emphasis added).
67   Adjin-Tettey, *supra* note 64.
68   *Restatement (Second) of Agency*, Section 214, Comment a (1958).
69   J. D. Schminky, 'The Liability of the Government under the Federal Tort Claims Act for the Breach of a Nondelegable Duty Arising from the Performance of a Government Procurement Contract', 36 *Air Force Law Review* (1992).

Indeed as an effect of the limited liability principle, the responsibility to maintain safety is currently delegated implicitly to affiliates together with the act of outsourcing; those affiliates harm vulnerable workers and local communities and thus fail in their responsibility to maintain safety. It is this complete shedding of responsibility to maintain safety and diligently handle risks that the core company performs that is blameworthy and not the general conduct of outsourcing and setting up subsidiaries. The core company is not a mere bystander that fails to act but an actor that delegated responsibility to maintain safety to its affiliates. So the result is a non-delegable responsibility to act to maintain safety imposed on the core company when operations are conducted by affiliates operating in zones characterised by risks of unremedied harm. Is this an obligation to *ensure* safety throughout affiliate operations or an obligation to *take steps* and act with reasonable care? In other words, a responsibility of result or a responsibility of conduct?

### 3.7. Nature of the Responsibility to Act

In tort law the duty to maintain safety can result in either vicarious liability independent of fault or in fault-based liability when the outsourcing entity was culpable. Both types of liability can be encountered.[70] What should be the standard proposed for the international CSR area and for core companies? Ruggie has rightly warned that no silver bullet exists in the business and human rights area. In this particular case of the core company's responsibility, a silver bullet would be the 'enterprise liability' doctrine proposing vicarious liability of the core company for its affiliate misconduct.[71] That would make the foundation for a responsibility to act as unrealistic as it would be indefensible to propose that the core company has no responsibility for what affili-

---

[70] C. Witting, 'Non-Delegable Duties and Roads Authorities, Leichhardt Municipal Council v Montgomery', 32 *Melbourne University Law Review* (2008) p. 332. *See also Restatement (First) of Torts*, §§ 416–429, introductory note (1934) stating that nondelegable duties "lie midway between absolute duties to provide safe conditions and duties which are satisfied by the exercise of personal care". Quoted in Schminky, *ibid*.

[71] Commenting on the Draft Norms, Catá Backer wrote: "Since the definition of TNC does not recognize the distinct legal personalities of the corporations that together constitute the TNC, the Norms essentially pierce the corporate veil... The Norms produce a standard incompatible with the domestic corporate laws of a majority of states. Yet the Norms make little effort either to recognize or resolve this conflict ... The Norms internationalize and adopt an enterprise liability model as the basis for determining the scope of liability for groups of related companies. This approach does, in a very simple way, eliminate one of the great complaints about globalization through large webs of interconnected but legally independent corporations forming one large economic enterprise. The problem, of course, is that, as a matter of the domestic law of most states, the autonomous legal personality of a corporation matters. Most states have developed very strong public policies in favor of legal autonomy." L. Catá Backer, 'Multinational Corporations, Transnational Law: The United Nations' Norms on the Responsibilities of Transnational Corporations as a Harbinger of Corporate Social Responsibility in International Law', 37 *Columbia Human Rights Law Review* (2005) (references omitted).

ates do. Between these extremes, the middle ground would be to argue in favour of a responsibility based on the fault of the core company. This supports Ruggie's choice to propose due diligence as the key expectation society has from companies. In a previous section I have already identified what appears as the blameworthy conduct of the core company.

In agreement with Ruggie, the nature of this responsibility to act will be to exercise reasonable care. In this vein he draws attention to the due diligence steps companies should take and draws sensible limitations on the scope of due diligence expected from companies.[72] There is no need to expand on these issues in a paper dealing with the foundations of RtR.[73] The required course of action is to exercise reasonable care at different stages of the business relationship to maintain safety against the foreseeable risks of human rights abuse present in that operational setting. The 'reasonable person' standard is flexible and adaptable and constitutes a key concept in negligence jurisprudence, which is packed with such suggestive provisions and formulations.[74]

## 4. Further Research and Outstanding Issues

### 4.1. Strengthening the Foundation of RtR by Using Tort Jurisprudence

Many interesting legal doctrines[75] are raised in ATCA cases.[76] But the doctrine of negligence is particularly well suited to the issues discussed in this chapter. Still, bringing

---

72 Ruggie discusses excellently the content and limits of due diligence in supply chain when the buyer company does not contribute to harm. He commendably selected this issue for in-depth treatment: "The remainder of this paper discusses the action the enterprise should take in the event that it is not contributing by its own actions or omissions, but is implicated by its link to the abuse through the product or services it procures". J. Ruggie, *The Corporate Responsibility to Respect Human Rights in Supply Chains*, Discussion Paper, 10th OECD Round Table Discussion on Corporate Responsibility, 2010, para. 7, <www.oecd.org/dataoecd/17/50/45535896.pdf>.

73 See Mares, *supra* note 23, for a discussion on the content of RtR and the choices a company has when discharging its RtR and conducting due diligence.

74 *Ibid.* See also R. Mares, 'Defining the Limits of Corporate Responsibilities against the Concept of Legal Positive Obligations', 40:4 *George Washington International Law Review* (2009).

75 In the *Chiquita* case (Columbia), the plaintiffs alleged in their complaint that the "Defendants are liable to Plaintiffs in that they aided and abetted, directed, ordered, requested, paid, were reckless in dealing with, participated in a joint criminal enterprise with, confirmed, ratified, and/or conspired with the AUC in bringing about the crimes against humanity committed against Plaintiffs". *Doe v. Chiquita Brands International*, 18 July 2007, p. 21, <www.earthrights.org/sites/default/files/legal/cbi-final-complaint-signed.pdf>.

76 For a comprehensive and recent list of cases, see Center for Constitutional Rights et al., Universal Periodic Review (United States of America), *Stakeholder Submission on United States Obligations to Respect, Protect and Remedy Human Rights in the Context of Business Activities*, 19 April 2010, <www.earthrights.org/sites/default/files/documents/escrnet-upr-april-19-2010.pdf>.

simply-worded, broadly applicable insights from a technical area such as the field of tort law into layman discussions of CSR is no easy task. This chapter aims to at least dismantle perceptions that jurisprudence indicates that no responsibility to act should be considered and that legal separation of entities is an unqualified principle. One need not hastily default in ethical or philosophical reasoning; instead jurisprudential precedents should be duly noted. It might be advisable to 1) draw on tort to explain the nature of the problem and reinforce the foundation of a responsibility to act by making use of accepted legal characterisations through careful analogy, and then 2) leave it to specialised multistakeholder settings to provide standards and guidance that flesh out what reasonable care and due diligence mean.

The foundation offered by reasoning in the shadow of negligence law could be further elaborated by taking a closer look at the main legal systems and delve deeper in the theories used, tensions encountered and promising ways forward. Among the concepts to be clarified would be some that were highlighted in this chapter: responsibility for third party conduct, blameworthy conduct when failing to act as third parties inflict harm, vulnerability, foreseeability and peculiarity of risks, and jurisprudential concepts similar to non-delegable obligations. Also it is important to see what space of manoeuvre exists in different systems when it comes to proximity and remoteness, foreseeability, causation, public policy, and too low standards of reasonableness. These obstacles can derail the RtR as applied to core companies.

This analysis could be foremost conducted to establish a clearer principled foundation for the responsibility to act, with all its complexities; such an analysis is not directed to inform litigation and create expectations that cases could be won. But, through clarity and persuasiveness, an analysis in the shadow of law could inform progressive law-making processes advancing a responsibility of core companies to act with care as well as social expectations. Basically anyone – lawmakers, non-governmental organisations, managers and researchers – asking the question: 'why really should the core company act?', could find such an analysis relevant and useful. The result would be consistent with Ruggie's ambition to lay down a foundation for a cumulative policy-making process.[77]

## 4.2. Two Relationships

This treatment of a core company's responsibilities prevents it from easily insulating itself from its affiliates' wrongdoings. There are two key relationships that need to be clarified when we argue for a core company's responsibility to act. On the one hand, there is the relationship with the separation of entities principle and its limited liability corollary; the difficulty for the RtR is one of *contradiction*. On the other hand, there is the relationship with the states' obligation to protect human rights under international law and the affiliate's own RtR; the difficulty for the RtR is one of *overlap*. The answers to these two relationships and the tensions they raise shape our understanding about the nature, content and limits of the core company's responsibility to act.

---

77  *Guiding Principles, supra* note 3, Introduction, para. 13.

On the relationship of RtR with the separation of entities principle, two issues could be highlighted here: one has to do with aiming for the conceptual middle ground and the other has to do with available alternatives to imposing a responsibility to act on core companies. On the first aspect, this chapter basically proposes a RtR for core companies based on own faulty conduct. It is a duty of care advanced as an exception to the no-liability rule grounded in the separation principle; as a result their relationship is one between rule and exception. Because of its exceptional status the core company's responsibility to act remains permanently vulnerable to attacks from the separation of entities norm with which it has an uneasy existence. This means that efforts to legally institutionalise this duty of care will always be challenged: less so when no legal liability follows misconduct (regulations requiring CSR reporting) or when the compulsion is optional (CSR clauses in contracts) but more so when liability for harm follows (a legal recognition of a duty of care owed by core companies to right holders) or when liability attaches to failures to take certain due diligence steps (legal obligations to conduct impact assessment or to implement management systems).[78]

The second aspect refers to whether a core company's responsibility to act is the right or only way of targeting abusive affiliates. This is particularly important given the contradiction mentioned in the previous paragraph. The responsibility to act of core companies is one among other policy levers to target affiliates. It should be remembered that this discussion covers core companies that do not contribute to harm, but merely fail to oversee, influence and/or distance themselves from abusive affiliates. There are policy choices to be made when it comes to how to target affiliates, which are companies incorporated under legislation of host states.[79] Such policy alternatives are highly relevant in the international CSR context; they would all fulfil a protective role. Sceptics of RtR could legitimately discuss: Should a responsibility to act be imposed on core companies? Should development aid be used to strengthen the legal systems of host states? Should host states be pressed harder under international law for discharging their obligation to protect human rights? Should consumers and investors be empowered with information in order to put pressure or boycott companies? And so on. There are alternatives to imposing a responsibility to act on core companies – state-centred international law, official development assistance, market choices – that could all reduce vulnerability of right holders in less developed countries. It is noteworthy that in tort jurisprudence alternative compensation schemes have displaced liability in tort.[80] Then the aforementioned policy alternatives, *if* effective, would be seen in a

---

78 Mares, *supra* note 23.
79 *See* the reasoning of the European Commission as it rejects any imposition of legal obligations or responsibilities on core companies. European Commission, *Implementing the Partnership for Growth and Jobs: Making Europe a Pole of Excellence on Corporate Social Responsibility*, COM(2006) 136 final (Brussels, 2006), pp. 5–7, <www.coess.org/documents/com_2006_0136.pdf>.
80 Elliot and Quinn noted that a hundred years ago tort was the way to get compensation for injury. Now, with the development of insurance and social security (for these, the issue of fault is irrelevant), the role of tort has declined. C. Elliot and F. Quinn, *Tort Law* (2009) p. 8.

way similar to the role that insurance and social security systems have played in classical tort. These notwithstanding it should be recalled that in this chapter the core company's responsibility is grounded in its own culpable conduct and that the core company might have a unique role and leverage over its affiliates that other entities might simply not have.

While *home* states have an irreplaceable role in establishing a core company's responsibility to act, it is *host* states that play a key role in shaping the way that the responsibility to act is discharged in more effective and sustainable ways. This brings the discussion to the relationship between the RtR and the responsibilities of actors in the host state. The difficulty here is one of overlap. From such overlap can result either strategic retreats by either states or companies, or fruitful interactions. Ruggie, in an effort to pre-empt any interpretation allowing strategic withdrawal by the states,[81] has gone at length to emphasise that the state's duty to protect stays no matter corporate responsibilities, that it is a 'pillar'. So it is the interaction between a core company's responsibility to act, on the one hand, and the host state's obligation to protect as well as the affiliate's own RtR, on the other hand, that will inform the content and limits of the responsibility to act: What due diligence steps should the core company be reasonably expected to take to monitor and influence its affiliates? How does the oversight the core company should assume interact with the oversight of the host state and civil society? What is the division of labour? What are creative ways of leveraging scarce oversight resources? What productive interaction and governance arrangements are better fit to move affiliates toward compliance?[82] These questions need to be answered pragmatically in light of the vulnerability experienced by right holders deprived of effective remedies. These relationships just reinforce the point that the core company has a responsibility to act with care and not to 'ensure' that rights are not violated. The burden is not meant to be unreasonable or unbearable. But a responsibility to act is warranted.

## 5. Conclusions

Ruggie addresses the RtR to all types of business entities. Core companies are explicitly covered in his Guiding Principles. Importantly he argues that core companies are responsible for what happens in their affiliate operations: not only when the core company took decisions that contributed to harm, but also when it did not take such decisions and was merely associated with the irresponsible affiliate. The latter situation triggered concerns detailed in this chapter. Why does a core company have to act where it apparently did not contribute to its affiliates' harmful impacts?

---

81   *Protect, Respect and Remedy, supra* note 10, para 55.
82   Ruggie deems soft law hybrid arrangements as promising and innovative governance arrangements; they could tackle systemic imbalances and provide sustainable solutions that corporate responsibility initiatives alone might not be able to deliver. J. G. Ruggie, 'Business and Human Rights: The Evolving International Agenda', 101 *American Journal of International Law* (2007) p. 819, at p. 839. *See also* the chapter by Skadegaard Thorsen and Andreasen in this volume.

This is the foundational question for which Ruggie does not offer a compelling answer. He deliberately refrains from presenting a theory of attribution of responsibility within business groups and networks. Furthermore, the separation of entities principle, though clearly acknowledged, is dealt with in Pillar 3 as a barrier to access to judicial remedies. With the separation principle banished from Pillar 2, Ruggie hopes his RtR conceptualisation will remain compellingly simple in presentation and not contaminated at its core by legal constructions or doctrinal disagreements. He is rightly mindful of the easiness with which companies can abuse legal form and take advantage of legal technicalities to shed liability. Unfortunately, Ruggie's account of the separation of entities principle fails to persuade a critical reader anchored in legal and business realities that a responsibility to act should be imposed on core companies.

There is a real danger that this part of the RtR will come to be seen as merely aspirational rather than having the imperative character given to the RtR by its definition as "the baseline expectation for all companies in all situations".[83] Despite being nominally applicable to multinational companies, the RtR is likely to succumb to the pressure of the separation of entities principle and become atomised into a collection of RtR of each entity in the business group or network; the core company will have a responsibility to act only when it 'contributed' to harm taken in affiliate operations but not when it was merely 'associated' to its affiliates.

Ruggie's RtR is commendable in its reach and is not flawed, but incomplete. He overlooked the support he could have drawn from an unlikely source: jurisprudence. There are provisions in negligence jurisprudence where the law recognises exceptions to the no-liability-for-third-parties-misconduct rule. In law, according to the ALI's Restatement of Torts, one might be liable for harm to another through the foreseeable action of a third person; that a core company who outsources operations might be liable for the 'negligent selection' of a contractor that poses foreseeable risks; and the hiring party might have to take 'special precautions' to maintain safety where a contractor poses a peculiar risk of harm. Thus drawing on concepts employed in jurisprudence – vulnerability, risk, culpable conduct – one can characterise familiar relationships between core companies and affiliates in a way that does not relieve the core company of all responsibility for human rights abuses.

The result is a core company's responsibility to act and to do so with reasonable care, which is completely in tune with Ruggie's precepts of due diligence. By combining the raw force of the societal expectations behind CSR with the normative validity of legal exceptions recognised by jurisprudence, one can more legitimately present a responsibility to act for core companies. This responsibility to act has an uneasy coexistence with the separation of entities principle, but it can acquire legitimacy and recognition based on concepts already validated by authoritative tort jurisprudence and carefully adapted to the specificities of the international business and human rights context.

---

83   *Protect, Respect and* Remedy, *supra* note 10, para. 24.

# 8 The Monster Under the Bed: Financial Services and the Ruggie Framework

Mary Dowell-Jones* and David Kinley**

## 1. Introduction

The work to develop the 'protect, respect and remedy' Framework governing the human rights impacts of business together with its 'operationalising' Guiding Principles has coincided with one of the worst financial crises to hit the global economy and financial system in many decades. The social and individual welfare impacts have been wide-ranging and devastating. Estimates suggest that over 27 million workers have lost their jobs;[1] the number of people in 'vulnerable employment' has risen to 1.5 billion;[2] 64 million more people are living in extreme poverty;[3] and over 1 billion people, or one-sixth of humanity, are now undernourished.[4] Flowing from these circumstances, a raft of human rights have been threatened or undermined, including: rights to food, water and an adequate standard of living, to health, education and adequate housing, to non-

---

\* Finance specialist and Research Fellow, University of Nottingham Human Rights Law Centre.
\*\* Chair in Human Rights Law, University of Sydney. Our thanks to Christine Ernst for her keen editorial assistance.
1 International Labour Organisation, *Global Employment Trends 2011: The challenge of a jobs recovery* (ILO, Geneva, 2011) p. ix.
2 *Ibid.*, p. 22. Vulnerable employment is defined as "own-account and unpaid family workers", and is characterised by "informal work arrangements including a lack of social protection, low pay and difficult working conditions in which fundamental rights may be undermined" (pp. 21–22).
3 World Bank, *Global Monitoring Report 2010: The MDGs after the crisis* (World Bank, Washington, 2010) p. 6.
4 Food and Agriculture Organization (FAO), '1.02 billion people hungry: One sixth of humanity undernourished – more than ever before', 19 June 2009, available at <www.fao.org/news/story/en/item/20568/icode/>. The FAO commented that: "The most recent increase in hunger is not the consequence of poor global harvests but is caused by the world economic crisis that has resulted in lower incomes and increased unemployment."

discrimination, to privacy, to bodily integrity, and to a fair trial (the poor are often on the margins or effectively excluded from rule of law processes), as well as health and safety in the workplace and the right to work itself.

In the advanced economies, the 'socialisation' of financial sector losses through state bailouts has in some cases tripled the debt burden on states, leading to sovereign debt problems and savage budget cuts that could undermine human rights enjoyment. The impact of the crisis on the USA economy has raised the deficit to a level not seen since 1945 that has pushed the country close to defaulting on its debts of USD 14.3 trillion, and resulted in planned spending cuts of roughly USD 3 trillion over the next decade.[5] European governments are also projected to make hundreds of billions of dollars worth of spending cuts over the next four years that will directly impact public services, employment and pensions, all of which are closely aligned with these states' obligations under international human rights law, in particular the International Covenant on Economic, Social and Cultural Rights.[6] The crisis has clearly demonstrated that in today's deeply integrated financial markets, accumulated failings in regulation, monetary policy, corporate governance and corporate behaviour can be catastrophic and far-reaching for human rights enjoyment. Human rights standards are inevitably drawn along in the slipstream of financial market malfunction. Lying between financial sector failings and the adverse human rights impacts they generate, there are layers of financial complexity in products, processes and corporate form, as well as the long extra-territorial reach of financial activity, that even regulators have struggled to monitor. This is the nature of the monster beneath the bed of the 'protect, respect and remedy' Framework into which none of the above complexity can be easily interpolated. As they stand, the Framework and attendant Guiding Principles provide, at best, benchmarks for arguing that the management of international financial markets should take into account their human rights impacts. Yet, given the dimensions of the problem, it is not easy to see what else they could do at this stage.

During his tenure as a Special Representative of the Secretary-General (SRSG), Professor Ruggie acknowledged the importance of the crisis as a context for his work and as a challenge for the operationalisation of the 'protect, respect and remedy' Framework, calling for states to recalibrate "the balance between market and state", and for corporations to "better integrate societal concerns into their long-term strategic goals".[7] In the realm of financial services, the real question is: how?

There are various dimensions to this question. In this chapter we will seek to explore some of the uncharted dimensions by examining the Ruggie Framework in

---

5   Congressional Budget Office, *CBO's 2011 Long-Term Budget Outlook June 2011*, p. 1, available at <www.cbo.gov/ftpdocs/122xx/doc12212/06-21-/Lomg-Term_Budget_Outlook.pdf>; 'Obama agrees deal to raise US debt limit', *Financial Times*, 1 August 2011.

6   BBC, 'EU austerity drive country by country', 31 March 2011, available at <www.bbc.co.uk/news/10162176>.

7   *Report of the Special Representative of the Secretary-General on the issue of human rights and transnational corporations and other business enterprises: Towards operationalising the "protect, respect and remedy" framework*, 22 April 2009, A/HRC/11/13, para. 10. On the crisis *see* paras. 7–11.

[Handwritten note at top: "Financial (banking) sector is particularly vulnerable to liability under broad interpretation of 'duty to respect.'"]

light of the types of complex financial issues, products and processes that underlay the devastating human rights impacts of the most recent financial crisis. Our focus is on the broad systemic, macro level harms that the finance sector can cause in aggregate to human rights worldwide, which is a largely unrecognised threat in much human rights literature. This has tended instead to focus on areas of direct, immediate impact of corporate acts on the rights of individuals or groups. The financial crisis highlights the distinctness of the financial sector in terms of causality and methods of interacting with human rights standards, and the difficulty of using the Ruggie Framework together with the Guiding Principles as an operational benchmark for addressing this. Although the subprime securitisation process at the heart of the financial meltdown did contain examples of the type of immediate corporate human rights harms that the business/human rights community is more familiar with – such as mis-selling, fraud and abuse on the part of mortgage brokers for subprime credit – a large part of the process of generating such a staggering economic, financial and human rights crisis lay well beyond the ambit of this causal model. Thus at the outset it is important to stress that even had the Ruggie Framework been available and able to address some of the more flagrant human rights abuses and fraudulent behaviour among mortgage lenders, it could not in and of itself have stemmed the tide of system-wide harm that engulfed the global economy.

The chapter is organised as follows: in section 2, we highlight how the integration of social and human rights criteria into financial sector practice has so far been shallow, despite the appearance of comprehensive coverage one might infer from the proliferation of codes of standards and initiatives over the last decade or so. As such, there is little of substance to be drawn on in applying the 'protect, respect and remedy' Framework to the financial sector as a whole. In section 3, we provide a brief overview of some key features of the subprime meltdown, including the way the subprime mortgage-backed securities at the heart of the crisis were created and sold. This is intended to give the reader an insight into the distinct way that human rights harms can be created and magnified in the financial sector. In section 4, we examine the three pillars of the Ruggie Framework in light of the subprime process and highlight some of the challenges that it raises for operationalisation of the Framework. This is intended to give a flavour of some of the largely unmapped problems that finance poses for the 'protect, respect and remedy' Framework, and for human rights standards more broadly. In section 5, we provide some thoughts on the way ahead, while section 6 concludes.

## 2. Financial Services and Human Rights: The State of Play

Are the human rights impacts of financial instability 'externalities' of market dysfunction that are beyond the scope of human rights due diligence in the financial sector? Or are they captured by the broad strokes of the SRSG's principles that challenge those tasked with operationalisation to think more extensively and more technically about the relationship between human rights and financial services?

The Framework's Guiding Principles would appear to sanction, indeed endorse, a comprehensive approach to preventing and mitigating human rights harm in the financial sector. In meeting their duty to protect against human rights abuse by business enterprises domiciled in their jurisdiction, states must enforce laws that require business enterprises to respect human rights, ensure that other laws and policies governing business enable them to respect human rights, and must ensure policy coherence across governmental departments and multilateral institutions that ensures respect for human rights.[8] This would *prima facie* appear to capture the legislative and regulatory architecture of the financial system within the ambit of the Guiding Principles as it played a key causal role in the crisis. In principle at least states need to ensure that this architecture provides "an environment conducive to business respect for human rights".[9] However, Ruggie concedes that the human rights implications of many business-related laws and policies "remain poorly understood",[10] and nowhere is this more so than in the governing architecture of international finance, which, as we shall explore below, is immensely technical and not easily harmonised with international human rights norms.[11]

Businesses' responsibility requires that they avoid causing or contributing to adverse human rights impacts through their own activities, or any that are linked to their operations through business relationships "even if they have not contributed to those impacts".[12] Insofar as the crisis emerged from toxic risk taking by financial corporations around the world, magnified by corporate governance failings and the highly interconnected nature of financial services firms, there is a strong case to argue that a comprehensive approach needs to be taken to examine the responsibility to respect human rights in financial activity, even if achieving this is a long-term objective.

However as we move beyond the broad scope of the Framework's Guiding Principles, there is little to draw on in applying human rights standards to financial services at an operational level because so far few technical areas of finance have been mapped to human rights standards.[13] Although there has been a proliferation of codes of principle, standards and initiatives in the finance and human rights, and environmental, social and governance (ESG) space over the last decade – the Equator

8   Report of the Special Representative of the Secretary-General on the issue of human rights and transnational corporations and other business enterprises, John Ruggie: Guiding Principles on Business and Human Rights: Implementing the United Nations "Protect, Respect and Remedy" Framework, UN Doc. A/HRC/17/31, 21 March 2011, Principles 1, 3, 8 and 10.
9   Ibid., p. 8, Commentary to Principle 3.
10  Ibid.
11  Studies into the crisis paint a picture of the extraordinary complexity involved. *See for example* Financial Crisis Inquiry Commission, *The Financial Crisis Inquiry Report: Final Report of the National Commission on the Causes of the Financial and Economic Crisis in the United States* (Public Affairs, New York, 2011); UK Financial Services Authority, *The Turner Review: A Regulatory Response to the Global Banking Crisis* (FSA, London, 2009).
12  *Guiding Principles on Business and Human Rights*, supra note 8, Principles 11 and 13.
13  M. Dowell-Jones and D. Kinley, 'Minding the Gap: Global Finance and Human Rights', 25:2 *Ethics & International Affairs* (2011) pp. 183–210.

Principles,[14] the Global Compact,[15] the Principles on Responsible Investment,[16] the United Nations Environment Programme Finance Initiative,[17] and the Wolfsberg Principles,[18] to name but a few – efforts have largely related to a few key areas where environmental and some human rights impacts are most visible and directly attributable to corporate activity. Project finance, prudential and ethical investing (though not always together), ESG/corporate social responsibility (CSR) issues, and corruption and transparency matters have been the main focus, though globally they cover only a fraction of financial activity. Crucially, none of these areas touch upon the structural dynamics and characteristics of the financial system that generate financial crises and wide-ranging adverse human rights impacts.

There can be a tendency to equate gross assets under management (AUM) of signatory institutions with the depth of coverage across financial activity of social criteria. For example, the 800+ signatory institutions of the Principles on Responsible Investment have combined AUM of USD 22 trillion.[19] This figure is somewhat misleading as an indicator of depth of penetration of social criteria into financial activity and the structure of financial markets for the following reasons: investment processes are still governed by modern financial theory, which has been heavily criticised for lacing instability through financial markets that have far-reaching and often adverse social impacts – both when markets are reaching euphoric highs (as we have seen with booming commodity and property markets) and when they are spiralling downwards;[20] these assets are themselves drawn along in the flow of financial fashion thanks to benchmarking[21] that in practice compounds market instability, causing negative social impacts; and the apparent size of this pool of assets is still a very small fraction of financial markets, which are worth in excess of USD 1,000 trillion and are made up of complex, interlocking layers of financial activity that, as we have seen with

---

14 <www.equator-principles.com>.
15 <www.unglobalcompact.org>.
16 <www.unpri.org>.
17 <www.unepfi.org>.
18 <www.wolfsberg-principles.com>.
19 Principles for Responsible Investment, *Annual Report of the PRI Initiative 2010*, p. 1, available at <www.unpri.org/files/annual_report2010.pdf>.
20 On the failings of modern financial theory *see* K. Dowd and M. Hutchinson, *Alchemists of Loss: How Modern Finance and Government Intervention Crashed the Financial System* (John Wiley, London, 2010).
21 Benchmarking refers to the practice of measuring a fund's performance against a target index, say, for example, the FTSE 100, on a quarterly or annual basis. This is then also used to weigh the fund's performance against its peer group. What this produces in practice is 'closet indexing', or a tendency to standardisation whereby funds will mimic the composition of the benchmark as closely as possible in order not to deviate too far from its performance. This exacerbates herding behaviour in financial markets, and partly accounts for the reality that actively managed funds rarely outperform index-tracking funds over anything but a very short-term time horizon, despite much higher fees being charged to investors.

[Handwritten annotation at top: authors would have held investment/trading firms accountable for human rights "abuses" resulting from global financial crises.]

the current crisis, serve to compound and magnify risk, not diversify it. This USD 22 trillion of assets sit within this context and is conditioned by it, no matter how high-sounding their social principles.

The unfolding of the subprime crisis provides a timely illustration of how the layers of complexity involved in modern finance and the linguistic incongruity between it and human rights concepts provide a substantial barrier to the comprehensive application of the 'protect, respect and remedy' Framework to global financial activity. What appeared to be a straightforward and laudable policy goal that would further human rights realisation (by expanding home loans to low income borrowers) became a vehicle for broad-based, global human rights harm thanks to deficiencies in financial engineering and layers of interconnected structural failings in the architecture of the financial system itself. Most of the critical failings were located in areas of the financial system that are currently off the human rights radar and that require substantial industry experience to decode,[22] and so the question can legitimately be posed: how far can we or should we go in including those failings within the 'protect, respect and remedy' Framework? Is trying to deepen the application of human rights principles to finance through focusing on more systemic issues stretching the Ruggie Framework too far?

It is worth stressing at this point that the subprime meltdown was not an isolated case of financial malfunction, but a manifestation of some of the ongoing problems that the financial system poses for global human rights enjoyment. It demonstrates how financial alchemy and complexity can transform a commendable goal of social justice and equity into a vehicle for adverse human rights impacts far beyond the epicentre of financial activity. As we will see below, the idiosyncratic and convoluted nature of the way 'human rights harms' are generated by financial activity suggests that important policy and operational choices will have to be made in determining the boundaries of the Ruggie Framework in relation to financial activity.

The 'protect, respect and remedy' Framework may require creative and sometimes counter-intuitive interpretation when applied to financial services. If a comprehensive and inclusive approach to 'human rights harm' is taken that includes the very extensive social welfare and human rights degradation that systemic financial instability causes, then a substantial body of work and financial expertise is going to be needed to translate the Ruggie Framework into a meaningful operational benchmark for the financial sector as a whole. The alternative approach of limiting it to those areas of finance that are currently well understood from a human rights point of view risks in-

---

22  Indeed, it is interesting to hear regulators talk openly about the "social costs of systemic risk" and that banking "risks endangering innocent bystanders within the wider economy", but you are unlikely to hear many human rights advocates talking directly about the human rights costs of systemic risk. 'The $100 billion question', Comments by Andrew Haldene, Executive Director, Financial Stability, Bank of England, at the Institute of Regulation & Risk, Hong Kong, 30 March 2010, available at <www.bis.org/review/r100406d.pdf?frames=0>.

advertently giving the financial sector a veneer of social responsibility while the more nefarious and socially-detrimental practices are continued beneath the radar.[23]

## 3. Understanding the Sub-Prime Process: Identifying Human Rights Harm

The trigger for the global financial meltdown of 2007–2009 was savage losses being incurred across the world's financial system on reasonably new, untested products called residential-mortgage-backed securities (RMBSs) and collateralised debt obligations (CDOs) linked to subprime US mortgages.[24] These losses triggered falls in similar products and in financial markets around the world, and a sharp contraction in economic and trade activity that had widespread adverse consequences for human rights. Although the losses on subprime products were not enough on their own to account for the enormous scale of the crisis, the failure of these products that had been at the vanguard of widely trumpeted 'financial innovation', combined with other structural interconnections and vulnerabilities "that bankers, government officials and others had missed or dismissed",[25] severely destabilised financial markets and brought the system as a whole to the point of collapse. The sharp contraction in global economic and financial activity, and enormous losses on financial assets, were devastating for the global poor whose incomes and livelihoods are precarious at best, and highly exposed to any adverse change in economic conditions. The *Financial Times* described them as the "[f]orgotten victims of the global downturn."[26]

This analysis is not intended to be a systematic review of the epidemiology of the crisis. Rather, we will focus on sketching out a few of the features of subprime RMBSs and CDOs, which we will then use to draw out key challenges that the 'protect, respect and remedy' Framework will face in financial services. Chief among these is the difficulty of pre-emptively identifying and remediating human rights harm among the complexity of financial products, processes and jargon.

A subprime RMBS is a collection of mortgages that were bundled together into a 'pool' and then the streams of repayments divided up and sold as separate financial assets. They were derivatives of the underlying mortgages that effectively sold on to investors the likelihood of being repaid. They were invented in the late 1990s as a way

---

23 As former Federal Reserve Chairman Alan Greenspan told the Financial Crisis Inquiry Commission, "partial supervision is dangerous because it creates a Good Housekeeping stamp". *The Financial Crisis Inquiry Report, supra* note 11, p. 95.
24 The process of securitisation is discussed below. CDOs were a sub-set of RMBSs that effectively 're-securitized' the lower-rated tranches of several RMBSs. For an example of how the processes worked *see* Goldman Sachs, *Effective Regulation: Part 1 Avoiding Another Meltdown*, March 2009, pp. 19–26, available at <www2.goldmansachs.com/ideas/global-markets-institute/featured-research/effective-re-part-1.pdf>.
25 *The Financial Crisis Inquiry Report, supra* note 11, p. 27.
26 'Forgotten victims of the global downturn', *Financial Times*, 10 March 2009.

of transforming the credit process to respond to different pressures coming from the legal and commercial operating environment.[27]

Prior to securitisation, customers who wanted a mortgage had to build up a long-term relationship with their bank and diligently save up a sizeable deposit even to be considered. Once the bank manager deemed them creditworthy and granted a mortgage, the bank would 'own' the loan for its duration, and monitor the repayments. Thus the 'credit risk', *i.e.* whether it would be repaid or not, was dealt with on a relational basis, largely by the bank getting to know the customer very well, and it was held by the bank for the 20–25 years of the loan. This gave the bank a huge incentive to manage its lending responsibly and carefully. The downside of this model was that there was a lot less credit available, there was a lower rate of home ownership, and it could be very difficult to obtain a mortgage for those on lower incomes or with a poor credit history because the risk was considered too great.

In the US context this tended to result in discriminatory lending practices towards poorer, often black and Hispanic neighbourhoods, which were largely excluded from access to home loans and other credit because they were deemed too high risk.[28] The US Community Reinvestment Act (CRA) of 1977 was enacted to address this discrimination and widen access to financial services for low income groups. This mandated that banks had to demonstrate that they were actively lending in such neighbourhoods if they wanted to benefit from federal deposit insurance.[29] The Financial Services Modernization Act of 1999 – which repealed parts of the Glass-Steagall Act of 1933[30] by allowing banks to become 'universal banks' offering all types of financial services under one roof – reinforced the CRA by specifying that a condition of being granted a license to become a 'universal bank' was that they had to demonstrate compliance with the CRA. In order to comply with the terms of the Act, and to generate public and regulatory support for the 'mega mergers' that dominated the US banking

---

27   For an analysis of the history and process of securitization *see Financial Crisis Inquiry Report, supra* note 11; G. Tett, *Fool's Gold: How Unrestrained Greed Corrupted a Dream, Shattered Global Markets, and Unleashed a Catastrophe* (Little Brown, London, 2009); M. Lewis, *The Big Short – Inside the Doomsday Machine* (Allen Lane, London, 2010); J. Kregel, 'Changes in the U.S. Financial System and the Subprime Crisis', The Levy Economics Institute of Bard College, *Working Paper* no. 530, April 2008.

28   So-called 'redlining'. *See* Illinois Legislative Investigating Commission, *Redlining: Discrimination in Residential Mortgage Loans: a report to the Illinois General Assembly* (Illinois General Assembly, Chicago, 1975); A. M. Regan, 'The Community Reinvestment Act Regulations: Another Attempt to Control Redlining', 28 *Catholic University Law Review* (1979) pp. 635–656. Housing discrimination was a key issue in the civil rights movement because it reinforced the economic segregation of racial groups in deprived, inner city ghettos. United States Commission on Civil Rights, Report 4: Housing, 1961, available at <www.law.maryland.edu/marshall/usccr/documents/cr11961bk4.pdf>.

29   For an analysis of the CRA's role in expanding access to financial services for low income groups *see* M. Barr, 'Credit Where it Counts: The Community Reinvestment Act and its Critics', 75 *New York University Law Review* (May 2005) pp. 101–233.

30   Which had been enacted in the aftermath of the Wall Street collapse of 1929 and which separated out bank functions into different financial entities.

landscape in the late 90s and 2000s, banks made hundreds of billions of dollars worth of 'community lending pledges' to support low- and moderate-income communities, including mortgages lending.³¹ In signing the 1999 Act into law, then President Bill Clinton declared:

> The Act establishes an important prospective principle: banking organizations seeking to conduct new ... activities must first demonstrate a satisfactory record of meeting the credit needs of all the communities they serve, including low- and moderate-income communities.³²

This legal and policy framework would seem to be highly consistent with the SRSG's Guiding Principles, which require states to "enforce laws that are aimed at, or have the effect of, requiring business enterprises to respect human rights".³³ Financial inclusion and the growth in lending to the poor (*e.g.* microcredit) have been lauded in human rights and development literature over the last decade as key tools in poverty reduction and human rights realisation. Indeed, much of a guide produced by the Federal Reserve Bank of Boston to aid mortgage originators in complying with the CRA could have been written with the Ruggie Framework in mind, such is its language of addressing discrimination by not rigidly sticking to old credit assessment practices that largely exclude lower-income borrowers.³⁴

However, in a system as complex as finance the law of unintended consequences generally applies, and this legislation interacted with other aspects of the legislative and policy architecture of international finance to usher in significant changes to the American mortgage industry and financial sector that ultimately cost many individuals dearly in terms of their social, personal and economic well being.³⁵ At the front end

---

31   For example, Bank of America committed to USD 750 billion in community lending over ten years during its merger with FleetBoston Financial Corp in 2004; Citigroup committed to USD 120 billion in community lending in 2002 when it merged with California Federal Bank. See *The Financial Crisis Inquiry Report*, supra note 11, p. 97. For an example of the way the Federal Reserve considered the issue of CRA compliance in granting mergers *see* Federal Reserve Board, *Press Release: Order Approving the Merger of Bank Holding Companies*, 15 December 2005, approving the merger of Bank of America with MBNA Corp, available at <www.federalreserve.gov/boarddocs/press/orders/2005/20051215/attachment.pdf>.

32   President William J. Clinton, 'Statement on Signing the Gramm-Leach-Bliley Act', 12 November 1999, available at <www.presidency.ucsb.edu/ws/index.php?pid=56922>.

33   *Guiding Principles on Business and Human Rights*, supra note 8, Principle 3 (a). Even the merging of financial services companies into 'universal banks' was supported at the time as a goal that would further efficiency and help enhance economic welfare.

34   Federal Reserve Bank of Boston, *{Closing The Gap:} A Guide to Equal Opportunity Lending*, (no date), available at <www.bos.frb.org/commdev/closing-the-gap/index.htm>.

35   The precise role that the CRA played in the subprime crisis is a matter of ongoing controversy. While not taking a clear view on the share of the blame to be accorded to the CRA, the Act did, at the very least, serve as a catalyst in opening up the subprime mortgage market by forcing banks to find ways to manage profitably the credit risk of subprime lending.

of mortgage origination, lending standards had to be relaxed because it was difficult to comply with the CRA using old credit risk tools that systematically excluded poorer borrowers.[36] The result was a proliferation of forms of mortgages and a slackening of standards of oversight that, when combined with the growing demand from investment banks for mortgages to package into RMBSs and CDOs, substantially increased mortgage lending and led to many of the abuses and frauds that are now synonymous with subprime.[37] This was one of the most direct and visible of the adverse human rights impacts that stemmed from the crisis. The tricking and cajoling of many subprime borrowers into mortgages they neither understood nor could afford violated their rights to speech (which includes the receipt of full and frank information where appropriate), to non-discrimination (across a range of gender, race and age categories united by being relatively poor), and fair trial and right to a remedy (the lack of adequate recourse to the courts for many mortgagees, either because they had questionable causes of action or, most frequently, because they lacked the resources to fund the litigation). Many have subsequently lost their homes or are unable to meet the repayments.[38] Such direct infringements would appear to be a relatively straightforward

> This paved the way for securitisation and the growth in other types of lenders moving into the subprime market. Testimony given to the Financial Crisis Inquiry Commission by a former Federal Reserve Governor noted, for example, that enforcing the CRA "had given the banks an incentive to invest in technology that would make lending to lower-income borrowers profitable by such means as creating credit scoring models customized to the market. Shadow banks not covered by the CRA would use these same credit scoring models, which could draw on now more substantial historical lending data for their estimates, to underwrite loans." *Financial Crisis Inquiry Report, supra* note 11, p. 74. For the purposes of analysing the Ruggie Framework, it provides a good example of how social goals can interact with other parts of the financial sector in unanticipated ways. See B. Bernanke: 'The Community Reinvestment Act: Its Evolution and New Challenges', speech at the Community Affairs Research Conference, Washington D.C., 30 March 2007, available at <www.federalreserve.gov/newsevents/speech/bernanke20070330a.htm>.

36   For a criticism of the role of government policy in producing lax underwriting standards see S. Liebowitz, 'Anatomy of a Train Wreck: Causes of the Mortgage Meltdown', in B. Powell and R. Halcomb, *Housing America: Building Out of A Crisis* (Transaction Publishers, New Jersey, 2009).

37   One of these was the 'option-ARMs' mortgages, or option-Adjustable Rate Mortgages, whereby borrowers would be sold a mortgage with very low 'teaser' rates of interest payments for the first few months or years, which made the mortgage appear affordable, but which would shift sharply upwards (or 'reset') to a much higher interest rate at the end of this period. Sometimes the monthly repayments under the reset rate were more than the income of the borrower. This type of mortgage was at the centre of investigations, for example, investigations by the California Attorney General into fraudulent practices at Countrywide Financial, which had been one of the biggest mortgage brokers in the US. See 'Atty. Gen. Brown Discloses New Evidence of Countrywide's Deceptive Practices', State of California Department of Justice, Office of the Attorney General, *Press Release*, 17 July 2008, available at <www.oag.ca.gov/news/press_release?id=1588&y=2008>.

38   The Financial Crisis Inquiry Commission found that four million families had lost their homes, and another four and a half million were either in the foreclosure process or were

type of human rights harm to pre-emptively identify and address through standard techniques as envisaged in the Ruggie Framework. Indeed, if mortgage brokers had in place robust human rights policies and due diligence procedures, could at least some of these abuses have been prevented?

In considering this question, it is worth bearing in mind the commercial environment that nurtured this exploitative behaviour. The credit process effectively fractured across different corporate entities as it was transformed by securitisation, meaning that it was no longer a binary relationship between borrower and lender but was rather a complex process involving many different corporate actors and activities. Credit production, repackaging and reselling became a highly leveraged and highly lucrative production line involving different corporate entities all engaged in a particular part of the process (the 'originate to distribute' model). This seriously diluted responsibility for credit and ethical standards as products were passed on so quickly from one corporate entity or legal vehicle to another, and the various stages of the process became highly specialised. Using due diligence to spot potential human rights harm in this environment is challenging to say the least, as the creation of the 'harm' is spread across different actors and different, highly technical, stages of the product creation process. Having said this, the clear cases of fraud, mis-selling and abuse by mortgage brokers could potentially have been subjected to human rights due diligence as these instances fall more obviously within the existing notion of human rights causality. Though even here, it must be said, the complexity of financial fraud makes it difficult to determine exactly when fraudulent behaviour by mortgage brokers becomes a human rights issue. Given the scale of the financial crisis, however, using the Ruggie Framework to weed out cases of the most egregious abuse in the mortgage market could not have stopped the housing and securitisation bubble in its tracks, and so it is important not to assume that the existing notion of corporate human rights causality provides a strong enough intellectual model from which to develop the practical means to pre-empt the depth and range of harms that can result from financial activity.

The subprime RMBSs and CDOs were created by investment banks in part in response to the increased credit risk that they now had to hold on their books thanks to CRA loans. This was problematic because of risk-based capital adequacy regulations that had been enacted after the Savings & Loans crisis of the 1980s that required banks to put aside more capital against these low quality credit risks compared to safer, higher-rated assets like treasury bonds.[39] The process of securitisation offered a way of transferring these assets onto other investors, earning a profit for doing so, and lowering the amount of capital that they had to hold against these assets.[40] It is this process of 'risk transfer' and regulatory capital arbitrage that was a prime cause of the adverse

---

behind on their mortgage payments. *Financial Crisis Inquiry Report*, *supra* note 11, ch. 22, pp. 402–410.

39   These were introduced in the first Basel Accord on international capital adequacy standards of 1988, and introduced in the USA in the Federal Deposit Insurance Corporation Improvement Act of 1991.

40   See *Effective Regulation: Part 1 Avoiding Another Meltdown*, *supra* note 24, which explains the way the regulatory capital framework applied to securitised mortgage assets.

global human rights impacts of the crisis, but in a much less obvious or transparent way than human rights lawyers are used to dealing with, and one that would be very difficult to deal with from a human rights due diligence point of view.

Securitisation relied on newly available developments in quantitative finance that provided a mathematical technique for pooling home loans together and calculating the overall credit risk – *i.e.* risk of loss on the pool of mortgages as a whole – and then dividing up that risk into separate parts (or 'tranches') for sale to investors.[41] Although this may not seem like a relevant issue for oversight of human rights effects, this is a good example of how the genesis of adverse human rights impacts in the financial sector may be remote from any existing notion of what is legitimately an issue of human rights concern. The method used to calculate the credit risk across a disparate pool of mortgages was central to the subprime edifice and its eventual collapse, with its wide-ranging human rights ramifications. The way the 'probability of default' (*i.e.* likelihood of loss on the mortgages) and the 'correlation' (*i.e.* the likelihood of the pooled assets defaulting in similar ways – if one borrower defaults, does it increase the chances of other borrowers doing the same?) were calculated was fundamental to the ability of banks to pool these assets together for sale to investors. This is a legitimate human rights concern because beyond the broad financial hardships felt by many as a consequence of this deep systemic failure, some individuals endured such severe financial stress that they lost many of the financial and social assets that provided them with a minimum tolerable level of social inclusion and individual respect and dignity, namely, jobs, savings, housing, voice, privacy, educational choices and access to adequate health care.

It also allowed rating agencies to award these products the now-infamous AAA-ratings, creating the illusion that such products carried only very low levels of risk but paid above-market rates of return. This rating was crucial to the subprime machine because many institutional investors were prevented by regulation from investing in assets with credit ratings below AAA.[42] It also enabled banks to hold RMBSs and CDOs themselves for treasury and investment purposes while requiring minimal capital under risk-based capital regulations. When the mortgages started defaulting, banks found themselves severely undercapitalised and could not absorb the savage losses on these products, intensifying the collapse of global markets in the face of extreme uncertainty as to the solvency of the world's financial system. Thus the mathematics at

---

41 The groundbreaking paper was D. Li, 'On Default Correlation: A Copula Function Approach', 9:4 *Journal of Fixed Income* (Spring 2000) pp. 43–54.

42 The Financial Crisis Inquiry Commission described the credit rating agencies as "essential cogs in the wheel of financial destruction. … The mortgage-related securities at the heart of the crisis could not have been marketed and sold without their seal of approval. Investors relied on them, often blindly. In some cases, they were obligated to use them, or regulatory capital standards were hinged on them. The crisis could not have happened without the rating agencies." The report also notes that between 2000 and 2007, Moody's rated nearly 45,000 mortgage-backed securities as AAA. In contrast, only six US companies carried this credit rating in 2010. *The Financial Crisis Inquiry Report*, *supra* note 11, p. xxv.

[authors: "complex quantitative analysis as human rights impact"]

the heart of securitisation enabled both the creation of the product and – when combined with the mathematics of risk and of capital adequacy – the creation of a global market for that product.

This combination proved toxic because it quadrupled the size of the subprime loan market in just four years: subprime mortgage origination rose from USD 130 billion in 2001 to USD 625 billion in 2005.[43] By 2007 there were 7.5 million subprime mortgages outstanding, with a combined value of USD 1.3 trillion.[44] This fuelled – and was fed by – an enormous and unsustainable housing boom that was not factored into the calculations on which RMBSs and CDOs were based, making the whole edifice severely vulnerable to a change in market conditions. By creating a global investment market for subprime RMBSs and CDOs, it transmitted the eventual damage right around the world, helping to spread the fallout from the crisis onto some of the world's poorest and most vulnerable people. It also undermined the ability of subprime borrowers to protect their own rights to information, procedural fairness and a remedy, because buyers of RMBSs and CDOs were now so remote from these original borrowers that there was no chance of them being able to approach their lenders to renegotiate terms if they found themselves in difficulty repaying their mortgages.

By replacing steady verification of the quality of the mortgages going into a RMBS or CDO (which could number in the thousands) the mathematical techniques effectively enabled the 'automation' of the securitisation process that allowed trillions of dollars worth of mortgages to be repackaged and resold in a short space of time, without proper checks. By using very sophisticated quantitative analytics, which were largely indecipherable to those without advanced quantitative skills, it created the illusion of safety in products that had not been tested in any period of market stress. Ordinarily, normal investor prudence should have reined in demand for these products, limiting their damage to the financial system and eventually human rights, but the combined forces of financial fashion, high rates of return being offered in a 'low yield' global environment, and a supporting backdrop of risk-based capital regulations, quantitative risk management techniques that were benchmarked to asset prices, the use of derivatives like credit default swaps to 'insure' any residual risk on the products, and 'mark-to-market' accounting standards set in train a global credit bubble of unprecedented proportions that was socially ruinous for many living on the margins and ultimately devastating for their human rights enjoyment.

The mathematics of credit risk, securitisation, and risk-based capital regulations allowed an illusion of certainty and sophistication to obfuscate the true level of risk across trillions of dollars worth of subprime mortgage-backed RMBSs and CDOs that were sold around the world to investors who did not fully understand or verify the risks they were exposing themselves to. The intellectually persuasive theoretical explanation for what was happening was even being widely trumpeted by regulators who

---

43   D. Greenlaw, J. Hatzius, A. Kashyap and H. S. Shin, *Leveraged Losses: Lessons from the Mortgage Market Meltdown*, US Monetary Policy Forum Conference Draft, 2008, p. 16, available at <research.Chicagobooth.edu/igm/events/docs/USMPF-final.pdf>.

44   Dowd and Hutchinson, *supra* note 20, p. 301.

> *This is the type of "creative" human rights impact analysis under the Guidelines which will transform free markets*

were supposed to monitor and control financial exuberance.[45] But ultimately the edifice proved to be fundamentally unstable, and the human rights impacts of its collapse were, for many, catastrophic.

It is difficult to shoehorn much of this into a traditional analysis of human rights causality, which depends on a reasonably direct, linear relationship between corporate actor/act and human rights harm on defined individuals. From a human rights perspective, it may indeed be countered that this description of the subprime process and its social, economic and human rights impacts is remote from and incidental to the Ruggie Framework and the Guiding Principles, that it is more the preserve of financiers than human rights lawyers. The complex, multi-layered nature of the causality involved across the world's financial sector and the difficulty of attributing causation to any individual corporate actor is very different to what is generally considered to fall within the normal boundaries of attribution of responsibility for human rights abuse. But in seeking to understand the wide-ranging human rights harm that was generated by the crisis and how this can be addressed from the standpoint of the 'protect, respect and remedy' Framework, it is important to venture off the beaten track and look at these structural factors.

The way RMBSs and CDOs were structured, the assumptions embedded in the quantitative models on which they were built, and the way they generated and spread complicated and largely unmeasurable risk through the global financial system under the watchful eyes of regulators and senior management provides an excellent example of the complex causality of human rights harm in today's colossal financial markets, and how closely it is bound up with systemic risk. It shows how in just a few years the financial supply chain turned one of the oldest and safest financial products (the home mortgage) into a crisis severe enough to imperil its own solvency and to leave lasting impacts on the socio-economic, and in some cases civil and political, rights of the poor.

### 4. Applying the Ruggie Framework to the Subprime Process

Although this is a rather slimmed down version of a very complex series of events, it has sought to highlight how convoluted the process of generating human rights harm can be in the financial sector once you move beyond more straightforward transactions where it is already reasonably well understood. Here we will attempt to apply some of the Guiding Principles to the subprime process, to illustrate in more detail some of the challenges that will be encountered in applying the 'protect, respect and remedy' Framework to financial services and in particular to the types of financial activity that collectively generate such broad-based human rights harms.

---

45   *Risk Transfer and Financial Stability*, remarks by Alan Greenspan to the Federal Reserve Bank of Chicago's Forty-First Annual Conference on Bank Structure, 5 May 2005, available at <www.federalreserve.gov/boarddocs/speeches/2005/20050505/default.htm>; *Regulation and Financial Innovation*, remarks by Ben Bernanke to the Federal Reserve Bank of Atlanta's 2007 Financial Markets Conference, 15 May 2007, available at <www.federalreserve.gov/newsevents/speech/bernanke20070515a.htm>.

### 4.1. The State Duty to Protect Human Rights

The first of the Framework's three pillars requires states to protect human rights from abuse by third parties, including business enterprises. This requires that they take "appropriate steps to prevent, investigate, punish and redress such abuse through effective policies, legislation, regulations and adjudication" and that they should "set out clearly the expectation that all business enterprises domiciled in their territory and/or jurisdiction respect human rights throughout their operations".[46] As straightforward as this may sound, it is anything but when applied to financial regulation.

At the very least, it would seem to require that policymakers and regulators can demonstrate that they have actively taken possible human rights impacts into account in regulating the financial system, and that overall the regulatory architecture of international financial markets should be designed so as to minimise their potential adverse human rights impacts. This is extremely difficult at this present juncture because it assumes: a) that regulators can foresee and predict how complex financial activity and systemic dynamics may generate adverse human rights impacts both in their own country and, through market contagion, in countries around the world; and b) that they can frame regulation of the entities over which they have jurisdiction so as to pre-empt these impacts. This is far easier said than done: regulators and policymakers have widely claimed after the event that they simply did not see or understand the extent of the risks building in financial markets during the subprime bubble.[47]

The financial system has grown in complexity to such a degree over recent years that there is no accepted understanding of how to measure and control either the financial or human rights risks it generates. Moreover, the 'model' on which financial regulation is built is based on theories that may be remote from human rights values because they assume that liberalised finance is socially optimal in aggregate, without looking at impacts on vulnerable individuals. The globalisation of financial services has not been accompanied by sustained attention to their impact on the global poor and marginalised through, for example, financial crises. Regulators and policymakers are also susceptible to the influence of industry narratives, and the same 'cognitive errors' as those they are meant to regulate.[48]

In the case of subprime, regulators and policymakers simply failed to look beyond enormous profits and the sophisticated quantitative analytics that were embedded in RMBSs and CDOs and the regulatory architecture itself to conjecture what risks were

---

46  *Guiding Principles on Business and Human Rights*, supra note 8, Principles 1 and 2.

47  As the Financial Crisis Inquiry Commission commented, "policy makers and regulators were caught off guard as the contagion spread, responding on an ad hoc basis … to put fingers in the dike. There was no comprehensive and strategic plan for containment, because they lacked a full understanding of the risks and interconnections in the financial markets. … We had allowed the system to race ahead of our ability to protect it." *Financial Crisis Inquiry Report*, supra note 11, p. xxi.

48  A. Pollock, 'Lots of Regulatory Expansion but Little Reform', 4 *Regulation Outlook* (June 2010), American Enterprise Institute for Public Policy Research, pp. 1–6, at p. 2.

piling up and what their impact would be beyond the financial markets.[49] Instead, they bought into the dominant intellectual paradigm, the belief that financial markets benefitted everyone by acting as the "risk managers for the economy"[50] and that the 'new model of risk transfer' strengthened the resilience of the financial sector and enhanced economic growth. Where regulators did raise concerns, they encountered industry 'pushback' because "it was difficult to express their concerns forcefully when financial institutions were generating record-level profits".[51] It is also worth stressing that in general securitisation occurred in compliance with various laws aimed at the financial sector;[52] and that the regulatory architecture – which had been developed around theories of finance for which Nobel prizes had been won[53] – proved to enhance financial fragility, not prevent it.

Against this backdrop, a comprehensive perspective on the state duty to protect human rights from abuse by financial services companies requires more than just an overlay of human rights-focused legislation or principle on the pre-existing regulatory framework to address issues such as financial inclusion. As we have seen with the Community Reinvestment Act, the law of unintended consequences applies, and mandating human rights goals can interact with other parts of the regulatory framework in unanticipated ways that can result in human rights harm down the line. In the long-term, the state duty to protect will require a recognition that adverse human rights impacts can be generated by failings in technical areas of financial regulation (like capital adequacy) that may initially seem remote from and indeed unrelated to human rights concerns. Scrutiny of the regulatory architecture of finance as a whole that takes into account the potential adverse impacts on the rights of the world's poorest and most vulnerable people from financial market activity and malfunction will

---

49  Under this risk-based approach, regulatory authorities acted more like 'consultants', who did not "attempt to restrict risk-taking but rather [to] determine whether banks identify, understand, and control the risks they assume". *Financial Crisis Inquiry Report*, supra note 11, p. 307, quoting the *OCC Large Bank Supervision Handbook*.

50  *Financial markets as risk managers for the economy: Main effects and side-effects*, remarks by Thomas Mayer, Chief European Economist at Deutsche Bank, at the ECB-Bundesbank-Cfs conference on financial system modernisation and economic growth in Europe, 28 September 2006, available at <www.eu-financial-system.org/fileadmin/content/Dokumente-Events/seventh-conference/Mayer.pdf>. This is an excellent example of the dominant industry logic prior to the collapse.

51  *Financial Crisis Inquiry Report*, supra note 11, p. 307.

52  Except in a few rare cases such as Lehmans' 'Repo 105' transactions. It is noteworthy how few criminal prosecutions have been launched against bankers in the aftermath of the credit crisis, in comparison to previous crises like the Savings & Loan crisis of the 1980s, and the dotcom collapse of 2001.

53  Modern Financial Theory, which "can be summarized as the application of the theories of mathematical statistics to finance". It includes the efficient markets hypothesis, modern portfolio theory, the Black-Scholes-Merton options pricing formula, and statistical/probability-based risk management. Dowd and Hutchinson, supra note 20, p. 65. For an overview and critique of Modern Financial Theory, see pp. 65–135.

be necessary. This may require a more prudent and possibly conservative attitude to financial markets than we have at present.

The complicating difficulty for the operationalisation of the State duty to protect, however, is elaborating how human rights values can be fitted into the technical detail of the regulatory framework, particularly where this may encounter industry resistance to rules that the industry feels may undermine competitiveness. The political muscle of the sector as a whole, and in particular of large, complex financial institutions (LCFIs) that are now designated as 'too big to fail', cannot be underestimated. Considering that in Washington D.C. there are reportedly more than three financial sector lobbyists for every member of the US Congress,[54] and that the technicality of markets and regulation mean that few outside the industry understand them, it is clear that the power of vested interests is extensive when it comes to lobbying in key policy and legislative hubs, and that the voice of the financial sector is invariably and carefully listened to.

### 4.2. The Corporate Responsibility to Respect Human Rights

The second of the Framework's three pillars is simply this: business enterprises should respect human rights. This is an "expected standard of conduct for all business enterprises wherever they operate."[55] Applying this to corporate activity beyond the areas that are currently the focus of finance-human rights related initiatives will require a substantial expansion of the understanding of the relationship between international financial markets and human rights, as well as how this understanding can be used to foster changes in industry-wide corporate practices.

Firstly, implementation of this principle will require the development of analysis that provides a template with which financial companies can assess the potential adverse impacts of their commercial activities across the board. So far, as we have noted, few areas of financial activity have been mapped against human rights principles and the areas that have been mapped have tended to be those where the relationship is most transparent. The subprime crisis has amply demonstrated that adverse human rights impacts can lurk in far less accessible corners of financial activity, like derivatives, structured finance, liquidity management and risk management where causation is far more difficult to pinpoint among the complexity of financial jargon and process. There is currently no template or benchmark that companies can use to evaluate potential human rights harm flowing from these more technical areas of their business – in fact they are likely to be very unwilling to concede that there is any connection between these parts of their operations and human rights principles.

---

54   Based on 2010 figures from the Centre for Responsive Politics at <www.opensecret.org> Lobbying> Industries. The Centre reports that a total of 1,629 lobbyists were reported as working for the following industries: securities and investment; commercial banks; finance/credit companies; insurance; credit unions; savings and loans; and miscellaneous finance.

55   *Guiding Principles on Business and Human Rights*, supra note 8, Principle 11 and Commentary.

Secondly, developing such a template will require a foray into systemic dynamics and the issue of collective action/collective responsibility. There are many cases in finance where what would be harmless activity when conducted by a few market participants in small numbers turns into a powder keg of risk for everyone, including the global poor, when it attracts large numbers of players. Securitisation and RMBSs/CDOs are a clear example. Practiced in small numbers, they may well have done what they were advertised to do: improving access to credit for poorer borrowers, transferring risk to financial entities most able to bare it, and easing the international flow of capital. But herding in financial markets is endemic – and partly driven by the homogenisation of processes like risk management, industry benchmarking and regulatory standards themselves – and is hugely destabilising. It is capable of turning time-honoured products such as home mortgages into a global financial catastrophe that reverberates through many communities, impacting especially detrimentally on the poorest and most vulnerable within them.

The Guiding Principles clearly state that the responsibility to respect human rights requires that corporate entities "seek to prevent or mitigate adverse human rights impacts that are directly linked to their operations, products or services by their business relationships, even if they have not contributed to those impacts".[56] This very expansive principle potentially does away with the collective action problem by imputing collective responsibility for systemic dynamics, and the role that their activities may play in systemic dynamics, to every corporate participant in financial markets. It would appear to suggest that companies cannot use the excuse that it was not their subprime deals that caused the collapse of world economic activity and its attendant human rights ills to deflect responsibility. It potentially imposes a very high standard of conduct on financial entities when reviewing their corporate strategies for potential human rights harm. However, in doing so it opens up a can of worms because the relationship between systemic risk, financial markets and human rights is neither well documented nor well understood, and so the attribution of responsibility will remain an incredibly difficult task to perform. The practicality of the Guiding Principles is, therefore, fundamentally challenged.

In the absence of any existing model or understanding of systemic risk that permits markets to be analysed and outcomes to be predicted with anything like reasonable certainty, the operationalisation of this principle is a steep uphill climb. In capturing all types of financial activity within its ambit, the principle is a weak base upon which to try to build a case for corporate responsibility in the financial sector. The complexity of financial markets not only provides lots of smoke and mirrors behind which they can hide, it also presents a formidable obstacle to understanding what this principle requires in practice even for those financial companies with high principles. For example, does it require that financial entities disinvest from certain markets that may be overheating because the attendant systemic risks may well prove extremely detrimental to human rights should they materialise, even in the face of huge uncertainty as to the likelihood of this? How does this interact with a bank's responsibilities

---

56   *Guiding Principles on Business and Human Rights*, supra note 8, Principle 13 (b).

to its shareholders? Would doing so only destabilise the markets sooner rather than later?

The breadth of the Guiding Principles would also appear to capture within their ambit the shadow banking system and its highly specialised financial activities that generally do not feature on the human rights agenda. The shadow banking system is effectively a "parallel financial system[s] of enormous scale"[57] that engages in very specialised, non-depository, financial activities – such as trading in money markets and currency exchanges, hedge fund investment, investment banking and insurance – alongside the traditional banking system. In 2008, this system was valued at roughly USD 20 trillion, compared to about USD 13 trillion for the traditional banking system with which human rights advocates are generally familiar.[58] The shadow banking system provided key aspects of the securitisation process and played a key role in transforming subprime mortgages into a global financial meltdown and human rights harm. Monoline bond insurers, for example, provided the credit default swaps that were used to 'insure' subprime CDOs to give the impression that any risk was virtually minimal. It was all part of the game of very sophisticated obfuscation that allowed the markets to overheat to such an extraordinary degree with the active support of industry leaders and regulators. Tying the shadow banking system to potential human rights harm is, however, another very substantial challenge for the operationalisation of the 'protect, respect and remedy' Framework in financial services.

The practical implementation of the notion of the corporate responsibility to respect hinges upon an ongoing process of human rights due diligence that requires businesses to "comprehensively and proactively attempt to uncover human rights risks, actual and potential, over the entire life cycle of a project or business activity".[59] If a comprehensive perspective on the meaning of the corporate responsibility to respect human rights in the financial sector is taken that includes potential human rights harm generated by any type of financial operation (*i.e.* not just those few areas where human rights analysis is currently focused), then there would be no immediate way in which human rights due diligence could be used to pre-empt such harms. Even where human rights due diligence is "included within broader enterprise risk-management systems"[60] within the financial sector, this is likely to be highly misleading and to fail to capture many human rights risks precisely because those risks may flow from failures in risk management systems themselves.

As we have highlighted above, it is very difficult to see how human rights due diligence could have been used in any pre-emptive way in the securitisation process, except where the process interacted most directly with the rights of subprime borrowers themselves. It is particularly difficult to see how human rights due diligence could have

---

57   *Financial Crisis Inquiry Report*, supra note 11, p. 28; on shadow banking *see* pp. 27–37.
58   Z. Pozsar, T. Adrian, A. Ashcroft and H. Boesky, *Shadow Banking*, Federal Reserve Bank of New York, *Staff Reports* no. 458, July 2010.
59   *Towards operationalising the "protect, respect and remedy" framework*, supra note 7, para. 71.
60   *Guiding Principles on Business and Human Rights*, supra note 8, Commentary to Principle 17, p. 16.

been applied to the process in any of its more technical stages. To use human rights due diligence in this context would require an understanding of deficiencies in quantitative finance and how this fed into broader market dynamics, as well as how all of this would impact upon the rights of the global poor through systemic interdependencies. Not only would this require substantial industry expertise – in practice it would need market experts more than human rights specialists – it would also require high-level influence within an organisation in order for any problems identified to be acted upon in the face of lucrative profit streams.

Although Principle 19 (ii) of the Guiding Principles states that the effective integration of human rights impact assessments requires that "[i]nternal decision-making, budget allocations and oversight processes [should] enable effective responses to" those impacts, in reality it is likely that responsibility for human rights due diligence will fall to CSR teams who are quite far removed from decisions on risk taking or the allocation of capital across business lines. Arguably, many CSR teams lack the product and process experience to apply due diligence to specialised areas of bank activities, particularly in large, complex financial institutions (LCFIs) and the more specialised financial vehicles in the shadow banking system. Even where such expertise is available within an institution and processes in place, it is difficult to see how human rights due diligence could have been applied to securitisation arms in a preventive way because it is often a matter of extreme controversy and expert judgement as to what the systemic implications are likely to be. Indeed, if concern among senior managers and traders at Lehman's failed to rein in excessive risk taking on the basis of potential losses, it is difficult to see how the logic of human rights harm and due diligence could currently achieve much strategic reorientation.[61] There is often at the very least a huge degree of uncertainty involved, which will water down the force of human rights due diligence.

Where a particular product or process is generating huge returns and appears justified by prevailing financial logic, as was the case with subprime RMBSs and CDOs, it is very doubtful whether a due diligence process could pre-empt or rein in the type of risk taking and speculative activity that appear likely to generate substantial human rights harms down the line. The success of this may also strongly depend on the organisation in question: human rights due diligence may perhaps have had more success at J.P. Morgan, which began scaling back its involvement in subprime in 2006, than at Citigroup, where its then Chief Executive, Chuck Prince, declared in July 2007, just a month before major problems started in the subprime market: "[A]s long as the music is playing, you've got to get up and dance. We're still dancing."[62] There is an awful lot of conceptual groundwork to lay before human rights due diligence could be used as a methodology at financial institutions to identify and mitigate human rights risks right across their businesses.

---

61   L. McDonald and P. Robinson, *A Colossal Failure of Common Sense: The Incredible Inside Story of the Collapse of Lehman Brothers* (Ebury Press, London, 2009).
62   Tett, *supra* note 27, pp. 168–169 and 174.

## 4.3. Access to Remedy

The third pillar of the Ruggie Framework requires that those affected by corporate human rights abuses should have access to an effective remedy. The aim of a grievance procedure is "to counteract or make good any human rights harms that have occurred", and it can include "apologies, restitution, rehabilitation, financial or non-financial compensation and punitive sanctions… as well as the prevention of harm through, for example, injunctions or guarantees of non-repetition".[63] The provision of an effective remedy at the corporate level requires an ability to trace, with reasonable certainty, the identified human rights harm from victim to causal corporate act. Where the causal nexus was diffused across millions of corporate actors and millions of individuals who suffered human rights harm around the world, it is difficult to see how this methodology could apply. It would be very difficult to try to isolate causality and responsibility for providing a remedy at the level of any individual corporate actor in the case of the subprime meltdown.

For example, as we noted at the opening of this chapter, the numbers of the poor and vulnerable who have been negatively impacted by the crisis have been staggering – 27.6 million alone who have lost their jobs, and 64 million more living in extreme poverty.[64] As such, one would face an enormous challenge trying to impute any of these impacts directly to any of the banks at the centre of the crisis in order to claim some form of restitution for victims, at least at this current juncture. Even though their actions were major catalysts for the crisis, the generation of these human rights harms also required contributing failings by many other actors that compounded those of the major banks, for example, other financial entities, retail investors, governmental regulators, policymakers and economic actors across a complex chain that reached from Wall Street and the City of London into the lives of factory workers in South East Asia. Many of the failings that led to the subprime crisis were overseen and endorsed by regulators and policymakers using orthodox financial theories who were widely trumpeting the apparent success of their policies. This failure of oversight complicates the task of apportioning blame and attributing a responsibility to provide a remedy to victims because corporate human rights abuse in this case has a profound systemic dimension.

It is also worth bearing in mind that the financial condition of many banks after the crisis may have limited their capacity to provide an effective remedy. In the case of Ireland, for example, the cost of rescuing the banking sector has amounted to roughly two-thirds of Irish Gross Domestic Product[65] as the banks have been crippled by losses on property loans. Basic economic and social rights of many people in Ireland are being negatively impacted by the substantial public sector budget cuts that

---

63   *Guiding Principles on Business and Human Rights*, supra note 8, Commentary to Principle 25, p. 22.
64   See first paragraph of this chapter.
65   'Irish Bow to Trichet on Bondholders as Rescue Hits $142 Billion', *Bloomberg Business Week*, 1 April 2011, available at <www.businessweek.com/news/2011-04-01/Irish-bow-to-trichet-on-bondholders-as-rescue-hits-142-billion.html>.

are in progress in order to meet the state costs of the financial sector rescue. In such circumstances, it is doubtful whether Irish banks are in a position to provide any sort of remedy to those people who are now being affected by the public sector cuts.

The access to remedy is unlikely to work in finance in the way it can work in other sectors where causal relationships are easier to identify. At least where causal dynamics are diffused across market participants, it can be extremely difficult to identify which corporate entities are responsible for what direct harm, something that may make it extremely difficult to claim any form of remedy from them. It may in fact be the case that providing a remedy for financial crises may take on a different form – perhaps some form of collective 'insurance fund' that all market participants contribute to and that can be held on standby to mitigate the impacts of market dislocation on the world's marginalised people.

## 5. The Way Ahead

While it is easy on first reading to feel pessimistic given how long and hard fought has been the battle to achieve even the current level of human rights awareness in financial services, there are two factors that should be borne in mind. Firstly, the true scale of the problem should spur human rights advocates into further action. Financial crises are an increasingly important menace to economic stability and global human rights enjoyment, particularly for those on the margins of society. Over the last 20 years as global markets have integrated and grown exponentially in both size and complexity, financial crises have occurred on a regular 5–7 year cycle, accompanied, each time, by seriously detrimental human rights impacts. The growing scale of financial crises also means that states' ability to take measures to protect the human rights of their citizens can be severely compromised by financial meltdown. Often, states are themselves overwhelmed by the scale of the meltdown and their ability to comply with their international human rights obligations, including the obligation of non-retrogression, is severely constrained.

Thus there is little room for complacency or scope for pessimism among human rights advocates as this is an issue that at some point, sooner rather than later, has to be addressed on the human rights agenda. The Ruggie Framework and Guiding Principles at least offer a solid starting point for this debate by establishing the principle that businesses have responsibilities towards human rights that span all aspects of their operations, not just those areas where human rights impacts are most immediately visible, and that governments have a duty to ensure that such responsibilities are recognised and enforced. Thus, the work of the SRSG provides a bedrock from which to challenge, on human rights grounds, the notion that international financial markets are too powerful or difficult to restrain. It is now up to the human rights community to make sure that his work is used effectively to deeply embed human rights values into the heart of the financial system. The very fact that the inherent instability of financial markets precipitates regular crises that decimate the basic rights of the most vulnerable members of humanity by undermining the economic and social conditions assumed in international law as prerequisites for the adequate protection of human rights means that we must not accept the status quo as reflective of the human rights responsibilities of the financial sector.

Secondly, the problem of financial system stability is one that is well-worn in the financial, economic and policy making literature. Admittedly, it is a complex topic, but there are many sources of information available, and it is subject to an ongoing process of negotiation and research in various international fora. The challenge for human rights advocates is to join this debate by raising the issue of the human rights aspects of systemic risk and asking, if not demanding, policymakers to consider their responsibilities to the global poor in managing the global financial system. Encouraging consideration of whether the human rights dimensions of crises change the way the issue of financial stability is dealt with, or at least modifies the attitude to key issues in banking and market regulation, is itself a good starting point.[66]

## 6. Conclusion

In his 2009 report, the SRSG declared that: "Human rights concerns remain poorly integrated into other policy domains that directly shape business practices. Therefore, a major objective of the Special Representative … [was] to assist Governments in recognizing those connections and advancing the business and human rights agenda beyond its currently narrow confines."[67] As we have highlighted above, only a narrow range of issues in the financial sector have so far been addressed from a human rights perspective, and many of the most far reaching issues have barely been touched at all. There are many outstanding issues that will need to be addressed in fitting the Ruggie Framework to the realities of today's financial system.

Here we have sought to tackle some of the less accessible but, for that very reason, no less important issues, in order to give readers an insight into some of the main problems and challenges that are likely to be encountered. What is certain, however, is that as financial markets continue to grow in both size and complexity, their ability to impact negatively the human rights of the world's poor and marginalised through periodic disruptions in the functioning of the world's economy and financial system will only grow in scale. That fact alone should give us cause to redouble our efforts to try to understand what are the human rights implications of global finance, how they are caused and what might feasibly be done to correct the situation, no matter how

---

66 And yet going beyond pontification to making practicable proposals as to how one might do this, proves to be extremely difficult. A recent *Report of the Independent Expert on the question of human rights and extreme poverty, Magdalena Sepúlveda Carmona* (A/HRC/17/34; 17 March 2011) exemplifies the problem, for while the Report repeatedly urges that human rights be taken into consideration in any restructuring of global finance, it provides only two or three brief pointers as to *how* that might be concretely achieved – namely, improved data collection; better and broader training of financial policy makers in governments; and greater participation of community and civil society organisations in processes of financial policy formulation: see paras.86, 88 and 90.

67 *Towards operationalising the "protect, respect and remedy" framework*, supra note 7, para.44.

demanding the task. Within global finance lies both the power and wherewithal to improve the lot of the world's poor and marginalised; so there is much to hope for. The Ruggie Framework and Guiding Principles still leave us some way from converting that hope into expectation, but now, at least, we can be in no doubt as to how difficult such alchemy will be to achieve.

# 9 Human Rights Norms for Business: The Missing Piece of the Ruggie Jigsaw – The Case of Institutional Investors

Rory Sullivan* and Nicolas Hachez**

## 1. Introduction

The United Nations (UN) Special Representative for Business and Human Rights, John Ruggie, has discussed at length the positive impact that companies over the world can have on human rights through foreign direct investment. He has, however, paid much less attention to the role that portfolio investment may play in respecting human rights. In this chapter, we not only argue that institutional investors (*e.g.* pension funds, investment managers, insurance companies) have a vitally important role to play but also explore the conditions under which they can most effectively play their part in this important agenda. We focus primarily on how institutional investors can – through their leverage and influence – contribute to the respect of human rights by other corporations.

Our starting point is that while issues such as climate change, health and safety, and bribery and corruption are progressively finding their way into investment decision-making and are increasingly being discussed in company-investor meetings, human rights considerations have nowhere near the same profile. It appears that investors are not systematically examining the human rights implications of their investment decisions, nor are they, with some exceptions, proactively encouraging companies to effectively manage their human rights impacts. In a world where the limitations of state-centric approaches to the realisation of human rights are ever more apparent, the lack of attention being paid by investors to human rights issues may well impact negatively on global efforts to protect and promote human rights.

The objectives of this chapter are to explain why investors are not currently paying attention to human rights and to offer some practical proposals on how this situation can be addressed. We begin by describing the role institutional investors could play in helping ensure business respect for human rights. We identify the central obstacle to

---

\* Senior Research Fellow, University of Leeds.
\*\* Research Fellow, Leuven Centre for Global Governance Studies and Institute for International Law, University of Leuven.

them playing this role as the lack of consensus and clarity around the human rights expectations of companies and, specifically, the absence of an agreed normative framework against which corporate human rights performance can be assessed. We then offer our views on what an effective accountability framework for business and human rights would look like. Finally, we consider the implications of our proposals in the context of the recommendations that have been made by the Special Representative.

## 2. Institutional Investors and Human Rights

To start with, we would like to set out four limits to the scope of our chapter. First, we focus on a particular segment of the finance sector, namely 'institutional investors'. These are entities that pool or manage financial resources with a view to investing them in equity, bonds or other investment products, and include pension funds, investment managers, insurance companies, investment banks, and sovereign wealth funds. We concentrate, in particular, on direct investors (*i.e.* those investors that make investment decisions rather than those that outsource investment decisions to others).[1] We recognise that institutional investors are just one type of investment decision-maker, and that investors are just one of many stakeholders in the business and human rights debate. However, the specific dilemmas and challenges faced by institutional investors in implementing human rights are indicative of the challenges faced by others seeking to deliver similar outcomes.

Second, we focus primarily on investments in equities (or shares), corporate debt and private equity, as these asset classes are those where there is the clearest link between investment and corporate activities. We acknowledge that these asset classes differ significantly in terms of the importance of human rights issues to the investor, the avenues (or mechanisms) of influence that are available and the actual influence that an individual investor can exert. Notwithstanding these differences, investors in these asset classes face broadly the same challenges when trying to assess corporate human rights performance, and the principles and issues we highlight in this chapter are broadly the same across these asset classes.[2]

Third, we pay limited attention to the so-called 'ethical' investors (*i.e.* investors that have explicitly ethical objective(s) that override financial objectives) as these rep-

---

[1] While not explicitly the subject of this article, any discussion around the role and responsibilities of institutional investors must be understood in the context of the demands and expectations placed on them by their clients, and the importance assigned by these clients to social, environmental and governance issues in their investment processes. *See generally* H. Viñes Fiestas, R. Sullivan and R. Crossley, *Better Returns in a Better World – Responsible Investment: Overcoming the Barriers and Seeing the Returns* (Oxfam, Oxford, 2010).

[2] The human rights implications of wider systemic issues in the financial services industry and of financial instruments such as derivatives are canvassed in the chapter by Dowell-Jones and Kinley in this volume, and M. Dowell-Jones and D. Kinley, 'Minding the Gap: Global Finance and Human Rights', 25:2 *Ethics and International Affairs* (June 2011).

resent a relatively small part of the overall investment market.³ Rather our focus is on how mainstream investors can internalise human rights issues in their investment practices and processes.

Fourth, we are explicitly concerned about the role of investors in the absence of regulation that clearly defines the human rights obligations of companies or that explicitly requires investors to take account of human rights issues in their investment processes.⁴ Clearly, if such regulation was to emerge (an eventuality we consider most unlikely over the next five or ten years), the terms of this discussion around the responsibilities of investors would alter, at least for those human rights that were covered by the regulation.

## 2.1. Why Should Institutional Investors Be Concerned about Human Rights?

There are four broad arguments for investors to be concerned about human rights. The first derives from the call in the 1948 Universal Declaration of Human Rights⁵ (UDHR) for "every individual and every organ of society" to respect and promote, to the extent of its capabilities, the rights set out in the UDHR. That is, all societal actors (a category that clearly includes investors) have an explicit obligation to respect and promote human rights.⁶ It is relevant to note here that despite the widely acknowledged status of – at least part of – the UDHR as customary international law, the UDHR does not impose binding human rights obligations directly on corporations or investors.⁷

---

3   Eurosif, *European SRI Study 2010* (Eurosif, Paris, 2010).

4   Expressed another way, we discuss the role and contribution of investors as a primarily voluntary activity, driven by societal (rather than regulatory) pressures and by the commercial and other interests of investors.

5   UN General Assembly, Universal Declaration of Human Rights, Resolution No. 217 A (III), 10 December 1948. We acknowledge that the UDHR, as a resolution of the UN General Assembly, is not *per se* legally binding.

6   For a more detailed treatment of this argument, see L. Henkin, 'The Universal Declaration of Human Rights at 50 and the Challenge of Global Markets', 25 *Brooklyn Journal of International Law* (1999) p. 25.

7   For discussions of the potential to directly attribute human rights obligations to corporations under international law, *see* D. Kinley and J. Tadaki, 'From Talk to Walk: The Emergence of Human Rights Responsibilities for Corporations at International Law', 44 *Virginia Journal of International Law* (2004); A. Clapham, *Human Rights Obligations of Non-State Actors* (Oxford University Press, Oxford, 2006); UN Human Rights Council, *Business and Human Rights: Mapping International Standards of Responsibility and Accountability for Corporate Acts. Report of the Special Representative of the Secretary-General (SRSG) on the Issue of Human Rights and Transnational Corporations and Other Business Enterprises*, 9 February 2007, UN Doc. No. A/HRC/4/035, paras. 35–41. While the UDHR does not impose binding human rights obligations on companies, specific obligations have been imposed on corporations in certain specific regimes (*see further* Clapham, this note, pp. 244 *et seq.*). It could be argued that sovereign wealth funds, as state actors, may be in a different position. For a cautious study of sovereign wealth fund accountability with regard to human rights under international law, *see* B. Demeyere, 'Sovereign

The second argument is that investors influence the actions of companies they choose to invest in and may, therefore, be considered to have a responsibility to take action to correct the negative consequences of these activities.[8] It has been argued that the pressure from investors to put short-term profits ahead of corporate responsibility and the failure of many investors to play the part of active owners (*i.e.* by not holding company boards properly to account for their governance) are often contributory factors to unethical behaviour by companies.[9] The manner in which institutional investors invest and discharge their responsibilities as the providers of capital and the owners of companies, therefore, has important consequences for society as a whole. As Mary Robinson, former UN High Commissioner for Human Rights and Chair of the Business Leaders Initiative for Human Rights (BLIHR), might argue: "with this kind of power comes responsibility".[10]

The third argument relates to the fiduciary duties of institutional investors, in that investment returns may be affected by human rights, among a range of other factors. While it is difficult to put figures on the business costs and benefits of hu-

---

Wealth Funds and (Un)Ethical Investment: Using Due Diligence as a Yardstick to Avoid Contributing to Human Rights Violations Committed by Companies in the Investment Portfolio', forthcoming in G. Nystue *et al.* (eds.), *Corporate Complicity, Human Rights Violations and Disinvestment: Legal and Philosophical Perspectives* (Cambridge University Press, Cambridge, 2011).

8 See Human Rights Council, *Report of the Special Representative of the Secretary-General on the Issue of Human Rights and Transnational Corporations and other Business Enterprises, John Ruggie – Guiding Principles for the Implementation of the United Nations 'Protect, Respect And Remedy' Framework* (hereafter 'Guiding Principles'), 21 March 2011, UN Doc. No. A/HRC/17/31, Principle 19(b), pp. 18–19, which states: "Where a business enterprise contributes or may contribute to an adverse human rights impact, it should take the necessary steps to cease or prevent its contribution and use its leverage to mitigate any remaining impact to the greatest extent possible. Leverage is considered to exist where the enterprise has the ability to effect change in the wrongful practices of an entity that causes harm. Where a business enterprise has not contributed to an adverse human rights impact, but that impact is nevertheless directly linked to its operations, products or services by its business relationship with another entity, the situation is more complex. Among the factors that will enter into the determination of the appropriate action in such situations are the enterprise's leverage over the entity concerned … If the business enterprise has leverage to prevent or mitigate the adverse impact, it should exercise it." On these notions of influence and leverage, *see also* Human Rights Council, *Clarifying the Concepts of "Sphere of Influence" and "Complicity" – Report of the Special Representative of the Secretary-General on the Issue of Human Rights and Transnational Corporations and other Business Enterprises, John Ruggie*, 15 May 2008, UN Doc. No. A/HRC/8/16.

9 C. Mackenzie, 'The Scope for Investor Activism on Corporate Social and Environmental Impacts', in R. Sullivan and C. Mackenzie (eds.), *Responsible Investment* (Greenleaf Publishing, Sheffield, 2006) pp. 20–38.

10 T. Slavin, 'Big Business Becomes Mrs Robinson's Affair', *The Observer*, 12 December 2004, available at <www.guardian.co.uk/business/2004/dec/12/theobserver.observerbusiness14>.

man rights, the broad connections are clear.[11] Companies that are perceived as being implicated in human rights violations may face litigation from employees or other stakeholders, or may be targeted by non-governmental organisations (NGOs) or the press, with consequent impacts on their brand or reputation, their share prices, their ability to access markets and their ability to recruit the best employees. Conversely, organisations with a good human rights record should be able to achieve a range of commercial benefits such as enhanced reputation and image, more secure 'licence to operate', improved employee recruitment and retention, reduced risk of litigation, new business opportunities and better stakeholder relationships. There may also be broader social benefits as a consequence of businesses operating in a responsible manner such as increased trust between business and the community or, depending on the country, a decline in social unrest. Expressed another way, it can be argued that companies striving to behave ethically are – all other things being equal – likely to represent better investments over the long-term.[12] As emphasized by Tessa Hebb, "[i]ncreasingly pension fund investors look to [environmental, social and governance] indicators as proxies for long-term performance".[13] Clearly, human rights form an important aspect of the social performance of companies.

Finally, quite apart from the investment and moral arguments for taking account of human rights in investment decisions, investors are facing increased scrutiny and pressure from governments, media and civil society to be transparent and accountable for the social and environmental impact of their investments. Perhaps the most high profile example in recent years has been the campaign for the international prohibition of cluster munitions, which has seen investors being explicitly targeted. These campaigns have been particularly successful in the Netherlands and Scandinavia where an increasing number of investors now have explicit prohibitions on investing in companies involved in the production of cluster munitions.[14]

## 2.2. What Can Investors Do?

Among mainstream investors, the major strategies for addressing environmental, social and governance issues in investment practice are: (a) enhancing mainstream investment processes to explicitly incorporate consideration of company performance on these issues, (b) using the formal rights (*e.g.* shareholder rights such as voting and calling emergency meetings) and informal influence available to investors to encourage companies to pay appropriate attention to the management of social, ethical and environmental issues, and (c) engagement with public policy makers and other stake-

---

11   R. Sullivan and P. Birtwell, 'CEO Briefing: Human Rights' (United Nations Environment Programme Finance Initiative, Geneva, 2008).
12   *See generally* G. Clark and T. Hebb, 'Why Should They Care? The Role of Institutional Investors in the Market for Corporate Global Responsibility', 37 *Environment and Planning* (2005).
13   T. Hebb, *No Small Change: Pension Funds and Corporate Engagement* (Cornell University Press, Ithaca, 2008) p. 9.
14   *See for example* the list presented in Viñes Fiestas *et al.*, *supra* note 1, p. 11.

holders to encourage them to regulate or take other actions to address the underlying causes of social or environmental problems. Recent years have seen a dramatic increase in the number of investors using these strategies.[15]

In relation to investment analysis, there are good reasons for thinking that investment decision-making influences corporate behaviour, with the investment decisions made by stock-market participants setting the share price for companies, which, in turn, affects company behaviour, both directly by affecting the cost of capital and indirectly by motivating boards and executive behaviour. If insufficient weight is given to the value of good corporate social and environmental performance or to the costs of poor performance, the capital markets may create incentives for companies to cause (or fail to prevent) harmful corporate impacts on society and the environment.[16]

There are many examples of where these issues have impacted directly on company financial performance through litigation (*e.g.* tobacco, asbestosis, product liability), regulation, taxation and other market instruments, and company failure as a consequence of probity failings (*e.g.* Enron). Over the past five years, there has been a significant amount of research focused on the investment implications of social and environmental factors; investors have examined issues such as HIV/AIDS in the Southern African mining industry, the effects of the European Union's Emission Trading Scheme on European electricity utility companies, the implications of obesity for food producers and retailers, and the effects of climate change on the insurance sector.[17] Such analysis avoids the legal controversy traditionally associated with ethical screening because its aims are directed at maximising financial returns for investors.[18] That is, there is no intention to place ethical considerations ahead of financial ones. Instead the intention is to improve on existing analysis and so deliver financial benefit to pension fund beneficiaries.

Shareholder activism involves shareholders using their unique power as the owners of companies to facilitate change. As shareholders, large institutional investors have a range of formal and informal rights and powers relating to companies. Formally, shareholders may directly influence the way the company is managed, through voting on matters such as appointments to the board of directors, the board's remuneration policy, the appointment of auditors and the annual report and accounts. They may also file shareholder resolutions at general meetings and may, under certain conditions, have the ability to call emergency general meetings (EGMs). Informally, institutional investors can exert influence through their ability to buy and sell shares and bonds (hence influencing share price and/or the cost of capital), through their relationships and frequent contact with management, by encouraging other investors to use their

---

15   Eurosif, *supra* note 3; Sullivan and Mackenzie, *supra* note 9; G. Clark and T. Hebb, 'Pension Fund Corporate Engagement – The Fifth Stage of Capitalism', 59 *Relations industrielles/Industrial Relations* (2004).

16   See Sullivan and Mackenzie, *supra* note 9 for a more detailed treatment of this argument.

17   See for example the sell-side (investment bank) research posted at <www.unpri.org/research/>.

18   B. Richardson, 'Do the Fiduciary Duties of Pension Funds Hinder Socially Responsible Investment?', 22 *Banking and Finance Law Review* (2007).

formal powers and by creating peer pressure (*e.g.* through benchmarking performance on specific corporate governance or corporate responsibility issues). The views that investors express in meetings and other communications with company management about social and environmental issues can have an important influence on the weight assigned by company management to these issues and the actions they decide to take. Over the past ten years, shareholders in many countries have used their influence to create longer-term incentive structures for directors,[19] increase board independence and executive accountability, create better risk management infrastructure (making it harder for incompetent or self-seeking managers to take unjustifiable risks with the business), and, more recently, to improve the quality of companies' policies, management systems and disclosures on issues such as climate change, bribery and corruption, supply chain labour standards, human rights and access to medicines. In some cases this has contributed to important outcomes such as dramatically reduced prices of AIDS medicines, the withdrawal of companies from unhelpful industry lobby groups, and improvements in labour conditions in retail supply chains.[20]

Public policy engagement involves investors working with policy makers and other actors to create the (regulatory) conditions whereby companies are encouraged to operate in a responsible manner. There are a number of examples where investors have sought to make this kind of contribution, most notably in relation to climate change (where investor groups have been at the forefront of calls for governments to establish a robust international framework for greenhouse gas emissions)[21] and revenue transparency where investors have played a leading role in the Extractive Industries Transparency Initiative (EITI).[22]

## 2.3. Will Investors Take Action?

The argument that investors have social and environmental responsibilities is increasingly accepted in the investment industry. Perhaps the most high-profile example is

---

[19] An increasing number of companies now link part of the bonuses paid to their senior managers to the social and environmental performance of the enterprise. See A. Williams, 'The Case for Greening Executive Bonus Packages', 18 May 2010, available at <www.businessgreen.com/bg/analysis/1807532/the-greening-executive-bonus-packages>.

[20] *See for example* the case studies in Sullivan and Mackenzie, *supra* note 9 and the views expressed in Viñes Fiestas *et al.*, *supra* note 1.

[21] Much of this has been under the auspices of the European Institutional Investors Group on Climate Change (IIGCC) (<www.iigcc.org>) and similar organisations in North America and Australia/New Zealand. *See further* S. Pfeifer and R. Sullivan, 'Public Policy, Institutional Investors and Climate Change: A UK Case-Study', No. 89 *Climatic Change* (2008) pp. 245–262; R. Sullivan and S. Pfeifer, 'Moving the Capital Markets: The EU Emissions Trading Scheme', Issue 33 *Journal of Corporate Citizenship* (Spring 2009) pp. 87–96; R. Sullivan and C. Mackenzie, 'Can Investor Activism Play a Meaningful Role in Addressing Market Failures?', Issue 31 *Journal of Corporate Citizenship* (Autumn 2008) pp. 77–88.

[22] Investors are identified, by the EITI, as one of its core supporters, there is an investor statement in support of the EITI, and investors are one of the stakeholder groups on the EITI's board. *See further* <eiti.org/supporters/investors>.

the UN-backed Principles for Responsible Investment (UNPRI).[23] As of early 2011, over 800 investment institutions (asset owners, investment managers and professional service providers) had become signatories to the UNPRI.[24] The Principles, established in 2006, are intended to develop and promote best practice in the area of responsible investment through facilitating the integration of environmental, social and governance (ESG) issues into mainstream investment practice. Signatories commit to incorporating these issues into their investment analysis and decision-making and to engaging with the companies in which they are invested to encourage high standards of corporate responsibility and corporate governance.

The annual progress reports produced by UNPRI[25] suggest that investors are increasing their capacity to address ESG issues in their investment processes, through adopting responsible investment policies, hiring dedicated staff, collaborating with other investors and building some consideration of ESG issues, including human rights, into their investment decisions. In addition, a number of the collaborative engagement programmes, facilitated by the UNPRI's Clearinghouse, have focused on social issues: 17 per cent of engagements between April 2009 and March 2010 covered poverty and development issues such as indigenous peoples' rights, revenue transparency or human rights.[26] For example, in 2010, a group of UNPRI signatories engaged with 14 North American, European and Japanese consumer electronics companies to ensure that the tin, tantalum and other minerals sourced from the Democratic Republic of Congo were not linked to armed groups responsible for serious and persistent human rights' abuses.[27]

A number of other initiatives aiming to foster sustainable and responsible investment have emerged in recent years. The majority of these have focused on transparency and disclosure in relation to a defined sustainability theme, a defined region or a defined economic sector. Examples include the European SRI Transparency Code,[28] the Carbon Disclosure Project,[29] the Forest Footprint Disclosure Project,[30] the Investor Statement on Sustainability Reporting in Emerging Markets,[31] and the Investors' Statement on Transparency in the Extractives Sector.[32] The rationale for focusing on disclosure is that if the functioning and performances of companies are thrown into

---

23   <www.unpri.org/>.

24   <www.unpri.org/signatories/>.

25   The most recent report is Principles for Responsible Investment, *Report on Progress 2010* (PRI, London, 2010), previous progress reports can be found at <www.unpri.org/publications/>.

26   <www.unpri.org/collaborations/>.

27   *Report on Progress 2010*, supra note 25.

28   <ww.eurosif.org/images/stories/pdf/european_sri_transparency_code.pdf>.

29   <www.cdproject.net/>.

30   <www.forestdisclosure.com/>.

31   <www.unpri.org/files/EMDP/2010%20-%20How%20to%20become%20a%20signatory%20to%20the%20investor%20statement.pdf>.

32   <eiti.org/files/Investors%27Statement%202010-04-21.pdf>.

bright light, investment markets, consumers or possibly public authorities will presumably be able to sanction or reward them as appropriate.[33] However, as we discuss further below, while transparency is an integral part of a global strategy for ensuring corporate accountability, disclosure processes relying mainly on reputational or market accountability are unlikely to achieve their purpose in the absence of clear substantive reference points.

### 2.4. What Makes Investor Action Effective? Clarity Around Expectations

The preceding discussion should provide some encouragement to those who wish to see investors playing a greater role in encouraging companies to adopt high standards of performance on human rights issues. There are financial, commercial, ethical and sometimes possibly legal reasons for investors to take action, there is evidence that such actions can be effective and, therefore, there is a growing consensus in the investment community that they should take these types of action. While there has been very significant progress on corporate governance and climate change (and, to an extent, environmental issues in general), investors face a series of practical challenges in integrating consideration of human rights issues into their investment processes. These include:[34]

- The requirement for materiality (or financial significance) to be proven before an issue will be considered relevant. Therefore, for a particular human rights issue to be explicitly considered in an investment decision, it would be necessary to explain how the issue affects recognised drivers of investment value for the company in question and the financial significance of these impacts.[35]
- A general lack of knowledge and understanding of human rights norms and issues in the financial sector.[36]
- The absence of a shared and uniform methodological framework for integrating social information into financial processes.

---

33   The central importance of disclosure was stressed by a group of 'Socially Responsible Investors' responding to the Special Representative's Protect Respect and Remedy framework in 2008. *See Statement by Socially Responsible Investors to the Eighth Session of the Human Rights Council on the Third Report of the Special Representative of the UN Secretary-General on Business and Human Rights*, 3 June 2008, available at <www.reports-and-materials.org/SRI-letter-re-Ruggie-report-3-Jun-2008.pdf>.

34   R. Roca and F. Manta, *Values Added: The Challenges of Integrating Human Rights into the Financial Sector* (The Danish Institute for Human Rights, Copenhagen, 2010).

35   R. Sullivan, *Valuing Corporate Responsibility: How Do Investors Really Use Corporate Responsibility Information?* (Greenleaf Publishing, Sheffield, 2011).

36   It is important to emphasise that this does not mean that human rights issues are not taken into account at all. In practice, investors have rules of thumb that allow them to account for these issues. For example, they frequently will have some sort of measure of 'country risk' or 'project risk' that accounts for a whole series of issues including human rights-related aspects such as freedom of expression, rule of law, security and freedom of association. *See further* Sullivan, *supra* note 35.

- The reality that social issues are generally presented in qualitative terms, making it difficult to integrate them into investment models.[37]

These are huge structural barriers and addressing them explicitly (*e.g.* through the development of human rights-related indicators, the raising of awareness across the entire finance sector, the development of clear relationships between human rights performance and measures of financial impact) would take many years to achieve.

There is, however, another way of approaching this problem. Investors are more likely to take specific social issues into account in their investment decisions and their engagements where the expectations of companies are clearly defined (*i.e.* it is possible to assess compliance/non-compliance in objective terms) and where there is a consensus around the standards of behaviour or performance that are expected.[38] From an investment perspective, the argument is that the risks to companies (in terms of damage to their reputation and consequent impacts on cash flows and profits) are greatest where they violate or risk violating agreed societal norms, *i.e.* where their behaviour can be characterised as 'unacceptable' or 'immoral'.[39] In practice, this means that investors will look out for those areas where companies breach agreed norms of good practice and are more likely to avoid those companies whose behaviour is, or could be seen as, unacceptable and so at greatest risk.

This is not just a theoretical argument. When we look at specific human rights-related issues, the areas where most progress has been made – labour standards, bribery and corruption, cluster bombs and controversial weapons – are those where specific and widely supported international norms exist, and therefore where there is clarity around the specific expectations of companies. Clarity around expectations also provides a basis for engagement, through enabling company performance to be assessed in a structured and objective manner, thereby enabling investors to encourage laggards to improve while also rewarding leaders.

One question that the arguments above inevitably raise is whether a normative framework around the human rights expectations of companies would be helpful to companies. While we acknowledge that companies have generally lobbied against any efforts to define specific human rights obligations that they should meet (including the very strong lobbying against the Draft Norms put forward by the UN Sub-Commission

---

37  A. Snyder, 'Holding Multinational Corporations Accountable: Is Non-Financial Disclosure the Answer?', *Columbia Business Law Review* (2007).

38  This was the central conclusion of Oxfam's Better Returns in a Better World project (BRBW), a two year research project from 2008 to 2010 which sought to understand the barriers to greater investor engagement with poverty alleviation and development issues (Viñes Fiestas *et al.*, *supra* note 1). The project was structured as a research partnership with the investment industry, involving seven workshops and a series of one-to-one interviews with investment sector representatives. In total, the project engaged with over 80 different investors across Europe and the United States.

39  Sullivan, *supra* note 35; Viñes Fiestas *et al.*, *supra* note 1.

on the Promotion and Protection of Human Rights),[40] we believe that the absence of an agreed normative framework makes it difficult for companies to clearly delineate the scope of their obligations. Moreover, this absence means that, even when companies have taken highly proactive approaches to managing human rights issues, it may be difficult for them to demonstrate that all human rights issues have been identified and properly managed. The establishment of an agreed normative framework could also help to address 'free rider' problems. It is predictable that not all states and not all firms will take the same care to observe fundamental human rights. In the absence of consensus around minimum standards or expectations, the more conscientious corporations that invest time and money into observing human rights, and make themselves accountable for their record in this field, may find themselves at a competitive disadvantage in relation to more unscrupulous corporations that do not undertake such actions. They may also lose business opportunities in countries with poor human rights records, as these host governments may not wish to do business with ethically-driven corporations. In this context, a recognised normative framework would help create a level playing field, facilitate assessments of corporate performance, and allow disparate pressures to be brought to bear on companies (*i.e.* enabling leaders to be recognised and rewarded and/or enabling laggards to be identified and sanctioned).

In the next section, we study how clarity around expectations could be achieved within the context of the work of the Special Representative.

## 3. Needed: A Normative Framework for Business and Human Rights

### 3.1. Accountability How? Process, Substance and the Special Representative's Framework

Despite our arguments above about the need for and value of a normative framework to investors and to companies, we recognise that the direction of travel in the business and human rights debate seems to be moving away from rather than towards developing such a body of human rights norms. Most of the discourse around the human rights responsibilities of companies has focused on the systems and processes that companies should have in place[41] rather than the substantive performance outcomes they should be seeking to achieve from these processes. This focus on processes rather than performance is reflected in the investment world where the vast majority of the collaborative initiatives supported by investors have focused on improving

---

40   UN Economic and Social Council, Commission on Human Rights, Sub-Commission on the Promotion and Protection of Human Rights, Norms on the Responsibilities of Transnational Corporations and Other Business Enterprises with Regard to Human Rights, 26 August 2003, UN Doc. No. E/CN.4/Sub.2/2003/12/Rev.2, hereinafter 'Norms'.

41   There is a general consensus around the management systems that companies should have in place to address their human rights issues. *See for example* Business Leaders Initiative for Human Rights, UN Global Compact and The Office of the High Commissioner for Human Rights, *A Guide for Integrating Human Rights into Business Management*, 2007, at <www.ohchr.org/Documents/Publications/GuideHRBusinessen.pdf>.

the 'transparency' of corporate operations. Even though the increased transparency of corporate activities is, clearly, an important element of corporate accountability, shedding light on corporate practices is of limited value if there is no clear standard to assess performance against and for accountability 'processes' (such as investor-induced market rewards and sanctions) to play out. Accountability 'processes'[42] cannot work in a vacuum; they need to operate in reference to a clear normative framework.[43] These problems with process rather than performance-based approaches are being recognised by other actors, most notably, the European Parliament, which has adopted a resolution[44] criticising the approach of the Commission to corporate social responsibility (CSR) as too process-oriented, and not sufficiently focused on results.[45]

Unfortunately, the work of the Special Representative epitomises this shift from substance to process.[46] As explained in the introduction to this volume, the Special Representative rightly states that corporations have a 'responsibility to respect human rights'. However, when asked about the normative framework in reference to which this responsibility to respect should be discharged and assessed, the Special Representative argues that, based on his extensive empirical observations, corporations should be concerned with all human rights, as they can potentially breach all of them. His conclusion is, therefore, that looking for a 'list of human rights obligations' specially directed at corporations is a useless, redundant and misguided exercise.[47]

---

42   For one (among very many) classifications of accountability 'mechanisms', 'processes' or 'channels', *see* R. Grant and R. Keohane, 'Accountability and Abuses of Power in World Politics', 99 *American Political Science Review* (2005) pp. 35–36.

43   For a study of the 'accountability processes' applicable to an important financial institution, the European Investment Bank, and of the substantive standards in reference to which those processes work, *see* N. Hachez and J. Wouters, 'A Responsible Lender? The European Investment Bank's Environmental, Social and Human Rights Accountability', *Leuven Centre for Global Governance Studies Working Paper* No. 72, September 2011, available at <papers.ssrn.com/sol3/papers.cfm?abstract_id=1923604>.

44   European Parliament, Resolution of 13 March 2007 on Corporate Social Responsibility: A New Partnership, EU Doc. No. 2006/2133(INI).

45   *See generally* J. Wouters and N. Hachez, 'The EU Corporate Social Responsibility Strategy: A Business-Driven, Voluntary and Process-Oriented Policy', 19 *Journal of European Social Policy* (2009).

46   *See for example* the argument made by Parker and Howe in this volume, that the "second pillar [of the Special Representative's framework] further distances the framework from the earlier Norms in the interest of diplomacy by defining corporations' human rights 'responsibilities' primarily in terms of 'due diligence' rather than substantive values, rights or goals that business must meet".

47   The Special Representative therefore concluded that there was no value in "defining a limited list of rights linked to imprecise and expansive responsibilities, rather than defining the specific responsibilities of companies with regard to all rights". Human Rights Council, *Protect, Respect and Remedy: a Framework for Business and Human Rights – Report of the Special Representative of the Secretary-General on the issue of human rights and transnational corporations and other business enterprises*, John Ruggie, 7 April 2008, A/HRC/8/5, p. 15, para. 51.

Admittedly, the Special Representative was appointed following the stalemate in the business and human rights debate that had been created by an attempt to identify a substantive body of corporate human rights obligations. Even though the 'Norms on the Responsibilities of Transnational Corporations and Other Business Enterprises with Regard to Human Rights'[48] were adopted in 2003 by the United Nations Sub-Commission on the Promotion and Protection of Human Rights, they failed to be ratified by the then Commission on Human Rights. Despite enthusiasm from civil society, which saw in the Norms a pathway to direct legal human rights obligations for businesses,[49] the corporate world lobbied intensively against the Norms, criticising the vague – though law-like – language in which they were drafted. Business groups were particularly concerned about how the Norms might be implemented, and the potential consequences of diverting human rights responsibilities from state actors to private persons.[50] With the business and human rights debate having stalled as a result of the demise of the Norms, the Special Representative was appointed in 2005 by Secretary-General Kofi Annan in order to get things moving again, which the Special Representative was able to achieve by advocating 'principled pragmatism.'[51] This entailed dismissing efforts to define a normative framework and focusing instead on the now well-known 'protect, respect and remedy' framework for corporate human rights accountability.

The protect-respect-remedy framework identifies three avenues for addressing the issue of corporate human rights violations: (i) the 'duty' of States to 'protect' their citizens against human rights violations (including those committed by corporations), (ii) the 'responsibility' of business to 'respect' human rights where they operate, and (iii) the necessity of ensuring that effective 'remedies' be available for victims of corporate human rights abuse.[52] Looking more closely at prong (ii) of the framework (the corporate responsibility to respect), while the Special Representative refers to 'all hu-

---

48  Norms, *supra* note 40.

49  See for example Amnesty International, *The UN Human Rights Norms for Business: Towards Legal Accountability*, 2004, available at <www.amnesty.org/en/library/asset/IOR42/002/2004/en/c17311f2-d629-11dd-ab95-a13b602c0642/ior420022004en.pdf>.

50  International Chamber of Commerce and International Organisation of Employers, *Joint Views of the IOE and ICC on the Draft "Norms on the Responsibilities of Transnational Corporations and other Business Enterprises with Regard to Human Rights"*, March 2004, available at <www.reports-and-materials.org/IOE-ICC-views-UN-norms-March-2004.doc>.

51  Commission on Human Rights, *Interim Report of the Special Representative of the Secretary-General on the Issue of Human Rights and Transnational Corporations and Other Business Enterprises*, 22 February 2006, UN Doc. No. E/CN.4/2006/97, para. 70.

52  Guiding Principles, *supra* note 8. Since 2008, the Special Representative and his team have produced a vast amount of documents aiming at 'operationalizing' the framework (*see for example*, the Special Representative's last two reports: Human Rights Council, *Business and Human Rights: Towards Operationalizing the "Protect, Respect and Remedy" Framework*, 22 April 2009, UN Doc. No. A/HRC/11/13; and Human Rights Council, *Business and Human Rights: Further Steps Toward the Operationalization of the "Protect, Respect and Remedy" Framework*, 9 April 2010, UN Doc. No. A/HRC/14/27). Most recently, *see* the

man rights', it appears that the practical intent is that corporations ought to comply with domestic laws on human rights where these are established, and where this is insufficient refer to the international framework, which 'at a minimum' encompasses the International Bill of Rights, and the Core ILO Conventions.[53] Based on those, companies must show 'due diligence', and establish 'policies and processes' to operationalise such due diligence and 'manage' their human rights impacts.[54] Those policies and processes are, of course, to be differentiated according to sectors, regions or types and sizes of corporations.[55]

To paraphrase the Special Representative, while it is true that we need 'specific responsibilities', this does not detract from the fact that we also need clear norms relating to those responsibilities.[56] The fact that all human rights may potentially be breached by corporations is something of a truism and should not be disputed. However, the reference by the Special Representative to 'all human rights' does not provide the required clarity around the normative framework for companies. We acknowledge the huge amount of work that the Special Representative and his team put into the protect-respect-remedy framework and the extensive consultation around this framework. Even though we agree with the broad 'protect, respect and remedy' framework, we find the absence of a normative description of corporate human rights obligations to be a major flaw in relation to the specific point of the corporate responsibility to respect. Our concern is that by discussing the 'corporate responsibility to respect' mostly in terms of an elusive and relative obligation of 'due diligence' rather than in terms of substance and outcomes (*i.e.* that human rights be respected as the fundamental social and legal norms that they are), the effect is to suggest that the responsibility of corporations with regard to human rights is more one to 'manage' than one to 'respect'. This is not merely a matter of semantics and, in fact, has serious practical consequences in terms of corporate accountability. As we have explained above, accountability for performance requires that there be clarity around expectations and responsibilities, which can easily be translated into a 'compliance/non-compliance'[57] assessment framework. The self-standing 'due diligence' requirement in the Ruggie framework, coupled with a vague reference to the general body of international human rights law, does not provide the level of specificity that we think is required.

---

Special Representative's 2011 *Guiding Principles for the Implementation of the United Nations 'Protect, Respect And Remedy' Framework*, supra note 8.

53   Guiding Principles, *supra* note 8, Principle 12, p. 13.

54   *Ibid.*, Principles 13–15, pp. 13–15.

55   *Ibid.*, Principle 14, p. 14.

56   This point has been stressed by institutional investors, who have said that they would find it helpful to have an internationally agreed framework on a series of corporate obligations, so as to be able to make better informed investment decisions. *See* Viñes Fiestas *et al.*, *supra* note 1, p. 28.

57   While we use the term compliance here, we do not intend that this is confined to an assessment of compliance with the law, but rather a more general assessment of whether companies meet or do not meet defined standards of performance.

This is true in respect of market-based accountability mechanisms (such as those induced by investors' activities), but also in those cases in which the Special Representative's framework could be used to define a standard of conduct for corporations in legal accountability mechanisms such as civil liability suits.[58] In broad terms, general civil liability regimes require the demonstration of a faulty behaviour on the part of the defendant. A claimant alleging that a corporation has violated his/her human rights should therefore demonstrate (among other elements) to the court that the behaviour of the corporation constitutes a 'fault' or a 'breach of its duty of care' in order for the corporation to be held legally liable.

Our intention here is not to promote a regime of strict liability in respect of human rights, or even an unattainable obligation of result in respect of human rights, even for those companies which can demonstrate responsible human rights conduct.[59] However, the very loose 'obligation-of-means-type' managerial approach used by the Special Representative arguably leaves much to be desired if corporations effectively are to be held accountable. We identify two main grounds for concern. The first is that it promotes the conception that human rights are just another business risk which corporations should manage as they would any other commercial risk.[60] The problem with this conception is that it moves human rights from the realm of ethics to the realm of costs and benefits. That is, defining corporate human rights responsibilities only in process-oriented terms could be seen as a perversion of the business and human rights debate, as it contributes to reinforcing, in the corporate minds, the idea that respect for human rights is a risk management issue, and not a responsibility in

---

58  While not explicitly the subject of this chapter, we also note that these weaknesses in the manner in which corporations' responsibility to respect are defined also negatively impacts on the third strand of the Ruggie framework (*i.e.* the right for victims of human rights abuses to have access to 'remedies' in case a corporation fails to live by its responsibility to respect).

59  In general regimes of civil liability, consequences will be attached to a human rights-related harm if it can be proven by the plaintiff that the defendant has committed a 'fault' or a breach of its 'duty of care' that caused the harm in question. Where harm has been suffered but no such fault or breach can be proven, no liability will be incurred. In contrast, in 'strict' liability regimes, liability will be incurred 'automatically' once harm has been suffered as a result of the occurrence of a certain type of event. Our view is that legislation on business and human rights (if adopted) is most likely to be based on fault-based liability rather than strict liability, with corporations being allowed to use the defence that they behaved 'as a reasonable person' or that they exercised 'reasonable care'. We also recognise that, given the very high legal and policy profile of human rights, corporations will have to demonstrate a high level of care in order to escape liability, especially when particularly grave violations are alleged. For a further discussion of this issue, *see* R. Mares, 'Defining the Limits of Corporate Responsibilities Against the Concept of Legal Positive Obligations', 40 *George Washington International Law Review* (2009) esp. pp. 1193 *et seq.*.

60  In this regard, see, however, the *proviso* made by the Special Representative in his 2010 report that "[h]uman rights risk management differs from commercial, technical and even political risk management in that it involves rights-holders. Therefore, it is an inherently dialogical process that involves engagement and communication, not simply calculating probabilities". *See* Human Rights Council (2010), *supra* note 52, para. 85, p. 17.

its own right. The second is that the emphasis on due diligence without reference to substantively strong and outcome-oriented obligations[61] is bound to lower the effectiveness of the accountability framework (see *infra*). Emphasis on general due diligence processes opens the door to corporations engaging in 'creative' or 'symbolic' compliance, *i.e.* where they design 'human rights impact management processes' primarily aimed at avoiding liability while being aware that abuses might still occur.[62] Indeed, the Special Representative's framework suggests (although this is yet to be tested) that a corporation faced with a legal claim could escape liability for causing or contributing to human rights abuses if it was able to argue that it had a convincing enough 'due diligence' policy, rather than because it could show a concrete absence of fault on its part and a sincere commitment to respecting human rights.[63]

---

61    In any case, the substantive obligations of corporations should be stronger than simply the obligation to 'do no harm', which was presented by the Special Representative (Human Rights Council, *supra* note 47, para. 24), and which he defines in the following terms: "To respect rights essentially means not to infringe on the rights of others – put simply, to do no harm. Because companies can affect virtually all internationally recognized rights, they should consider the responsibility to respect in relation to all such rights, although some may require greater attention in particular contexts. There are situations in which companies may have additional responsibilities – for example, where they perform certain public functions, or because they have undertaken additional commitments voluntarily. But the responsibility to respect is the baseline expectation for all companies in all situations." In this regard, and while acknowledging the particularly contentious way the Norms dealt with the issue of the scope of corporate human rights obligations, we note that certain authors have found it disappointing that the Special Representative did not reflect more on the extent to which corporations have more 'proactive' responsibilities than a mere responsibility to 'respect'. The disconnect, notably, with the state obligations to 'protect, respect and fulfill' human rights, is emphasised. In this regard, *see* J. L. Cernic, 'United Nations and the Corporate Responsibility for Human Rights', 8 *Miskolc Journal of International Law* (2011) pp. 28–29.

62    For an interesting discussion on 'creative compliance', albeit from the field of tax rather than human rights law, *see* D. McBarnet. 'When Compliance is not the Solution but the Problem: From Changes in Law to Changes in Attitude', in V. Braithwaite (ed.), *Taxing Democracy* (Ashgate, Aldershot, 2002), who, at p. 229, notes: "creative compliance involves finding ways to accomplish compliance with the letter of the law while totally undermining the policy behind the words". We are not suggesting that corporations will focus primarily on designing the most credible-looking due diligence process rather than proactively engaging with the human rights issues faced by the corporation. However, we see it as a central limitation of the Special Representative's framework that it allows this possibility, and may even appear to encourage corporations to act in this manner. We note that the literature suggests that creative compliance has been identified as finding its source in a certain attitude towards law, which is notably encouraged by a certain way of drafting and designing norms (pp. 240–241).

63    The diversity in civil liability regimes is too great for a complete analysis to be conducted here, but it may be noted, on a general level, that the due diligence model could allow the alleged violator to argue that the required 'policies and procedures' were in place, rather than requiring a concrete, actual and proactive concern for human rights issues. That is, attention would be diverted from the outcome (whether or not human rights viola-

In conclusion, we find the approach referring to 'all human rights' for the substance, and creating, for the rest, 'due diligence' processes, to be overly optimistic about the self-explanatory character of the international human rights regime and the way it is supposed to be interpreted and applied by business. Furthermore, it waters down the social and legal standard of conduct that business is expected to live by, and fails to clarify its concrete responsibilities. As a result, the 'due diligence' standard alone is unsuited for both market-based and investor-induced accountability, as well as for the application of civil liability mechanisms. We believe that an effective accountability framework should, before moving to compliance processes, first *spell out* the substance of the obligations of corporations in respect of human rights, for example in the form of a detailed, comprehensive 'Code'.[64] In this respect, as we have noted above, simply cross-referencing general human rights instruments that were written with states in mind, is not enough. While the Special Representative undoubtedly makes very sensible proposals as to how to operationalise corporate due diligence (proposals that, in fact, fit comfortably within the enlightened and proactive approach to social issues management that investors expect of companies), the due diligence approach alone does not deal with the performance question. Specifically, in the absence of clearly spelled out substantive obligations, it is left to companies to define the outcomes that they wish to achieve.[65] In this sense, it perhaps places corporations in too comfortable a position given the stakes involved. Self-regulation by reference to vague principles or agendas has clear limits and, with regard to human rights, such strategy seems a bit thin when considering the few incentives that businesses have to mend their ways, and the relative freedom they have not to.[66]

In the next sections we further describe the kind of normative framework that we envision and offer some reflections and proposals as to how it may complement the Special Representative's work.

---

tions occurred) to the process (*i.e.* the presence or absence of due diligence procedures). In this regard, *see however* the statement in the Special Representative's 2010 report that he "would not support proposals that conducting human rights due diligence, by itself, should automatically and fully absolve a company from Alien Tort Statute or similar liability". See Human Rights Council (2010), *supra* note 52, para. 86, pp. 17–18.

64  The emphasis on substance rather than process would make this Code very different from the very bland and PR-oriented 'Codes of Conduct' that many corporations have adopted.

65  As the Special Representative himself rightly underlines: "the standards that business initiatives incorporate are typically self-defined rather than tracking internationally recognized human rights" (Draft Guiding Principles, para. 9, p. 3).

66  We acknowledge that there are fundamental questions around the role and effectiveness of self-regulation in public policy, even in situations where there is a clear normative framework in place. For a critical analysis of self-regulation, *see* R. Sullivan, *Rethinking Voluntary Approaches in Environmental Policy* (Edward Elgar, Cheltenham, 2005).

## 3.2. What Substance?

Based on the above considerations, in broad terms, we think that a credible normative framework should – perhaps self-evidently – reflect the major sources of international human rights expectations, be sufficiently clear so that corporate performance can be assessed objectively and should focus on standards and performance (*i.e.* human rights outcomes) rather than just management systems and processes (such as due diligence).

Before moving on to the question of the substance of such a framework, we first wish to respond briefly to the commonly used business argument against such frameworks (and one that was heavily deployed against the Sub-Commission's Draft Norms), namely that they are a precursor to binding regulation. We acknowledge this argument, but do not think it has particular relevance for three reasons. The first is, as we note at the beginning of this chapter, that our chapter is explicitly concerned about the question of how we can make progress in the absence of regulation. Second, we do not believe that, even if there was some degree of consensus around human rights norms, regulation would automatically follow. In fact, we are sceptical that we will see anything that resembles a comprehensive human rights treaty being adopted within the next decade. Third, even if such a treaty or international agreement was adopted, ensuring the effective implementation of such a treaty presents a whole series of additional problems.[67] That is, we are of the view that we are a very long way from seeing a comprehensive and effectively enforced treaty on business and human rights.

Perhaps the closest to a suitable and robust framework for this purpose is that developed by the Business Leaders Initiative on Human Rights (BLIHR).[68] The Initiative was established by a group of international businesses (including Barclays, Novartis and Novo Nordisk) with the aim of helping further integrate human rights into business policies and practices. The BLIHR member companies viewed international human rights standards as an important part of the global governance debate, as these would provide guidance in defining the respective human rights responsibilities of government, business, NGOs and other societal actors. A central element of the BLIHR programme was testing the value of the UN Sub-Commission's Draft Norms and developing practical tools and guidance on their implementation.

While BLIHR acknowledged that the expectations on businesses are very sector-specific and reflect factors such as the size of the business, its markets, its activities, its geography and its history,[69] one of its central conclusions was that it is important to develop a bedrock of essential obligations that any company has, and of essential steps

---

67 See J. Zerk, *Multinationals and Corporate Social Responsibility – Limitations and Opportunities in International Law* (Cambridge University Press, Cambridge, 2006) pp. 83 *et seq.*; E. De Brabandere, 'Human Rights and Transnational Corporations – The Limits of Direct Corporate Social Responsibility', 4 *Human Rights & International Legal Discourse* (2010).
68 For further information on BLIHR, see <www.blihr.org/>.
69 Business Leaders Initiative on Human Rights (BLIHR), *Business Leaders Initiative on Human Rights: Policy Report 4* (BLIHR, London, 2009) p. 8.

that any company should take regardless of its size, location or nature of its business.[70] It therefore proposed a framework – which was based on the UN Sub-Commission's Draft Norms – that contained both minimum standards (what it referred to as 'essential' business behaviour in relation to specific human rights) as well as examples of performance that are expected by wider society that can be classed as 'expected' or 'desirable'. BLIHR proposed that companies have responsibilities to respect the human rights listed in Annex 1. For each of these, BLIHR set out a series of 'essential steps' that virtually all companies should take if they were to meet their responsibilities in relation to that human right. To illustrate the BLIHR approach, Box 1 presents the example of the right to privacy.

Box 1: Essential steps in relation to the right to privacy[71]

In respecting this right, the BLIHR companies see the following as essential steps:

- Ensuring that, upon request, individuals will be made aware of personal information that the business maintains on them, where it is held and how it can be corrected;
- Not asking workers about their health or pregnancy status except when the status is directly relevant to the performance of job duties, and seeking to keep such information confidential;
- Ensuring adequate protection of personal information held by the company;
- Only providing an individual's personal or other information to government authorities to the extent required by law and upon request, or with the individual's permission;
- Seeking to minimise the use of monitoring, surveillance and security measures that may invade the privacy of individuals to the extent practicable, and using such measures solely for the legitimate business purpose of protecting its assets and the safety of its workers or others.

In the context of our argument about the importance of norms, the BLIHR approach is attractive as an operationalisation of the corporate responsibility to respect as it combines the substance, process and performance elements that we have identified as essential to an effective human rights framework for business. The list of rights and obligations provides a substantive reference on which corporations could base their objectives, and the essential steps delineate in a detailed and nuanced manner the various ways in which corporations are to reach those objectives. With the BLIHR approach as a framework, the objective of bringing clarity to the obligations of businesses and the expectations stakeholders (and among them institutional investors) have of them can more easily be reached. On the legal accountability side, when a liability claim is made in practice by a harmed stakeholder, the framework allows both the standard of conduct for appreciating the existence of a breach of duty of care and the limiting factors

---

70   Ibid., p. 11.
71   Ibid., p. 16.

(*e.g.* foreseeability, proximity, causation[72]) to be determined in a reasonably objective manner. At the same time, when a corporation makes a claim of compliance with its human rights responsibilities, it can do so by reference to a solid normative framework, and not only on the basis of self-defined risk-mitigating processes.

Finally, we wish to stress that our purpose is not to discard the framework put forward by the Special Representative altogether, and also that we do not view the BLIHR framework as an alternative to the Ruggie framework. In fact, we see the two approaches as compatible, with the BLIHR addressing the major gaps in the Special Representative's view of the corporate responsibility to respect. The BLIHR framework's contribution is to explicitly enumerate the human rights applicable to corporate activities,[73] thereby clarifying the scope and substance of corporate responsibilities in that respect, and to provide guidance on practicalities of discharging those responsibilities by exploring, right by right, what concrete actions are required of corporations. The BLIHR approach connects to the Special Representative's due diligence approach, but it improves on it in two major ways: (i) it makes it relative to a clear, concrete and finite code of human rights obligations; and (ii) it discusses due diligence processes not in an open-ended or self-reflective way, but in an applied and rights-specific way, delineating clear outcomes that need to be achieved by corporations.[74] From the perspective of investors, the BLIHR framework provides a clear and detailed benchmark that they can use to clearly and objectively assess corporate performance. Moreover, the fact that the BLIHR framework was developed and tested by companies gives it a degree of credibility and legitimacy, at least in the business community.

### 3.3. *The Recipe for Success: Legitimacy and Effectiveness*

In order to be recognised as relevant, authoritative and valid, any normative framework would need to be effective and have legitimacy.[75] By effectiveness, we mean the ability of the framework to actually reach its intended purpose. Expressed another way, the result should be increased respect for human rights by those businesses us-

---

72    Mares, *supra* note 59, pp. 1188 *et seq.*

73    Hereby putting substance (and nuance) on Ruggie's claim that corporations are liable to breach all human rights.

74    The intensity of the requirements delineated in the 'steps' varies from results-oriented steps ('ensure that …') to more means-oriented ones ('seek to minimize …'). In this regard, the BLIHR framework reflects the complexity of human rights responsibilities of business, while, at the same time, not giving companies complete freedom to define for themselves the level of outcomes they will seek. Arguably, the extent of the defenses that a corporations could be able to present are more limited in this model than in the much vaguer 'due diligence' model presented by the Special Representative.

75    On the value of effectiveness and legitimacy for the 'validity' of a norm, *see* F. Ost and M. van de Kerchove, *De la Pyramide au Réseau? Pour une Théorie Dialectique du Droit* (Publications des Facultés Universitaires Saint-Louis, Brussels, 2000) pp. 309 *et seq.* On the determinants of the 'authority' acquired by private actors in global governance, *see* R. B. Hall and Thomas Biersteker (eds.), *The Emergence of Private Authority in Global Governance* (Cambridge University Press, Cambridge, 2002).

ing the framework. By legitimacy, we mean that the framework should be recognised as 'appropriate' or 'the right thing to do' by a wide circle of stakeholders.[76] These two characteristics are of course mutually reinforcing,[77] and depend on a number of elements, ranging from their compatibility with agreed societal norms to the existence of practical mechanisms for accountability.

There are several reasons why we think the BLIHR framework could be both effective and legitimate. The first is that it is clearly based on both core international human rights law principles and the work of the UN Sub-Commission. The second is that it has been applied in practice by companies. Based on this experience, BLIHR developed a series of guidance tools and materials to support their implementation.[78] That is, the principles are in a form that allows companies to use them as a basis for managing their human rights impacts. Third, the framework allows reasonably objective assessments of corporate performance to be made. This, in turn, would allow investors to make an assessment of whether the company is exposed to specific human rights risks (and to make an assessment of the significance of these risks), to assess how well the company is managing its human rights issues, and to engage with the company (and, in turn, objectively assess the quality of the company's response to that engagement).

The BLIHR framework also has a number of limitations. In particular, we recognise that the sources and the testing of these, as with any other sets of principles, is not enough. If the framework is to be agreed as the definitive normative framework for business and human rights, it needs endorsement across business and civil society. In relation to business, we would be surprised if there was particular opposition to this framework; in fact, if we look at the debates around the UN Sub-Commission Norms, the major objections from business seemed to relate to whether and how the Norms would be enforced rather than to the fact that business had specific responsibilities with regard to human rights.

In addition to the need for broad support and endorsement for the framework, we also believe that credible monitoring, assessment and redress mechanisms would be critical to the success of the framework.[79] Such accountability is a crucial element of the effectiveness and of the legitimacy of any global governance instrument, all the more when designed and operated by private actors[80] and when domestic legal rem-

---

76   *See generally* M. Zürn, 'Global Governance and Legitimacy Problems', 39 *Government and Opposition* (2004) pp. 260-261.

77   *See* J. Black, 'Legitimacy and the Competition for Regulatory Share', *LSE Law, Society and Economy Working Paper Series,* WPS 14-2009, July 2009, available at <www.lse.ac.uk/collections/law/wps/WPS2009-14_Black.pdf>.

78   *See further* <www.blihr.org/>.

79   This speaks to the 'due diligence' policies and processes that the Special Representative advocates.

80   *See* N. Hachez and J. Wouters, 'A Glimpse at the Democratic Legitimacy of Private Standards: Democratic Legitimacy as Public Accountability – The Case of GLOBAL G.A.P.', 14:3 *Journal of International Economic Law* (forthcoming 2011).

edies are absent or ineffective.[81] In its current state, the BLIHR framework is overly reliant on self-evaluation and reporting. As we have discussed above, while institutional investors would have a role to play in scrutinising corporate performance and perhaps holding companies to account for their performance, this falls short of structurally effective accountability in the business and human rights regulatory regime. The market is indeed powerless against the majority of corporate human rights violations: those committed by less visible corporations (*e.g.* those subcontractors buried deep down in the supply chain), those which are not disclosed voluntarily, *etc*.[82] To address the shortcomings of market-based accountability, less diffuse accountability mechanisms would therefore be needed.

## 4. Assessment of the Proposed Framework

We recognise that our argument in favour of a corporation-specific and substance-oriented normative framework may shake the consensus that has been reached around the protect-respect-remedy proposals that have been advanced by the Special Representative. We also recognise that there are a number of objections that could be raised about our proposals. We engage with what we see as the most substantive of these here as we believe that these challenges provide important insights to the design and effective implementation of a normative framework.

### 4.1. The Norms Were Rejected and There Is a Consensus Around the Protect-Respect-Remedy Framework

Our analysis above suggests that, if we want investors to make a meaningful contribution to the protection and promotion of human rights, they need a clearly defined normative framework, supported by civil society and backed up by effective institutions. The question is not one of intellectual purity; it is one of how the capital markets can be harnessed to support the delivery of international human rights.

In this context, it is important not to overestimate the consensus formed around the Special Representative's framework. While many stakeholders are happy that the Special Representative was able to jumpstart the debate after the stalemate caused by the Norms, many also regret the Special Representative's lack of ambition, seeing the protect-respect-remedy framework primarily as a clarification effort (whereas the Norms were seen as an important political breakthrough), and take issue with a number of important points, notably the total abandonment of a 'list of human rights obligations' approach.[83]

---

81  *See* the 'access to remedies' part of the 'Protect, Respect and Remedy' framework of the Special Representative', at Human Rights Council, *supra* note 47, paras. 82 *et seq.*, pp. 22 *et seq.*

82  Market accountability can be described as 'diffuse', *i.e.* characterised by a high degree of relativity and uncertainty.

83  *See* Human Rights Council, *supra* note 47, para. 51, pp. 14–15. Admittedly, the sort of 'list of human rights obligations' contained in the Norms was much shorter and much vaguer

## 4.2. Even If There Was a Normative Framework Would Investors Use It and Would It Be Effective?

We see this as a much more important question and one that we cannot provide a definitive answer to. We recognise that even if there was a clear human rights normative framework and even if investors did integrate human rights factors into their investment decisions, human rights issues would probably continue to be underplayed in investment analysis and decision-making. There are three broad reasons.[84] First, investment models typically only look three years or, sometimes, five years forwards; impacts that occur outside these types of timeframes are generally ignored. Second, impacts that occur in the future are generally assigned a lower importance than similar impacts today. Third, as many significant social and environmental impacts are simply not financially material (*i.e.* they have a modest effect on companies' earnings or profits), they tend to be excluded from investment analysis. The consequence is that, on its own, investment analysis is unlikely to be enough to incentivise companies to improve their human rights performance. However, if this integration is supplemented by engagement, where investors explain to companies how human rights issues are factored into their investment decisions and clearly communicate their expectations of companies' human rights performance, we can see a very different dynamic at play, where the incentives for companies to improve their performance would be significantly increased.

The creation of an agreed normative framework would also help bypass some of the problems presented by the general lack of knowledge about human rights issues in the investment world. It is likely that investors would articulate their expectations of companies by reference to 'compliance with' the framework and would look to companies to have the systems and processes in place to comply with (and demonstrate compliance with) the framework. That is, rather than requiring investors to become specialists in human rights issues, such a framework would allow investors to define their expectations by reference to compliance with a widely recognised standard.

We acknowledge that there are, at present, few incentives for investors to engage proactively with the companies in which they are invested. This is a well recognised problem.[85] While there may be arguments for investors to take a more proactive approach, the transaction costs of taking action and the reality that the benefits are difficult to measure and accrue to the investment industry as a whole (rather than to the individual investor) limit the level of willingness and interest of individual investors to commit significant resources to this area. There are other obstacles as well, including: a general scepticism about the investment benefits of focusing on human rights; a

---

than that put forward by the BLIHR. For a summary of the reception of the framework, see J. Wouters and N. Hachez, 'Business and Human Rights in EU External Relations – Making the EU a Leader at Home and Internationally', Research Study for the European Parliament, April 2009, available at <www.europarl.europa.eu/activities/committees/studies/download.do?language=en&file=25533>, pp. 14–18.

84  *See generally* Sullivan, *supra* note 35.
85  *See generally* Viñes Fiestas *et. al.*, *supra* note 1.

general lack of understanding of how and why human rights issues could be relevant to investment; a reluctance to be seen as a 'social activist' or 'campaigning NGO'; a lack of pressure from clients, stakeholders or industry peers to take action on these issues; an unwillingness to take a leadership position; and a perception that focusing on these issues would entail incurring additional costs or risk damaging investment performance.

Some of these obstacles may well be overcome if we see a greater focus on human rights in existing legal obligations or voluntary initiatives, in particular in the environmental space. Domestic legislation in some countries, for example, now seeks to induce, with more or less success, institutional investors to at least consider sustainable development issues in their operations, notably by requiring them to report on their social and environmental impacts.[86] Certain states also explicitly require their national pension funds to take such factors into account. The most prominent example is that of Norway's Government Pension Fund, which is managed according to strict ethical guidelines adopted by the Norwegian government, and under the oversight of a Council of Ethics.[87] This is a good example of how national legislation and global private initiatives could interact: as domestic legislation requires investors to take human rights factors into account in their investment decisions, a framework such as that developed by BLIHR may be used as a reference instrument in discharging this legal obligation.

### 4.3. A Normative Framework Cannot Cover Every Eventuality

We recognise that not all eventualities will be covered by a normative framework such as the one that we propose here. Yet, the Special Representative's approach relying on all-encompassing but overly general human rights instruments is no solution either. We believe that seeing the proposed normative framework as a set of adaptable (though not relative!) principles should overcome the difficulties resulting from the limited character of the framework. Not all aspects of behaviour can be prescribed for any actor in society and, therefore, a periodic review of the framework should allow gaps to be filled as they appear.

We also recognise that the development of any sort of normative framework such as that proposed here will inevitably mean that many of the important subtleties and nuances in the debate around the human rights responsibilities of business will be obscured. However, there are two responses. The first is that if investors' influence is to be

---

86   See E. de Cannart d'Hamale et al., *La Responsabilité sociale des Entreprises (Corporate Social Responsibility) – Concept, Pratiques et Droit* (Vanden Broele, Brugge, 2006) p. 151.

87   For information on the legal framework for the fund, see <www.regjeringen.no/en/dep/fin/Selected-topics/the-government-pension-fund/responsible-investments/the-council-on-ethics-for-the-government.html?id=447010>. For an analysis of the social and environmental governance impacts of the fund's investment activities, see L. Cata Backer, 'Sovereign Wealth Funds as Regulatory Chameleons: The Norwegian Sovereign Wealth Funds and Public Global Governance through Private Global Investment', 41 *Georgetown Journal of International Law* (2010).

harnessed, some compromises and simplifications will inevitably be needed. Second, any normative framework will develop and evolve over time, reflecting changing circumstances as well as experience in the application of the framework.

## 4.4. Would Such a Framework Be Legitimate?

There are a number of dimensions to the legitimacy of any framework – the sources of the framework, the expertise of its authors, its alignment with prevailing societal norms, the process with which it was adopted, whether it is perceived as effective, *etc*. The specific point we wish to address here is whether any such framework would succeed in gathering sufficiently widespread support to be seen as a credible and appropriate framework. We are actually quite optimistic on this point. We see the fact that many NGOs explicitly supported the UN Sub-Commission's Norms as an indication that creating such wide-spread buy-in is feasible, although we fear that this may be more difficult than it was in 2003/2004 given that the Norms have effectively been sidelined and many NGOs have subsequently engaged with the Special Representative's process.

There is a second reason why such legitimacy is important, and it relates to the role that investors can and could play in influencing corporate human rights practice. At present, the lack of a consistent view across the NGO community about the human rights expectations of companies and the relative lack of focus on the role that institutional investors can play in protecting and promoting human rights has meant that there has been limited pressure on investors to engage with companies on human rights issues. Moreover, the absence of consensus around a normative framework has meant that where such discussions have taken place, they have tended to focus on management processes rather than outcomes.

## 5. Concluding Comments

We acknowledge the challenge that our arguments present both to the UN Special Representative and to the international community. We recognise the consensus that has been painstakingly built up around the protect-respect-remedy formulation and the high level of global engagement with the Special Representative. That said, our central question is whether all of this work has moved us any closer to a coherent, practical framework that investors – and, indeed, other stakeholders – can use to assess the human rights performance of companies and to hold them to account for their performance against this framework. If this is the proper test of the work of the Special Representative, then our answer must be that the debate around business and human rights has, at best, stalled, and more likely regressed since the Special Representative was appointed.

In his protect, respect and remedy framework, the Special Representative emphasises the role of states in ensuring respect for human rights by corporations. However, in a world where the ability of the nation state to effectively control the activities of companies is severely constrained, we need to look beyond conventional regulatory approaches and consider how the influence of other actors can be harnessed. In our view, this requires putting in place credible accountability mechanisms aimed at keeping corporate conduct in check, using the resources of all actors available, including corporations themselves, and their investors. Such accountability mechanisms should be based on clear normative references for judging behaviour, and on effective processes for operationalising those norms and sanctioning misbehavers. In this light, our criticism of the Special Representative's framework pertains mainly to the fact that, notably because of his rejection of the substance-oriented approach of the Norms and his exclusive focus on corporate due diligence, the conceptual effort toward corporate human rights accountability has been diverted into a search for management and disclosure processes, which, though useful *per se*, are unlikely to function effectively in the absence of a normative framework that clearly defines and delineates corporate human rights obligations. The fact that we do not have such a normative framework, in our view, weakens the pressures for companies to manage their human rights impacts effectively and makes it harder for the accountability mechanisms identified by the protect, respect and remedy framework to operate.

In relation to institutional investors and the ways in which they can contribute to increased accountability from business, we have, as a consequence, gone from a situation where a number of mainstream investors were proactively communicating the Norms to the companies in which they were invested and encouraging these companies to ensure that they met the letter and spirit of the Norms, to one where human rights are practically off the agenda. Our proposals are directed at changing this situation as quickly as possible. The priority is the development of a credible normative framework such as that provided by BLIHR. Given that this process would take some time, the immediate action should be for institutional investors (or at least a group – which could be relatively modest in terms of numbers – of large institutions) to endorse the BLIHR framework as the most credible human rights framework that is currently available. For their part, governments and civil society should lend their support to this agenda. This support has two dimensions. The first is to press the Working Group on business and human rights to develop such a framework, and the second is to lend their support to the framework through pressing companies and investors to support and ensure the effective implementation of such a framework once it has been developed.

Finally, while the focus of this chapter is on the role that institutional investors can play in the protection and promotion of human rights in the business community, it is not our intention to argue that investors are the only or the most important actor. Companies face pressure from a range of stakeholders (governments, NGOs, the media, employees, *etc.*), of whom investors are just one. We also recognise that investors may not be best placed to be the arbiters of company performance, either in terms of defining what is acceptable corporate behaviour or in holding companies to account for failings in their performance. Therefore, other types of accountability mechanisms will be needed as well. That said, we are also very aware of the realities of the limitations of international human rights law as it applies to business (in particular its limitations in holding companies to account for their human rights performance). Investors – at least in theory – offer the potential of stimulating moves towards the 'regulation' of companies, through encouraging the development of effective corporate self-regulatory regimes as well as increasing the pressure on governments to take action to complement or supplement these self-regulatory initiatives. We therefore see this chapter as part of the wider discussion around the potential for non-state actors to create the right incentives for companies to take proper account of their human rights impacts.

## Annex 1  Scope of Companies' Human Rights Responsibilities[88]

| | |
|---|---|
| 1 | Responsibilities in relation to the right to non-discrimination |
| 2 | Responsibilities in relation to the right to life |
| 3 | Responsibilities in relation to the right to prohibition against torture, and cruel, inhuman or degrading treatment or punishment and the right to consent to scientific and medical experimentation |
| 4 | Responsibilities in relation to the prohibition against slave, forced or compulsory labour |
| 5 | Responsibilities in relation to the right to liberty and security of person |
| 6 | Responsibilities in relation to the right to liberty of movement and freedom to choose residence |
| 7 | Responsibilities in relation to the right to privacy |
| 8 | Responsibilities in relation to the right to freedom of thought, conscience and religion |
| 9 | Responsibilities in relation to the right to hold opinions and the right to freedom of expression and information |
| 10 | Responsibilities in relation to the right to the prohibition against incitement of national, racial or religious hatred. |
| 11 | Responsibilities in relation to the right to the right of peaceful assembly |
| 12 | Responsibilities in relation to freedom of association, including the right to form and join trade unions and the right to strike |
| 13 | Responsibilities in relation to the right to take part in the conduct of public affairs |
| 14 | Responsibilities in relation to the rights of persons to their culture, religious practice and language |
| 15 | Responsibilities in relation to the right to just and favourable conditions of work |
| 16 | Responsibilities in relation to the right to a fair wage and decent living |
| 17 | Responsibilities in relation to the right to safe and healthy working conditions |
| 18 | Responsibilities in relation to the right to rest, leisure and holidays |
| 19 | Responsibilities in relation to the right to social security, including social insurance |
| 20 | Responsibilities in relation to the right to a family life |
| 21 | Responsibilities in relation to the prohibition against exploitative child labour |
| 22 | Responsibilities in relation to the right to an adequate standard of living, including adequate food, clothing and housing |
| 23 | Responsibilities in relation to the right to the highest attainable standard of physical and mental health |
| 24 | Responsibilities in relation to the right to education |

---

88  BLIHR, *supra* note 69, pp. 13–20.

| 25 | Responsibilities in relation to the right to take part in cultural life |
| 26 | Responsibilities in relation to the right to enjoy scientific progress |
| 27 | Responsibilities in relation to the right to protection of the benefits resulting from scientific, literary or artistic productions |
| 28 | Responsibilities in relation to the actions of others (avoiding complicity) |

# 10 Pushing the Boundaries: The Role of National Human Rights Institutions in Operationalising the 'Protect, Respect and Remedy' Framework

Meg Brodie*

## 1. Introduction

National human rights institutions (NHRIs) have emerged as unique actors in the business and human rights field. As independent statutorily established bodies, NHRIs have traditionally focused on state violations; however recently and increasingly these state based bodies are mobilising their human rights expertise and mandate to address private-sector human rights abuse. In an open letter to NHRIs the United Nations (UN) Special Representative of the Secretary-General (SRSG) for Business and Human Rights, John Ruggie, noted that he had "long taken an interest in the vital role of NHRIs in advancing human rights in practice".[1] When the SRSG first set out the 'Protect, Respect and Remedy' Framework in 2008,[2] he made clear his view that the contribution of NHRIs was valuable: "The actual and potential importance of these institutions cannot be overstated."[3] By doing so, he galvanised NHRI networks and individual institutions to more concertedly consider their potential contribution, and to share what they were already doing to deal with business-related violations.

---

* National Human Rights Institutions Fellow, The Raoul Wallenberg Institute of Human Rights and Humanitarian Law, Lund, Sweden.
1 J. Ruggie, *Message from the Special Representative of the Secretary General for Business and Human Rights to NHRIs Worldwide*, 28 January 2009.
2 For information and analysis of the history and context of the Ruggie mandate, *see* the chapters in this volume by Mares; Buhmann; Knox; and Melish and Meidinger. In 2008 the SRSG presented the UN Human Rights Council with a framework intended to provide a focal point for all stakeholders to advance thinking and action on business and human rights. The Framework rests on three pillars – the state's duty to protect against human rights violations, corporations' responsibility to respect human rights, and effective access to remedies (*see* Human Rights Council, *Protect, Respect and Remedy: A Framework for Business and Human Rights: Report of the Special Representative of the Secretary-General on the Issue of Human Rights and Transnational Corporations and Other Business Enterprises*, John Ruggie, A/HRC/8/5, 7 April 2008, (*Protect, Respect and Remedy*)).
3 *Ibid.*, para. 97.

There are many examples of NHRIs addressing business-related human rights violations including, for example, making orders and recommendations directly to both companies and states for implementation;[4] facilitating access to judicial mechanisms for resolution;[5] convening stakeholders for dialogue;[6] and supporting businesses to understand their human rights responsibilities.[7] However, while these types of activities are encouraging examples of NHRI innovation and willingness to engage with business-related human rights violations, the reality is that *contra* Ruggie the potential contribution of NHRIs *can* be overstated. In 2011, Ruggie released a set of Guiding

---

[4] The Kenyan National Commission on Human Rights utilised a national inquiry process to make orders and recommendations to remedy the harm experienced by coastal communities as a result of human rights violations committed by salt companies in collusion with public institutions: Kenyan National Commission on Human Rights, *Report of a Public Inquiry into Allegations of Human Rights Violations in Magarina, Malindi*, 2006; F. Simbiri-Jaoko, 'The Experience of Kenya National Commission on Business and Human Rights', *Presentation to the Side Event on Business and Human Rights*, 31 May 2010. In France, the Commission Nationale Consultive des Droits de l'Homme undertook a review of corporate social responsibility, providing a series of recommendations in an opinion to the government about exercising France's state duty to protect: Commission Nationale Consultative Des Droit De L'Homme, *Opinion on Corporate Human Rights Responsibility*, 24 April 2008. For further examples, see Deva on the experiences of the National Human Rights Commission of India in dealing with business related violations: S. Deva, 'Corporate human rights abuses: what role for national human rights violations', in H. Nasu and B. Saul (eds.), *Human Rights in the Asia-Pacific Region: Towards Institution Building* (Routledge, Milton Park, 2011) pp. 244–247.

[5] In Bolivia, the Pilcomayo river basin was contaminated by a series of mines, including a company owned by the President. The Bolivian Defensor del Pueblo and civil society joined together to present a complaint before the Inter-American Court of Human Rights: Presentation to Working Group on Business, Environment and Human Rights, 10th International Conference of NHRIs, Human Rights and Business: The Role of NHRIs, Edinburgh, Scotland, 8–10 October 2010.

[6] In Korea, the National Human Rights Commission began the process of engaging with business and human rights issues, developing strategic plans and policies for its own action and convening multiple business stakeholders: National Human Rights Commission of Korea, *New Challenges and New Chances for NHRIs: Introduction of NHRCK's Activities in the Area of Business and Human Rights and the Prospects of Future Initiative*, Paper presented at the 10th International Conference of NHRIs, Human Rights and Business: The Role of NHRIs, Edinburgh, Scotland, 8–10 October 2010.

[7] In Australia, business executives' reluctance to dialogue on 'human rights obligations' prompted the Australian Human Rights Commission to undertake to 'translate' international human rights instruments into language familiar and accessible to the corporate stakeholders: Australian Human Rights Commission, *NHRIs and the Corporate Responsibility to Respect*, Paper presented at the 10th International Conference of NHRIs, Human Rights and Business: The Role of NHRIs, Edinburgh, Scotland, 8–10 October 2010. The Danish Institute of Human Rights has produced a commercial tool that allows businesses to assess their human rights compliance: Danish Institute of Human Rights, *Human Rights Compliance Assessment Tool*, <www.humanrightsbusiness.org>, visited on 15 May 2011.

Principles that seek to operationalise the 'Protect, Respect, Remedy' Framework.⁸ These Principles envisage that NHRI's primary contribution will be as a state-based non-judicial grievance mechanism providing effective and accessible remedies for business-related harm.⁹ However, while some NHRIs have complaints handling mechanisms and powers to both investigate and hand down enforceable orders,¹⁰ many have limited or no powers to order binding remedies that "counteract or make good any human rights harms that have occurred".¹¹

To understand the true value of NHRIs in dealing with business-related human rights violations, a more integrated vision of NHRI engagement is required than that explicitly provided by the Guiding Principles. NHRIs, with limited exceptions, are not likely in the short term to provide the effective remedies envisaged by the Guiding Principles unless and until there is a concerted effort by states to equip NHRIs with the necessary powers and resources to perform this non-judicial grievance mechanism role. Nevertheless, the Guiding Principles do provide a platform to articulate further the crucial contribution NHRIs must make to provide protection and redress to victims of business-related human rights violations. As such, NHRIs' most significant immediate contribution to the advancement of the Guiding Principles will be supporting the operationalisation of the state duty to protect and corporate responsibility to respect human rights.

In this chapter I firstly describe the unique position of NHRIs, highlighting how interaction with business creates new accountabilities for these independent institutions. Secondly, I consider the extent of NHRIs' business and human rights mandate under international standards, the Paris Principles. Thirdly, I outline how NHRIs have participated in the development of the 'Protect, Respect, Remedy' Framework and analyse how the Guiding Principles position the role of NHRIs. Fourthly, I look at the challenges limiting NHRIs' capacity to deliver effective remedies, focusing in particular on how the proliferation of diverse forms of NHRIs has created a sharp divide between institutions that can hear individual complaints and those that cannot. I also review the kinds of remedy that are open to NHRIs to provide. Fifthly, I explore how NHRIs' experiences conducting national inquiries demonstrate the potential for these institutions to play a role in supporting the operationalisation of each pillar of the Framework. Sixthly, I conclude by pointing to the key opportunities for NHRIs to address business-related NHRI harm.

---

8   Human Rights Council, *Report of the Special Representative of the Secretary-General on the Issue of Human Rights and Transnational Corporations and Other Business Enterprises, John Ruggie: Guiding Principles on Business and Human Rights: Implementing the United Nations "Protect, Respect and Remedy" Framework*, A/HRC/17/31, 21 March 2011, (*Guiding Principles*).

9   While the Guiding Principles make mention of NHRIs under all three pillars, NHRIs' contribution as a state-based non-judicial grievance measure is regarded as "particularly important". See *Guiding Principles*, supra note 8, para. 27, commentary.

10  See Office of the High Commissioner for Human Rights, *Business and Human Rights: A Survey of NHRI Practices*, July 2008, (*Survey*).

11  *Guiding Principles*, supra note 8, para. 25, commentary.

NHRIs have collectively made extensive commitments to engage in the promotion and protection of human rights threatened by business-related violations. These institutions have already begun to answer the SRSG's call for NHRIs to "push the boundaries of what they can contribute".[12] Efforts to maintain the momentum generated by the SRSG must persuade states to properly equip NHRIs to provide effective remedies for business-related human rights harm; manage stakeholder expectations of NHRIs; and encourage NHRIs to continue to strive to utilise the Guiding Principles as a platform for further and creative protection against rights violations by businesses.

## 2. Positioning NHRIs: Standing Apart but Alongside Other Actors

A NHRI is an independent statutory body, established by a state to promote and protect human rights within its jurisdiction.[13] They were conceived in order to bridge the gap between the aspirations of international human rights law and its domestic realisation,[14] as well as to complement existing international, regional and national mechanisms.[15] NHRIs are often seen as occupying a unique, but difficult, position between government and civil society,[16] opening them up to multiple sites of accountability. Smith argues that these accountabilities are both "'downwards' to their partners, beneficiaries, staff and supporters; and 'upwards' to their funders, parliaments and host governments".[17] Additionally, NHRIs increasingly have accountabilities beyond the state to the International Coordinating Committee for National Institutions for the Promotion and Protection of Human Rights (ICC), the body of NHRI peers responsible for accrediting institutions for participation in international fora.[18]

However, NHRIs' increased focus on human rights violations by businesses creates a new potential site of accountability. While it does not necessarily follow that the accountabilities described above are disrupted by NHRI engagement with the private

---

12   J. Ruggie, *Outline of Remarks by SRSG John Ruggie*, 'Human Rights and Business: The Role of National Human Rights Institutions', Geneva, 31 May 2010, p. 4.

13   United Nations Centre for Human Rights, *National Human Rights Institutions: A Handbook on the Establishment and Strengthening of National Institutions for the Promotion and Protection of Human Rights* (1995).

14   Report of the Secretary General, *Strengthening of the United Nations: An Agenda for Further Change* (2002) A/57/387, [50]; A. Pohjolainen, *The Evolution of National Human Rights Institutions – The Role of the United Nations* (Danish Institute for Human Rights, Copenhagen, 2006).

15   B. Burdekin, *National Human Rights Institutions in the Asia-Pacific Region* (Martinus Nijhoff Publishers, The Hague, 2007), p. 5.

16   A. Smith, 'The Unique Position of National Human Rights Institutions: A Mixed Blessing?', 28 *Human Rights Quarterly* (2006) p. 937.

17   *Ibid.*, p. 906.

18   M. Brodie, 'Progressing Norm Socialisation: Membership Matters. The Impact of the Accreditation Process of the International Coordinating Committee of National Institutions for the Promotion and Protection of Human Rights', 80 *Nordic Journal of International Law* (2011) p. 161.

sector, a shift in the current conceptualisation of NHRIs positioned independently between the government and civil society is required in order to accommodate another actor. Business enterprises are not just stakeholders – the potential role of business as both a supporter and violator of human rights requires NHRIs to maintain the independence required to sanction business, while winning a degree of 'private sector legitimacy'.¹⁹ This has implications for the way NHRIs choose to engage with business. In view of these dual roles, "NHRIs and the corporate sector … should regard each other as potential allies and partners".²⁰ However, NHRIs are also called to play an important role in holding businesses that violate human rights to account.

Balancing these tensions with respect to other actors, including the state and civil society organisations, is already recognised as a major challenge facing NHRIs.²¹ Much of NHRIs' ability to navigate these relationships relies on their actual and perceived independence, ²² the scope of their mandate and the choices they make in exercising it. The SRSG believes that NHRIs have a critical and unique role to play in operationalising the 'Protect, Respect, Remedy' Framework.²³ However the operationalisation will only be effected if the commensurate "need to ensure all NHRIs' mandates are adequate to allow them to fulfil this role in practice"²⁴ is met. This begins with compliance with the international minimum standards for NHRI establishment.

## 3. Reading the Paris Principles for a Business and Human Rights Mandate

The accepted reference point²⁵ for describing the mandate of NHRIs is the 'Principles Relating to the Status and Functioning of National Institutions for the Protection and Promotion of Human Rights'.²⁶ Negotiated in Paris in 1991 and adopted by the

---

19   Smith, *supra* note 16, p. 906. Smith discusses the interaction between NHRIs and NGOs and the pursuant 'public sector legitimacy'.
20   Danish Institute for Human Rights, *Report from the Roundtable of National Human Rights Institutions on the Issue of Business and Human Rights*, Copenhagen, 1–2 July 2008, p. 3, (*Roundtable July 2008*)
21   Smith, *supra* note 16.
22   See e.g. Human Rights Watch, *Protectors or Pretenders? Government Human Rights Commissions in Africa* (2001), <www.hrw.org/reports/2001/africa/overview/factors.html>, visited 26 August 2008.
23   Ruggie, *Outline of Remarks*, *supra* note 12.
24   ICC Working Group on Business and Human Rights, *Interim Report to ICC Bureau*, Rabat, Morocco, 1 November 2009, p. 2, (*Interim Report*).
25   The historical context for the development of NHRIs and the reasons for their rapid proliferation have been extensively canvassed: Pohjolainen, *supra* note 14; S. Cardenas, 'Emerging Global Actors: The United Nations and National Human Rights Institutions', 9:1 *Global Governance* (2003) p. 23; T. Pegram, 'Diffusion Across Political Systems: The Global Spread of National Human Rights Institutions', 32:3 *Human Rights Quarterly* (2010) p. 729.
26   *United Nations Principles Relating to the Status of National Institutions* (*Paris Principles*), Annex to the GA Resolution 48/134 of 20 December 1993 (*Paris Principles*). This article

United Nations General Assembly in 1993, the standards became known as the Paris Principles. The core tenants of the Paris Principles are that NHRIs are established with a broad human rights mandate; independence from government guaranteed by the constitution or statute; membership composed of pluralist representation, secured by official appointment; sufficient resources; and a range of monitoring and advisory functions, supported by powers to operationalise them.[27] The Paris Principles clearly envisage that NHRIs will seek to protect and promote all human rights and address violations irrespective of the perpetrator. While the Principles do not expressly require that NHRIs engage with non-state violations,[28] they nevertheless encourage NHRI action on business-related abuse in four specific ways.

Firstly, under the competencies and responsibilities granted to NHRIs, the Paris Principles are clear that institutions "shall be vested with competence to promote and protect human rights"[29] and they are required to "be given as broad a mandate as possible".[30] This means that, provided a NHRI's establishing legislation does not seek to prescribe a more limited sphere of competence for the institution, it may deal with "any situation of violation of human rights".[31]

Secondly, the Paris Principles contemplate under 'methods of operation' that NHRIs will engage, and need to be empowered to engage, with both state and non-state actors.[32] The Principles provide that an institution shall "freely consider *any* questions falling within its competence"[33] and "hear *any* person and obtain *any* information and *any* documents necessary for assessing situations falling within its competence".[34] Enactment of these provisions is crucial to the capacity of a NHRI to seek information from, and about, businesses, particularly where there are alleged vio-

---

does not consider other state-based human rights mechanisms such as Parliamentary Committees and single issue Commissions and Ombudsmen. These types of bodies may also do important work on business and human rights issues, see e.g. United Kingdom House of Lords, House of Commons Joint Committee on Human Rights, *Any of Our Business? Human Rights and the UK Private Sector*, First Report of the Session 2009–2010, 24 November 2009. However, the *Guiding Principles* make it clear that NHRIs are institutions that are Paris Principles compliant, *Guiding Principles*, *supra* note 8, para. 3, commentary.

27   *Paris Principles*, *supra* note 26.
28   Surya Deva attributes the Paris Principles' silence on business violations to the "state centric bias of human rights law": Deva, *supra* note 4, p. 241.
29   *Paris Principles.*, *supra* note 26, Competence and responsibilities, Article 1.
30   *Ibid.*, Competence and responsibilities, Article 2.
31   *Ibid.*, Competence and responsibilities, Article 3(a)(ii).
32   Business enterprises are often captured under the term 'non-state actors', a tendency of international and human rights law to define all actors in relation to states. See P. Alston, 'The "Not-a-Cat" Syndrome: Can the International Human Rights Regime Accommodate Non-State Actors', in P. Alston (ed.), *Non-State Actors and Human Rights* (OUP, Oxford, 2005) p. 3.
33   *Paris Principles*, *supra* note 26, Methods of operation, Article (a).
34   *Ibid.*, Methods of operation, Article (b) (emphasis added).

lations. Importantly the Paris Principles foresee that NHRIs will need to seek, and at times compel, the production of information from actors from all sectors.

Thirdly, the Paris Principles require NHRIs to "maintain consultation with other bodies, whether jurisdictional or otherwise, responsible for the promotion and protection of human rights (in particular ombudsmen, mediators and similar institutions)".[35] The Principles thus recognise that NHRIs do not operate in isolation and that there is often a complex system of other mechanisms with which NHRIs should consult. The institutions specifically contemplated – the judiciary, ombudsmen and mediators – are those that the SRSG's Framework also envisages will play a central role in dealing with business-related human rights violations. Further, the Paris Principles allow for interaction with other mechanisms, thus taking into account NHRI cooperation with Organisation for Economic Co-operation and Development (OECD) National Contact Points (NCPs),[36] UN Global Compact local networks[37] and other state or non-state based mechanisms that ultimately contribute to the operationalisation of the Guiding Principles.[38]

Fourthly, the Paris Principles arguably provide for business engagement in the process of determining the composition of a NHRI. Consultation with various representative groups is viewed as an important part of legitimising NHRI leadership and helping to ensure both the plurality of its representation and its independence from any one actor, particularly government. Business representatives are not specifically mentioned, but the Paris Principles include amongst the groups that may contribute "professional organizations, for example, associations of lawyers, doctors, journalists and eminent scientists".[39] An extended interpretation of this group could theoretically include peak business or representative corporate social responsibility umbrella organisations. If involved in this way, business may regard itself and be regarded as a stakeholder. Business participation in the process may also encourage private sector acceptance of the authority of a NHRI.

---

35  *Ibid.*, Methods of operation, Article (f).

36  *International Coordinating Committee of National Human Rights Institutions, Review of OECD Guidelines for Multinational Enterprises: Submission of International Coordinating Committee of National Human Rights Institutions*, 25 November 2010.

37  Global Compact Human Rights Working Group, Meeting Summary Report, London, 17 November 2010, <www.unglobalcompact.org/docs/issues_doc/human_rights/Meetings_x_events/HRWG_17Nov10_MeetingReport.pdf>, visited 10 June 2011.

38  It is outside the scope of this chapter to address the issues that may arise when there are multiple avenues for seeking redress, including in particular jurisdiction confusion or overlap. NHRIs already experience this tension in relation to their interaction with the courts. Where there are multiple grievance mechanisms for making complaints about violations of businesses, clarity around jurisdiction, mandate and power to order remedies will be vital.

39  *Paris Principles*, supra note 26, Composition, Article 1(a).

The establishing legislation[40] of a NHRI should seek to give effect to the Paris Principles' core components and be reflexive to evolving international standards. Based on the above reading of the Paris Principles, at best, the instrument establishing a NHRI should clearly set out a mandate to deal with business-related violations. At the least, in order to comply with the broad mandate envisaged by the Paris Principles, establishing legislation should not exclude business, or particular human rights from a NHRI's mandate.

Compliance with the Paris Principles is assessed by the ICC's Sub-Committee on Accreditation (ICC SCA),[41] and a positive ranking as a 'fully compliant' institution will confer international and domestic legitimacy on the NHRI, as well as credibility on the state that created it.[42] In addition to their individual findings on particular applications, the ICC SCA also issues 'General Observations' that seek to clarify the interpretation of the Paris Principles. To date, the ICC SCA has not issued any observations that deal specifically with a NHRI's mandate to deal with business-related violations, although this course would be open to it. In particular the ICC SCA could advise that legislative restrictions on a NHRI's competence to deal with business are potentially in violation of the Paris Principles requirement for a broad human rights mandate.[43] Decisions of the ICC SCA have driven increased specificity of the content of the Paris Principles, and at the same time garnered acceptance for the legitimacy of the Sub-Committee's interpretations.[44] Over time this same process may influence the adoption of a refined interpretation of the NHRI mandate as one that requires an explicit provision for business-related violations. This process may gradually help realise the need for expanded mandates, and place pressure on states to enact reform as necessary.

Even if it does not become an explicit requirement, the Paris Principles do implicitly grant a mandate for NHRIs to deal with business-related human rights violations. This provides grounds for NHRIs to creatively draw on the full range of their functions and powers in addressing actual and potential corporate violations. Some institutions have embraced broad interpretation of the extent of its mandate where a NHRI's estab-

---

40  In some instances NHRIs are established using other mechanisms such as by executive decree. However it is now accepted that a Paris Principles compliant institution must be established in either a constitutional or legal text to protect its independence and permanency. See International Coordinating Committee of National Institutions for the Promotion and Protection of Human Rights, *General Observations*, 2007, para. 1.1, (*General Observations*).

41  *International Coordinating Committee of National Institutions for the Promotion and Protection of Human Rights, Rules of Procedure for the Sub-Committee on Accreditation*, adopted 14 September 2004, (*ICC SCA Rules of Procedure*)

42  Cardenas, *supra* note 25.

43  The process of issuing General Observations is currently under review: 'Discussion Paper on the Proposed Review of the General Observations Developed by the ICC Sub-Committee on Accreditation', Annex IV ICC Sub-Committee on Accreditation Report, March 2010.

44  Brodie, *supra* note 18, p. 143.

lishing legislation is silent on the same. For instance, the Chair of the Kenyan National Commission on Human Rights argues that she is

> not sure that NHRIs would need a specific mandate to deal with business, given that it already fits neatly into work done with government, business, and civil society in relation to economic, cultural and social rights. The choice of whether to engage business directly is a choice of the institution – if we ignore business, [we] cannot deliver on [our] wide mandate.[45]

Ruggie too, believes that NHRI engagement is often a decision to change institutional priorities, rather than one necessarily prescribed by a limited mandate: "While the mandates of some NHRIs may currently preclude them from work on business and human rights, for many it has been a question of choice, tradition or capacity."[46] National institutions agree. In October 2010 at the ICC's 10th International Conference, the 80 NHRIs present unanimously agreed that they would "actively consider how their mandates under the Paris Principles can be applied or where necessary strengthened, in order to promote and protect human rights as they relate to business".[47] Further, and specific to the SRSG's Framework, NHRIs committed "to proactively consider new ways in which NHRIs' mandates can be used to advance the 'protect, respect and remedy' framework".[48] Leveraging the Paris Principles provision for a broad mandate, NHRIs are clearly prepared to heed the SRSG's call to 'push the boundaries' of their engagement with business and human rights. In the absence of explicit statements, NHRIs' willingness to creatively interpret the extent of their mandate provides a foundation for engaging with business and human rights issues. This is exactly what NHRIs have sought to do.

## 4. Developing the 'Protect, Respect and Remedy' Framework: The Involvement of NHRIs

National human rights institutions mobilised quickly to participate in the mandate of the SRSG on business and human rights. Other actors were "struck … by the willingness [of NHRIs] to address these issues … even where they had not done so in the

---

45  *Report on the ICC and OHCHR Side Event: Engaging NHRIs in securing the promotion and protection of human rights in business*, held during the Human Rights Council, 11th Session, 2–18 June 2009, p. 7.

46  Human Rights Council, *Business and Human Rights: Towards Operationalizing the "Protect, Respect and Remedy" Framework, Report of the Special Representative of the Secretary-General on the Issue of Human Rights and Transnational Corporations and Other Business Enterprises, John Ruggie*, A/HRC/11/13, 22 April 2009, para. 103.

47  International Coordinating Committee of National Institutions for the Promotion and Protection of Human Rights, *The Edinburgh Declaration*, 10 October 2010, para. 16, (*Edinburgh Declaration*).

48  *Ibid.*, para. 17.

past".[49] While NHRIs have long engaged with issues raised by business-related human rights violations, it is true to say that NHRIs' general and conceptual role in this space is only just emerging.[50]

The establishment and exercise of Ruggie's mandate coincided with the maturing and solidifying of the NHRI international and regional networks. As expectations on NHRI members increase[51] and opportunities for engagement in international fora deepen,[52] the secretariats of the international NHRI network, the ICC, and one regional NHRI network,[53] the Asia Pacific Forum of National Human Rights Institutions (APF), have facilitated a collective focus on business and human rights.

During the period of the SRSG's mandate, members of both the ICC and the APF have endorsed and employed the 'Protect, Respect and Remedy' Framework,[54] seeking to better understand the contribution that NHRIs must make in dealing with business-related violations.[55] The ICC sought to institutionalise its response to the Ruggie mandate. In July 2008 the Danish Institute for Human Rights convened the first ICC roundtable on business and human rights. Since that time, the ICC has partnered and independently hosted many fora to facilitate NHRI collaboration and raise awareness of the role of NHRIs on business and human rights.[56] Further, the ICC members de-

---

49   Report on the ICC and OHCHR Side Event, supra note 45, p. 6.
50   Ibid., p. 1. For instance, the controversial predecessor to the Ruggie mandate did not discuss the role of NHRIs beyond mentioning that 'national mechanisms' will engage in monitoring application of the norms: Norms on the responsibilities of transnational corporations and other business enterprises with regard to human rights, E/CN.4/Sub.2/2003/12/Rev.2, 26 August 2003, para. 16.
51   For instance the ICC has implemented a reaccreditation process for all 'A' accredited institutions on a five year rotating basis: ICC Working Group on Accreditation, Decision Paper on the Review of ICC Accreditation Procedures for National Human Rights Institutions, March 2008.
52   A. Müller and F. Seidensticker, Handbook: The Role of National Human Rights Institutions in the United Nations Treaty Body Process, German Institute for Human Rights, 2007; see also ICC position papers on NHRIs and the Human Rights Council, Universal Periodic Review and Special Procedures, available at <www.nhri.net/default.asp?PID=363&DID=0>, visited 20 April 2011.
53   There are NHRI regional networks in Asia <www.asiapacificforum.net>, Africa <www.nanhri.org>, Europe <www.ihrc.ie/international/euronhrigroups.html> and the Americas < www.rindhca.org.ve>, visited on 21 April 2011. The APF is the most advanced network. See C. Renshaw 'The Role of Networks in the Implementation of Human Rights in the Asia-Pacific Region', in Nasu and Saul, supra note 4, p. 185.
54   The SRSG notes in Introduction to the Guiding Principles that NHRIs have been among the stakeholders who have endorsed or employed the 'Protect, Respect and Remedy' Framework: Human Rights Council, Guiding Principles, supra note 8, para. 7, commentary.
55   See e.g. Asia Pacific Forum of National Human Rights Institutions, Advisory Council of Jurists, ACJ Reference on Human Rights, Corporate Accountability and Government Responsibility, 27–31 July 2008.
56   A listing of hosted fora may be found at <www.nhri.net>, visited 10 May 2011.

cided to establish the Working Group on Business and Human Rights to guide and prioritise NHRIs individually and collectively.[57] The permanent nature of the ICC Working Group on Business and Human Rights allows for ongoing activity, as well as a focal point for other actors to engage with NHRIs on this issue. It also illustrates how seriously the ICC is taking this issue – this is the first thematic working group to be established by the organisation.

The ICC and individual NHRIs have also taken the opportunity to engage with the SRSG's consultations. For NHRIs globally, the decision to thematically focus the 10th International Conference of NHRIs on business and human rights provided the opportunity for all NHRIs to seek to understand the Ruggie mandate. The conference culminated in the Edinburgh Declaration, which affirms NHRIs' active support of the 'Protect, Respect and Remedy' Framework. This represented a significant shift from the prevailing tendency for NHRIs to focus on state violations. National institutions recognised this:

> The Edinburgh meeting ... showed how far NHRIs have come in a relatively short time in acknowledging that despite the difference in our mandates and country contexts we are working on the impacts of corporate human rights abuses, particularly on vulnerable individuals and communities, in our work every day.[58]

The acknowledgement that business and human rights issues are part of the NHRI daily experience, moves NHRIs away from reasons not to act and prepares them for embracing a role in the operationalisation of the SRSG's 'Protect, Respect and Remedy' Framework.

## 5. How do the Guiding Principles Position the Role of NHRIs?

The Guiding Principles have begun to articulate what NHRIs are expected to contribute to the operationalisation of the 'Protect, Respect, Remedy' Framework. In this section I look at the limited role envisaged for NHRIs under the first two pillars – the state's duty to protect and corporations' responsibility to respect. I then examine the

---

57 See e.g. NHRI Steering Committee on Business and Human Rights, *Proposal for the Establishment of a NHRI Working Group on the Issue of Business and Human Rights*, March 2009; International Coordinating Committee of National Institutions for the Promotion and Protection of Human Rights, *Operationalizing human rights in the private sector – what role, priorities and strategies for NHRIs?: Report of the ICC Working Group on Business and Human Rights Side Event at OHCHR Consultation on Business and Human Rights, Operationalizing the 'Protect, Respect, Remedy' Framework*, Geneva, 5–6 October 2009; *Interim Report*, supra note 24.

58 Intervention on behalf of six NHRIs from Canada, Denmark, Malaysia, Korea, New Zealand and Venezuela following the Edinburgh Conference, on behalf of the International Coordinating Committee of National Institutions for the Promotion and Protection of Human rights and the Office of the High Commissioner for Human Rights, Geneva, 12 October 2010.

challenge set under pillar three, namely that as a state-based non-judicial grievance mechanism NHRIs will provide access to effective remedies.

## 5.1. The Limited Role for NHRIs in Pillars One and Two: A Missed Opportunity?

The SRSG has sought to keep the contribution of NHRIs firmly within the third pillar of the 'Protect, Respect and Remedy' Framework. In the Draft Guiding Principles released for consultation in November 2010, there was only one passing reference to NHRIs outside of the Principles relating to remedy.[59] The SRSG's decision to essentially exclude mention of NHRIs from the first two pillars, came in spite of NHRI lobbying and the reiteration in the Edinburgh Declaration of NHRIs' agreement "to call on the SRSG in his Guiding Principles to recognise the centrality of NHRIs in business and human rights under all three pillars of the 'protect, respect, remedy framework'".[60] The final Guiding Principles shift from this position slightly. In the Introduction to the Principles, NHRIs are part of the narrative about engaged stakeholders.[61] Now, for the first time, NHRIs are explicitly included under pillar one, the state duty to protect. Under the general state regulatory and policy functions principle the commentary provides:

> National human rights institutions that comply with the Paris Principles have an important role to play in helping States identify whether relevant laws are aligned with their human rights obligations and are being effectively enforced and in providing guidance on human rights also to business enterprises and other non-State actors.[62]

In adding this commentary at the 11th hour, the SRSG makes explicit two things in relation to the role of NHRIs in operationalising the 'Protect, Respect and Remedy' Framework. Firstly, by referencing the Paris Principles, the SRSG indicates that the credibility, legitimacy and independence of NHRIs are important. The inference is that a Paris Principles compliant NHRI is considered to have sufficient independence and the relevant functions and powers needed to perform the tasks asked of it by the Guiding Principles. Secondly, under the state duty to protect pillar NHRIs have three primary supportive tasks. The first is to assist states to assess the alignment of state

---

59  In the *Draft Guiding Principles*, under the corporate responsibility to respect, business enterprises were advised "to consult externally with respected experts, including from governments, civil society and national human rights institutions" for advice on complex contextual operating environments such as conflict affected areas. (*Draft Guiding Principles for the Implementation of the United Nations "Protect, Respect and Remedy" Framework*, 22 November 2010, para. 21, commentary.)

60  *Edinburgh Declaration*, supra note 47, para. 18.

61  NHRIs have endorsed and employed the Framework, and the ICC's Edinburgh conference was part of the extensive consultations undertaken by the SRSG: *Guiding Principles*, supra note 8, paras. 7 and 12, commentary.

62  Ibid., para. 3, commentary.

laws with human rights obligations, and by extension ensuring that the laws seek to protect against third party human rights violations. The second task is to monitor to ensure effective enforcement of those laws. The third task allocated to NHRIs as a state-established body is to assist the state to fulfil its duty to protect by providing human rights guidance to businesses and other non-state actors. National institutions and indeed Ruggie himself see this guidance as an important part of supporting corporations to meet their responsibilities under pillar two.[63] NHRIs may use their promotion functions and powers to support and educate both businesses and other relevant stakeholders. This gives NHRIs a proactive role where they may themselves initiate promotion and other activities relevant to guiding and supporting business. This may be distinguished from the only reference to NHRIs contained under pillar two, which like its counterpart under the Draft Guiding Principles encourages businesses to approach NHRIs as one avenue for credible, independent, expert advice.[64]

These references to NHRIs under the first two pillars serve to underline the interrelated nature of the pillars and the difficulty in separating distinct roles for actors that are neither states nor businesses. However the SRSG missed the opportunity to include clearer, more comprehensive statements about the contribution NHRIs can make to the operationalisation of the Framework. Further, the SRSG is also highly aware and indeed encouraging of NHRIs' contribution: "NHRIs have a critical – if not unique – role to play … across all three pillars of the Framework."[65] Speaking at a UN Human Rights Council side event on business, human rights and the role of NHRIs, Ruggie expanded on some of the ways that he envisaged NHRIs would contribute. Under pillar one, he highlighted scrutiny of law, scrutiny of the law's implementation and enforcement, and scrutiny of the human rights performance of state-owned enterprises or private companies delivering public services. These first two suggestions feature as last minute additions to pillar one, but the final one does not. Under pillar two he offers suggestions for NHRIs' crucial role in helping businesses understand human rights. Beyond the 'guidance' role ultimately recognised in the Principles, Ruggie envisaged awareness raising, the creation and dissemination of learning tools, a convening role, capacity building and training.

In particular, the decision not to underline the role of NHRIs as a convenor of actors will now mean that NHRIs will themselves have to carve out legitimacy in this space. The Guiding Principles were an opportunity to educate by explaining the various realistic and potential roles and contributions of different actors.[66] The Guiding Principles could never set these out exhaustively.[67] Neither should the Guiding Principles be prescriptive to the extent that it precludes bottom up engagement and

---

63    J. Ruggie, *Outline of Remarks*, supra note 12.
64    *Guiding Principles*, supra note 8, para. 23, commentary.
65    Ruggie, *Outline of Remarks*, supra note 12.
66    International Coordinating Committee of National Institutions for the Promotion and Protect of Human Rights, *Submission of the ICC to the UN Special Representative on Business and Human Rights' Draft Guiding Principles*, 2011.
67    Ruggie's Report to the Human Rights Council setting out the Guiding Principles was limited by the Council's procedural requirements to a maximum of 30 pages. Others argue

[handwritten annotation at top: "John Ruggie may have been concerned about calling for too strong a role for NHRIs holding businesses accountable"]

participant led initiatives. However, clear and comprehensive statements about the role of NHRIs under each pillar would have assisted NHRIs by preparing state and business actors to accept the inevitable linkages that will occur.[68] Moving forward, if the Guiding Principles remain the key departure point for addressing business and human rights, then NHRIs should seek to read and implement them in ways that reinforce their inter-related nature and build acceptance for practical interpretations that recognise the necessity of NHRI involvement. States and business enterprises will be better able to operationalise their respective duty to protect and responsibility to respect by accepting and, where necessary, facilitating NHRI engagement.

### 5.2. Access to Remedy: The Big Ask of NHRIs

The Guiding Principles envisage a central role for NHRIs under the third pillar of the Framework, access to remedy. The SRSG is careful to maintain the burden for providing effective remedy on the state, but uses the Guiding Principles to outline a variety of avenues for redress of business-related human rights harm. The Principles distinguish firstly between judicial and non-judicial grievance mechanisms. It is clear that "effective judicial mechanisms are at the core of ensuring access to remedy".[69] Non-judicial grievance mechanisms are separated between state-based and non-state-based mechanisms. The former are, as the name suggests, either administered by the state or set up by the state to operate independently of it. The latter may include mechanisms established by business or regional and international human rights bodies.[70]

The Guiding Principles list a range of examples of state-based non-judicial mechanisms that might contribute to providing access to remedy including labour tribu-

---

that the Guiding Principles also fail to account for some actors altogether, particularly the role of civil society. *See* the chapter by Melish and Meidinger in this volume.

68  *See* strong statements by a range of actors supporting operationalisation of the NHRI role under all three pillars, including by the former ICC Chairperson, High Commissioner for Human Rights, the Chief Commissioner of the Scottish Human Rights Commission and host of the ICC 10th International Conference on Business and Human Rights, a group of NHRIs, and the Convenor of the ICC Working Group on Business and Human Rights: J. Lynch, *Statement to OHCHR Consultation on Business and Human Rights Operationalizing the 'Protect, Respect, Remedy' Framework*, delivered on behalf of the ICC/ICC Working Group on Business and Human Rights, 5–6 October 2009; N. Pillay, *Opening Statement, Side Event Human Rights and Business: The Role of NHRIs*, Geneva, 31 May 2010; Scottish Human Rights Commission, *Consultation on UN Special Representative of the United Nations Secretary-General for Business and Human Rights Draft Guiding Principles for the Implementation of the UN 'Protect, Respect and Remedy' Framework*, 2011; Statement by the International Coordinating Committee of National Institutions for the Promotion and Protection of Human Rights, Human Rights Council, 11th Session, 2–18 June 2009; and C. Methven O'Brien, *Opening Statement and Welcome: Engaging NHRIs in Securing the Promotion and Protection of Human Rights in Business*, Side Event to the UN Human Rights Council, Geneva, 5 June 2009.

69  *Guiding Principles*, *supra* note 8, para. 26, commentary.

70  *Ibid.*, para. 28, commentary.

nals, NCPs, ombudsperson offices and government run complaints offices.[71] Guiding Principle 27 establishes the state obligation to "provide effective and appropriate non-judicial grievance mechanisms alongside judicial mechanisms, as part of a comprehensive State-based system for the remedy of business-related human rights abuse".[72] The only specific mechanism listed in the commentary to this Principle is the NHRI.[73]

While NHRIs are not envisaged as the sole avenue for state-based non-judicial redress, through Guiding Principle 27 they are nevertheless promoted as the forum of choice. This has implications. Recall that the international minimum standards for NHRIs, the Paris Principles, do not exclude NHRIs from addressing violations by businesses. Nevertheless, in reality because the Paris Principles do not specify the mandate, functions and powers required to deal with business-related human rights violations, many NHRIs may not have the capacity to do so. The commentary to the Guiding Principles does recognise that the mandates of existing mechanisms may need to be expanded in order to operate as grievance mechanisms.[74] However, the true significance of the reach of that statement is only revealed on examination of the basis for a NHRI mandate to engage with and provide *remedy* for business-related human rights harm. In the section that follows I examine the challenges for NHRI engagement on business and human rights, including in particular the diffusion of a range of different institutional models, and the related differences in mandates.

## 6. Challenges to NHRIs' Engagement with Business and Human Rights

There are multiple challenges that impact the capacity of NHRIs to effectively address violations by businesses. These include the context in which a NHRI operates, particularly where there are low levels of compliance and a weak existing enforcement framework;[75] the paucity of resources available for a NHRI to dedicate to business issues and a commensurate lack of capacity or knowledge to operate in this area;[76] and the underdevelopment of non-judicial mechanisms, including the relationship and in-

---

71  *Ibid.*, para. 25, commentary.

72  *Ibid*, para. 27.

73  *Ibid.*, commentary.

74  *Ibid.*

75  See e.g. Simbiri-Jaoko, *supra* note 4, p. 5. Similarly, Macdonald argues that many of the barriers to redress in transnational situations are "products of deeper underlying features of the social, political and institutional environments within host countries". K. Macdonald, *The Reality of Rights: Barriers to Accessing Remedies when Business Operates Beyond Borders* (The Corporate Responsibility Coalition, London, 2009) p. 39. This mirrors the findings of the SRSG on the worst cases of corporate violations occurring where governance challenges are the greatest, *Protect, Respect and Remedy*, *supra* note 2, para. 16.

76  For example, the South African Human Rights Commission, with one dedicated staff member, is considered best practice: *Report on the ICC and OHCHR Side Event*, *supra* note 45, p. 7.

teraction between NHRIs and other relevant actors.[77] All of these issues must be taken into account as NHRIs are called on to deal with violations by businesses. However, one of the most immediate challenges relates to the structure and form of NHRIs themselves, including the proliferation of institutions without complaints handling functions and the remedies that NHRIs are empowered to provide.

### 6.1. Diversity of Form

The Paris Principles do not prescribe the form a NHRI must take in order to meet the international minimum standards and as a result there is significant diversity in the institutional model. There are a number of typographies that outline the spectrum of institutions regarded as NHRIs.[78] Definitions are sometimes contested,[79] but generally included are three main types of institution: multiple member bodies such as Human Rights Commissions; single member bodies such as an Ombudsman, usually with a specific human rights mandate; and hybrid institutions combining these forms, including some institutions with an emphasis on advisory and research functions. One of the most important distinguishing features between institutional forms is whether or not the NHRI has been granted the power to receive individual complaints.

The Paris Principles reflect the political compromise that was made when the standards were drafted. Representatives involved in the negotiations came from a diverse range of countries and institution types. Unable to agree on whether or not quasi-judicial functions should be mandatory, the final text included them as additional principles, optional for those institutions granted powers to receive complaints and investigate them.[80] The effect of that decision means that many Paris Principles compliant institutions, while regarded as meeting the minimum international standards, do not have the competence to receive or investigate complaints. This has been minimised by the Guiding Principle's emphasis on the NHRI as a particularly important state-based grievance mechanism.

---

77   *Protect, Respect and Remedy*, supra note 2; A. Miller, *Presentation Human Rights and Business: The Role of NHRIs*, Geneva, 31 May 2010.

78   See e.g. L. C. Reif, 'Building Democratic Institutions: The Role of National Human Rights Institutions in Good Governance and Human Rights Protection', 13 *Harvard Human Rights Journal* (2000) p. 3; International Council on Human Rights Policy, *Assessing the Effectiveness of National Human Rights Institutions* (2005).

79   For example, Reif argues for inclusion of the classical ombudsman model, despite these institutions often not possessing a specific human rights mandate, *ibid*. Burdekin distinguishes the classic ombudsman model (generally concerned with public administration) from multi-member institutions that may promote and protect human rights in both the public and private sectors, Burdekin, *supra* note 15, pp. 86–87.

80   Burdekin provides a firsthand account of the disagreement. Note too that the final text of the Paris Principles used the term 'quasi-jurisdictional competence', when it was likely that 'quasi-judicial competence' was meant. Burdekin, *supra* note 15, p. 24.

## 6.2. The 'Additional Principles' – The Optional Mandate

In 2007–2008 the Office of the High Commissioner for Human Rights (OHCHR) surveyed NHRIs on behalf of the SRSG to ascertain their practices with respect to business and human rights.[81] The survey's results on the complaints mechanisms of NHRIs are widely quoted[82] and used by the SRSG to bolster the idea that NHRIs that are able to address grievances involving companies "can provide a means to hold business accountable".[83] This is of course true – *if* an institution has a complaints handling function it can utilise that function and any associated powers to investigate, gather information, and potentially adjudicate, mediate or recommend a resolution. However, a realistic assessment of the extent of institutions with complaints handling functions to deal with business-related violations, as well as a deeper reflection about the kinds of mechanisms available in particular states, reveals the paucity of NHRIs ready to perform a grievance mechanism role.

According to the publicly released survey data,[84] 43 NHRIs responded to requests for information about their mandate and capacity to deal with business-related human rights violations. Of these NHRIs 29 were Paris Principles accredited. When the survey was conducted there were a total of 85 NHRIs with ICC membership, with 61 of these institutions considered fully Paris Principles compliant.[85] This means that only a little over 50 per cent of NHRIs responded to the survey. Of those institutions, a total of 20 Paris Principles compliant institutions could accept some sort of business-related complaints. Only eight Paris Principles compliant NHRIs had complaints mechanisms available to deal with any type of company and all human rights.[86] A further seven Paris Principles compliant NHRIs could accept complaints with regard to any kind of company but only on certain rights issues.[87] There were five Paris Principles

---

81   *Survey, supra* note 10.
82   Pillay, *supra* note 68, p. 3.
83   *Protect, Respect and Remedy, supra* note 8, para. 97.
84   Note that the only available version of the survey released in the first half of 2008 notes that it is still accepting responses with a finalised version to be released later in the same year. All references, including those by the UN High Commissioner on Human Rights as well as the SRSG indicate that further responses were not incorporated into the aggregated data. There are some minor discrepancies. Ruggie refers to 31 institutions as being Paris Principles compliant. Pillay states that there were 41 responses.
85   International Coordinating Committee for National Institutions for the Promotion and Protection of Human Rights, *Chart of the Status of National Institutions Accredited by the ICC*, December 2007.
86   These were Egypt, Jordan, Kenya, Mongolia, Philippines, Niger, Paraguay and Rwanda. It was also reported that Nigeria, a non-Paris Principles compliant NHRI, had such a complaints mechanism.
87   These included Australia, Canada, Denmark, Mauritius, New Zealand, Republic of Korea and Sweden. Two non-Paris Principles compliant institutions could also accept these kinds of complaints, the Netherlands and Slovakia.

compliant institutions that could accept complaints with regard to any kind of rights but only certain kinds of companies.[88]

Before even reaching the point of assessing the capacity of a NHRI to provide effective remedy out of a self-administered grievance mechanism, it is clear that relief is only accessible in a limited number of states. This becomes particularly important when the alleged violation is the responsibility of a transnational corporation. In one typical scenario, the violation occurs in a developing country – the 'host' state where the business investments have been made – while the corporation is domiciled in a developed 'home' state. Rees observes that "'home' states [are] typically OECD members with an NCP, which place[s] the government in the role of convenor between company and complainant. 'Host' states [are] typically not OECD members but often [have] a human rights institution (ombudsman or commission)."[89] Her analysis is borne out by the OHCHR survey data on NHRIs and business. Cross-referenced against data on NHRIs in OECD member states and countries adhering to the OECD Guidelines for Multinational Enterprises[90] many of the states found to have no complaints mechanisms for dealing with business-related human rights violations are in fact OECD ones. Of the 34 OECD member states and Guideline adhering states, eight have no NHRI and a further ten have non-Paris Principles compliant institutions. Of the remaining 16 institutions, five may take complaints only on certain rights issues, usually equality, two may receive complaints concerning particular companies related to the state and seven have no complaints mechanism.

Based on this analysis[91] the number of NHRIs mandated to accept complaints of business-related human rights violations is discouraging. It is concerning that NHRIs, one of the key non-judicial mechanisms touted by the SRSG Guiding Principles, can offer only limited protection via complaints mechanisms in OECD countries and their reach beyond that is not extensive.

There are two further limiting factors linked to a NHRI's mandate that must also be borne in mind. Firstly, the definition of human rights differs from one NHRI to another. Many will not live up to even the minimum requirement of the Guiding Principles that business enterprises respect rights contained in the Universal Declaration of Human Rights, the International Covenant on Civil and Political

---

88  These included Argentina, Bolivia, Peru, Spain and Togo. Five non-compliant institutions could accept these kinds of complaints, Antigua and Barbuda, Hungary, Puerto Rico, Romania and Trinidad and Tobago.

89  C. Rees, *Access to Remedies for Corporate Human Rights Impacts: Improving Non-Judicial Mechanisms*, Corporate Social Responsibility Initiative, Harvard Kennedy School, Report No. 32, November 2008.

90  *OECD Guidelines*, supra note 36, p.17.

91  Note that the survey data may not fully capture the momentum created by the SRSG's mandate. By relying on NHRI responses alone, and not supplementing the results of the survey with further analysis of institutions' establishing legislation, some institutions' complaints mechanisms were not counted. For instance in the Asia-Pacific region there are a further five NHRIs with complaint mechanisms that may allow them to address business violations. *See* Burdekin *supra* note 15.

Rights, the International Covenant on Economic, Social and Cultural Rights and the fundamental rights in the eight International Labour Organization (ILO) core conventions as set out in the Declaration on Fundamental Principles and Rights at Work.⁹² For example, Burdekin demonstrates that there are ten different formulations of the definition of 'human rights' in the establishing legislation of NHRIs in the Asia-Pacific.⁹³ It may often be the case that a NHRI is not mandated to deal with rights that the Guiding Principles require that business enterprises respect. This of course means that they cannot provide any remedy for breach of that right. On a related point, a NHRI might enjoy a broad human rights mandate, but as seen in the survey data above, the institution is limited with respect to the types of rights on which they may receive complaints. These will invariably be narrower than the rights provided for under the Guiding Principles.

Secondly, the complaints handling function of NHRIs tends to be one of the most prescriptive components of their establishing legislation. One particularly relevant potential limitation may be the standing of those who can bring a complaint. For example the Afghanistan Commission only recognises the human rights of Afghan citizens.⁹⁴ While this may not prevent a complaint against a non-national party, similar standing restrictions and other prescriptive requirements for dealing with complaints may complicate a NHRI's capacity to deal with complex cases of transnational corporation violations that cross borders and involve actors from multiple jurisdictions.

### 6.3. The Right Remedies?

The Guiding Principles call for effective remedies for business-related human rights violations. The remedies should be both procedurally sound and provide a just substantive outcome. The remedies envisaged include "apologies, restitution, rehabilitation, financial or non-financial compensation and punitive sanctions (whether criminal or administrative, such as fines) as well as the prevention of harm through, for example, injunctions or guarantees of non-repetition".⁹⁵

The Paris Principles establish four principles to provide guidance on how NHRIs may hear and consider complaints. First, the Paris Principles encourage amicable settlement, conciliation, the possibility of binding decisions and confidentiality where necessary. Second, the Principles ask that the petitioner be informed of their rights and the remedies available to them. Access to remedies should also be promoted. Third, the NHRI should hear complaints or transmit them to the relevant authority. Fourth, the NHRI should resolve complaints by making recommendations that may include proposing amendments and law reform.⁹⁶

---

92  *Guiding Principles, supra* note 8, para. 12, commentary.
93  Burdekin, *supra* note 15, p.31.
94  *Law on the Structure, Duties and Mandate of the Afghan Independent Human Rights Commission* (2005), Article 4.
95  *Guiding Principles, supra* note 8, para. 25, commentary.
96  *Paris Principles, supra* note 26, Additional Principles (a)–(d).

Aggregation of the data collected from the survey of NHRI practice suggests there are many varied ways that NHRIs seek to provide redress. There are over 30 different mechanisms that NHRIs reported they may activate in the process of investigating or resolving a business-related complaint, including, for instance, mediation, on-site visits, compelling production of documents, information and witnesses, obtaining expert opinions, monitoring implementation of recommendations, conducting public inquiries and hearings, and requesting state official assistance. This diversity suggests that institutions generally have a range of mechanisms on which they rely, including complementary judicial mechanisms.[97]

According to the survey data, NHRIs may seek to give effect to the following types of remedy: apology, change to business or government policy, recommendations to government, recommendations to the parties, provision of legal aid, recommendation of monetary compensation, release of public statements, reports to parliament, referral to a judicial body, representation before a court, referral to a government agency, referral to a prosecutor, settlement, and orders enforceable by the courts. While there are genuine avenues provided by NHRIs for remedy of business-related rights violations, the overwhelming number of remedies that rely on recommendations alone may limit actual or perceived access to effective remedies.

Further evidence suggests that the inability to give effect to binding remedies discourages affected parties from even seeking redress from NHRIs. Examining case studies of transnational corporate violations in developing countries, Macdonald notes that the limited capacity or weak powers of the Human Rights Commissions in Kenya, India and Georgia to enforce recommendations deterred affected parties from seeking their assistance.[98] In contrast to Macdonald's findings the Kenyan National Human Rights Commission is often exemplified as a best practice NHRI dealing with business: "The Kenya Human Rights Commission, I think it is fair to say, has been in the very vanguard of national human rights institutions engaging with the business agenda."[99] The experiences of affected parties such as those studied by Macdonald challenge NHRIs and those championing their role as grievance mechanisms to realistically assess what they currently offer in order to better protect and promote human rights.

The remedial role of NHRIs may emphasise an institution's duty to protect and prevent human rights violations, along with its contribution to shaping public policy.[100] The grievance mechanism model envisages that each of these objectives will be advanced by providing a forum for the complaints of affected parties. Further, Macdonald's research suggests that affected parties want decisions on those complaints to be binding and enforceable. It is imperative that states acknowledge that their duty to provide effective access to remedies may require them to enhance the mandate, functions and powers of NHRIs to fulfil this role. In many instances, to

---

97 Rees, *supra* note 89.
98 Macdonald, *supra* note 75.
99 Methven O'Brien, *supra* note 68.
100 M. Marmorat, 'Non-Judicial Remedies in Norway for Corporate Social Responsibility Abroad', *Fafo Discussion Paper*, No. 14, 2009, p. 9.

secure the independence and functional operationality of a NHRI performing a grievance mechanism role, legislative change and allocation of sufficient resources will be required. In June 2011 the United Nations Human Rights Council (HRC) affirmed the importance of independent and autonomous Paris Principles compliant NHRIs. The HRC also went further noting "with satisfaction the efforts of those Member States that have provided their national institutions with more autonomy and independence, including by giving them an investigative role or enhancing such a role, and encourages other Governments to consider taking similar steps".[101] This statement is a clear indication of the HRC's position that states must improve the mandates of NHRIs to enable more effective promotion and protection of human rights.

Despite the increasing recognition of the need to strengthen NHRIs it would be a mistake for national institutions not to use the full extent of their existing mandate, functions and powers to bring about compliance and change. The experiences of a number of NHRIs creatively utilising their resources to deal with systemic corporate abuses provide inspiration for the potential role of NHRIs in supporting the operationalisation of each pillar of the 'Protect, Respect and Remedy' Framework. This is the focus of the next section.

## 7. Opportunities for NHRIs to Operationalise the 'Protect, Respect and Remedy' Framework

With limited exceptions, NHRIs' inability to make binding recommendations may lead stakeholders to wrongly dismiss their value in protecting and promoting human rights. However, NHRIs increasingly recognise that they can take action on business-related human rights violations.[102] The Ruggie 'Protect, Respect and Remedy' Framework and Guiding Principles provide the necessary basis for continuing to define the role of NHRIs. National institutions may use the intention and language of the Framework to pursue good human rights outcomes by supporting and holding both states and business enterprises to account under each of the pillars. The following examples of national inquiries conducted by the New Zealand and Ghanaian Human Rights Commissions demonstrate the potential for NHRIs to address systemic business-related violations even where binding remedies are not part of the solution.

---

101  Human Rights Council, *Follow-up and implementation of the Vienna Declaration and Program of Action: National Institutions for the promotion and protection of human rights*, A/HRC/17/L.18, 10 June 2011, para. 9.

102  The ICC Working Group on Business and Human Rights recently conducted a Baseline assessment on the interest, activities and potential for NHRIs to engage with business-related violations. The key issues of importance nominated by NHRIs included "discrimination, environmental degradation (right to food and water), labour (especially child labour) rights, indigenous rights, privatization (particularly in the Americas) and exploitation of natural resources (particularly in Africa)". Miller, *supra* note 77.

### 7.1. National Inquiries – Dealing with Systemic Human Rights Violations

National inquiries conducted by NHRIs are comprehensive investigations into widespread or systemic human rights violations. Commissioners conducting national inquiries regard them as one of the most effective ways to fulfil a NHRI's mandate to promote and protect human rights.[103] This view is supported by evidence that national inquiries lead to tangible progressive human rights change.[104] National inquiries intentionally involve a vast range of actors, and unless specifically restricted, NHRIs can use this methodology to publicise, engage and seek resolution for business-related harm. The first example from New Zealand demonstrates how actors from the private, public and community sectors were all brought into the national inquiry process to deal with discrimination in access to public services. The second example from Ghana shows the importance of official public documentation of violations in order to start the long-term process of human rights protection.

#### 7.1.1. Seeking Solutions through Collaboration: Access and Discrimination

In September 2003 the New Zealand Human Rights Commission (NZHRC) launched a national inquiry into the accessibility of public land transport for people with disabilities.[105] While it was clear that the rights of people with disabilities were being violated, split ownership and management of the transport service between the private sector and the government had enabled both actors to eschew their respective duties and responsibilities. The NZHRC's *Accessible Journey* national inquiry was collaborative in nature, undertaken "with the express objective of ensuring that the views of all stakeholders were sought and taken into account throughout the process".[106]

One strength of the NZHRC's inquiry was getting all of the stakeholders in the same room to work together on solutions. To do so the Chief Commissioner, Rosslyn Noonan, made a conscious decision not to rely on any of the Commission's formal powers to compel responses by state and non-state actors.[107] In the view of one of the inquiry Commissioners, Robyn Hunt, "the recommendations of the Human Rights

---

103 Interview with Chief Commissioner Rosslyn Noonan, New Zealand National Human Rights Commission (Wellington, New Zealand 30 June 2009); Interview with Oyunchimeg, Commissioner, National Human Rights Commission of Mongolia (Ulaanbaatar, Mongolia, 21 September 2007); Burdekin, *supra* note 15.
104 *See* Government Responses since the Inquiry Began, Human Rights and Equal Opportunity Commission, *Human Rights and Mental Illness: Report of the National Inquiry into the Human Rights of People with Mental Illness*, Vol. 1 and Vol. 2, 1993.
105 New Zealand Human Rights Commission, *The Accessible Journey: Report of the Inquiry into Accessible Public Land Transport*, 2007.
106 *Ibid.*, p. 128.
107 Asia Pacific Forum, *Going Public: Strategies for an Effective National Inquiry*, 2007.

Commission Inquiry into Accessible Land Transport have had far more impact than any individual complaints".[108]

The national inquiry methodology reflects key aspects of the Guiding Principles. As "States do not relinquish their international human rights law obligations when they privatize the delivery of services that may impact upon the enjoyment of human rights,"[109] the NZHRC used the inquiry to both clarify expectations and provide "adequate independent monitoring" [110] of the provision of public transport. The NZHRC assisted the state to identify where relevant laws were not aligned with human rights obligations to people with disabilities and how they were not being effectively enforced.[111] The Commission contributed by providing "effective guidance to business enterprises on how to respect human rights throughout their operations".[112]

The collaborative process convened by the NZHRC facilitated "informal engagement with affected stakeholders",[113] including civil society groups representing the concerns of people with disabilities. This led to "meaningful consultation with potentially affected groups and other relevant stakeholders"[114] in urban and regional areas to assess the human rights risks. Fundamentally, the national inquiry reaffirmed that "business enterprises should respect human rights". However, as part of the stakeholder discussions, legitimate business concerns including the economic costs of implementing particular measures were allowed on the table. This enabled the NZHRC to bring businesses into a process where they were heard and understood, tempered by the understanding that the NZHRC's role was to ensure that businesses addressed the "adverse human rights impacts with which they [were] involved".[115]

Remedies took a number of forms, commensurate with the systemic nature of the human rights violations. New laws, policies and procedures[116] to ensure human rights compliance, by both state and businesses, were a component of the resolution of the national inquiry. They included new vehicle quality standards for urban buses; the development of a New Zealand Transport Strategy that "is committed to the concept of a fully accessible journey"; the enactment of the *Public Transport Management Act 2008* that regulates commercial public transport operators and requires disabled people be consulted in transport planning; taxi fleets must now display signs in Braille inside the front door of taxis; and new training regulations have been introduced for taxi and

---

108  R. Hunt, 'From Strategy to Convention: Implementing Disability Human Rights in New Zealand', Key Note Address delivered at the Australian Federation of Disability Organisations Policy About Us For Us Conference, Melbourne, 29 May 2009.
109  *Guiding Principles*, supra note 8, para. 5, commentary.
110  *Ibid.*
111  *Ibid*, para. 3, commentary.
112  *Ibid.*, para. 3(c).
113  *Ibid.*
114  *Ibid.*, para. 18.
115  *Ibid.*, para. 11.
116  *Ibid.*, para. 16.

bus drivers that require that they complete special needs awareness training in order to receive a licence.[117]

The national inquiry process did not result in individuals being granted enforceable remedies. Yet the process of dealing with the structural problems that were leading to systemic human rights violations by both business enterprises and the state produced change. Aspects of the role played by the NZHRC indicate actions in support of all three pillars, and outcomes that have led to the state better upholding its duty to protect by regulating and guiding businesses to understand and implement their responsibility to protect. This has resulted in remedies that seek to prevent ongoing violations.

### 7.1.2. Bringing Systemic Violations to Light: Experiences of Mining Communities

In December 2006 the Ghana Commission on Human Rights and Administrative Justice (CHRAJ) launched a national inquiry into the human rights of people living in mining communities in Ghana. The CHRAJ identified that "the causes of the violations of human rights appear systemic in nature requiring, in part, a solution that will tackle the systemic causes".[118] The terms of reference for this inquiry were not geared towards relief for individuals; it was "not a fault finding"[119] investigation, rather one that sought to give "all role players ... an opportunity to address the issues with the Commission in a cooperative manner".[120] The key tasks the CHRAJ set itself were to assess and identify the human rights situation in mining communities, to make recommendations to curtail violations, and to promote awareness of human rights in mining communities including cordial relations between different interest groups in those communities.[121]

The CHRAJ produced a comprehensive report that extensively documents violations in over 40 communities with investigations involving 11 key target groups.[122] In most communities the CHRAJ addressed issues including water and water sources, dust and chemical pollution, health and related issues, blasting, safety and security,

---

117 New Zealand Human Rights Commission, *Legislation and Policy Developments*, <www.hrc.co.nz/home/hrc/disabledpeople/inquiryintoaccessiblepubliclandtransport/legislationandpolicydevelopments.php>, visited 24 May 2010.

118 Commission on Human Rights and Administrative Justice, *The State of Human Rights in Mining Communities in Ghana*, March 2008, p. 11.

119 *Ibid.*, p. 12. Note that in parallel to the investigation of systemic causes of violations in mining communities, the CHRAJ also took individual complaints as part of its routine and ongoing complaint handling function.

120 *Ibid.*, p. 13.

121 *Ibid.*, p. 26.

122 *Ibid.*, pp. 27–29. The target groups covered included women, farmers, Unit Committees of District Assemblies, small scale miners, galamsey groups, victims of cyanide spillage, mining companies, regulatory institutions and agencies, traditional leaders and chiefs, youth groups and associations, and civil society organisations.

resettlement and compensation, livelihoods and employment, illegal artisanal mining (galamsey), royalties, and development projects. The CHRAJ's conclusions and recommendations are directed to mining companies and private security agencies, as well as government agencies and departments.[123]

The CHRAJ's national inquiry report began an important process in documenting violations, highlighting in particular where the Ghanaian state is failing in its duty to protect human rights. For example, the "[i]nvestigations show that state institutions with regulatory and monitoring responsibility for the mining sector have not performed optimally due to capacity constraints ... [and] ... [c]ommunities have expressed little confidence in the ability of the [environmental protection] agency".[124] The report also clearly evidences the disregard of mining companies operating in Ghana for their responsibility to respect. While the national inquiry did not provide immediate remedy or prevent all ongoing abuse,[125] it has nevertheless been an important component in a long-term process of seeking protection for mining communities in Ghana. According to WACAM, a NGO advocating the rights of Ghanaian communities affected by mining,[126] "[t]he CHRAJ Report has contributed immensely to the ongoing reforms in the Mining Sector and has become a reference point globally for bringing out the human rights challenges confronting resource rich developing countries".[127]

National institutions have a clear role to play in supporting the operationalisation of all three pillars of the 'Protect, Respect and Remedy' Framework. These two examples of national inquiries help to highlight the work a NHRI may do as a convenor of stakeholders that engages the state, business enterprises and affected parties to seek resolutions for human rights violations. It is indicative of the creativity that NHRIs may bring to bear in answering the SRSG's call to push the boundaries of their contribution.

## 8.  Conclusions: Answering the Call – Pushing the Boundaries

In many respects the role of NHRIs in addressing business-related human rights violations is "just starting to be articulated".[128] National institutions have been willing participants in international efforts to define and clarify the duties and responsibilities of states and business enterprises in protecting and respecting human rights. In a very

---

123  *Ibid.*, pp. 172-195: these included the Environment Protection Agency, Ministry of Health, police, military, Office of the Administrator of Stool Lands, Ministry responsible for Minerals and Mining, District Administration, and the Youth Employment Scheme.

124  *Ibid.*, p.173.

125  For evidence of ongoing problems *see* United States Department of State, *2010 Human Rights Report: Ghana*, 8 April 2011.

126  *See* <www.wacamghana.com>, visited 10 June 2011.

127  Ghana News Agency, 'Bossman: Ghana should not make money ... at the expense of human rights', *Ghana News Agency*, 1 June 2011.

128  J. Lynch, *Addressing the Parallel Meeting of the Advisory Council of Jurists during the 13th Annual Meeting of the Asia Pacific Forum of National Human Rights Institutions*, Kuala Lumpur, Malaysia, 29 July 2008, p. 2.

short period of time NHRIs have leveraged their maturing international and regional networks to collectively recognise their vital role. They have influenced and been influenced by the development of Ruggie's 'Protect, Respect and Remedy' Framework and have been contributors to the final Guiding Principles.

While the SRSG called on NHRIs to "push the boundaries of what they can contribute",[129] he was reluctant to give effect to the repeated requests of NHRIs to more comprehensively incorporate their role into all three pillars of the 'Protect, Respect and Remedy' Framework. Ruggie did, however, firmly place the burden on states to enable NHRIs through expanded mandates and sufficient resources.[130] This is extremely important because, as currently constituted, for many NHRIs their role in providing effective remedies has been overstated. Collectively and as individual institutions, NHRIs must use all avenues at their disposal to pressure states to strengthen NHRIs. This could include utilising ICC accreditation procedures and international fora where Paris Principles compliant institutions have speaking rights, mobilising domestic constituencies to advocate on their behalf, and working with regional and international civil society networks to highlight inadequacies in NHRIs' mandates and resources.

One of the most important contributions NHRIs will make is to continue to define their own role in addressing business-related violations and articulate what is required to facilitate it. There are four key opportunities for NHRIs to act. Firstly, moving forward, states and NHRIs should actively seek to improve and refine the operationality of NHRIs' grievance mechanisms based on evidence of best practice[131] in securing positive human rights outcomes for individuals and communities affected by business-related violations.

Secondly, the unique position of NHRIs to convene stakeholders and activate networks must be leveraged. Systemic or widespread violations by businesses may require solutions that operate on multiple levels, including for example political, legal, social and commercial elements. National institutions can provide a forum where human rights remain paramount yet allow for these different perspectives to be accommodated. This can also help to overcome polarised positions that lead to government,

---

129   Ibid., p. 4.
130   *Guiding Principles, supra* note 8, para. 27.
131   There are two sets of criteria relevant to revising and assessing NHRI grievance mechanisms. Firstly the Guiding Principles establish a set of effectiveness criteria for non-judicial grievance mechanisms. *See Guiding Principles, supra* note 8, para. 31. Secondly, research on NHRI effectiveness as well as the effectives of non-judicial mechanisms provides further crucial insight into relevant factors to be considered. *See* International Council on Human Rights Policy, *supra* note 78; The Corporate Responsibility (CORE) Coalition, *Protecting rights, repairing harm: How state-based non-judicial mechanisms can help fill gaps in existing frameworks for the protection of human rights of people affected by corporate activities – A briefing paper prepared for the UN Secretary General's Special Representative on Business and Human Rights on behalf of The Corporate Responsibility (CORE) Coalition*, November 2010; and forthcoming research The University of Melbourne, Corporate Accountability Project <www.corporateaccountabilityresearch.net>, visited 5 June 2011.

business and civil society not talking to one another.[132] NHRIs also have the advantage of being a local mechanism[133] as well as the ability to establish and maintain effective international[134] and regional[135] networks.

Thirdly, NHRIs have the potential to become centres of knowledge and research on business and human rights issues. Utilising their research mandates NHRIs may increase information about and understanding of business-related human rights violations in their jurisdiction, informed by local experiences and evidence of root causes. This information may then be shared with affected parties, civil society and other relevant stakeholders. In this way a NHRI may become a hub for information, including for businesses seeking to better understand the human rights context of the environment in which they operate.

Fourthly, NHRIs may play a crucial role in changing the attitude and behaviour of stakeholders through education and training, and the provision of advice and encouragement. NHRIs may act as a catalyst for changing corporate culture, policies and practice,[136] and they may also assist vertical and horizontal coherence in the state implementation of human rights obligations.[137]

In Edinburgh, NHRIs gave their unanimous support "to proactively consider new ways in which NHRIs' mandates can be used to advance the 'protect, respect and remedy' framework."[138] However, they also recognised "the need for its further development and alignment with international human rights standards".[139] On 15 June 2011

---

132 C. Avery, Business and Human Rights Resource Centre, quoted in *Report on the ICC and OHCHR Side Event*, supra note 45, p. 6.

133 Rees, *supra* note 89.

134 This may include NHRIs utilising their special role in UN fora or mobilising through the ICC to cooperate and share information on developing consistent international standards. See O. Maurel, 'Building Corporate Human Rights Responsibility: Between Confidence and Justice. Possible NHRI Contributions to "the State Duty to Protect," the First Pillar of Corporate Human Rights Responsibility', Paper presented at the 10th International Conference of NHRIs, Human Rights and Business: The Role of NHRIs, Edinburgh, Scotland, 8–10 October 2010.

135 There is great potential for NHRIs to develop existing cooperation at a regional level to deal with transnational human rights issues. For example, in the Asia-Pacific the Philippines Commission has agreements with the Korean and Malaysian Commissions to alert each other when transnational migrant worker issues arise. See *ACJ Reference on Human Rights, Corporate Accountability and Government Responsibility*, supra note 55, p. 19.

136 For example, both the Danish Institute for Human Rights and the Canadian Human Rights Commission have developed tools to help business enterprises assess human rights risks. See *Report on the ICC and OHCHR Side Event*, supra note 45, p. 5; Human Rights Compliance Assessment Tool, *supra* note 7.

137 For instance, NHRIs may assist by running programs to increase inter-departmental cooperation and include training officials in government departments that may not routinely consider human rights issues but whose mandates may have significant human rights impacts such as trade or investment.

138 *Edinburgh Declaration*, supra note 47, para. 17.

139 *Ibid*.

the HRC endorsed the Guiding Principles and decided to establish a Working Group to promote their implementation.[140] In doing so, the HRC recognised the central role of Paris Principles compliant NHRIs as a partner in this process.[141] Specifically the HRC encouraged NHRIs "to further develop their capacity to fulfil that role effectively, including with the support of the Office of the High Commissioner and in addressing all relevant actors".[142] With the Guiding Principles in hand, NHRIs must continue to advance and advocate protection of and remedy for business-related human rights harm. They have much to offer to this process.

---

140   Human Rights Council, 17th Session, *Human Rights and Transnational Corporations and other Business Enterprises*, A/HRC/17/L.17/Rev.1, 15 June 2011.
141   Ibid., para. 6(b) and (h), 11, 14.
142   Ibid., para 11.

# 11 Ruggie's Diplomatic Project and Its Missing Regulatory Infrastructure

Christine Parker* and John Howe**

## 1. Introduction

This chapter evaluates John Ruggie's legacy from the standpoint of the sociology and politics of business regulation and compliance. We argue that Ruggie has successfully conducted a political and diplomatic project to connect[1] international human rights law language and methods to practical discourses of corporate social responsibility (CSR) at the United Nations (UN). The "Protect, Respect and Remedy" Framework's[2] (the Framework) success at making connections on a diplomatic level, however, comes at the expense of recognising the more radical implications of applying human rights to business. The Framework connects international human rights law with business' CSR practices – but only by the use of vague and ambiguous language. This language puts distance between the crises of legitimacy caused by businesses' adverse human rights impacts on the one hand and any "authoritative" statement of business obligations to respect human rights on the other hand.

---

\* Professor and ARC Research Fellow, Law School, University of Melbourne (to 30 June 2011); Professor, Centre for Regulatory Studies and Law Faculty, Monash University (from 18 July 2011).

\*\* Associate Professor, Law School, University of Melbourne. We are grateful to participants at a workshop on Corporate Social Responsibility at the University of Melbourne for their comments on our proposed paper, especially Ronen Shamir. We are also grateful to John Knox and Radu Mares for helpful comments on the first draft of this paper, and to Jane Brophy for editorial assistance in finalising the paper. The opinions expressed here remain the authors' own.

1 See notes 25–27 and accompanying text for an explanation of why we use the term "connect" here.

2 J. Ruggie, *Report of the Special Representative of the Secretary-General on the Issue of Human Rights and Transnational Corporations and Other Business Enterprises: Guiding Principles on Business and Human Rights: Implementing the United Nations "Protect, Respect and Remedy" Framework*, A/HRC/17/31 (*Final Report*) (2011).

Section 2 of this chapter sets out our analytical framework. We suggest that the Framework necessarily formalises – and thus potentially ossifies – what could be agreed by the UN, business and human rights activists at one point in time. Its diplomacy therefore constrains it to be consistent with the "practicalities" of business, and to avoid or neutralise more radical critiques of business.[3] Indeed the chief diplomatic genius of the Framework is in establishing that it is primarily states that have *legal* duties in relation to the application of human rights to business. Ruggie's reports have repeatedly emphasised that for the most part businesses do not have international law obligations to respect human rights: instead their responsibilities are largely based on the much softer, more nebulous notion of "social expectations".[4] Thus the Framework underestimates (whether intentionally or not) what is required to push corporate responsibility for human rights beyond due diligence processes and the redress of individual grievances.

As currently stated, the Framework could easily become the basis for a lukewarm, even counter-productive, set of practices around business and human rights. Yet it is also possible that the Framework might open up small opportunities for further contestation, crisis and hence political leverage that would make businesses transform their practices in substance to not only remedy abuses of human rights on an individual basis, but also to transform power differentials and address inequalities (that is to address distributive injustice) that allow human rights to be abused on a regular basis.[5]

In sections 3 and 4 of this chapter we therefore provide comments on the Framework in the spirit of contestation and critique. We also suggest how its ongoing implementation could be adjusted and developed to encourage, or at least allow for, greater accountability for the justice and human rights implications of business activities on people and environments. We draw on our own and others' empirical and theoretical research on business regulation and compliance to analyse two specific ways in

---

[3] O. Perez, 'Private Environmental Governance as Ensemble Regulation: A Critical Exploration of Sustainability Indexes and the New Ensemble Politics', *Theoretical Inquiries in Law* (forthcoming 2011) p. 34, available at <ssrn.com/abstract=1710639>; R. Shamir, 'Capitalism, Governance and Authority: The Case of Corporate Social Responsibility', 6 *Annual Review of Law & Social Sciences* (2010) pp. 531–553; R. Shamir, 'Corporate Social Responsibility: A Case of Hegemony and Counter-Hegemony', in B. de Sousa Santos and C. A. Rodriguez-Garavito (eds.), *Law and Globalization from Below* (Cambridge University Press, Cambridge, 2005) pp. 92–117.

[4] J. Ruggie, *Report of the Special Representative of the Secretary-General on the issue of Human Rights and Transnational Corporations and Other Business Enterprises – Protect, Respect and Remedy: A Framework for Business and Human Rights*, A/HRC/8/5 (2008) (*Main Report*), para. 9.

[5] See C. A. Rodriguez-Garavito, 'Global Governance and Labor Rights: Codes of Conduct and Anti-Sweatshop Struggles in Global Apparel Factories in Mexico and Guatemala', 33:2 *Politics and Society* (2005) pp. 203–233 (a case study of workers, local unions and transnational advocacy networks gaining political traction to improve both the protection and participation of workers in apparel factories that supplied to major Western brand names through the power of shaming and the support of government regulation even though the relevant codes of conduct were inadequate to address rights of participation).

which the Ruggie Framework does not recognise the potential for its own radicalism and to make some suggestions for its further development.

We argue that Ruggie's Framework underestimates the radical nature of what is required for *states* to take "appropriate steps" to regulate business respect for human rights including the role of the state in "regulatory space" interacting with other actors especially where the state itself is directly involved in subsidising or operating business. Ruggie does recognise that the state's duty to protect should extend to where states are "doing business with business"; that is, outsourcing, procurement, investment and export promotion. We argue that states should use their role as market actors to subvert businesses' "economic licenses" by using the deployment of wealth and contractual provisions to regulate against human rights abuses.[6]

We go on to argue that Ruggie's Framework equally underestimates what is required for businesses to take "due diligence" to discharge their responsibility to respect (RtR) human rights, and provide victims with access to remedies. We argue that businesses will always seek to neutralise critiques of their adverse human rights impacts and to bring any new initiatives to regulate business and human rights back within the rubric of the "business case" and "risk management" since this provides greater opportunity for management discretion and profit-orientation in the way they respond to human rights concerns.[7] We use literature on corporate self-regulation and compliance management systems[8] to argue that the Framework underestimates the degree of corporate commitment, capacity and skill required to take due diligence processes seriously. More fundamentally, it ignores the need for due diligence processes to be designed and, importantly, implemented in such a way that they open themselves up to radical critique of the substantive injustices and human and environmental impacts of business. We argue that due diligence processes to protect human rights only have value to the extent that they continually make business managers more open to critique by local and international activists as well as "victims" of their whole model of business decision-making and its substantive results. If this does not occur, and often it does not, corporate management will tend to use due diligence as a risk management technique that papers over the conflict between "business as usual" and the steps that must be taken to change business operations and decision-making to address the injustices, inequalities and power differentials that allow human rights to be abused on a regular basis.[9]

---

6   See J. Howe, 'The Regulatory Impact of Using Public Procurement to Promote Better Labour Standards in Corporate Supply Chains', in K. Macdonald and S. Marshall (eds.), *Fair Trade, Corporate Accountability and Beyond: Experiments in Globalising Justice* (Ashgate, Aldershot, 2010).

7   Shamir, 'Capitalism, Governance and Authority', *supra* note 3, pp. 531–553; Shamir, 'Corporate Social Responsibility', *supra* note 3, pp. 92–117.

8   See C. Parker, *The Open Corporation: Effective Self-Regulation and Democracy* (Cambridge University Press, Cambridge, 2002).

9   Here we draw on de Sousa Santos' analysis of the counter-hegemonic politics of subaltern cosmopolitan legality: B. de Sousa Santos, 'Law, Politics and the Subaltern in Counter-Hegemonic Globalization', in B. de Sousa Santos and C. A. Rodriguez-Garavito (eds.),

## 2. Ruggie's Diplomatic Project: Creating an Ambiguous Shared Discourse of Business and Human Rights

### 2.1. A Diplomatic Solution to Conflict Over Business and Human Rights

Each of Ruggie's various reports to the UN and his own explanations of his role[10] explicitly state that his appointment as Special Representative in 2005 was intended to move beyond the conflict between business and human rights advocacy groups in relation to the "Draft Norms on the Responsibilities of Transnational Corporations and Other Business Enterprises with regard to Human Rights" (the Draft Norms) that had been proposed by the Sub-Commission of the then UN Commission on Human Rights (later the Human Rights Council) in 2004.[11] As Ruggie's *Final Report* in 2011 explains, this conflict over the Draft Norms was itself prefigured by "heightened social awareness of businesses' impact on human rights" in the 1990s because of "the dramatic worldwide expansion of the private sector at the time."[12] Dissent, critique and confrontation had become a political reality for transnational corporations generally, and spurred a crisis of legitimacy for global corporate capitalism.[13] A diplomatic venture was needed to resolve the crisis without radically changing global corporate capitalism or the nature of international law. The Draft Norms had failed because they tried to do both these things.

Ruggie's diplomatic solution has been to draw on hitherto primarily theoretical and scholarly applications of international human rights law to business[14] to create a

---

*Law and Globalization from Below* (Cambridge University Press, Cambridge, 2005) pp. 1–26.

10   *See for example* 'Introduction by the Special Representative' (July 2009) available at the UN Special Representative portal at <www.business-humanrights.org/> (accessed 5 May 2011).

11   "This proposal [*i.e.* the Draft Norms] triggered a deeply divisive debate between the business community and human rights advocacy groups while evoking little support from Governments. The [UN Commission on Human Rights] declined to act on the proposal. Instead in 2005 it established a mandate for a Special Representative of the Secretary-General 'on the issue of human rights and transnational corporations and other business enterprises' to undertake a new process …": Ruggie, *Final Report, supra* note 2, para. 3. For accounts of this conflict and the subsequent appointment of Ruggie, *see also* B. Horrigan, *Corporate Social Responsibility in the 21st Century: Debates, Models and Practices Across Government, Law and Business* (Edward Elgar, Cheltenham, 2010) pp. 317–321; D. Kinley, J. Nolan and N. Zerial, "'The Norms are Dead! Long Live the Norms!" The Politics Behind the UN Human Rights Norms for Corporations', in D. McBarnet, A. Voiculescu and T. Campbell (eds.), *The New Corporate Accountability: Corporate Social Responsibility and the Law* (Cambridge University Press, Cambridge, 2007) pp. 459–475.

12   Ruggie, *Final Report, supra* note 2, para. 1.

13   *See* Shamir, 'Capitalism, Governance and Authority', *supra* note 3. *See also* L. Boltanski and E. Chiapello, *The New Spirit of Capitalism* (Verso, London, 2005).

14   For example, D. Kinley and J. Tadaki, 'From Talk to Walk: The Emergence of Human Rights Responsibilities for Corporations at International Law', 44 *Virginia Journal of In-*

Framework that could be, as it indeed was, "unanimously" "welcomed"[15] at the UN itself. This Framework is presented[16] as having been subject to a "widespread positive reception"[17] by both business and human rights groups, despite the fact they had been at loggerheads over the Draft Norms. As Ruggie comments,

> In 2005, there was little that counted as shared knowledge across different stakeholder groups in the business and human rights domain ... [The research of the Special Representative] has provided a broader and more solid factual basis for the ongoing business and human rights discourse ...[18]

The Framework then becomes the "authoritative focal point [for business and human rights] that had been missing."[19] Its genius is to exhaustively explicate, interpret and apply the existing language of international human rights law to mediate between the concerns of the UN, corporate capitalism and activists.

---

*ternational Law* (2004) pp. 931–1023; D. Kinley and J. Nolan, 'Human Rights, Corporations and the Global Economy: An International Law Perspective', in A. G. Scherer and G. Palazzo (eds.), *Handbook of Research on Global Corporate Citizenship* (Edwar Elgar, Cheltenham, 2008) pp. 343–373; P. Muchlinski, 'Corporate Social Responsibility and International Law: The Case of Human Rights and Multinational Enterprises', in D. McBarnet, A. Voiculescu and T. Campbell (eds.), *The New Corporate Accountability: Corporate Social Responsibility and the Law* (Cambridge University Press, Cambridge, 2007) pp. 431–458. See also J. Ruggie, 'Business and Human Rights: The Evolving International Agenda', 101:4 *American Journal of International Law* (October 2007) pp. 819–940; J. Ruggie, 'Taking Embedded Liberalism Global: The Corporate Connection', in D. Held and M. Koenig-Archibugi (eds.), *Taming Globalization: Frontiers of Governance* (Polity Press, Cambridge, 2003); B. Kytle and J. Ruggie, *Corporate Social Responsibility as Risk Management: A Model for Multinationals*, Corporate Social Responsibility Initiative, Kennedy School of Governance, *Working Paper #4* (March 2005); J. Ruggie, 'The Theory and Practice of Learning Networks: Corporate Social Responsibility and the Global Impact', 5 *Journal of Corporate Citizenship* (Spring 2005) pp. 27–36. The chapter by Melish and Meidinger in this volume summarises well Ruggie's own scholarly contribution to the literature on international human rights law and business.

15 Ruggie, *Final Report, supra* note 2, para. 5.
16 The first author has heard a number of reports of advocacy organisations dismissing the value of the Ruggie Framework informally despite the appearance of support for it in their formal statements.
17 Ruggie, *Final Report, supra* note 2, para. 8.
18 Ruggie, *Final Report, supra* note 2, para. 4.
19 Ruggie, *Final Report, supra* note 2, para. 5. For empirical evidence that this authoritative focal point for human rights and business was missing not only at the UN, but also among CSR practitioners, see J. Conley and C. A. Williams, 'Engage, Embed and Embellish: Theory Versus Practice in the Corporate Social Responsibility Movement', 31 *Journal of Corporate Law* (2005) pp. 1–38; R. Shamir, 'Mind the Gap: The Commodification of Corporate Social Responsibility', 28 *Symbolic Interaction* (2005) pp. 229–253.

## 2.2. An Ambiguous Discourse

Thus Ruggie has created a shared discourse around business and human rights at the United Nations that can lead on to the creation of practices – "institutions, initiatives, instruments, symbols, rituals, procedures and texts"[20] – for the regulation of corporate impacts on human rights. The practical international politics of corporate human rights responsibility have previously been framed largely around discretionary, "soft" law initiatives.[21] These initiatives see corporate responsibilities for human rights as a matter of management discretion and authority in response to risks to reputation, social and political legitimacy, and ultimately to profit.[22] That is, they are based on the "business case" for CSR (that CSR is directly or indirectly good for profits)[23] and risk management (that seeks to avert crises of social, political and economic legitimacy for the corporation).[24]

Ruggie created a discourse for business and human rights that uses the language of international law obligation to appear to move beyond "soft law", and therefore address activists' concerns about lack of legal accountability, yet, as we shall see, without necessarily challenging business managers' discretion to deal with human rights as they wish. It is in this way that Ruggie's Framework has succeeded where the Draft Norms failed in bridging the division between business, human rights advocates and government. It therefore enables the connections between CSR and international hu-

20  R. Shamir and D. Weiss, 'Corporations, Indicators, and Human Rights: A Material Semiotics View', in K. Davis, A. Fisher, B. Kingsbury and S. Merry (eds), *Governance by Indicators: Global Power through Data* (Oxford University Press, Oxford, forthcoming 2012) p. 2. See P. Bourdieu, *The Logic of Practice*, transl. R. Nice (Polity Press, Cambridge, 1980/1990) p. 53.

21  Although there is also a patchwork of state involvement in encouraging CSR: see Horrigan, *supra* note 11, chs. 4–6, for a good overview of developments in both state regulation and soft law. See also P. Zumbansen, 'The Conundrum of Corporate Social Responsibility: Reflections on the Changing Nature of Firms and States', in R. Miller and R. Bratspies (eds.), *Transboundary Harm: Lessons from the Train Smelter Arbitration* (Cambridge University Press, 2006).

22  See Shamir, 'Capitalism, Governance and Authority', *supra* note 3; Shamir, 'Corporate Social Responsibility', *supra* note 3, p. 371; D. Vogel, *The Market for Virtue: The Potential and Limits of Corporate Social Responsibility* (Brookings Institution, Washington DC, 2005).

23  Hence the incredible effort expended to try and scientifically "prove" that corporate social responsibility is good for business: *see* Vogel, *supra* note 22, ch. 2; A. B. Carroll and K. M. Shabana, 'The Business Case for Corporate Social Responsibility: A Review of Concepts, Research and Practice', 12 *International Journal of Management Reviews* (2010) p. 85.

24  This is often reflected in triaging (or "assessing") the magnitude of risks to the corporation's reputation (not necessarily to those outside the corporation who are affected; and addressing the risk via managing people's perceptions not necessarily addressing the underlying risk: Parker, *The Open Corporation*, *supra* note 8, pp. 64–65; Shamir and Weiss, *supra* note 20. See also M. Power, *Organized Uncertainty: Designing a World of Risk Management* (Oxford University Press, Oxford, 2007); R. Rosen, 'Risk Management and Corporate Governance: The Case of Enron', 35 *Connecticut Law Review* (2003) pp. 1157–1184.

man rights law discourse necessary for a new "field",[25] "network"[26] or "community" of regulation of human rights in business.[27] Moreover the human rights language of the Framework seems to add the possibility of an "authoritative", regulatory dimension to CSR discourse. Yet since the Framework is essentially a diplomatic project, it remains vague and ambiguous about this authoritative, legal dimension to human rights in business.[28] Ruggie's task was to stabilise or neutralise dissent and critique within the diplomatic realm of the UN Commission on Human Rights, later the Human Rights Council, and reach a solution acceptable to all. Diplomacy achieved this by "encompassing" both sides of the debate inside the (ambiguous) language of the Framework.[29] In evaluating the Framework then, the question is where do the ambiguities and diplomatic elisions in the language of the Framework occur? And what does this mean for how the practices and institutions for corporate human rights responsibility that the Framework enables are conceived and practiced?

In the remainder of this section we argue that Ruggie's diplomatic success has been achieved by "distancing"[30] the Framework (that is, the authoritative focal point for business and human rights in the UN) from radical, substantive business accountability and responsibility for human rights; that is, from any absolute (or authoritative) obligations on business to achieve certain substantive obligations in relation to human rights in particular circumstances. Moreover, it avoids placing any obligation on business managers to limit their own discretion by empowering those affected by those decisions (e.g. unions representing workers or councils representing local communi-

---

25  Bourdieu, *supra* note 20; L. Edelman and S. Talesh, 'To Comply or Not to Comply – That Isn't the Question: How Organizations Construct the Meaning of Compliance', in C. Parker and V. L. Nielsen, *Explaining Compliance: Business Responses to Regulation* (Edward Elgar, Cheltenham, forthcoming 2011).

26  See J. Braithwaite and P. Drahos, *Global Business Regulation* (Cambridge University Press, Cambridge, 2000).

27  See J. Black, *Rules and Regulators* (Clarendon Press, Oxford, 1997). The citations in notes 25–27 are all different social and regulatory theorists' conceptualisations of how different state and non-state actors can connect together into a new area of regulation. See also Perez on an "ensemble" of regulation: Perez, *supra* note 3; and Shamir and Weiss' adoption of Latour's actor-network-theory: Shamir and Weiss, *supra* note 20; B. Latour, *Re-assembling the Social: An Introduction to Actor-Network-Theory* (Oxford University Press, Oxford, 2005).

28  Indeed since it is successful at "translating" between business executives, CSR practitioners, human rights advocates, UN bureaucrats, governments and so on, we expect a degree of vagueness, ambiguity and multiplicity in the language of the Framework. See Latour, ibid., p. 39; N. Brunsson, *The Organization of Hypocrisy: Talk, Decisions and Actions in Organizations* (Abstrakt Forlag, Oslo, 2002); Edelman and Talesh, *supra* note 25.

29  M. Fourcade and K. Healy, 'Moral Views of Market Society', 33 *Annual Review of Sociology* (2007) pp. 285–311, p. 305.

30  Here we are following Shamir and Weiss' analysis of "distancing" in the use of corporate human rights indicators: Shamir and Weiss, *supra* note 20. We might equally have used the language of "neutralization", "elision" or "bracketing".

ties) to participate in deciding what human rights should be addressed and how they should be addressed.[31]

### 2.3. Putting Distance Between Legal Obligations and Business Responsibilities

In order to move beyond the political conflict between advocates and business, Ruggie's Framework and the associated consultation process "distanced" the UN Commission on Human Rights from taking responsibility for preventing, punishing or even exposing and evaluating the *substantive* results of business conduct in terms of actual human rights impacts on human beings and broader social and environmental inequalities and injustices. It had been the very attempt to enumerate substantive norms for corporate conduct so as to hold corporations legally accountable for the actual results of their conduct of business that led to the dissensus around the Norms.[32] Therefore this is what needed to be distanced or made ambiguous for Ruggie's Framework to achieve diplomatic success. Ruggie therefore adopted a legal discourse that emphasises first *a legal obligation on the state* (not business) to provide formal justice for individual victims in relation to human rights abuse by business (rather than distributive justice for groups and systems); and then, as the second priority, a social responsibility on business via *processes* of due diligence (rather than accountability for the results of business conduct or empowerment of those affected by business operations). As the Ruggie process evolved, this distancing became more complete, although there is not space to demonstrate this shift here. In short, the original substantive critiques disappear from the formal reports and become subject to case studies and so on available via the web portal. Over the same time period, the language of the Framework itself becomes more formal and legalistic, and therefore appears more neutral in its assumptions about the responsibility of business for human rights abuses and injustices.[33]

This distancing is quite clear in the language of the three pillars of "Protect, Respect, and Remedy" in the Framework, which are stated as:

> The first is the state *duty* to protect against human rights abuses by third parties, including business enterprises, through *appropriate* policies, regulation and adjudication.
>
> The second is the corporate *responsibility* to respect human rights, which means that business enterprises should act with *due diligence* to avoid infringing on the rights of others and to address adverse impacts with which they are involved.

---

31  See Rodriguez-Garavito, *supra* note 5, p. 205.

32  Ruggie's *Main Report* criticises the Draft Norms for emphasising "precisely the wrong side of the equation: defining a limited list of rights linked to imprecise and expansive responsibilities, rather than defining the specific responsibilities of companies with regard to all rights." Ruggie, *Main Report*, *supra* note 4, para. 51.

33  Compare the report that preceded the Draft Guiding Principles issued in 2010 with the introduction to the *Final Report* (incorporating the Guiding Principles) issued in 2011. In this analysis we focus on the most final and complete form of the Framework in the 2011 *Final Report*.

The third is the need for greater *access* by *victims* to effective remedy, both judicial and non-judicial.

Each pillar is an essential component in an inter-related and dynamic system of preventative and remedial measures: the state duty to protect because it lies at the very core of the international human rights regime; the corporate responsibility to respect because it is the basic expectation society has of business in relation to human rights; and access to remedy because even the most concerted efforts cannot prevent all abuse.[34]

The language of giving states "duties" while corporations have "responsibilities" in the first and second pillars is a political decision. It clearly indicates that businesses' "responsibilities" for human rights are of a different order to states' "duties". It diplomatically distances the Framework (addressed primarily to states) from the controversy and conflict created by the earlier Norms (which were addressed to business). Its aim is to "clarify",[35] and in so doing to reinforce, the international law status quo that states have international legal obligations while businesses do not. Businesses' "responsibilities" are stated to be based on the much more vague and ambiguous social obligations and the possibility that international law might evolve in the future to hold them accountable.[36] This language creates a holding pattern between purely discretionary CSR (seen as inadequate by activists) and the more radical attempt of the Norms to create new international human rights law that would apply to business (seen as unacceptable by business and the UN). Ruggie's Framework therefore represents, so to speak, a more practical, reasonable and therefore diplomatic approach than that of the Norms.

The Framework's first pillar does extend traditional CSR discourse beyond discretion and the business case by calling for authoritative state-based regulation of corporate human rights. Nevertheless, as we argue in section 3 below, it does not adequately recognise the nature of "regulatory space"[37] and the dynamic relationship between state and business in constructing the meaning of regulation and therefore of the human rights obligations of business.[38] Moreover, as we argue in section 4 below, the Framework's call for state-based regulation of human rights in business is rather light in its touch. The duty of states is expressed as using "appropriate" policies, regulation and adjudication, creating further opportunities for the business case and business influence to moderate the way human rights in business is actually regulated in practice.

The second pillar further distances the Framework from the earlier Norms in the interests of diplomacy by defining corporations' human rights "responsibilities" primarily in terms of a process of "due diligence" rather than accountability for the substantive impacts of their behaviour on human rights and justice. One of the main

---

34 Ruggie, *Final Report*, supra note 2, para. 6.
35 Ruggie, *Main Report*, supra note 4, para. 4.
36 Ruggie, *Main Report*, supra note 4, para. 9.
37 C. Scott, 'Analysing Regulatory Space: Fragmented Resources and Institutional Design', *Public Law* (2001) p. 329.
38 *See also* R. Shamir, 'Socially Responsible Private Regulation: World-Culture or World-Capitalism?', 45:2 *Law and Society Review* (forthcoming 2011).

reasons that the Norms caused conflict was because they attempted to specify the substantive human rights obligations that business must meet. This would inevitably bring to the forefront of attention specific ways in which human rights would challenge business as usual. In the Framework this confrontation between substantive human rights and business as usual is successfully backgrounded by saying only that the RtR covers "the entire spectrum of internationally recognized human rights" without showing the bad taste of specifying it in substance.[39] The foreground focus of the Framework is on specifying the formal, legal dimensions (and limits) of the responsibility of the due diligence process; that is, "taking adequate measures for [the] prevention, mitigation and, where appropriate, remediation" of "adverse human rights impacts".[40] "Due diligence" can hence be interpreted as a complement to management discretion in relation to CSR and human rights, not necessarily a corrective.

In section 4 of this chapter we argue that a process of due diligence for human rights on the part of business will only begin to address the human rights and global justice agenda if it is designed and practiced in such a way as to make business management open to substantive and radical critique from the outside of the impacts of specific business conduct. That is, it must contain within itself the seeds for its own substantive and radical critique. However the ongoing operationalisation of the Framework is to take the form of "guiding principles" to be developed "in the same research-based and consultative manner that had characterised [Ruggie's] mandate all along". It is also said to bring together civil society and experts in law and policy including "road-testing" in order to provide guidance that is "practical" and "informed by actual practice".[41] We suggest that this indicates an intention to base further operationalisation on examining current corporate practices as reported by CSR practitioners, lawyers and business managers and therefore not departing too greatly from what corporations can accept according to a business case or risk management rationale.

Putting together the first and second pillars, the Framework states only that a state has a "duty" to take "appropriate measures" to ensure that business takes "responsibility" for a "due diligence" process to meet human rights standards. The accomplishment of Ruggie's Framework – and also its potential weakness – is therefore to translate the language of risk management and the business case (preserving management discretion) into the legal language of "due diligence", a concept that has been used extensively in corporate law to provide a defence for business management discretion against claims that they have failed to take "reasonable care".[42] Here, then, is the ambiguity: the language of the Framework appears to put a positive duty on business to show respect for human rights through "due diligence". But in practice the very concept of due diligence is a defensive one that corporate lawyers, CSR practitioners

---

39 Ruggie, *Final Report, supra* note 2, p. 13. This does not of course preclude or discourage states from adopting treaties and laws that do seek to hold corporations substantively accountable. But it takes the focus of these substantive accountabilities in the UN.
40 Ruggie, *Final Report, supra* note 2, p. 13.
41 See Ruggie, *Final Report, supra* note 2, paras. 10 and 11.
42 See L. Spedding, *The Due Diligence Handbook: Corporate Governance, Risk Management and Business Planning* (CIMA, Amersterdam, 2009).

and risk management experts can use to head off the legitimacy crisis of business human rights responsibility by showing that enough has been done. It does not extend and challenge the discourse of CSR with a more "authoritative" and far-reaching sense of obligation for human rights.[43]

The final step in the process of distancing the Framework from radical corporate accountability for human rights is evident in the third pillar of the Framework, "remedy". Those who suffer at the hands of corporate conduct are defined as "victims" who require "access" to a remedy. The language of "victims" suggests individuals[44] who can identify some individual right that has been trampled and therefore should be able to access an individual remedy that can be "adjudicated" in formal legal terms. The remedies available are stated to include "compensation, restitution, guarantees of non-repetition, changes in relevant law and public apologies". This puts the focus on the remedy that the individual victim should be able to access, rather than putting the focus on activism and dissent to identify radical and systemic changes that the business should make to its mode of operation. We suggest that while victim access to remedies might be an important aspect of applying human rights to business, it is even more important that "business as usual" be made accountable for the social and environmental injustice of a whole model of doing business. "Remedies" are primarily about justice defined in an individualistic and often legalistic way.[45] Putting the focus on individual remedies is therefore another way in which the Framework distances itself from the distributive justice concerns of activists and local communities that motivated the crisis that prompted the Ruggie process.

In the following two sections we discuss in further detail how an understanding of the sociology and politics of business regulation and compliance might extend and, to a certain extent, radicalise the Framework's understanding first of state responsibilities for regulation, and second of corporate due diligence and access to justice for human rights abuses.

## 3. A More Radical Approach to State Regulation and Coherence?

### 3.1. Regulatory Space

Ruggie's Framework provides that states, corporations and civil society have a role in the prevention of, and remedy for, harms to human rights by corporations. That is, he assumes that state-based regulation of business is appropriate, in conjunction with more voluntary and civil society forms of regulation. This goes some way towards recognising what we know from regulation and compliance literature about how regu-

---

43 See references at *supra* notes 22–24.
44 Although this might perhaps include groups of individuals.
45 As Melish and Meidinger note in their contribution to this volume, "the SRSG's discussion of state and corporate duties to remedy is focused almost exclusively on the provision of grievance procedures for 'victims' … Community members are conceived principally as 'objects' of potential abuse, not as 'subjects' of decision making processes and impact assessments concerning activities that may affect their lives." (p. 332).

lation works. Regulation and compliance researchers have long noticed that it is more useful to understand the impact and effectiveness of regulation in terms of how it operates in a "regulatory space" in which many parties exercise regulatory capacity. It is not useful to focus purely on the state exercising its authority to regulate behaviour through law and administrative oversight. The regulatory space metaphor points out

> that resources relevant to holding of regulatory power and exercising of capacities are dispersed or fragmented. These resources are not restricted to formal, state authority derived from legislation or contracts, but also information, wealth and organisational capacities. The possession of these resources is fragmented between state and non-state bodies.[46]

One of the strengths of Ruggie's Framework is that it does take a broad view of the "state duty to protect" pillar, suggesting that it extends beyond the use of formal law to require business to respect human rights to include circumstances where the state transfers its wealth resource to business in pursuit of public policy goals. Ruggie has noted that "the State's role as an economic actor is a key – but under-utilised – leverage point in promoting corporate human rights awareness and preventing abuses".[47] Grouped under the heading "The State-business nexus" (in an earlier report, Ruggie referred to the activities in question as states "doing business with business"[48]), Ruggie's Guiding Principles address circumstances where businesses are either owned, controlled or supported by the state. Three areas of particular concern highlighted by Ruggie are examples of state support for business: investment promotion, export credit and public procurement.

Ruggie has also argued that state neglect of human rights concerns when doing business with business is an area where there is "horizontal policy incoherence" in relation to the state duty to protect, or "where economic or business-focused departments and agencies that directly shape business practices – including trade, investment, export credit and insurance, corporate law, and securities regulation – conduct their work in isolation from and largely uninformed by their Government's human rights agencies and obligations".[49] In other words, states should not say that they are

---

46   Scott, *supra* note 37, p. 330.

47   J. Ruggie, *Report of the Special Representative of the Secretary-General on the issue of Human Rights and Transnational Corporations and Other Business Enterprises – Business and Human Rights: Further Steps Toward the Operationalization of the "Protect, Respect and Remedy" Framework*, A/HRC/14/27 (2010) (*2010 Report*), para. 32, p. 8. Ruggie has argued that it is the proximity of business to the state which justifies the inclusion of doing business with business within the state duty to protect: "The closer a business enterprise is to the State, or the more it relies on statutory authority or taxpayer support, the stronger the State's policy rationale becomes for ensuring that the enterprise respects human rights": Ruggie, *Final Report, supra* note 2, para. 4.

48   Ruggie, *2010 Report, ibid.*, p. 7.

49   J. Ruggie, *Report of the Special Representative of the Secretary-General on the issue of Human Rights and Transnational Corporations and Other Business Enterprises – Business and Human Rights: Towards Operationalizing the "Protect, Respect and Remedy" Frame-

protecting human rights in one policy area and asking business to do the same, and then in another area (such as investment or export promotion) exclude human rights from consideration.

However, Ruggie does not necessarily recognise that all or most of the actions discussed under the "state duty to protect" pillar are ways of "regulating" business to do the right thing. Further, Ruggie's Framework inadequately understands the variety of ways in which state regulation, voluntary or civil society regulation, and business responsibility interact with and mutually constitute each other. The diplomatic nature of Ruggie's Framework tends to emphasise that states act through "law" and other actors regulate through "social obligation". But a "regulatory" perspective points out that states regulate in many ways and with many partners. In regulatory space, regulation is "any set of processes by which norms are established, the behavior of those subject to the norms are monitored and fed back into the regime, and for which there are mechanisms for holding the behavior of regulated actors within the acceptable limits of the regime".[50] By contemplating that wealth transfers offer states leverage in promoting human rights abuses, Ruggie is acknowledging the potential for government expenditure to operate as a regulatory instrument in the achievement of greater business respect for human rights.[51] Nevertheless, he does not expressly consider that the effectiveness of these norms in preventing human rights abuses will depend to some extent on business cooperation, and on the enrolment or involvement of stakeholders – interested state and non-state organisations other than "regulator" and "regulatee" – to hold business accountable.

### 3.2. Public Wealth Transfers and Subversion of Businesses' Economic License to Operate

To further explore the implications of this analysis, we turn to Ruggie's consideration of investment promotion, export credit and public procurement as elements of the state duty to protect in more detail. In identifying the potential for government to make public wealth transfers conditional upon business respect for human rights, Ruggie is consistent with a number of studies concerned with the extent to which procurement, investment promotion and export credit is, or should be, linked with social concerns such as human rights, labour standards and environmental sustainability.[52] However, Ruggie is careful to avoid suggesting that procurement and invest-

---

work A/HRC/11/13 (2009) (2009 Report), para. 18, p. 8; see also Ruggie, 2010 Report, supra note 47, para. 16, p. 5.

50   Scott, supra note 37, p. 331.
51   For a comprehensive discussion of government wealth transfers as a form of regulation, see T. Daintith, 'Regulation', in International Association of Legal Science, *International Encyclopedia of Comparative Law*, vol. XVII (Mohr Siebeck, Tubingen, 1997) p. 48.
52   See for example, in relation to procurement, C. McCrudden, *Buying Social Justice: Equality, Government Procurement and Legal Change* (Oxford University Press, Oxford, 2007); Howe, supra note 6; and K. Zeisel, 'The Promotion of Human Rights by Selective Public Procurement Under International Trade Law', in O. de Schutter (ed.), *Transnational*

ment promotion should be conditional upon business *compliance* with human rights obligations. In relation to procurement, the final version of the Guiding Principles says that states should *promote* "awareness of and respect for human rights by [contracted enterprises], with due regard to States relevant obligations under national and international law".[53] He goes a little further when discussing that a range of agencies linked to the state may provide support and services to business activities, including export credit agencies, official investment insurance or guarantee agencies, development agencies and development finance institutions:

> Where these agencies do not explicitly consider the actual and potential adverse impacts on human rights or beneficiary enterprises, they put themselves at risk – in reputational, financial, political and potentially legal terms – for supporting any such harm, and they may add to the human rights challenges faced by the recipient State. Given these risks, *States should encourage and, where appropriate, require human rights due diligence* by the agencies themselves and by those business enterprises or projects receiving their support.[54]

What is apparent from this language is that Ruggie wants to elide the "regulatory" aspect of what the state does in the context of wealth transfers as much as possible. Once again, this may be related to the politics of gaining acceptance for his proposals. Consistent with our argument in sections 2 and 3 of this chapter, Ruggie is suggesting that the state has a responsibility to do something authoritative when it does business with business – to make human rights an explicit concern in relation to public expenditure – but that business owes something less than a legal obligation in return. At best, he is suggesting that states could require business to engage in a form of self-regulation concerning human rights. At worst, he is assuming that business will voluntarily give greater attention to their human rights practices in the context of wealth transfers.

Notwithstanding Ruggie's efforts to avoid suggesting that businesses should comply with human rights norms in return for state wealth transfers, Ruggie's proposals concerning investment promotion, export credit and public procurement have some fundamental implications for business regulation if they were taken seriously. Although Ruggie presents the incorporation of human rights norms for business in

---

*Corporations and Human Rights* (Hart Publishing, Oxford, Portland, 2006) pp. 361–391. On investment promotion, see T. Bartik, 'Solving the Problem of Economic Development Incentives', 36 *Growth and Change* (2005) p. 139; J. Howe and I. Landau, 'Do Investment Attraction Incentives Create Decent Jobs? A Study of Labour Conditions in Industry Assistance Contracts', 19:3 *Labour & Industry* (2009) pp. 97–136. On export finance, see F. Haines, 'Political Risk, Green Governance & the Challenge of Resetting The Government/Business Relationship: Exploring the Role of Export Credit Agencies', Climate and Environmental Governance Network Working Paper No. 11 (Regulatory Institutions Network, ANU, Canberra, 2011); and Jubilee Australia, 'Risky Business: Shining a Spotlight on Australia's Export Credit Agency' (Jubilee Australia, Sydney, 2009).

53   Ruggie, *Final Report*, supra note 2, para. 6.
54   Ruggie, *Final Report*, supra note 2, principle 4 commentary (emphasis added).

state wealth transfers as an unproblematic extension of the duty to protect, there is an extensive literature concerning the regulatory nature and impact of economic instruments which suggests otherwise.

The assumption underpinning the use of deployment of wealth as a regulatory instrument is that it is an attractive alternative to mandatory legal regulation ("command and control"). Instead of mandating a change of behaviour, with punishment for non-compliance, economic instruments offer the firm an incentive to comply with desired behaviour, whether by making access to a market or financial support conditional upon the business meeting certain goals. The idea is that the conditional transfer of funds from the state will subvert the firm's "economic license to operate". Neil Gunningham, Robert Kagan and Dorothy Thornton have argued that the concept of the license to operate best explains the external pressures that shape the extent to which an enterprise is socially responsible.[55] Their concept is broader than the conventional understanding of a license as expressing a company's legal obligations, encompassing three broad categories of license: legal, social and economic. The notion of the social license to operate expresses the demands of social actors and stakeholders such as communities, activists and the voting public. However, Gunningham argues that a business' license to operate also includes:

> 'economic reality' requirements such as the need to meet debt obligations, show growth in earnings, and maximise shareholder return on investment (or at least to provide a reasonable rate of return). The terms of this *economic license* – what is an adequate rate of return on investment or level of profitability – are not written down in detail like a regulatory permit, of course; they may vary over time, 'tightening' and 'loosening' with market conditions and each firm's economic performance.[56]

The economic license can act either as a brake on, or as a spur to, compliance or "beyond compliance" behaviour. Where the state makes transfers of wealth conditional upon, for example, human rights performance, the regulatory license is intended to directly impact on the company's economic license to operate. It is anticipated that the lure of government expenditure will make it easier for the firm's managers to ensure that the business respects human rights in circumstances where in the absence of an economic incentive such activity would be inconsistent with market demands or the profit maximisation goal.[57]

---

55  N. Gunningham, R. Kagan and D. Thornton, *Shades of Green: Business, Regulation and the Environment* (Stanford University Press, California, 2003).

56  N. Gunningham, 'Corporate Environmental Responsibility: Law and the Limits of Voluntarism', in D. McBarnet, A. Voiculescu, and T. Campbell (eds.), *The New Corporate Accountability: Corporate Social Responsibility and the Law* (Cambridge University Press, Cambridge, 2007) p. 482.

57  See R. Howse, 'Retrenchment, Reform or Revolution? The Shift to Incentives and the Future of the Regulatory State', 31 *Alberta Law Review* (1993) pp. 455–492; P. Grabosky, 'Regulation by Reward: On the Use of Incentives as Regulatory Instruments', 17:3 *Law and Policy* (1996) pp. 256–281.

We suggest that these assumptions are not without difficulty. For example, although many governments already make eligibility for procurement contracts dependent on businesses demonstrating compliance with labour standards and environmental sustainability criteria (Ruggie cites examples from the United States and the Netherlands), the use of procurement policy in this way is still very much contested, especially in the context of free trade agreements.[58] Linkages between procurement and social policy objectives are contested both within government and by business on a number of grounds. Chief among government objections is the argument that government's primary concern in the deployment of public wealth should be economic and not social concerns (*i.e.* value for money). On the business side the argument is made that linkages are anti-competitive as they are unfair to organisations dependent on government assistance or contracts that are in competition with businesses not dependent on government.[59] Conditional transfers are far less common and even more contested in the context of export finance and investment promotion, where similar objections are made more successfully.[60]

It also cannot be assumed that applying human rights criteria to deployment of wealth is necessarily a more effective way of preventing human rights abuses than legal regulation. There is very little empirical research concerning the effectiveness of deployment of wealth transfers in achieving social policy or CSR goals. Braithwaite and others have noted that as a regulatory technique, regulation by reward may in fact be counterproductive.[61] The attraction of government funding creates the risk of "creative compliance" and other rent-seeking behaviour. In other words, conditional government funding may generate only superficial attempts to meet funding criteria, as many firms will be tempted to pursue their own goals at the expense of public objectives. Ruggie's Framework does not adequately address conflict and competition between frameworks or rationales for CSR and business regulation, such as the power of the economic license to operate for business. The evidence from studies of the use of wealth transfers as a form of business regulation suggests it cannot be assumed that the use of these mechanisms to promote business observance of human rights will successfully subvert the economic license to operate of firms in the absence of a certain regulatory infrastructure.[62]

---

58  *See for example* J. Dunoff, 'Linking International Markets and Global Justice', 107 *Michigan Law Review* (2009) pp. 1039–1058; Zeisal, *supra* note 52.

59  For a summary of the arguments against procurement linkages, see McCrudden, *supra* note 52, pp. 114–122, while a useful discussion of business opposition to the linking of procurement with social policy in the context of European Corporate Social Responsibility policy debates can be found on pp. 382–384. For discussion in the context of other forms of industry assistance, *see* Howe and Landau, *supra* note 52.

60  Jubilee Australia, *supra* note 52; Howe and Landau, *supra* note 52.

61  J. Braithwaite, 'Rewards and Regulation', 29 *Journal of Law and Society* (2002) pp. 12–26; *see also* Howse, *supra* note 57.

62  Howse, *supra* note 57; K. Webb, 'Thumbs, Fingers and Pushing on String: Legal Accountability in the Use of Federal Financial Incentives', 31 *Alberta Law Review* (1993) pp. 501–535.

At a minimum, state use of wealth transfers to promote human rights observance should operate as an incentive to corporations to internalise human rights norms through development of internal systems, involving multiple stakeholders.⁶³ While this might be achieved by states requiring that business carry out human rights due diligence in return for wealth transfers, as flagged by Ruggie in relation to export credit agencies, careful attention must be paid to how due diligence is designed and carried out. The appropriate use and design of due diligence is explored in greater detail in the following section of the paper.

Beyond this, regulatory compliance scholarship suggests that maximising the effectiveness and accountability of conditional transfers requires monitoring and enforcement mechanisms of one form or another. Ruggie acknowledges the need for monitoring and evaluation in the context of contracting-out of public service delivery when he says that "States should ensure that they can effectively oversee [the delivery of previously public services by private enterprises], including through the provision of adequate independent monitoring and accountability mechanisms".⁶⁴ However, he does not seem to recognise the importance of monitoring and oversight of human rights conditions set through procurement, investment promotion and export credit expenditure. For example, in arguing as he does that export credit agencies should require due diligence from companies receiving assistance, it is not clear that Ruggie understands that successful self-regulation may also require independent monitoring and evaluation by third parties to ensure that self-regulatory regimes are not merely self-serving.⁶⁵

Consistent with regulatory space analysis and some New Governance literature,⁶⁶ a number of studies have emphasised the importance of the state "enrolling", "harnessing" or collaborating with non-state actors who are "third parties" to the regulatory process in the oversight of both the assessment of eligibility for wealth transfers and business observance of human rights criteria after the receipt of public funds.⁶⁷ The enrolment of third party actors should be complementary to state regulation; that is, the involvement of third parties should supplement state regulation rather than signifying

---

63  Parker, *supra* note 8, p. 29.
64  Ruggie, *Final Report*, *supra* note 2, principle 5.
65  Howse, *supra* note 57; C. Parker, 'Meta-regulation: Legal Accountability for Corporate Social Responsibility', in D. McBarnet, A.Voiculescu, and T. Campbell (eds.), *The New Corporate Accountability: Corporate Social Responsibility and the Law* (Cambridge University Press, Cambridge, 2007) p. 228.
66  See the chapter by Melish and Meidinger in this volume.
67  J. Black, 'Enrolling Actors in Regulatory Systems: Examples from UK Financial Services Regulation', *Public Law* (2003) pp. 63–91; V. L. Nielson and C Parker, 'To What Extent do Third Parties Influence Business Compliance', 35 *Journal of Law and Society* (2008) pp. 309–340; J. Fine and J. Gordon, 'Strengthening Labor Standards Enforcement through Partnerships with Workers' Organisations', 38:4 *Politics & Society* (2010) pp. 552–585; Howse, *supra* note 57, p. 476. P. Grabosky, 'Using Non-Governmental Resources to Foster Regulatory Compliance', 8:4 *Governance* (1995) pp. 527–529.

state abdication from regulation.⁶⁸ In other words, state regulation can be enhanced or supplemented by "institutional designs that facilitate the entering of countervailing voices"⁶⁹ such as worker organisations or human rights groups. While there have been mixed assessments of so-called private monitoring systems such as corporate codes of practice, independent monitoring of regulatory compliance by third parties in conjunction with state regulation has been shown to have greater potential in achieving corporate accountability to labour standards and other social criteria.⁷⁰ The use of third party certification and monitoring has already been adopted with some success in the context of some public procurement regimes where compliance with labour standards is a condition of business participation.⁷¹ We concur with Melish and Meidinger in this volume, who argue that Ruggie does not place enough emphasis on the role of civil society in the implementation of the duties owed by the state and business under his Framework. They suggest that the addition of a fourth pillar to the Ruggie Framework, representing the civic duty of civil society to "participate", would help to legitimate and mobilise the involvement of civil society actors in functions such as monitoring and evaluation processes.

Where third party monitoring is not incorporated within the regulatory regime, non-state actors may nevertheless employ their own resources to secure corporate accountability to human rights norms in the context of expenditure transfers. Returning to the concept of a business "licence to operate", it is important to recognise that the regulatory, economic and social licenses are not mutually exclusive, and each may be monitored by a variety of stakeholders.

> Environmental groups not only enforce the terms of the social license directly (e.g. through shaming and adverse publicity) but also seek to influence the terms of the economic license (e.g. generating consumer boycotts of environmentally damaging products) and of the regulatory license (e.g. through citizen suits or political pressure for regulatory initiatives).⁷²

---

68  Rodriguez-Garavito, *supra* note 5, p. 206. An example of where private monitoring by non-governmental organisations has been used to supplement state regulation of labour standards through procurement is the City of Los Angeles Sweatfree Procurement Ordinance, described in Howe, *supra* note 6, pp. 340–343. See also M. Amengual, 'Complementary Labor Regulation: The Uncoordinated Combination of State and Private Regulators in the Dominican Republic', 38:3 *World Development* (2010) pp. 405–414.

69  Rodriguez-Garavito, *supra* note 5, p. 219.

70  See for example ibid.; Fine and Gordon, *supra* note 67; K. Kolben, 'Intergrative Linkage: Combining Public and Private Regulatory Approaches in the Design of Trade and Labor Regimes', 48 *Harvard International Law Journal* (2007) pp. 203–56; Grabosky, 'Using Non-Governmental Resources', *supra* note 67, pp. 530–531; D. Weil 'Public Enforcement/Private Monitoring: Evaluating a New Approach to Regulating the Minimum Wage', 58 *Industrial and Labor Relations Review* (2005) pp. 238–257.

71  See Howe, *supra* note 6.

72  Gunningham, Kagan and Thornton, *supra* note 55, p. 37.

In other words, Ruggie's recommendation of incorporating human rights criteria in wealth transfers presents an opportunity for non-state actors to pressure states to adopt such initiatives, and to highlight any non-observance of these norms by business recipients of wealth transfers. In this way, what Ruggie presents as a social obligation for business may become more like a legal obligation in the sense that managerial discretion to deal with human rights issues may be "regulated" by enforcement of the social license, or pressure on the economic license. This sort of "uncoordinated" action by non-state regulators is nevertheless complementary to state regulation which links human rights norms to wealth transfers.[73]

A major obstacle to monitoring and scrutiny of government expenditure and incentive-based regulation by non-state actors external to the regulatory process is a lack of transparency. There is a tendency for governments to treat wealth transfers as commercially sensitive, and to keep transfer conditions and/or implementation of social or environmental criteria confidential. For example, export credit agencies such as Australia's Export Finance Investment Corporation (EFIC) have been heavily criticised in this respect.[74] Greater transparency of state deployment of wealth to business would therefore be an important element in extending business respect for human rights conditions, something that would likely be strongly resisted by both states and business.

As argued earlier in the paper, part of the value of Ruggie's Framework is its potential to create a coherent, coordinating rationale for business regulation and responsibility that is not just about management discretion and trade and profits. However, horizontal policy incoherence of the kind identified by Ruggie has been a particularly intractable problem in relation to public wealth transfers.[75] It would be easy to add public procurement, where value for money has tended to trump social and human rights criteria in government purchasing decisions. Ultimately one might hope that the Ruggie Framework could lead to a coherent, international understanding of the basic responsibilities of business that ought to be protected, respected and remedied in domestic law and international law (and not derogated from by other laws and policies). However, the Framework gives little guidance as to the process by which historical resistance to policy coherence between public wealth transfers and human rights might be overcome. The goal of policy coherence may in part be achieved by states attaching human rights criteria to public wealth transfers, but some mechanism is needed to ensure that these criteria are not trumped by the economic policy goals behind transfers and the economic license to operate of firms.

---

73  Amengual describes how monitoring processes under a corporate code of conduct supported enforcement activity by a state labour inspectorate in factories in the Dominican Republic: Amengual, *supra* note 68.

74  Jubilee Australia, *supra* note 52; Haines, *supra* note 52.

75  Ruggie has identified investment promotion in the case of host states and export credit in the case of home states as examples of where policy incoherence arises: Ruggie, *Main Report*, *supra* note 4, pp. 11–12.

## 4. A More Radical Approach to Justice? Due Diligence and Access to Justice

### 4.1. The Ambiguity of Due Diligence

Ruggie's Framework suggests that businesses' "baseline responsibilities for human rights" are to comply with national laws[76] and to "respect" human rights: the "responsibility to respect" is discharged via "due diligence".[77] Ruggie explains that the concept of due diligence "describes the steps a company must take to become aware of, prevent and address adverse human rights impacts" and comments that "comparable processes are typically already embedded in companies because in many countries they are legally required to have information and control systems in place to assess and manage financial and related risks."[78]

There is an extensive empirical and theoretical literature in the field of regulation and compliance on what it means for companies to take their social and legal responsibilities (including human rights responsibilities) seriously by building them into their everyday practices.[79] For example, in *The Open Corporation*, Parker summarised what her own and others' empirical research suggests about what makes for effective, "open" and accountable corporate self-regulation of social and legal responsibilities

---

76 Note that the Guiding Principles in the *Final Report* comments that "[t]he failure to enforce existing laws that directly or indirectly regulate business respect for human rights is a significant legal gap in current State practice. Such laws might range from non-discrimination and labor laws to environmental, property or privacy laws. It is therefore important for States to consider which relevant laws are not currently being effectively enforced, why this is the case, and what measures may reasonably correct the situation." Ruggie, *Final Report, supra* note 2, para. 5. There is not space to canvas these issues in this paper but it is important to notice that there is a huge empirical and theoretical literature on regulatory enforcement and regulatory agency discretion that is relevant to these issues, and that what amounts to "effective" enforcement and why regulatory agencies do not always engage in effective enforcement is heavily contested: I. Ayres and J. Braithwaite, *Responsive Regulation: Transcending the Deregulation Debate* (Oxford University Press, New York, 1992); R. A. Kagan, 'Regulatory Enforcement', in D. Rosenbloom and R. Schwartz (eds.), *Handbook of Regulation and Administrative Law* (Marcel Dekker Inc, New York, 1994) pp. 383–422; P. May and S. Winter, 'Regulatory Enforcement Styles and Compliance', in C. Parker and V. L. Nielsen (eds.), *Explaining Compliance: Business Responses to Regulation* (Edward Elgar, Cheltenham, forthcoming 2011).

77 Ruggie, *Main Report, supra* note 4, paras. 54 to 56.

78 Ibid., para. 56. Both the *Main Report* and the *Guiding Principles for Implementation* in the *Final Report* go on to set out some of the main elements of due diligence for avoiding adverse human rights impacts.

79 See Parker, *supra* note 8; C. Parker and S. Gilad, 'Internal Corporate Compliance Management Systems: Structure, Culture and Agency', in C. Parker and V. L. Nielsen (eds.), *Explaining Compliance: Business Responses to Regulation* (Edward Elgar, Cheltenham, forthcoming 2011); C. Coglianese and D. Lazer, 'Management-Based Regulation: Prescribing Private Management to Achieve Public Goals', 37 *Law & Society Review* (2003) pp. 691–730.

as shown in Box 1.[80] Ruggie's discussion of due diligence is broadly consistent with these principles, although even a cursory reading of the literature on corporate compliance, self-regulation and social responsibility management systems shows that the level of senior management commitment, capacity, resources and skill needed to take such due diligence schemes seriously is immense. Moreover it is extremely difficult to evaluate whether such schemes are in fact effective at achieving the policy outcomes they are apparently supposed to achieve. Many critics point out that self-regulating organisations and sectors may engage in activity that looks impressive, but does not actually achieve public policy goals such as respect for human rights. Rather it neutralises critique of human rights abuses by appearing to do something about them while at the same time maintaining business priorities.[81]

Box 1: Elements of Effective, Open Self-regulation for a Business Firm

(1) There should be clearly defined responsibility for self-regulation that is shared between:
- a specialised self-regulation function with sufficient authority to determine strategies and priorities for legal and social responsibility issues, monitor compliance, receive complaints from internal and external stakeholders, and be responsible for coordinating reporting on the company's responsibility performance to government agencies and the public. The chief self-regulation staff member should generally have a level of seniority (*e.g.* direct reporting line to Board or Board Committee) and employment protections (*e.g.* no termination of the contract without a Board review).
- a clear Board-level self-regulation oversight agenda. This might be achieved by a Board Audit or Compliance Committee, a designated Board member (as is the custom in Germany), or simply by making the self-regulation/compliance programme a standing agenda item on normal Board meetings. The Board should receive reports on social and legal responsibility issues, review compliance management strategy and priorities, and act on policy issues raised by compliance management activity. Certain categories of stakeholder might be represented on a Board Audit, Compliance or Social Responsibility Committee.
- reporting lines and job descriptions that make compliance with self-regulation part of everybody's job, and make clear pathways for compliance performance and problems to be taken directly to the top through a reporting line independent of line management. All employees and managers should have clear access to the self-regulation/compliance function to receive advice and raise issues. The chief self-regulation/compliance person should have senior management status, and a direct reporting line to the CEO and the Board. This means that the self-regulation/compliance function can bypass uncooperative line management, has access to intelligence about conflicts and problems at every level, and the power to put them on the agenda at the highest level.

---

80  Box 1 is based on Parker, *supra* note 8, pp. 197–244.
81  *See* K. Krawiec, 'Cosmetic Compliance and the Failure of Negotiated Governance', 81 *Washington University Law Review* (2003) pp. 487–544; W. Laufer, 'Corporate Liability, Risk Shifting, and the Paradox of Compliance', 54 *Vanderbilt Law Review* (1999) pp. 1343–1420.

> (2) The company's internal discipline system must articulate with the compliance system – *i.e.* management and employees should be regularly and swiftly disciplined for any misconduct under the company's compliance system (and also rewarded via performance evaluations for positive contributions). This disciplinary action should be designed in such a way that it respects employees' integrity, connects with employees' values and allows the company as a whole to learn from individual mistakes and misbehaviours in order to prevent them recurring.
> 
> (3) The company should have a Justice Plan for engagement with external stakeholders – *i.e.* systems for identifying its obligations under law, and any other standards it wishes to voluntarily adopt (such as certain ethical or social responsibility principles, or broader human rights principles), and have systems that allow external stakeholders to use those rights to contest corporate actions and decision-making. These should include at the very least a complaints handling system with a capacity to identify patterns of complaint, and to report those issues to someone who can resolve them. Best practice Justice Plans should also include a pathway, and where necessary financial support, for stakeholders to take their complaints to an external, independent decision-maker in circumstances where they cannot be resolved within the corporation.
> 
> (4) There must be regular evaluation of corporate self-regulation processes and performance. This should include the extent of implementation of self-regulation processes, whether their scope and strategy remain appropriate for the organisation, verification of reports of activity and performance produced internally, and assessment of performance and outcomes of the whole approach to self-regulation within the corporation.

For example, in a series of studies of corporate responses to civil rights legislation, Lauren Edelman has shown that employers have created "a variety of symbolic forms of compliance" such as anti discrimination rules, civil rights offices, and grievance procedures that are "more attentive to managerial prerogatives than to legal ideals" and did not produce much substantive change.[82] Equal employment opportunity programmes, for example, did not change the representation of women and minorities in the workplace and grievance procedures "managerialised" and internalised disputes about civil rights in the workplace rather than encouraging employees to use their legal rights to achieve the outcomes the law sought to guarantee for them. Edelman also shows how legal (and human rights) concepts of equitable gender and racial representation in the workplace where transformed into a concern with "diversity management" that aimed at using diversity for productive, profit-making potential rather than protecting rights. Edelman goes on to show how corporations are able to influence the

---

82  Edelman and Talesh, *supra* note 25. Edelman and Talesh summarise a number of studies by Edelman and colleagues.

application of the law by courts, tribunals and regulators so that their own constructions of the law to suit management purposes become the dominant interpretation of the meaning of compliance.

Similarly, Sharon Gilad[83] studied United Kingdom financial services firms' responses to "Treating Customers Fairly" (TCF) regulatory requirements, which required them to engage in a due diligence process to avoid mis-selling financial products. Gilad finds that most firms did not change anything substantive at first. Indeed many of the firms continued to engage in selling products with exactly the features that had given rise to earlier mis-selling scandals in the financial services industry. Instead of changing their practices, these firms made an effort to create measures and evidence that they could report to the regulator to show that they were "already" complying. Once they were forced to make greater changes by the regulator, most firms reframed TCF as a business issue that related to their "customer experience" programmes; that is, as something intended to enhance customer loyalty and promotion to family and friends, rather than a matter of legal rights. All but two of the major banks still continued to sell the types of products that had been mis-sold in the past, despite a continued high level of customer complaints about them and regulatory investigation and enforcement activity.

Finally corporate due diligence processes can often be used to create an evidence trail that obscures top-management or entity responsibility for breaches and instead scapegoats individuals. Christine Parker reports on the case of a major gas facility where the environmental, health and safety management system was designed to allow management to blame powerless employees for the explosion that killed them.[84] Garry Gray also reports a number of ways in which health and safety systems are used to "responsibilise" individual employees and avoid employers being the target of the law.[85]

### 4.2. *Under-estimation of Due Diligence*

We suggest that there are two ways in particular in which Ruggie's discussion ignores or underestimates the capacity for failure of corporate due diligence approaches to human rights (and other social and legal responsibilities).

First, Ruggie's discussion of due diligence processes reads like something that can be "added on" when a company is considering operations in another country that may have an inadequate human rights framework. Thus, in the *Main Report*, Ruggie describes the due diligence process as follows:

> Companies should consider three sets of factors. The first is the country contexts in which their business activities take place, to highlight any specific human rights challenges they

---

83  S. Gilad, 'Reframing and Delegation in the Institutionalization of Regulation', *Regulation and Governance* (forthcoming 2011).
84  Parker, *supra* note 8, p. 154.
85  G. Gray, 'The Responsibilization Strategy of Health and Safety: Neo-Liberalism and the Reconfiguration of Individual Responsibility for Risk', 49 *British Journal of Criminology* (2009) pp. 326–342.

may pose. The second is what human rights impacts their own activities may have within that context – for example, in their capacity as producers, service providers, employers and neighbours. The third is whether they might contribute to abuse through the relationships connected to their activities, such as with business partners, suppliers, State agencies, and other non-State actors. How far or how deep this process must go will depend on the circumstances.[86]

This suggests that human rights due diligence is a limited, definable assessment to be done on the basis of assessments of the risk of human rights abuse in particular foreign countries. However human rights are not just something to worry about in "other" countries. Neither is due diligence to ensure people's human rights are being respected something that can be cordoned off as an "add on" in relation to specific projects that are thought to raise particular risks. If one thing is clear from regulation and compliance literature on corporate compliance with social and legal responsibilities in other contexts (such as environmental and health and safety responsibilities), it is that these responsibilities must be fundamental to all aspects of business strategy and operations if they are to make any difference.

Ruggie's Framework does pay lip service to the notion that "the integration of human rights policies throughout a company [and we might add its supply chain] may be the biggest challenge in fulfilling the corporate responsibility to respect".[87] This may well go beyond previous corporate social responsibility instruments at the international level.[88] But still the energy in the language of Ruggie's diplomatic project goes into defining the limits of business responsibility for human rights. For example it is made clear that there is only a "responsibility" to avoid *directly* causing or contributing to adverse human impacts through the business enterprises' own activities. There is a lesser obligation to "seek to prevent or mitigate" human rights abuses that are only "directly linked to their operations, products or services" as a result of business relationships.[89] Yet this distinction between human rights abuses directly "caused" and those more indirectly "linked" to a particular corporation is the very issue that caused conflicts over business' human rights responsibility in the first place – and thus gave rise to the Draft Norms and then Ruggie's mandate. These issues include "poor working conditions in global supply chains" and the expansion of oil, gas and mining companies "into increasingly difficult areas", code for compromised, but often indirect, relationships with corrupt governments or government owned enterprises in Africa and elsewhere.[90] Indeed, in contemporary capitalism, it is these complex chains of supply and production chains and corporate group relationships that have been used to distance

---

86  Ruggie, *Main Report, supra* note 4, para. 57, p. 17.
87  *See for example ibid.*, para. 62 on 'Integration'.
88  *See* the chapter by Mares in this volume ('Responsibility to Respect: Why the Core Company Should Act When Affiliates Infringe Human Rights'); *also* R. Mares, 'The Limits of Supply Chain Responsibility – A Critical Analysis of CSR Instruments', 79:2 *Nordic Journal of International Law* (2010).
89  Ruggie, *Final Report, supra* note 2, p. 14.
90  *See* cases discussed by Shamir, *supra* note 3.

businesses and consumer brands in the "Global North" from responsibility for human rights and other abuses in the "Global South" and even among less powerful workers and local communities in their own countries.[91]

Moreover the apparent simplicity of the three sets of factors that should be considered by companies according to the quotation from Ruggie two paragraphs above belies the complexity of identifying and resolving human rights issues in the real world – as if one could get a handle on any real trouble cases as easily as "1, 2, 3". A formal United Nations document like Ruggie's Framework that seeks to specify business responsibility necessarily has to distance itself from the tangled mess of participation in and contribution to injustice in the real world.[92] Consider for example the case of two major Israeli banks that exclusively provided financial services to banks operating in the West Bank and Gaza Strip, thus allowing Palestinian civilians to conduct essential financial transactions in the Israeli currency (on which they were dependent).[93] Both banks eventually decided to terminate their services to Palestinian banks because of Israel's anti-terror law forbidding transactions that may enable acts of terrorism and the (illegal) declaration by Israel that Gaza was a "hostile territory" after the election of the Hamas-led government. At first the state regulator for the banks, the Bank of Israel, tried to prevent this. Various other parties brought conflicting petitions to the High Court of Justice both for and against the severance of ties with the Palestinian banks. The Israeli High Court of Justice eventually confirmed that Israel had a humanitarian obligation to facilitate currency transfers by Palestinians. This decision suggests that if the banks were to respect human rights, they should not cease services to the Palestinians. But it is hard to imagine how the banks' managements could have used Ruggie's three-step due diligence process to legitimately and elegantly come to this same conclusion on their own. The complexity of many human rights problem cases requires the participation of many voices in transparent, open and accountable public deliberation and decision-making processes. The Framework on its own raises the danger of ossification. It is the implementation through regulation and compliance infrastructures that could make all the difference.

Second, Ruggie's approach does not adequately recognise that effective internal "due diligence processes" will only occur where both states and stakeholders or activists continually critique businesses' human rights performance and regulate and hold them accountable for their actual due diligence processes.[94] Ruggie recognises this to some extent when he says:

---

91  See C. Estlund, *Regoverning the Workplace: From Self-Regulation to Co-Regulation* (Yale University Press, New Haven, 2010); F. Haines, *Corporate Regulation: Beyond 'Punish or Persuade'* (Clarendon Press, Oxford, 1997); D. Harvey, *The Condition of Postmodernity: An Enquiry into the Origins of Cultural Change* (Wiley-Blackwell, Oxford, 1990).

92  See L. May, *Sharing Responsibility* (University of Chicago Press, Chicago, 1992).

93  This example is taken from D. Weiss and R. Shamir, 'Corporate Accountability to Human Rights: The Case of the Gaza Strip', 24 *Harvard Human Rights Journal* (2011).

94  See Parker, *supra* note 8; C. Rodriguez-Garavito, 'Nike's Law: The Anti-Sweatshop Movement, Transnational Corporations, and the Struggle over International Labor Rights in

In order to gauge human rights risks, business enterprises should identify and assess any actual or potential adverse human rights impacts with which they may be involved either through their own activities or as a result of their business relationships. This process should: (a) Draw on internal and/or independent external human rights expertise; (b) Involve meaningful consultation with potentially affected groups and other relevant stakeholders, as appropriate to the size of the business enterprise and the nature and context of the operation.[95]

However, once again, this model of "stakeholder engagement" as part of corporate due diligence implies that it is a matter of corporate management discretion and authority to identify and assess human rights impact with the assistance of external expertise and stakeholder consultation, as deemed appropriate by corporate management themselves as a matter of reaching *from the inside out*. However, the whole reason why business responsibility for human rights is an issue at all is that affected communities and activists have wanted to identify and assess businesses and their model of doing business for themselves by penetrating the corporate shell *from the outside in*.[96] The thrust of "due diligence" is about controlling or "containing" relationships with stakeholders from the inside out. The language of "due diligence" does not prioritise attending to countervailing critique from the outside in. It might be suggested that the first pillar, the state duty to protect, and the third pillar, access by victims, should provide this "outside in" perspective. However, even if both pillars were strong,[97] they are meaningless if the very conceptualisation of the corporate obligation of due diligence is one that is all about maintaining management discretion to reframe and translate these outside critiques and attempts at enforcement into managerial priorities. Melish and Meidinger argue in their contribution to this volume that there should be a fourth pillar of "participation". We argue that due diligence should be reconceptualised to require outside participation, and therefore contain the seeds of its own critique.

People, organisations and sectors regulate themselves according to the social, market and other pressures they feel, and their own internal values or priorities. They might have the capacity to self-regulate in accord with democratically defined objectives and outcomes, but not necessarily the will to do so. There must continually be renewed radical critique of business activity in order for business to be held accountable and responsible, because business will constantly neutralise critique by institutionalising it. Merely adhering to particular procedures, such as a due diligence process, is unlikely to inject dynamism and life into business' responsibility for human rights. Rather, it is the political environment that can motivate company management to do the right thing. State regulation of human rights and adherence to due diligence processes will lack dynamism and "grip" if the company's external environment is not

---

the Americas', in B. de Sousa Santos and C. Rodriguez-Garavito (eds.), *Law and Globalization from Below* (Cambridge University Press, Cambridge, 2005) pp. 64–91.

95  Ruggie, *Final Report*, supra note 2, para. 18.
96  The need for both sides of this equation is the central premise of Parker, *supra* note 8.
97  Note that we argue above (in relation to the first pillar) and below (in relation to the third pillar) that both are seriously flawed.

continually making and remaking human rights into a strategic issue for corporate management. It is only "the heat of popular protests, consumer boycotts, legal suits, and a variety of public shaming campaigns"[98] that has made the field of human rights regulation of business emerge in the first place. And it is only the "counter-hegemonic politics and subaltern cosmopolitan legality" of those outside corporate management that can "erode the ideology and coercive institutions that sustain and naturalize the hegemony of dominant classes and groups" and "offer new understandings and practices capable of replacing the dominant ones."[99]

This makes the degree to which activists and "victims" have access to corporations to contest injustice and human rights abuses the crucial ingredient in influencing the nature of business' due diligence for human rights. This is recognised, albeit very weakly, by the Framework's third pillar – victim access to remedies. For Ruggie, this third pillar of the Framework is concerned with states providing formal judicial mechanisms[100] for rectifying individual injustices according to formal justice. It is also concerned with defining the formal legal justice standards that should be met by non-judicial grievance mechanisms, including self-regulatory corporate and industry-level dispute resolution mechanisms.[101] Indeed, internal corporate grievance mechanisms are encouraged[102] explicitly in order to avoid the current "primary means through which grievances against companies play out"; that is, "litigation and public campaigns". This is seen as desirable since "[f]or a company to take a bet on winning lawsuits or successfully countering hostile campaigns is at best optimistic risk management. Companies should identify and address grievances early, before they escalate." There is a great danger here of privatising, individualising and depoliticising conflicts that have much wider, public and distributive justice implications.[103] Once again, the focus has shifted from human rights obligations to allowing a purely discretionary, business-case based approach to corporate human rights responsibility. Corporate responsibility for human rights is bound to remain purely voluntary without sustained political pressure from outside.[104]

Parker has made a more radical proposal that companies above a certain size should be required by state regulation to have "access to justice plans" for those affected by their power.[105] Each Justice Plan would incorporate means of handling disputes relating to all the company's legal and social responsibilities, including human rights.

---

98  Shamir, *supra* note 9, p. 93; *see also* Rodriguez-Garavito, *supra* note 94.

99  De Sousa Santos, *supra* note 9, p. 18.

100 Ruggie, Final Report, *supra* note 2, p. 23.

101 Ibid., p. 24.

102 Ibid., pp. 24–25.

103 See L. Edelman, H. Erlanger and J. Lande, 'Internal Dispute Resolution: The Transformation of Civil Rights in the Workplace', 27:3 *Law and Society Review* (1993) pp. 497–534, at p. 528.

104 Rodriguez-Garavito, *supra* note 94.

105 C. Parker, *Just Lawyers: Regulation and Access to Justice* (Oxford University Press, Oxford, 1999) pp. 174–204.

This should include allowing stakeholders who represent broader interests (*e.g.* public interest groups) to contest corporate decision-making on both individual and distributive justice grounds. It is appropriate, just and right that corporate management be required to remedy wrongs done to particular stakeholders in breach of existing legal obligations (whether laid down in regimes of business regulation or in the general law of torts, equity or contract), and other obligations voluntarily accepted by the company (for example by signing on to an industry code of practice or promulgating their own codes of conduct) or generally accepted in international law (such as human rights). However, as is well known, the realities and technicalities of the corporate form and its governance, and of inequality of access to the formal court system, often make it hard to hold companies accountable for their wrongs. The right to access justice – to be able to make claims against individuals and institutions in order to advance shared ideals of social and political life and to rectify relations that have gone wrong – is an essential part of citizenship in contemporary democracies.

In order to make corporate due diligence a true way of discharging the RtR, it should be open, transparent and accountable to the broader community, including "victims" and activists in the following ways:[106]

- *Due diligence must include mechanisms for participation* by stakeholders in designing and implementing due diligence processes.[107] This should include consultation on the criteria to be used for evaluating and reporting information about the processes and performance of due diligence. Wherever possible, stakeholders should also participate in the actual decision-making about due diligence. Vague commitments to stakeholder "consultation" are not sufficient. It is easy to "consult" without granting stakeholders their legitimate entitlements to justice. It is when people really have a grievance about a company decision or action that true "stakeholder relations" become obvious.
- *Due diligence must include systematic policies and procedures for allowing stakeholders to contest decisions that affect them* on the basis of either state-based legal rights, or international law, or other standards the self-regulator has voluntarily adopted. These might include complaints handling and dispute resolution schemes, but they should go beyond these to include mechanisms in which companies re-think business operations and management styles. One of the most significant things companies could do to make themselves good "stakeholder corporations" is to ensure that they give real rights, including rights to take grievances to external courts and other agencies, to stakeholders (and stakeholder groups) with legitimate complaints about the company.
- *The corporation must publicly disclose information* that government and stakeholders can use to engage with due diligence processes and hold it accountable. There must be public reporting of information about due diligence processes and performance. This can assist states and activists to re-politicise grievances that might otherwise be treated as private and individual by corporate management,

---

106   Based on Parker, *supra* note 8, pp. 213–233.
107   This is consistent with the chapter by Melish and Meidinger in this volume.

and to make claims to rectify structures and patterns of injustice that arise from corporate practices including intra-corporate management of justice.
- As argued already above, the management of corporations *need to be aware that there is continually the possibility and indeed actuality of greater government coercion and/or public criticism* if they do the wrong thing. Due diligence processes motivated by anything else are a waste of time.

## 5.  Conclusion

We have argued that the main thrust of Ruggie's Framework is diplomatic – to provide an authoritative focal point for business and human rights within the UN and in the language of international law. But at the same time there is the danger that the diplomatic project of the Framework will mean that it does not go far enough in radically challenging the management discretion of the business case and a risk management approach to adverse human rights impacts. In particular, we have argued that the Framework underestimates both the role of the state in regulating human rights, and the challenges it faces in doing so in a regulatory space in which many actors seek to regulate business, and businesses themselves seek to influence and shape regulation. We have also argued that the Framework underestimates how radical and serious a commitment to due diligence for human rights must be in transforming corporate management. Most importantly, it underestimates the capacity of business to neutralise, deradicalise, individualise and formalise critique, and therefore the constant need to nurture voices that will claim justice on an individual and distributive level against corporate human rights abuses.

# 12    Protect, Respect, Remedy *and Participate*: 'New Governance' Lessons for the Ruggie Framework

Tara J. Melish* and Errol Meidinger**

## 1.    Introduction

John Gerard Ruggie has contributed enormously to the field of international law and public policy throughout his eminent career, both as public law scholar and international public servant. Nowhere is this more evident than in his recent work as Special Representative of the Secretary-General (SRSG) on the issue of human rights and transnational corporations, a United Nations mandate he held from 2005 to 2011.[1] Under that mandate Professor Ruggie and his accomplished team have succeeded in crafting a principles-based conceptual and policy framework for addressing business-related human rights harm that has not only raised the international prominence of human rights responsibilities for business entities, but has done so in terms that have been widely endorsed by a broad range of key stakeholders – especially states and business associations,[2] but also many civil society organisations.[3] Following on the heels of the

---

\*    Associate Professor and Director of the Buffalo Human Rights Center, University at Buffalo School of Law, The State University of New York.

\*\*    Professor and Director of the Baldy Center for Law and Social Policy, University at Buffalo School of Law, The State University of New York.

1    UN Doc. E/CN.4/2005/L.87, para. 1 (15 April 2005) (establishing mandate).

2    In June 2008, the UN Human Rights Council unanimously endorsed the PRR policy framework. See UN Doc. A/HRC/8/5. As Ruggie has underscored, that endorsement marked the first time the Council or its predecessor had taken an express policy position on business and human rights. The framework has likewise been endorsed by the world's largest business associations, the International Council on Mining and Metals, the Business Leaders Initiative on Human Rights, and scores of socially responsible investment funds. See J. G. Ruggie, 'Protect, Respect and Remedy: A United Nations Policy Framework for Business and Human Rights', 103 *American Society of International Law Proceedings* (2009) pp. 282, 287.

3    The value of the framework has been recognised by Amnesty International and large numbers of other civil society organisations (CSOs) in individual and joint submissions to the Human Rights Council. See UN Doc. A/HRC/8/NGO/5; Ruggie, *supra* note 2, p. 287.

more coolly-received Draft Norms,[4] such broad endorsement constitutes a significant political and diplomatic achievement for the Special Representative, essential for moving forward the international agenda on business and human rights.

Despite this important achievement, we nonetheless believe that there are serious shortcomings in the SRSG's 'Protect, Respect, Remedy' (PRR) framework. In this chapter, we interrogate the theoretical underpinnings of the PRR framework and query whether a conceptually and operationally more effective framework might have been produced had Ruggie and his team approached the task from a new governance or new accountability perspective.[5] While it is unclear whether Professor Ruggie would consider himself a new governance scholar, it is clear that much of his work closely parallels the emergence of the new governance perspective. Thus, over the same period that he was developing the precepts of social constructivism, embedded liberalism, and the global public domain, 'new governance' was taking form as a framework for understanding modern policy making. As described below, it likewise seeks to articulate a new nonreductionist understanding of institutional change and to document a richer set of actors and processes in global governance.

We recognise that attention to these actors and processes has been an important part of the SRSG's work during the second phase of his mandate.[6] Drawing on

---

Nevertheless, a large number of other CSOs, especially from the global south, have been more critical, urging the Human Rights Council to reject the Draft Guiding Principles. See e.g. Statement to the Delegations on the Human Rights Council 2011, 17th Session, Agenda Item 3 (30 May 2011), <www.fian.org/news/press-releases/CSOs-respond-to-ruggies-guiding-principles-regarding-human-rights-and-transnational-corporations/pdf>.

4   Norms on the Responsibilities of Transnational Corporations and Other Business Enterprises with Regard to Human Rights, UN Doc. E/CN.4/Sub.2/2003/12/Rev.2 (26 August 2003). While the UN Human Rights Commission's decision to table the Draft Norms can be understood from a variety of perspectives, much of the criticism focused on claims that the Norms inappropriately sought to extend to corporations many of the same human rights responsibilities that applied to states did so without adequately attending to the differences between the two types of actors or between 'voluntary' and 'non-voluntary' duties, and engaged in conceptual ambiguities and certain doctrinal excesses that extended international law beyond its present scope. See e.g. UN Doc. E/CN.4/2006/97 ("[I]n the SRSG's view the divisive debate over the norms obscures rather than illuminates promising areas of consensus and cooperation among business, civil society, governments, and international institutions with respect to human rights"); J. G. Ruggie, 'Business and Human Rights: The Evolving International Agenda', 101 American Journal of International Law (2007) pp. 819–840.

5   The term 'new accountability' has been used to describe the parallel trend in the human rights context to the uptake of 'new governance' in the regulatory field. See T. Melish, 'Maximum Feasible Participation of the Poor: New Governance, New Accountability and a 21st Century War on the Sources of Poverty', 13 Yale Human Rights & Development Law Journal (2010) pp. 1–133. It is best understood as a type of new governance, and hence is not differentiated from new governance here.

6   See UN Doc. A/HRC/RES/8/7 (extending Ruggie's mandate by three years and tasking him with 'operationalising' the framework by providing 'practical recommendations' and 'concrete guidance' to states, businesses, and other social actors on its implementation).

new governance scholarship and Ruggie's own theoretical work in the area of social constructivism and the global public domain, we nonetheless suggest that the SRSG's decision to include reference to the duties and responsibilities of only states and businesses in the PRR framework was ultimately a mistake. Explicit inclusion of the participatory roles and responsibilities of civil society organisations and multistakeholder initiatives – recognised as tantamount in importance and complementary to those of states and businesses at all levels of global governance – would have made a stronger conceptual policy framework and, critically, one with more and better opportunities for operationalisation on the ground. Recognition of this important participatory role is particularly critical, we contend, given the nature of the governance gaps, and the misaligned incentive structures that underlie them, that Ruggie himself identifies as the 'root cause' of the business and human rights predicament we face today.[7]

New governance scholarship provides important insights into this problem, from both normative and instrumental perspectives. In the following four sections we thus offer a constructive critique of the Ruggie proposal from a new governance perspective. After situating Ruggie's PRR policy framework within the sociological institutionalist tradition of understanding systemic transformation, we describe the insights that a new governance approach adds to the picture, particularly for filling the governance gaps created by globalisation in the business and human rights context. We then suggest the utility of updating the schema by adding a fourth 'participation' pillar as the basis for moving forward and offer elements to support this shift from a dyadic-unidirectional to triadic-multidirectional structure of shared responsibility in the global public domain.

## 2. The Ruggie PRR Policy Framework: A Sociological Institutionalist Approach to System Transformation

In his work as SRSG, Professor Ruggie has identified his mandate's primary objective as "reduc[ing] or compensat[ing] for the governance gaps created by globalization" in the area of business and human rights.[8] Such gaps have grown particularly wide over the last several decades as business entities have amassed increasingly expansive rights within the global economic structure. Such rights, together with new technologies and the increasing ease of transborder migration, have allowed business interests to circumvent, override, capture or dis-incentivise state regulatory authority with increasing facility. Correspondingly, Ruggie defines 'governance gaps' in terms of the growing gulf "between the scope and impact of economic forces and actors, and the capacity of societies to manage their adverse consequences".[9] Recalling his earlier work on embedded liberalism,[10] he underscores that "markets work optimally only if they are embedded within rules, customs and institutions", and that, as history teaches us,

---

7   UN Doc. A/HRC/8/5, p. 3; Ruggie, *supra* note 2, p. 287.
8   UN Doc. A/HRC/8/5, p. 3.
9   Ibid.
10  See e.g. J. G. Ruggie, 'International regimes, transactions, and change: Embedded liberalism in the postwar economic order', 26 *International Organization* (1982) pp. 379–415.

"markets pose the greatest risks – to society and business itself – when their scope and power far exceed the reach of the institutional underpinnings that allow them to function smoothly and ensure their political sustainability".[11] "How to narrow and ultimately bridge the[se governance] gaps in relation to human rights", he concludes, "is our fundamental challenge".[12]

The PRR framework is the policy prescription Ruggie sets forth for meeting this challenge. It seeks to establish a new common conceptual and policy framework for understanding the human rights duties and responsibilities of state and business actors. By embedding these shared understandings within corporate culture and state practice, he hopes to establish a solid foundation (congruent with the 'embedded liberalism' he understands to have characterised state-market relationships in the post-war economic order) for solving the collective action problems that have allowed abusive corporate activities to proliferate. Ruggie ascribes these problems in large part to the deontic 'confusion' he believes currently dominates the field, one in which states and businesses remain uncertain about the precise nature and scope of the duties they hold. Such confusion, Ruggie suggests, has led to endless strategic gaming. It has, correspondingly, hindered development of the underlying rules, customs and institutions within business culture and practice necessary to constrain corporate excesses. Such embedded normative and prescriptive institutional understandings are, in Ruggie's view, essential for achieving each of the dual challenges presented by the business and human rights conundrum: one, ensuring the smooth functioning of competitive markets and business operations and, two, protecting society from their negative externalities.[13] Achieving the appropriate accommodation between these two important policy goals defines Ruggie's business-friendly normative project.

Significantly, in its construction, the PRR framework closely tracks Ruggie's intellectual commitments in the field of international relations (IR), a point we believe is important to highlight for understanding both its strengths and weaknesses as a global project. As a scholar, Professor Ruggie has long been a prominent critic of neo-utilitarian or rational choice models of IR, charging that, in their individualistic methodologies and focus on narrow material or economic interests, they fail to take account of the broader cultural, institutional and ideational forms and processes that shape social actors' outlooks and behaviour.[14] Being an intellectual progenitor of social constructivism, he has thus endorsed a theoretically-informed approach to the study of international relations that focuses on how the identities and interests of individual actors, such as corporate entities or state representatives, are in fact socially constructed in international life.[15] Such construction, he theorises, occurs through

---

11   UN Doc. A/HRC/8/5, p. 3.
12   *Ibid.* Such gaps "provide the permissive environment for wrongful acts by companies of all kinds without adequate sanctioning or reparation" (*ibid.*).
13   *Cf.* Ruggie, *supra* note 10.
14   J.G. Ruggie, 'What Makes the World Hang Together? Neo-utilitarianism and the Social Constructivist Challenge', 52:4 *International Organization* (1998) pp. 855–885.
15   *Ibid.*, p. 856 ("Constructivism is about human consciousness and its role in international life").

the proliferation of global norms or shared cultural understandings. These shared or 'intersubjective' beliefs ultimately become embedded in human consciousness where they construct the interests and identities of purposive actors. Once embedded, such normative understandings become 'constitutive rules' or new 'social facts' that constitute and prestructure the domains of action within which individuals operate and understand their world. Within these domains, 'socially knowledgeable and discursively competent actors' strategically create and recreate international structure, engaging in an active process of interpretation and construction of reality'.[16] It is toward the creation of such new constitutive rules in state and business culture that Ruggie's project is authoritatively directed.

According to Ruggie, such constitutive rules serve two distinct functions at the level of the international polity. At an interpretive level, they may take the form of "international regimes that limit strictly interest-based self-interpretation of appropriate behavior by their members".[17] At a deontic level, they "may create rights and responsibilities in a manner that is not simply determined by the material interests of the dominant power(s)".[18] Through the global construction and embedding of constitutive rules in corporate culture, a rule-based 'logic of appropriateness' may thus come to supplant a rational interest-based 'logic of consequences' as the direct driver of policy action, a development Ruggie views as key to normative success.

Importantly, following from this theoretical understanding of how social change is effectuated in the world, Ruggie's intellectual attention is focused less on the concrete mechanisms through which the material interests of powerful actors can be leveraged by less powerful actors to promote socially accountable behaviour, than on the more nebulous international socialisation processes through which powerful actors, such as states and businesses, are acculturated into new understandings of socially appropriate behaviour. His focus is "the general process by which actors adopt the beliefs and behavioral patterns of the surrounding culture".[19] This distinction between 'social accountability' dynamics and 'social acculturation' processes is critical, we believe, for understanding the nature of the Ruggie project. In particular, it explains why that project is focused so narrowly on the normative clarification of the duties and responsibilities of states and businesses in terms they will find acceptable and consistent with their interests, rather than on the critical role of other non-state actors in holding states and businesses concretely to account for their conduct.

Consistent with the PRR framework, corporate actors should thus have human rights compliance systems in place with five standard components: a formally articulated human rights policy; a commitment to undertaking 'impact assessments' as a risk management tool; the integration of the company's human rights policy into operational practice guides; a way to track performance; and internal redress mechanisms

---

16   Ibid., p. 879.
17   Ibid.
18   Ibid.
19   R. Goodman and D. Jinks, 'How to Influence States: Socialization and International Human Rights Law', 54 Duke Law Journal (2004) pp. 621-703, 626 (defining 'sociological acculturation').

to ensure appropriate remedies where unjustified harm occurs.[20] Likewise, states must have systems in place to address three component areas: more effective policy alignment, both vertically and horizontally; market incentives aimed at promoting a corporate human rights culture; and available systems of human rights redress.[21]

Such compliance systems track closely what states and corporations already do or understand their obligations to be. Provided such compliance systems are in place, the PRR framework suggests that states and corporate entities satisfy their international duties and responsibilities in the business and human rights context. The challenge from the framework's perspective is to ensure that such systems are in fact replicated, standardised and, ultimately, internalised in business and government policies around the globe, a process in which states and businesses appear to be the primary actors. Indeed, although the system script does integrate certain incentive-based elements, the driving impulse behind the framework is one in which states and corporate actors voluntarily conform to the behavioural expectations of the wider culture as a result of the varying degrees of cognitive and social pressures that accompany identification with their global reference group.[22]

To facilitate this process of voluntary uptake and group social conformity, Ruggie engages in several important framing tactics. Perhaps most importantly, he avoids identifying corporate duties as 'legally' mandated or compulsory, preferring to identify them simply as 'responsibilities' or 'social duties' emanating from the 'social license' businesses need to operate.[23] The primary frame of compliance for business, then, is not legal regulation or judicial oversight, but rather shareholder, consumer and societal preferences. Distinguishing corporate 'social responsibilities' from both 'moral' and 'legal' duties, Ruggie reserves the latter exclusively for states, albeit under a reduced set of prescriptions that emphasise market-based promotional measures and the provision of post-hoc, individual-oriented grievance procedures. At the same time, Ruggie organises the framework principally around highly definitionally-malleable policy concepts such as 'due diligence' and 'risk management systems' that are already widely used and accepted in corporate culture and/or state-oriented human rights practice. Both framing tactics are designed to facilitate a familiarity and comfort with the framework that will promote voluntary buy-in and elite engagement with the new international regime, while allowing a large degree of creative ambiguity about what such engagement must in fact entail. The Guiding Principles, though providing some degree of policy direction, allow a similar measure of flexibility and business-determined discretion.[24]

---

20   UN Doc. A/HRC/8/5 (2008).
21   Ibid.
22   Cf. R. Goodman and D. Jinks, 'Incomplete Internalization and Compliance with Human Rights Law', 19 *European Journal of International Law* (2008) pp. 725–748, 726 (describing driving forces behind acculturative mechanisms of international law).
23   UN Doc. A/HRC/8/5; UN Doc. E/CN.4/2006/97.
24   UN Doc. A/HRC/17/31.

While Ruggie and other constructivists affirm that social constructivism is not itself a theory of international relations,[25] Ruggie's approach nests comfortably within institutional theory. Specifically, it represents an expression of 'sociological institutionalism'[26] or 'idealist institutionalism'.[27] These approaches share the central contention of institutional theory that "[w]orldwide models define and legitimate agendas for local action, shaping the structures and policies of nation-states and other national and local actors in virtually all of the domains of rationalized social life".[28] Unlike other 'new institutionalisms' associated with political science and economics, which Ruggie criticises as 'neo-utilitarian', they nonetheless do not draw expressly on rational choice theory and material interest as the driver of policy action. Rather, emphasising norms and the political process dynamics that lead to norm emergence, sociological institutionalists attribute the causal behaviour of social actors to their context or to higher-order factors, such as scripts or schemas drawn from shared cultural systems. Standard research designs in the field thus seek to document the effect of the world polity and global norms on national policy and structure, showing how 'world culture' reconfigures state and other policies in a range of policy arenas.[29]

Viewed within this broader theoretical frame Ruggie's PRR project makes particular sense. It is designed to create, in Ruggie's words, "an authoritative focal point" – a common global script for worldwide diffusion and adoption – on what human rights compliance systems look like within both corporate and state entities. Once approved, that global script would henceforth be made available for global diffusion and, through internationally organised processes of persuasion and socialisation, individual actor mimicry, uptake and internalisation. Thus, Ruggie aims to stimulate an international socialisation process through which the individual components of his global script are embedded as a new set of constitutive rules that define and prestructure the scope

---

25 Ruggie, *supra* note 14; M. Finnemore and K. Sikkink, 'Taking Stock: The Constructivist Research Program in International Relations and Comparative Politics', 4 *Annual Review of Political Science* (2001) pp. 391–416.

26 See M. Schneiberg and E. Clemens, 'The Typical Tools for the Job: Research Strategies in Institutional Analysis', 24:3 *Sociological Theory* (2006) pp. 195–227 (defining 'sociological institutionalism').

27 L. Fransen, 'Competition and Convergence in Private Governance: A Political-Institutional Analysis of Transnational Labour Standards Regulation', in *Governance: An International Journal of Policy, Administration and Institutions* (forthcoming 2011) pp. 1–40 (defining idealist institutionalism).

28 J. W. Meyer et al., 'World Society and the Nation-State', 103 *American Journal of Sociology* (1997) p. 145.

29 Schneiberg and Clemens, *supra* note 26; M. Finnemore, 'Norms, Culture and World Politics: Insights from Sociology's Institutionalism', 50 *International Organization* (1996) pp. 325–347; Meyer et al., *ibid.*, pp. 144–181; J. W. Meyer and M. T. Hannan (eds.), *National Development and the World-System: Educational, Economic and Political Change, 1950–1970* (Univ. of Chicago Press, Chicago, 1979). Countertrends nonetheless appear within 'critical constructivism'. See M. Barnett and K. Sikkink, 'From International Relations to Global Society', *The Oxford Handbook of International Relations* (2008) pp. 62–83 (citing examples).

of socially-acceptable corporate conduct. When this occurs, the 'life-cycle' of the underlying norms will have been completed, having passed through the iterative stages of persuasion, socialisation and ultimately internalisation.[30] The resulting taken-for-granted quality of the underlying norms would henceforth address the misaligned incentive structure and collective action problems that Ruggie currently attributes to the absence of consensus regarding appropriate policy forms and outcomes. Like the social consensus around business conduct that Ruggie has identified in his work on 'embedded liberalism' in the post-war economic era, such a consensus would resolve the modern governance gaps that define today's business and human rights context.

In this regard, consistent with social constructivist approaches more generally, the PRR framework does not attempt to make claims about the content of the relevant social structures or the nature of the agents at work in these processes.[31] It merely assumes or understands that these complex processes of persuasion and socialisation take place somewhere and somehow. The framework can thus best be seen as a policy expression, not of any particular set of mechanisms for causing social change, but rather of a particular social theory about the nature and causal direction of social change: that it is shaped primarily by ideational factors rather than material ones, and that the most important of these are 'intersubjective' beliefs widely shared across world culture.[32]

This theoretical approach is undoubtedly a necessary complement to neorealist and neoliberal approaches to international relations that have traditionally focused too heavily on materialist perspectives and individualist methodologies. Social constructivism has correspondingly played an important role in explaining worldwide institutional change that cannot be accounted for exclusively or even primarily by reference to rational material self-interest of distinct social actors or to the effects of coercion or persuasion-based models alone.[33] This is particularly true with respect to human rights norms.[34] Nevertheless, constructivist or sociological institutionalist approaches suffer from serious shortcomings when ideational factors become the exclusive or near exclusive focus of policy analysis or regime design, letting the important insights of economic institutionalism and the 'logic of consequences' recede to the margins. By failing to take more explicit account of the actual mechanics of and actors involved in

---

30   M. Finnemore and K. Sikkink, 'International Norm Dynamics and Political Change', 52 *International Organization* (1998).
31   *Ibid.* (discussing social constructivist approaches).
32   Ruggie, *supra* note 14; Finnemore and Sikkink, *supra* note 30.
33   Goodman and Jinks, *supra* note 22, pp. 725–727 (defending acculturation-based models, both descriptively and empirically, on the ground that neither coercion- nor persuasion-based accounts of social influence explain the twin observed patterns of structural isomorphism and decoupling that exist in the world with respect to states' embrace of international law norms).
34   T. Risse *et al.* (eds.), *The Power of Human Rights: International Norms and Domestic Change* (Cambridge University Press, Cambridge, 1999); O. Hathaway, 'Do Human Rights Treaties Make a Difference?', 111 *Yale Law Journal* (2002) pp. 1935–2042.

effectuating social change, we believe the PRR project has drifted dangerously in this direction.

In this regard, there are several discomfiting aspects of the Ruggie PRR framework and approach, two of which we highlight. Both spring from the framework's basis in acculturation-based models of social change and corresponding overemphasis on promoting a 'logic of appropriateness' from above, while paying insufficient attention to the operational structures and mechanics necessary to create a corresponding 'logic of consequences' from below. While certain scholars defend this focus on the ground that acculturative processes may indirectly promote opportunities for the emergence of domestic-level social movements,[35] we believe that any regime design that fails to take such essential social actors into specific operational account is a deficient and incomplete one.

The first concerning aspect of the Ruggie PRR framework lies in its central focus on the diffusion of a singular global human rights script as the solution to the lack of consensus around appropriate policy forms in the corporate accountability context. There are two principle risks associated with this search for a definitive authoritative centre, especially with its accompanying trend toward orthodoxy and institutional isomorphism. Most directly, an overemphasis on institutional isomorphism as the basis of human rights compliance tends inevitably to lead to strategically calculated and formalistic uptake practices, extensively described in the literature on 'decoupling'[36] and 'creative compliance'.[37] This phenomenon, popularly known as 'paper compliance' or 'greenwashing', has been widely observed in the corporate accountability context and is the principle criticism lodged against acculturation-based models of social influence. In his recent study of private governance arrangements in the garment industry, for example, Luc Fransen has documented how companies have used formal policy uptake to avoid exposure by activists, while failing to engage in the more difficult and expensive process of actual implementation.[38] He has also demonstrated that while corporate-led private governance initiatives have achieved a high level of policy convergence, they have generally done so by defining requirements in ways that require very little actual change in corporate operations. These decoupling processes are also common in other fields,[39] although they can be countered by effective competitor programmes and social monitoring.[40]

---

35   Goodman and Jinks, *supra* note 22, pp. 733–743.

36   J. W. Meyer et al., 'World Society and the Nation-State', 103 *American Journal of Sociology* (1997) p. 144; Goodman and Jinks, *supra* note 19, pp. 651–655.

37   C. Whelan and D. McBarnet, *Creative Accounting and the Cross-Eyed Javelin Thrower* (John Wiley and Sons, New York, 1999).

38   Fransen, *supra* note 27.

39   See sources in *supra* note 36 (citing examples).

40   See e.g. W. Laufer, 'Social Accountability and Corporate Greenwashing', 43:3 *Journal of Business Ethics* (2003) pp. 253–261; A. Lubitow and M. Davis, 'Pastel Injustice: The Corporate Use of Pinkwashing for Profit', 4:2 *Environmental Justice* (2011) pp. 139–144; C. Marquis and M. Toffel, 'The Globalization of Corporate Environmental Disclosure: Ac-

At a different level, an overemphasis on an authoritative centre allows for certain 'strategies of resistance' from businesses wishing to avoid real change. An example of this phenomenon is documented in the important fieldwork-based contribution in this volume by Haines, MacDonald and Balaton-Chrimes, who detail the justificatory strategies of businesses in the Indian tea sector for failing to comply in practice with human rights safeguards that they nonetheless steadfastly affirm their adherence to and compliance with as universal norms.[41] In the absence of institutionally-recognised mechanisms for affected communities and other civil society monitors to contest the empirical basis of such justificatory narratives and to assert their own understandings of how community rights are affected, it is difficult to expect the PRR framework, as a universalising global script, to lead to anything but suboptimal localised implementation. It is for this reason that we disagree with Sullivan and Hachez's contribution in this volume, in which they reproach the Ruggie project not for its inattention to civil society participation processes, but rather because it does not create a more detailed standardised check-list for corporations to voluntarily adhere to.[42] Again, in the absence of a role for participatory verification, monitoring, assessment and reconstruction by affected stakeholders themselves, reliance on such standardised checklists for uniform compliance is unlikely to facilitate much more than paper compliance and other shallow or superficial institutional reform efforts.

In this latter respect, an overemphasis on individual mimicry of standardised global forms tends likewise to lead to decontextualised systems that are unresponsive to localised problems or particular community needs. This is particularly problematic in the human rights context, where human rights requirements must be defined not by standardised texts, but according to the varied conditions and evolving perspectives of affected communities.[43] Although Ruggie cautions that the framework is not intended to serve as a "tool kit, simply to be taken off the shelf and plugged in",[44] there is no serious attempt to specify how due diligence and other requirements should be structured to be able to flexibly and responsively take account of varying contexts and the multiple voices that may be affected by corporate conduct in discrete circumstances.[45] The remedy pillar, though nominally established to achieve this end, is inadequate for ad-

---

countability or Greenwashing?', *Harvard Business School Working Paper* No. 11-115 (2011), <papers.ssrn.com/sol3/papers.cfm?abstract_id=1836472>.

41  *See* the chapter by Haines, MacDonald and Balaton-Chrimes in this volume.
42  *See* the chapter by Sullivan and Hachez in this volume.
43  *See generally* B. Rajagopal, *International Law from Below: Development, Social Movements and Third World Resistance* (Cambridge University Press, Cambridge, 2003); M. Mutua, 'Standard Setting in Human Rights: Critique and Prognosis', 29 *Human Rights Quarterly* (2007) pp. 547–630 (critiquing lack of third world perspectives in mainstream human rights standard-setting processes).
44  UN Doc. A/HRC/17/31 (2011), para. 15.
45  Although Ruggie's 2011 Guiding Principles do recognise the importance of transparency and participation in due diligence reporting, these aspects remain largely undeveloped and are not structured in a way so that they can be invoked as rights. *Ibid.*

dressing the varied and multiple means through which civil society actors participate in the construction, contestation and reconstruction of both local and global norms.

A second troubling aspect of the PRR framework, closely related to the first, is its embrace of an understanding of systemic transformation that is predominantly unidirectional in causation. That is, individual actors in the world polity adopt new rules, customs and institutions *in response to* a global framework. While political process dynamics are key to sociological institutional theory,[46] the causal imagery tends to move in one primary direction: from 'higher' international frameworks to 'lower' individual actors. This is true even as the precise mechanisms through which that unidirectional causality occurs are rarely described in the theory-based literature.[47] This leads to several important blind-spots, each apparent in the PRR framework. First, it overlooks the ways that global norms are constituted and reconstituted from below – a process particularly characteristic of human rights claims, which inevitably arise as historically- and contextually contingent challenges to power.[48] Similarly, it fails to identify feedback effects from local agents onto global structures. In these ways, sociological institutional approaches can, in Finnemore and Sikkink's evocative words, "begin to treat international norms as a global 'oobleck' that covers the planet and homogenizes us all".[49] Such approaches tend, correspondingly, to undervalue the critical role of local actors in both creating relevant human rights meaning in accordance with local values, mores and conditions and, equally important, in holding actors accountable to such meanings in locally effective and meaningful ways. They tend likewise to be insufficiently attentive to the importance of dynamic learning processes, competitive experimentalism, and how 'best' and 'worst' practices at the individual actor level must be tracked, systematised and disseminated for global learning and responsive adaptation in distinct local contexts. All of these processes are necessarily multidirectional, involving multiple stakeholders in constantly evolving communication, contestation and informational exchange.

This is not to say that sociological institutional or acculturation-based approaches to social influence are irrelevant to the design of effective international human rights regimes. To the contrary, we believe that they are critical, especially in understanding

---

46   Ruggie, *supra* note 14.
47   Exceptions appear in the works of Keck, Sikkink, Finnemore, Roppe and Risse, who have analysed the techniques used by activist groups, including strategic use of information, symbolic politics, leverage and accountability politics, issue framing and shaming. See e.g. M.E. Keck and K. Sikkink, *Activists Beyond Borders: Advocacy Networks in International Politics* (Cornell University Press, Ithaca, 1998); T. Risse *et al.* (eds.), *The Power of Human Rights: International Norms and Domestic Change* (Cambridge University Press, Cambridge, 1999). Such scholars nevertheless tend to recognise the limitations of social constructivist theories, especially in their more recent work, and the strengths of alternative theories in explaining evolving institutional behavior. See e.g. Barnett and Sikkink, *supra* note 29, p. 63.
48   See e.g. E. Kamenka, 'Human Rights, Peoples' Rights', in James Crawford (ed.), *The Rights of Peoples* (Clarendon, Oxford, 1988); Rajagopal, *supra* note 43.
49   Finnemore and Sikkink, *supra* note 25, p. 397 (citing Dr. Seuss's 1970 *Bartholomew and the Oobleck*).

the multiple causal pathways by which diverse actors come to respect international human rights norms. However, as even sociological institutionalism's most ardent defenders acknowledge, acculturative forces do not inevitably increase respect for human rights norms; indeed, they may produce highly negative results.[50] Designing a human rights regime exclusively or even primarily around such forces can thus be short-sighted and counterproductive. Rather, optimal human rights regime design requires that express attention be given to the multiple and evolving sets of actors and institutions that can take up global human rights scripts to press for compliance within domestic political and legal systems, using a variety of persuasion- and coercion-based incentive systems. It requires attention not only to interest discovery among elite players, but also to interest conflict and how less powerful actors seek to narrow power asymmetries through organised mechanisms of social leverage.

Clearly missing from the PRR framework, then, is concerted attention to *how* processes of socialisation and institutional change in fact occur. Through what mechanisms or channels? Which actors are most important in such processes and why? While other social constructivist theorists, such as Sikkink, Finnemore, Risse and Keck, have spent significantly more time unpacking these processes of social change, especially with regard to the critical role played by civil society in global governance,[51] attention to ensuring the on-the-ground operation of such processes is notably absent from Ruggie's PRR framework. This is true even as Ruggie in his scholarly work has himself broadly observed the rising role of new actors in reconstituting the 'global public domain'.[52]

In this respect, we remain unconvinced by framework supporters who argue that this participatory governance concern is effectively addressed by the 'remedy' pillar. Not only was that pillar hard-fought by the human rights community, which lobbied throughout the SRSG's mandate for more attention to mechanisms of civil society-directed accountability processes,[53] the remedy pillar is one that focuses on post-hoc, individual-oriented grievance procedures within state and corporate institutions. It is also one directed primarily at breaches of 'legal' rules, substantially limiting its direct application to the 'social duties' of businesses. Although critically important, such judicial and non-judicial 'remedial' mechanisms are only one set of tools in a much

---

50 R. Goodman and D. Jinks, 'Incomplete Internalization and Compliance with Human Rights Law: A Rejoinder to Roda Muchkat', 20 *European Journal of International Law* (2009) pp. 443–44 ("Acculturation often produces negative results such as dangerous national security practices, dysfunctional environmental laws, exorbitant administrative bureaucracies, and rights-based policies that are poorly suited to local needs"). As such, Goodman and Jinks disavow that "acculturation is the ideal or preferable social mechanism around which to design international human rights regimes", even as it should be "part of the larger conversation". Goodman and Jinks, *supra* note 22, note 10.

51 See *supra* note 47.

52 J. G. Ruggie, 'Reconstituting the Global Public Domain: Issues, Actors and Practices', 10 *European Journal of International Relations* (December 2004) pp. 499–531.

53 Interview with Irene Khan, Secretary-General of Amnesty International from 2001–2009 (May 2011).

broader toolbox of strategies and tactics increasingly used by non-governmental organisations (NGOs) and other civil society groups for holding state and corporate actors to account for human rights harm.[54] Such strategies are widely recognised as key to promoting actual on-the-ground change in corporate conduct, especially in line with new governance approaches. The failure to recognise these additional strategies and actors directly within the PRR framework, we contend, is a serious shortcoming in its construction.

The foregoing operational limitations are, we suggest, not merely a 'pragmatic' or 'diplomatic' concession to promote state and business compliance (as many commentators suggest), but also a direct reflection of the framework's theoretical underpinnings. As discussed, those underpinnings are grounded in the understanding that, through complex processes of elite socialisation around group norms, rational interest-based calculations of individual actors may come to take a backseat to embedded understandings of appropriate social conduct. This assumption is nonetheless made without addressing precisely *how* that process is to be effectuated, especially given the SRSG's explicit recognition of the governance gaps that have heretofore made state regulation and voluntary corporate social responsibility initiatives by themselves ineffective at promoting change. As a result, the Ruggie PRR framework pays insufficient attention to the need for new kinds of actors and accountability systems capable of leveraging the material interests of corporate actors and aligning their material and extra-material interests. This may be its greatest weakness. While we agree with Ruggie that norms and reputation matter for interests, and often matter greatly, there is a need in the PRR framework for greater attention to creating mechanisms that can ensure that a 'logic of consequences' (economic institutionalism) accompanies the 'logic of appropriateness' (sociological institutionalism) approach of Ruggie.[55]

New governance scholarship, which relies on both sociological and economic models of institutionalism, provides important insights into each of these key limitations in the Ruggie PRR framework.

### 3. A New Governance Perspective on Institutional Transformation: Recognising and Legitimating the Roles and Responsibilities of New Actors and Processes

'New governance' scholarship reflects a growing recognition that the assumptions of an authoritative centre and unidirectional causation do not reflect some of the most important lessons of regulatory governance gleaned in the past several decades. New governance approaches have, in this sense, emerged as a corrective to prior models of regulatory governance that assumed that legalised compliance with uniform rules generated and enforced from the centre was the most effective way of regulating public

---

54 Melish, *supra* note 5, pp. 55–59, 68–110.
55 Accord Goodman and Jinks, *supra* note 19, p. 444 (citing ambition of scholarly project as contributing to the development of an integrated theory of human rights regime design – one that, by definition, accounts for all mechanisms of social influence, including acculturation, persuasion, coercion and managerialism).

and private conduct. Emanating from the conviction that centralised regulatory control too often stifles innovation, competition, creativity, economic efficiency and local responsiveness, new governance approaches reject that view. They draw on a more varied set of actors and more varied set of techniques that emphasise regulatory fit, adaptability, efficiency, competition, stakeholder negotiation and continuously revised performance measures. They correspondingly tend to deemphasise reliance on formal rules, investing a more decentralised, often increasingly non-governmental set of agents with substantial discretion in determining the means through which goal-specific performance indicators will be met.

At the same time, new governance models seek to incorporate new mechanisms of stakeholder participation and public accountability as a way to retain democratic legitimacy and ensure community responsiveness. A principal way of doing so is through incentive and result-based performance evaluation systems that impose information-generation and disclosure requirements and reward entities for meeting performance benchmarks. It is expected that material incentives, together with stakeholder-accessible performance evaluation, will lead to greater local competition, the scaling up of best practices, and the potential for constant renewal and responsiveness to changing circumstances and the diversity of local needs. New governance regimes thus seek to redefine state-society interactions, with multiple stakeholders assuming traditional roles of governance.

Variously described in the literature as 'reflexive law', 'collaborative governance', 'decentred regulation' and 'democratic experimentalism', among other descriptors,[56] new governance approaches are highly influential in almost all fields of governance, at both national and global levels. International financial institutions and national civil service sectors, for their part, embrace the model under a 'new public management' rubric, while the European Union (EU) applies it as a supranational governance tool through the Open Method of Coordination.[57]

Indeed, in almost every field of governance, many types of actors play increasingly important authoritative roles, as is described in more detail below. It is now likewise understood that effective governance institutions must be responsive and dynamic: they must be committed to the transparent production and disclosure of information, learn from experience, listen to stakeholders, and adapt to particular circumstances. To accommodate these basic insights, new governance scholarship often lists a broad set of institutional changes that are reframing how governance structures are, can be, and should be exercised in the 21st century. These include: increasing decentralisation and subsidiarity; growing roles for non-state actors; widespread stakeholder participation; growing use of flexible and adaptable mechanisms such as information production and sharing duties, soft law, framework agreements, voluntary standards and open coordination; and stress on dynamic governance mechanisms such as compe-

---

56 Others include 'soft law', 'outsourcing regulation', 'reconstitutive law', 'revitalizing regulation', 'regulatory pluralism', 'meta-regulation', 'negotiated governance', 'responsive regulation' and 'post-regulatory law'.

57 For citations, *see* Melish, *supra* note 5, pp. 32–33, notes 131–133.

tition, organisational management systems, performance monitoring, experimental implementation mechanisms, and the like.[58]

Discussion of these new governance approaches is useful for understanding the limitations of the Ruggie PRR framework and how it might conceptually and operationally be enhanced. This is particularly true with respect to three core components of new governance regimes: (1) the critical role played by civil society actors in systems of global governance; (2) new and innovative processes for holding a broader set of social actors to account for achieving or failing to achieve distinct sets of social goals, targets or benchmarks; (3) and the necessity of institutionalising systems and processes of orchestration for the facilitation of cross-sector social learning and information exchange. We address each in turn.

### 3.1. New Actors, Decentred Processes and Widespread Stakeholder Participation

While it was once assumed that states played the exclusive, or at least controlling, role in governance systems, it is increasingly recognised that global governance is today conducted through the operation of ever more dense and interconnected networks of actors. These actors include not only states and businesses, but also all levels of civil society and civil society organisations (CSOs) – from individual norm entrepreneurs, to grassroots community-based organisations, to issue- or identity-motivated NGOs, to religious groups, labour organisations, and consumer or credit associations, on to a wide range of transnational advocacy networks and multistakeholder initiatives. Often working closely with intergovernmental organisations and industry networks, such actors have become increasingly active in every facet of regulatory policy, from standard setting and lawmaking through adjudication, monitoring and enforcement, at local and global levels alike. As their respective interests, networks and capabilities continuously evolve, the roles they play can vary significantly over both time and space. Their involvement has in fact become so important to the production and revision of multilayered governance structures that international law and governance institutions are recognised to "increasingly become part of the problem if they cannot somehow adapt to this current reality".[59]

---

[58] See e.g. O. Lobel, 'The Renew Deal: The Fall of Regulation and the Rise of Governance in Contemporary Legal Thought', 89 *Minnesota Law Review* (2004) pp. 342–470. For applications in the transnational sphere, see e.g. K. W. Abbott and D. Snidal, 'Strengthening International Regulation Through Transnational New Governance: Overcoming the Orchestration Deficit, 42 *Vanderbilt Journal of Transnational Law* (2009) pp. 501–578; E. Meidinger, 'Private Import Safety Regulation and Transnational New Governance', in C. Coglianese, A. Finkel and D. Zaring, *Import Safety: Regulatory Governance in the Global Economy* (University of Pennsylvania, Philadelphia, 2009) pp. 233–256; Melish, *supra* note 5; J. Scott and D. Trubek, 'Mind the Gap: Law and New Approaches to Governance in the European Union', 1 *European Law Journal* (2002) pp. 1–18.

[59] M. L. Schweitz, 'NGO Participation in International Governance: The Question of Legitimacy', 89 *Proceedings of the Annual Meeting (American Society of International Law), Structures of World Order* (April 5-8, 1995), pp. 415–420.

New governance regimes rely heavily on such actors for the legitimacy, efficiency and accountability of their operations. Indeed, traditional state-centred regulatory systems have already manifested a decades-long movement toward expanded public participation, deliberation, consultation and transparency; so it is not surprising that increasingly pluralistic regulatory systems would adopt similar practices. The primary traditional justifications have been efficacy and legitimacy: (1) the more information and feedback a regulatory programme garners, the more likely its activities are to be fitting and effective;[60] (2) the more regulated parties and beneficiaries participate in and understand a regulatory programme, the more likely they are to view it as appropriate and legitimate.[61] CSOs bring essential knowledge and expertise to global problem-solving and, by relying on their global networks and communication strategies, they are able to amplify local voices, spotlight problems and spread awareness in ways scarcely imaginable a generation ago.

In this way, CSOs likewise play essential accountability roles, holding other social actors, both public and private, to their social, policy and legal commitments and to other community standards of socially acceptable conduct. Accountability implies, in this regard, "that some actors have the right to hold other actors to a set of standards, to judge whether they have fulfilled their responsibilities in light of these standards, and to impose sanctions if they determine that these responsibilities have not been met".[62] Drawing on these core elements – especially those of information transparency, social actor responsibility, performance measures and social sanction – civil society groups have increasingly insisted on the right of communities most affected by human rights misconduct to hold other community members and social actors to a set of rights-based performance standards related to those rights, to independently monitor and assess compliance with those standards, and to impose some form of penalty or sanction where performance is objectively inadequate or where justificatory or process requirements are not met.[63] To establish the normative and institutional framework within which to do this, such movements draw directly on the substantive and procedural standards of international human rights law, particularly the legal process and accountability relationships it creates between distinct social actors, both public and private.[64]

They do this through a variety of strategies. They collect and channel information, lobby and advocate, educate and set agendas, participate in dispute resolution, implement policies and programmes, collaborate in policy and lawmaking, monitor and assess conduct through impact assessments, fact-finding and reporting, and impose positive and negative incentives on behaviour through certification, grading and

---

60  *E.g.* J. Freeman, 'Collaborative Governance in the Administrative State', 45:1 *UCLA Law Review* (1987).

61  T. Tyler, *Why People Obey the Law* (Yale University Press, New Haven, 1990).

62  R. W. Grant and R. O. Keohane, 'Accountability and Abuses of Power in World Politics', 99 *American Political Science Review* (2005) p. 29.

63  Melish, *supra* note 5, pp. 57–58.

64  Ibid.

auditing strategies – strategies that rely increasingly on social and consumer power in the marketplace.

Perhaps the most striking expansion in non-state activity has been in performance monitoring and enforcement. Thus, civil society actors play a critical role in developing indicators and benchmarks capable of measuring priority concerns, assessing social actor conduct against those measures, and widely publicising successes and failures in meeting appropriate benchmarks. Such strategies have been particularly important in the human rights context, where civil society actors engage in 'shadow reporting' under human rights treaties to independently assess government conduct in accordance with local experience and otherwise seek to hold a wide range of actors to account for conduct that fails to accord with minimum standards of socially-appropriate conduct.

At the same time, provisions for 'citizen suit' enforcement have proliferated in many fields of law, from environment to competition, in both common and civil law systems.[65] The rise of non-governmental enforcement mechanisms has been driven in many ways by resource concerns, but also by a desire to provide a check on state discretion. Governments simply cannot deploy sufficient enforcement resources across the broad sweep of activities that must be regulated by modern governance systems. They have learned to partly ameliorate this problem by authorising enforcement suits by non-governmental actors and offering incentives (either reimbursement of litigation costs or portions of penalties) for successful suits. This has the twin benefits of forcing violators to internalise a larger proportion of total enforcement costs and removing those costs from state budgets. Many private enforcement provisions are also driven by an implicit or explicit desire to limit the absolute discretion of government officials over regulatory enforcement. By creating an alternative enforcement mechanism, they create an additional accountability mechanism that can lead to increased predictability and legitimacy of the system.[66] In different situations, non-governmental enforcers can be civil society groups, business associations or even competitors.[67]

Non-state actors have also become very active in the development, promulgation and adjudication of standards. The modern version of this practice is often traced back to the founding of the International Organization for Standardization (ISO) after World War II to define transnational product standards to facilitate trade, although there are earlier examples.[68] The ISO system provides not only for the development of standards outside governmental processes, but also for their adjudication. That is, in-

---

65  E.g. B. Boyer and E. Meidinger, 'Privatizing Regulatory Enforcement: A Preliminary Assessment of Citizen Suits Under Federal Environmental Laws,' 35 *Buffalo Law Review* (1985) pp. 834–965; S. Casey-Lefkowitz *et al.*, 'The Evolving Role of Citizens in Environmental Enforcement', Fourth International Conference on Environment and Enforcement (Chiang Mai, Thailand, 1996), <www.inece.org/4thvol1/futrell.pdf>.

66  I. Ayres and J. Braithwaite, *Responsive Regulation: Transcending the Deregulation Debate* (Oxford, New York, 1992).

67  *Ibid.*, p. 158.

68  E.g. standards for organic food developed in Germany in the 1920s and standards for electrical products before then. *See e.g.* Meidinger, *supra* note 58, pp. 233–256.

dependent non-governmental actors, often contracted by either a producer or a buyer, determine that products and manufacturing processes conform to the standards. They thus provide the same kind of 'trust' in the producer that a government regulatory approval might provide.

Examples of regulation by non-state actors abound across industries and issue areas.[69] A prominent example is the Forest Stewardship Council, which certifies sustainable forestry around the world. It is a multi-stakeholder initiative comprised of social, economic and environmental chambers that provides its own mechanisms for setting global, national and subnational forest management standards, as well as for certifying compliance and sanctioning non-compliance.[70] The standards incorporate global, national and local expectations for proper forest management, including human rights and environmental ones. The sanctioning process is largely driven by independent CSOs that monitor producer behaviour and seek to leverage transnational product chains and consumer expectations to promote adoption and compliance by firms.[71]

While non-governmental standards typically begin as 'voluntary', they often become effectively compulsory through incorporation in powerful market chains. Moreover, it is not uncommon for state legislatures and agencies to adopt and make them legally compulsory.[72] Thus, many modern governance standards are produced, promulgated and implemented by varying combinations of private and governmental actors. This expanded panoply of actors, however, is only part of the story. Equally important is the growing reliance on new governance processes.

### 3.2. New Governance Accountability Processes

The incorporation of multiple kinds of actors into legislative, adjudicatory, monitoring and enforcement roles has been accompanied by a growing focus on participatory and process-oriented dimensions of governance. This development corresponds to an understanding that compliance with fixed rules applied uniformly across contexts can lead to suboptimal outcomes. Not only does it frequently fail to take localised circumstances into account, but it may fail to draw on community resources and expertise in ways that promote democratic control and legitimacy. This is particularly true given the contextual and evolving nature of problems faced by distinct communities, requiring often unique and targeted solutions that one-size-fits-all solutions determined from above generally cannot fully accommodate. Such participatory and process-oriented approaches likewise prioritise mechanisms for policy learning, adaptation and constant improvement in result-oriented goals.

---

69 Abbott and Snidal, *supra* note 58 (governance triangle).

70 E. Meidinger, 'Multi-Interest Self-Governance through Global Product Certification Programs', in O. Dilling, M. Herberg and G. Winter (eds.), *Responsible Business? Self- Governance in Transnational Economic Transactions* (Hart, Oxford, 2008) pp. 259–291.

71 M. Conroy, *Branded: How the Certification Revolution is Transforming Global Corporations* (New Society, New York, 2007).

72 H. Schepel, *The Constitution of Private Governance: Product Standards in the Regulation of Integrating Markets* (Hart Publishing, Oxford, 2005).

One of the most important of these participatory processes is performance monitoring.⁷³ Following the maxim that it is not possible to manage what is not measured, the monitoring of practices and impacts has become a near universal criterion for new governance. Performance monitoring in this regard entails several steps. First, it requires that an entity or community determine the goals of positive performance. It then requires the establishment of a set of indicators to measure whether progress is or is not being made toward those performance goals. By determining a baseline and establishing a set of benchmarks or targets to indicate the level of performance expected by a given time, performance monitoring provides a mechanism by which distinct social actors can assess other social actors' relative success in making improvements in performance measures, such as the enjoyment of human rights for particularly affected communities.⁷⁴

In this regard, information transparency and disclosure is essential. It provides the basis for a wide range of interested actors to call attention to unjustified backtracking with respect to priority goals or policies, arbitrary or discriminatory impacts, or insufficient progress in achieving locally agreed benchmarks or other performance goals. It likewise encourages the timely identification and assessment of such problems as they arise, facilitating social input as to their causes and the generation of community-based ideas for how distinct policies may be reconstructed or redirected to better serve human rights ends. Under this approach, less priority may be given to standardised policy uptake or to the precise means chosen to achieve any particular socially-sanctioned end, than to the progress (or lack thereof) that is in fact being made on core human rights indicators, particularly for the most vulnerable.

Under new governance arrangements, performance monitoring should accordingly be undertaken both by the organisation carrying out a given policy and external organisations of affected stakeholders or other interested monitors. Internal monitoring is central to the family of 'management systems' techniques that have been widely adopted by both governmental and non-governmental organisations over the past two decades. Exemplified and propagated by the ISO 9000 series of management standards, the management systems approach requires an organisation to define the impacts in which it is interested, develop mechanisms for consistently monitoring them – including making specific officers responsible for doing so – and look regularly for shortcomings and ways of making improvements.⁷⁵ The rapid uptake of management systems techniques worldwide appears to be driven both by the belief that organisations using them are more profitable and successful than their competitors and by tendencies toward organisational isomorphism, in which organisations are drawn to

---

73   The following description draws from Melish, *supra* note 5.
74   An exemplary organisation committed to such community-based performance monitoring is the Participation and Practice of Rights (PPR) Project, a new accountability initiative operating in Northern Belfast and North Inner City Dublin. See <www.pprproject.org>.
75   *E.g.* M. Potoski and A. Prakash, 'Information Asymmetries as Trade Barriers: ISO 9000 Increases International Commerce', 28:2 *Journal of Policy Analysis and Management* (2009) pp. 221–238.

imitate the practices of their most prominent or successful peers. It also seems to be generally assumed that when an organisation adopts a new routine based on incentives, that routine is likely to eventually become a taken-for-granted part of its operations, thus moving from a logic of consequences to a logic of appropriateness.

The management systems approach fits well with the PRR stress on corporate due diligence as a way of institutionalising human rights protection. It essentially provides a systematic approach to routinising that process. As we have suggested, however, by itself this will often be inadequate to achieve satisfactory human rights protection, for several reasons. First, internal management systems work best when organisations have material incentives [threat of lawsuits, penalties, regulation] to make them successful,[76] which will often not be the case for human rights if there are not sustained external pressures to perform well. Second, in other arenas even where appropriate internal incentives are present, organisational management systems are often complemented by external monitoring or certification systems. The external systems serve several important functions. The most obvious being to verify for interested constituencies that the organisation being reviewed is actually performing as it claims.

At the same time, it is important that an external check be available to verify that the measures being used to evaluate performance in fact correspond to community or social priorities or goals.[77] Where they do not, external monitoring processes are essential for bringing attention to the inappropriateness of the indicators chosen and for publicising the results of independent monitoring under the more appropriate performance measures. Through shaming, negative publicity or other ways of incentivising material interests, they may correspondingly bring pressure on an entity to change its measures and hence to improve its own internal process. Indeed, experience has shown that when governments and corporate actors are left to select and define their own indicators, those measurements often do not coincide with the real concerns and priorities of the local populations. The process thus runs the risk of measuring the wrong things – i.e., raw service delivery targets or narrow outcome indicators that tell a partial, even skewed story of what is in fact happening on the ground.[78] For this reason, it is critical that local communities and other stakeholders have a role in defining the broader goals of performance systems, as well as the particular indicators or measures used to evaluate performance toward those goals.

---

76   C. Coglianese and J. Nash, *Regulating from the Inside: Can Environmental Management Systems Achieve Policy Goals?* (Resources For the Future, Washington, D.C., 2001); N. Gunningham and P. Grabosky, *Smart Regulation: Designing Environmental Policy* (Clarendon, Oxford, 1998) p. 247.

77   D. O'Rourke, 'Multi-stakeholder Regulation: Privatizing or Socializing Global Labor Standards?', 34:5 *World Development* (2006) pp. 800–918; C. Rodriguez-Garavito, 'Global Governance and Labor Rights: Codes of Conduct and Anti-Sweatshop Struggles in Global Apparel Factories in Mexico and Guatemala', 33:2 *Politics & Society* (2005) pp. 203–333.

78   A. Rosga and M. Satterthwaite, 'The Trust in Indicators: Measuring Human Rights', 27:2 *Berkeley Journal of International Law* (2009) pp. 253–315; Melish, *supra* note 5, pp. 43–46, 94–99.

Less obvious, but extremely important, is that external monitoring and certification organisations can serve as essential communication and learning mechanisms. They are able to transfer information about best practices and emergent problems among business enterprises, and also to hold public discussions and deliberations about the best ways to achieve governance goals. Most importantly, they can serve as fora for deliberating what practices are appropriate for a given locale and type of industry. Although government agencies could in principle perform these deliberative functions, in practice they rarely do. Instead, these functions have become highly dispersed among transnational, national and local actors. The PRR framework does not propose a method for linking such discussions in a way that will help business enterprises know or achieve appropriate levels of protection in variable and changing circumstances.

Other participation-enhancing, process-oriented tactics used by large numbers of CSOs in new governance regimes include the organised use of civil society 'report cards', 'testing' processes, shadow reports, social auditing and certification schemes and the development of alternative budgets.[79] While many of these auditing and certification processes have initially been developed in the environmental arena, they are increasingly being used in the labour, education, health and other fields of new governance. This is done in a concerted effort to engage ordinary people in directly monitoring the quality and impacts of a range of public services by both public and private actors. By explicitly identifying areas of satisfactory and unsatisfactory service delivery, competitively rating providers, and then assessing 'grades', rankings or minimum standards for social certification, CSOs create new and socially-driven accountability frameworks that can impel direct rights-based improvements in public service delivery and access.[80]

In so doing, they aim to ensure that best and worst performers are publicly and transparently named, that processes exist through which consumers are provided valuable information about which businesses comply or fail to comply with minimum standards of human rights protection, and – most importantly – that all such information is widely and transparently accessible to the broad range of citizens and consumers that are in a position to act on it in making choices about how to spend their money, support political candidates, pursue their interests and otherwise organise their day-to-day lives.[81]

Two other kinds of new governance procedures are particularly relevant to human rights protection. Both often involve competition. The first is exemplified in the European Union's 'Open Method of Coordination' (OMC). In this method of govern-

---

79  Melish, *supra* note 5, p. 89.
80  See e.g. R. Jenkins and A. M. Goetz, 'Accounts and Accountability: Theoretical Implications of the Right-to-Information Movement in India', 20 *Third World Quarterly* (1999) pp. 603, 608 (discussing use of the 'report card' method in which public opinion surveys are conducted in low income neighbourhoods to report on the perceived quality and appropriateness of a range of public services, using the results as social leverage for improving service delivery performance).
81  Melish, *supra* note 5, pp. 105–106.

ance the EU establishes short, medium and long-term policy goals together with a broad set of quantitative and qualitative indicators for them. Individual countries translate the goals into context-appropriate national and regional policies, which are subject to regular monitoring, evaluation and peer review. National experiences are compared, peer reviewed and debated, and, over time, national policies are adjusted to reflect those discussions and the experiences of other countries.[82] The OMC thus eschews strict regulatory requirements in favour of broad goals and seeks to establish an iterative process of mutual learning based on monitoring and comparison of national reform experiments adapted to local circumstances.[83]

The OMC, however, requires a relatively powerful central authority to set goals and assess monitoring and reporting, conditions generally not met in global human rights governance. Although the international human rights field has moderately authoritative international actors that have articulated many broad principles of human rights over time, they lack the regulatory authority of the EU. The human rights field thus resembles many other areas of global governance, although it may be blessed with an unusually rich set of governing principles and rules. Like many other fields, human rights have multiple, sometimes competing authorities engaged in converting those principles and standards into binding localised rules and enforcement mechanisms. The most obvious ones are nation states, but they are continually assisted, supplemented and challenged by non-governmental organisations that are also engaged in the articulation and enforcement of rules. Like similar bodies in many other fields (*e.g.*, forestry, fisheries and mining) these non-governmental organisations typically have relatively elaborate procedures for defining standards, adjudicating ('certifying') compliance, and taking action against noncompliance – the latter often through public campaigns.[84] Many of these processes parallel those developed by the ISO and used by other organisations, particularly those in the ISEAL Alliance.[85] Multi-stakeholder standard setting, publication of standards, rules and procedures, public comment on policy determinations, third party certification proceedings, peer review and so on are the guiding norms, although some organisations adhere to them more closely than others.

---

82  D. Trubek and L. Trubek, 'Hard and Soft Law in the Construction of Social Europe: the Role of the Open Method of Coordination,' 11 *European Law Journal* (2005) pp. 343–364.

83  B. Eberlein and D. Kerwer, 'New Governance in the European Union: A Theoretical Perspective', 42 *J. Com. Mkt. Stud.* (2004) pp. 121–142, at p. 123; C. Sabel and J. Zeitlin, 'Learning from Difference: The New Architecture of Experimentalist Governance in the European Union', 14:3 *European Law Journal* (2008) pp. 271–327.

84  *E.g.* E. Meidinger, 'The Administrative Law of Global Private-Public Regulation: the Case of Forestry', 17 *European Journal of International Law* (2006) pp. 47–87.

85  The ISEAL Alliance is a global association of non-governmental standard setting and certification organisations that seeks to provide and promote guidance for best practices in standard setting. Originally founded by eight organisations, including the FSC, FLO and IFOAM, its membership is slowly growing and currently includes 11 full members and 8 associate members. See <www.isealalliance.org/>.

A critical additional point is that these organisations compete with each other and even with states for adherents, policy influence and public legitimacy. They desire that their systems of standards and enforcement will be more widely respected and adopted than others and thus have decisive influence in the field. This process is particularly evident in the field of international labour standards, where a number of significant transnational non-governmental organisations, including the Fair Labor Association (FLA), Social Accountability International (SAI), Ethical Trading Initiative (ETI), Workers Rights Consortium (WRC), Worldwide Responsible Apparel Production Program (WRAP), and Business Social Compliance Initiative (BSCI), currently compete to define and certify proper labour practices.[86] While they share many attributes and all rely heavily on the body of labour standards associated with the UN-based International Labour Organization (ILO), these organisations differ considerably in their requirements and methods of enforcement. At present, however, there appear to be few institutionalised mechanisms for judging or reconciling their competition.

### 3.3.  Human Rights Governance Ensembles and the Need for Orchestration

A third basic tenet of new governance is legal orchestration. Legal orchestration, it is said, is what separates the new governance model from flat processes of devolution and deregulation.[87] That is, following the subsidiarity principle, it functions to prevent the isolation or abandonment of decentralised initiatives, ensuring that they are linked together within a supportive 'higher' framework. Through that framework, the plurality of proliferating norm-generating practices that emerge in the market and civil society can be gathered, coordinated, sorted and made available for observation, allowing different actors to learn from other experiences, replicate success stories, scale-up where appropriate, and hence to engage in constant innovation and improvement.

Orchestration is particularly important in the human rights field. Indeed, human rights governance is carried out by many types of organisations and networks engaged in complex relationships and processes that the PRR framework neither directly accounts for nor utilises. At the bottom, organisations such as FLA, SAI, WRC and others exist because the system of states and corporations on which the PRR framework relies has not translated the body of international human rights laws into effective protections for workers in developing countries. Consequently, these non-governmental organisations have sought to impose their own standard setting and enforcement processes to persuade international customers to buy only products produced under acceptable conditions. Moreover, many other types of organisations are engaged in monitoring of human rights practices and advocacy of human rights regulations.[88]

---

86  Fransen, *supra* note 27. (The ETI does not certify firms, but instead focuses on setting standards that firms can use in self-certification.) For a general discussion of legitimacy competition, *see* J. Black, 'Constructing and Contesting Legitimacy and Accountability in Polycentric Regulatory Regimes', 2 *Regulation and Governance* (2008) pp. 137–164.
87  Lobel, *supra* note 58, p. 400.
88  P. Nelson and E. Dorsey, 'New Rights Advocacy in a Global Public Domain', 13 *European Journal of International Relations* (2007) pp. 187–216.

Overall, then, the system of human rights governance involves several types of actors whose activities are more interdependent than the PRR framework would suggest. Human rights rulemaking, adjudication and enforcement are carried out in many processes beyond state law making and corporate due diligence analyses. If one were to visualise the human rights governance system in any given locale one would see a complex mix of local, national, regional and international state and non-state agencies engaged in overlapping and intertwined rule making, adjudication, monitoring and enforcement activities. Similar configurations in other fields have been termed regimes,[89] regime complexes,[90] ecosystems,[91] and ensembles.[92] Each term is helpful, but 'ensembles' may be the most instructive for this analysis. It conveys the presence of multiple performers whose roles are interrelated and should be coordinated and harmonised, but who also have an inherent degree of autonomy. These players currently lack both a detailed score and an effective conductor. Because of the variable and changing conditions of their performance, a detailed score is not plausible. Nor, given the current state of the PRR framework, has a conductor been created. At present we have many necessary players groping toward an effective governance system, but limited understanding of how to orchestrate them. The implicit constructivist hope that orchestration might emerge from continuing efforts to give content to human rights norms by states and corporations has not adequately contended with the need to incorporate CSOs in the many facets of human rights governance, nor with how to adequately orchestrate that process.

There can be little doubt under present circumstances that the involvement of actors beyond states and corporations is desirable, and even necessary, given the limited resources and complex motivations of states and corporations. However, this is not to say that the system is functioning optimally. At present there is considerable fragmentation and conflict regarding what the human rights duties of corporations are. FLA and WRAP, for example, promote significantly different standards for corporate behaviour and implement them in different ways. Efforts to harmonise the standards and practices of these CSOs have often been difficult and contentious, leading commentators sometimes to declare failure.[93] Progress seems to be continuing, however, with all of the labour standards organisations recently having agreed to minimum and

---

89   Abbott and Snidal, *supra* note 58.

90   K. Raustiala and D. G. Victor 'The Regime Complex for Plant Genetic Resources', 58:2 *International Organization* (2004) pp. 277–309.

91   Meidinger, *supra* note 58. This term reflects the tendency for programmes to find niches in which they seem to have comparative advantages and to cooperate and compete with each other depending on their relative advantages. It was developed to characterise food governance in particular.

92   Perez uses this term to describe environmental governance structures around sustainability indexes. O. Perez, 'Private Environmental Governance as Ensemble Regulation: A Critical Exploration of Sustainability Indexes and the New Ensemble Politics', *Theoretical Inquiries in Law* (forthcoming 2011).

93   Fransen, *supra* note 27.

living wage requirements, and generally tending to 'harmonise up'.[94] While this process appears similar to the better documented 'ratcheting up' in forestry standards,[95] it is not clear that this is happening in the broader field of human rights standards, where efforts often remain localised and isolated. Accordingly, both the contributions of individual programs and the functioning of the larger system seem likely to remain suboptimal and to require greater attention than they have thus far received.

In sum, although CSOs make valuable and necessary contributions to an otherwise incomplete system for human rights protection, there is a pressing need for mechanisms to orchestrate and harmonise their activities, and to integrate the lessons they have learned into the larger process of human rights governance. A critical complement to the PRR framework, therefore, will be to produce studies and recommendations regarding how to learn from and flexibly orchestrate the activities of the full set of actors in the system, ensuring that their insights can be used to promote responsive adaptation, fit and scale in all localised human rights implementation efforts.

## 4. Operationalising the Business and Human Rights Framework: The Utility of Updating the Schema

We recognise that Ruggie does not entirely ignore the critical role of civil society actors or broader learning and sharing processes. His attention to these actors and processes has, however, largely been limited to the second phase of his mandate, under which he was tasked by the Human Rights Council specifically with offering concrete guidance to states, businesses and other social actors on how to 'operationalise' the PRR framework.[96] His 2007 Mapping report to the Human Rights Council on the PRR framework described selected multi-stakeholder initiatives, public-private hybrids that combine mandatory with voluntary measures, and examples of industry and company self-regulation.[97] Likewise, his 2008 report concluded that the intent behind the PRR framework is to help expand the number and scale of initiatives, promote cross-learning, and help cohere individual measures/initiatives into a more systemic response with cumulative effects.[98] Nonetheless, his PRR framework fails to create a conceptual or policy basis for *how* these initiatives may either be *promoted* by appropriate actors or *orchestrated* to in fact promote cross-learning, scaling up and competitive races to the top.

---

94   D. Doorey, 'Contestation, Authorizations, Collaboration in Labour Code Initiatives: The Case of the Living Wage', Draft Paper for the Workshop on Transnational Business Governance Interactions, Florence, Italy, May 2011. It should be noted that while the living wage has been accepted in principle by the certifying organisations, it still seems quite far from being achieved in practice.

95   C. Overdevest, 'Comparing Forest Certification Schemes: the Case of Ratcheting Standards in the Forest Sector', 8:1 *Socio-Econ, Rev.* (2010) pp. 47–76.

96   UN Doc. A/HRC/RES/8/7.

97   UN Doc. A/HRC/4/035.

98   UN Doc. A/HRC/8/5, paras. 105–106

We believe this failure is a significant design flaw, one carrying major conceptual and operational costs for the effectiveness of the project. An operationally more effective framework, we believe, would have incorporated a fourth pillar, one designed to recognise and affirm the central role played by civil society actors and affected stakeholders in human rights governance and accountability processes. Under the heading 'Participate', that pillar – or final 'P' – would have complemented the 'Protect, Respect, Remedy' framework by legitimating and spotlighting one of the key mechanisms through which human rights harms in the business context are contextually identified and defined and, critically, by which states and businesses are held to their international duties and responsibilities in practice. A 'PRRP' framework would correspondingly have recognised the equal instrumental importance of civil society actors to states and businesses in protecting against human rights harms in the business sector. Such recognition is critical, we believe, for ensuring that such actors have the social leveraging tools and international legitimation necessary for effective independent monitoring and accountability processes.

In proposing this fourth pillar, we recognise that a global framework of the PRR sort requires a certain presentational simplicity. Such presentational simplicity will, in turn, necessarily veil many important details the framework intends to encompass, both conceptually and operationally. In this regard, it is important to underscore that we do not take issue here with Ruggie's choice to focus his framework on the state duty to 'protect', the corporate duty to 'respect' and the overlapping duty to 'remedy' claimed breaches of said duties. We understand and appreciate the utility of this conceptual framework from both a legal and operational perspective, including for the important acculturation-based processes it promotes. In particular, unlike some other critics, we are convinced that the framework neither limits the legal duties held by states outside the 'business and human rights' context nor restrains the corporate duty to 'respect' to its 'negative' orientation. Accordingly, we believe the formal articulation of the PRR duties in an international framework that has received broad stakeholder endorsement is a useful and important contribution to advocacy and progress in the business and human rights field.

Where we do take issue, and where we believe a new governance approach provides key insight, is with respect to Ruggie's choice to focus his framework on the duties and responsibilities of *only* states and corporate entities and, specifically, to do so in a way that suggests that states and businesses are the central actors in human rights compliance regimes. Missing is the critical role and key responsibilities of civil society actors in global governance, particularly in defining, monitoring, evaluating, participating in, assessing and (re)constructing the operational elements of state and business duties in the business and human rights context. Without the incorporation of these critical actors – and a corresponding emphasis on independent civil society accountability processes as a complement to state-based remediation and voluntary enforcement efforts – we do not believe it is possible to close the 'governance gaps' that Ruggie identifies as the root cause of the business and human rights conundrum.

Indeed, Ruggie specifically acknowledges the basis of these governance gaps in the lack of sufficient accountability incentives faced by states and businesses today. He thus recognises that state authorities are not able to effectively regulate corporate conduct in light of the political and economic incentives they currently face in the globalised economy. At the same time, businesses are not able to effectively regulate themselves. As the SRSG affirms, '[t]he Achilles heel of self-regulatory arrangements to date is their undeveloped accountability mechanisms".[99] It remains unclear, then, how simply better articulating the normative duties or responsibilities of these actors in pillars 1, 2 and 3 – duties the respective actors already understood themselves to hold under international human rights law – will change the incentive structures they face or improve their internal accountability systems. Some type of independent and external monitoring and accountability is essential, it would seem, to disrupt and reshape the material incentives facing states and businesses in their day-to-day conduct as it affects human rights. That is, additional actors, with distinct ways of leveraging power over corporate and state conduct, must be explicitly brought into the framework for it to be effective in closing the current governance gaps. The 'participate' pillar would have addressed this critical concern by supplementing Ruggie's current emphasis on promoting a 'logic of appropriateness' from above with a corresponding 'logic of consequences' from below.

The inclusion of a fourth pillar would likewise have served to respond to the central critique lodged by scholarly commentators against acculturation-based models of regime design: that acculturative models promote only shallow and superficial reforms by targeted actors and hence should never form the basis for regime design.[100] Indeed, the problem of institutional isomorphism (manifested in high numbers of treaty ratifications and other formal human rights commitments) accompanied by deep and widespread patterns of 'decoupling' between those commitments and actual undertakings has long been a major problem in the human rights field. It has led commentators to insist that the problem with human rights law is not that it is insufficiently acculturative, but rather that it is under-enforced.[101] On this view, greater emphasis needs to be placed on new and innovative mechanisms of enforcement for human rights law and on how to hold state and business actors to account, socially, legally and politically (through a variety of incentive-based mechanisms), for policies and practices that threaten human rights harm.

Authoritative recognition of a fourth 'participation' pillar would have helped to address this central human rights concern by more accurately representing the complex social dynamic of interaction between interested actors that is necessary for institutional transformation to in fact take place within corporate culture and state practice. Specifically, it would have served to provide civil society actors with a critical set of leverage tools for asserting their voice and socially amplifying their power through a broad combination of persuasion, coercion and acculturation-based strategies to help close gaps between formal commitments and actual undertakings. As previously underscored, this range of strategies far exceeds those covered under a narrow 'remedy'

---

99   J. G. Ruggie, 'Business and Human Rights: The Evolving International Agenda', 101 *American Journal of International Law* (2007) p. 836.

100  Goodman and Jinks, *supra* note 22, p. 725 (noting critique).

101  *Ibid.*

prong.[102] A 'PRRP' framework would correspondingly reflect the growing understanding that while acculturation-based models must be a "part of the larger conversation", by themselves they are "not the ideal or preferable social mechanism around which to design international human rights regimes", a fact acknowledged even by sociological institutionalism's most dedicated defenders.[103]

The insights of both new governance and economic institutionalism are thus as critical to institutional transformation in the business and human rights context as is Ruggie's more idealist emphasis on the social embedding of norms. These approaches emphasise the necessity of ensuring social accountability systems that can effectively and sustainably leverage interests by embedding a logic of consequences within institutional structures. Hence, even if one would expect a rule-based logic of appropriateness to at some point become so embedded in corporate conduct as to supplant a logic of consequences as the effective driver of policy action, it is difficult to expect such embedding to occur in the absence of active processes of leverage and interest-based organising on the part of distinct social actors, especially those in civil society most directly impacted by state and corporate conduct. Express attention to these actors, processes and mechanics is thus essential to any effective accountability or governance regime.

In proposing a fourth 'participate' pillar we do anticipate counterarguments. This is especially so given the amount of time and resources already invested in the PRR framework and hence the resistance that will likely follow the prospect of updating it so soon. Specifically, we foresee four principle counterarguments: two question its necessity, two its advisability.

### 4.1. The Necessity of a Fourth 'Participate' Pillar

First, we anticipate that many framework supporters will defend the current structure by arguing that a 'participate' pillar is simply not necessary. Two arguments can be expected in this regard. First, civil society participation is already suggested in the Guiding Principles and hence need not be incorporated in the framework itself. Second, civil society will organise and participate regardless of what the framework looks like. We believe that neither argument is persuasive. Indeed, both take insufficient account of the very real power asymmetries that characterise human rights struggles, asymmetries that function in practice to substantially inhibit, limit or even preclude community-based civil society engagement in monitoring and accountability processes. By contrast, formal recognition in an authoritative international policy design of the right of stakeholders to participate in human rights governance and ac-

---

102  They likewise include active engagement in the conduct of human rights impact assessments, independent performance monitoring of businesses and states under locally-defined human rights indicators, the assessment of corporate and state policies, the publicising of setbacks, lack of progress, or abusive policies, and the active gathering and sharing of information related to all aspects of corporate-related human rights abuse, among many others.

103  Goodman and Jinks, *supra* note 22, note 10.

countability processes would provide a critical set of legal resources and leveraging tools to affected communities – both for mobilising less powerful actors to engage systems of abuse and for legitimating their participation *vis-à-vis* more powerful actors.

The instrumental importance of such recognition cannot be underestimated. Although the Guiding Principles do call for transparency and participation in the conduct of corporate due diligence responsibilities, such participation is not neither required under the framework, nor can it be asserted by civil society groups as a 'right' conferred under the framework. Under the current conceptual framework, a business can legitimately claim that it need not allow for civil society participation in external monitoring of any of the aforementioned due diligence activities. This apparent corporate right of control over who has access to relevant information for human rights monitoring and impact assessment and who can speak on behalf of communities in voluntary consultation processes is a major operational gap in the Ruggie framework. Indeed, corporate actors are unlikely, at least in the short-term, to see external monitoring of their operations on the human rights of affected communities as consistent with their economic interest. As has been noted with respect to private governance organisations in the garment industries, the degree of control over implementation and compliance procedures is a major source of division. Those initiatives, such as WRAP and BSCI, that are predominantly business-controlled, favour compliance systems in which the division of tasks between social and business actors is heavily weighted toward business actors. They thus select auditors themselves, preferring professional auditing firms; do not allow audited information to be released to the public; and insist that complaints and grievances be dealt with internally by firm representatives.[104]

Businesses that adopt policies such as these may be in formal compliance with the PRR framework, while in fact impeding real change in their corporate approach to respecting human rights. In this sense, by not incorporating a 'participate' pillar, the PRR framework may unwittingly contribute to a system in which corporate human rights policies are allowed to be used strategically by businesses to signal compliance to the market (thereby enhancing reputational interests), while simultaneously impeding production of and access to the information necessary for ensuring that the corresponding social reputation markets are functioning properly. If this were the case, the PRR framework could in practice serve to weaken, rather than enhance, corporate social accountability processes. The kind of mutual competition and monitoring by external actors that we have argued for would of course help to resolve these problems.

A fourth 'participate' pillar would play a critical legitimation role in this regard by validating civil society requests to access information from business entities about their policies, guidelines, impact assessments and performance tracking systems, while promoting greater business reliance on external, independent and community-based monitoring and assessment systems. It would correspondingly allow civil society actors to use the framework proactively, as an operational sword, to demand active spaces for their participation where it is otherwise denied.

---

104  Fransen, *supra* note 27. It should be noted that we are not arguing that it is never appropriate for firms to choose their own auditors in social accountability systems, only that the practice has serious risks unless counterbalanced by other accountability mechanisms.

In addition to its legitimating role, the inclusion of a 'participate' prong would also serve an essential mobilising function. It is important to recall in this regard that human rights law is designed specifically to protect and enhance the participatory agency of individuals to stand up and defend their own rights when threatened by external actors, whether public or private.[105] The international human rights architecture has correspondingly made protecting and promoting the right to participatory inclusion by individuals and groups in decision-making processes that affect their lives an increasing priority in its work.[106] A 'participate' pillar would assist civil society actors in organising themselves and mobilising internal resources to demand active engagement in increasingly creative and novel ways. By focusing on corporate and state actors only, the current PRR framework does not provide this critical resource to other community actors, as a human rights-based approach would require.

It has been suggested that Ruggie intended for the 'remedy' prong of the PRR framework to serve this role. Yet, the SRSG's discussion of state and corporate duties to remedy is focused almost exclusively on the provision of grievance procedures for 'victims' of human rights abuse. Although he refers to the importance of both judicial and non-judicial mechanisms, both types of mechanisms are directed toward ex-post redress for harms that have occurred in the corporate context. Community members are conceived principally as 'objects' of potential abuse, not as 'subjects' of decision-making processes and impact assessments concerning activities that may affect their lives. The 'remedy' prong is thus insufficient for addressing the distinct issues that arise from the right and responsibility of citizens to 'participate' in system accountability processes.

An effective regime for compliance with human rights norms must correspondingly focus much more explicitly on mechanisms of community participation and assessment that take effect before significant harm occurs. Such mobilisation of participation, as an internationally-recognised right of civil society actors, would likewise serve to counteract what has come to be known as the 'participation industry,' often called the fastest growing sector of the governance business. It would thus provide a framework of mobilisation to communities in ensuring, against token company exercises of 'stakeholder participation' that rely exclusively on limited 'consultations' or 'focus groups' with affected communities, the inclusion of a 'representative' of marginalised affected groups on advisory boards, or the creation of self-help groups or users' associations under program guidelines.[107] Rather, it would provide the tools for in-

---

105   See e.g. M. Ignatieff, 'Human Rights as Politics', in A. Gutman (ed.), *Human Rights as Politics and Idolatry* (Princeton University Press, Princeton, 2001) p. 4; P. Alston, 'International Law and the Human Right to Food' in P. Alston and K. Tomasevski (eds.), *The Right to Food* (Martinus Nijhoff, Leiden, 1984) p. 62.

106   See e.g. UN ECOSOC, Comm. On Econ., Soc. & Cultural Rights, General Comment No. 14, *The Right to the Highest Attainable Standard of Health*, para. 54, 22nd Sess., UN Doc. E/C.12/2000.4 (2000).

107   See e.g. The World Bank Group, *The World Bank Participation Sourcebook* (1996) pp. 145–146. While these kinds of participatory mechanisms can sometimes also spur increased community participation (M. Tysiachniouk and E. Meidinger, 'Importing Democracy:

sisting on the creation of new mechanisms through which affected communities may *independently* monitor the performance of decision-makers, not by invitation, but by their own power to identify minimum standards of appropriate community conduct (consistent with human rights values) and to exert social sanction where performance does not meet those standards.[108]

A second major counter-argument to the addition of a 'participate' pillar is that civil society will organise and participate regardless of the framework's precise elements. Defenders of acculturation-based international law regimes often highlight this argument, stressing that, by creating a global script that can be called upon in mobilisation campaigns, acculturative processes may indirectly promote opportunities for the emergence of domestic-level social movements.[109] While we do not disagree, we believe the argument only reinforces the importance of civil society mobilisation and participatory engagement for ensuring systemic transformation. It underscores – not diminishes – the utility of a fourth pillar to strengthen and promote this essential social dynamic in the business and human rights context.

In addressing this concern, we emphasise that we do not presume that Ruggie fails to appreciate the importance of civil society actors and processes. We believe that he assumes and expects them to operate. Nonetheless, consistent with his broader theoretical commitments, he understands them as ancillary to, or definitionally subsumed within, the larger process of norm acculturation or socialisation that he seeks to promote within the operations of states and global business entities. Our concern is that, by failing to recognise such actors and processes expressly, Ruggie undermines their very ability to mobilise and operate as legitimate actors within his framework. Accordingly, we believe that any regime design that fails to take such essential social actors into specific operational account is incomplete and deficient.

### 4.2. The Advisability of a Fourth 'Participate' Pillar

A second set of likely counterarguments to a fourth pillar arises from a desire to avoid the political divisiveness caused by business opposition to the Draft Norms. These arguments focus not on the utility of a 'participate' pillar, but rather on its advisability. On this view, any added instrumental utility to a PRRP framework should be sacrificed in favour of strong business sector buy-in and engagement with a more limited PRR framework.

Whether the business community would in fact oppose framework recognition of the role of civil society in human rights governance is nonetheless an empirical question. Interestingly, it is one that has not appeared to bear itself out in practice. According to inner members of the Ruggie team, a repeated question posed to the

---

Promoting Participatory Decision Making in Russian Forest Communities,' in C. Claeys and M. Jacqué, *Environmental Democracy: Facing Uncertainty* (Peter Lang Publishers, London and Brussels, 2011), they are often used to dampen and control community participatory processes.

108  Melish, *supra* note 5, p. 92.
109  Goodman and Jinks, *supra* note 22, pp. 733–743.

SRSG by business sector representatives in the SRSG's extensive global stakeholder consultations was why states and businesses were the only social actors addressed under the PRR framework.[110] They wondered why the roles and responsibilities of civil society were not likewise addressed. It does not appear, then, that the business community was broadly, or even marginally, opposed to explicit references in the framework to civil society rights and responsibilities. They may in fact have highly welcomed them.[111] We do not, then, believe that 'anticipated business opposition' is a persuasive argument for avoiding a fourth pillar.

A second potential, but equally unpersuasive, argument is that the addition of a 'participate' pillar would exceed the SRSG's mandate by recognising a right or duty that extends beyond current international law principles. Claims of such doctrinal excess were indeed a major motivation for broad business opposition to the Draft Norms. Whether or not such excess in fact characterised the Norms, it does not characterise our proposed fourth pillar. The right of civil society to participate in decision-making processes that impact their lives has consistently been recognised by international treaty bodies and tribunals. UN human rights treaty bodies, for example, expressly recognise the right to participatory inclusion by affected individuals and groups as "an integral component of any policy, programme or strategy development to discharge governmental [human rights] obligations …".[112] The effective enjoyment of human rights, such expert bodies insist, can only be secured if the "right to participate in public decision-making" is ensured to all groups in society.[113]

This important principle has likewise been recognised by the regional human rights tribunals. In the specific context of business and indigenous rights, regional tribunals have, for example, repeatedly recognised that states may not move forward with plans or concessions to private business regarding development, investment, exploration or resource extraction on indigenous lands without first ensuring the right to 'effective participation' of affected communities in the decision-making process. At the same time, required human rights safeguards include the obligation to ensure the performance of a prior social and environmental impact assessment *by an independent*

---

110  R. Davis, 'Ethical and Practical Challenges for Corporate Lawyers Advising Clients on Human Rights', 105 *Proceedings of the Annual Meeting (American Society of International Law), Harmony & Dissonance in International Law* (23–26 March 2011) (audio transcript).

111  Perhaps ironically, it was the civil society sector participating in the consultations that was most opposed to taking the emphasis of the framework off of states and businesses. Ibid.

112  UN ECOSOC, Comm. On Econ., Soc. & Cultural Rights, General Comment No. 14, *The Right to the Highest Attainable Standard of Health*, para. 54, 22nd Sess., UN Doc. E/C.12/2000.4 (2000).

113  See e.g. ibid. ("Effective provision of health services can only be assured if people's participation is secured by States"); UN ECOSOC, Comm. On Econ., Soc. & Cultural Rights, General Comment No. 4, *The Right to Adequate Housing*, para. 9, 6th Sess., UN Doc. E/1992/23 (1991) ("[T]he right to participate in public decision-making—is indispensable if the right to adequate housing is to be realized and maintained by all groups in society").

*entity*.[114] That is, international human rights tribunals have recognised that impact assessments conducted by economically interested parties often are not trustworthy indicators of likely human rights impacts. Attention to who is to conduct human rights impact assessments, under what conditions, and on the basis of what standards is an area of critical concern in the human rights context. It remains markedly under-specified in the Ruggie PRR framework.[115]

## 5. Conclusion: Moving Forward

In providing the foregoing critique and proposal, new governance lessons have been particularly influential to our analysis. As discussed, new governance approaches seek to maximise policy responsiveness and adaptability to agreed public goals by incorporating new channels for stakeholder participation and new processes of transparency, accountability and orchestration. These channels and processes are seen as necessary for both ensuring the legitimacy and operational effectiveness of public and private programs and for ensuring that 'compliance' or 'implementation gaps' are identified and closed as needed. At the same time, they do not seek mimicry or orthodoxy in forms, but rather encourage experimentation and competition for results in line with local diversity, priorities and experience.

Correspondingly, new governance approaches provide important insight into how an international human rights regime might be designed to both respect contextual diversity in the global community and to close the 'governance gaps' that the SRSG himself has identified as the root cause of the global business and human rights conundrum. Such approaches are in this regard consistent with Ruggie's social constructivist perspective, even while extending beyond it to expressly incorporate more instrumentalist elements. Indeed, by focusing not only on norms, but also on the political process dynamics that create and recreate them, Ruggie's theoretical approach has always emphasised the importance of actors engaging in that "active process of interpretation and construction of reality".[116] That process is not one that involves the deployment of norms alone, however. It necessarily relies on the strategic leverage of economic and other material interests by norm entrepreneurs as a means of instantiating new normative understandings or priorities in social actor conduct. As we have

---

114  See e.g. *Saramaka People v. Suriname*, Judgment of 28 November 2007, Inter-Am. Ct. (Ser. C), para. 129; *Center for Minority Rights Development (Kenya) and Minority Rights Group International on behalf of the Endorois Welfare Council v. Kenya*, Communication 276/2003, Afr. Comm'n on Hum. & Peoples' Rts (2010).

115  In recognising the foundational basis of our proposal in mainstream international law principles and jurisprudence, we underscore that we do not and would not characterise our proposal as 'radical', as do Parker and Howe with respect to their similar participatory proposal in this volume. While our proposal does necessarily address issues of power and interest conflict, such questions are fundamentally what human rights are about and hence should not, in our view, be understood as representing anything outside of mainstream acceptance.

116  Ruggie, *supra* note 14.

suggested, the construction of relevant human rights norms in any particular context cannot legitimately or effectively occur without the direct and active participation of those whose human rights are at stake. Hence, the need to both ensure and promote the direct participation of those and other supporting actors in corporate social accountability processes.

To help fill this critical gap in the PRR framework, this chapter has proposed an important fourth pillar – civil society participation – upon which processes of this sort could have been advanced through the SRSG's mandate. Developing and institutionalising these ideas, including those related to effective orchestration of the lessons and informational outputs produced by the proliferation of such participatory processes, will be a necessary next step in creating an effective human rights governance system. We urge the new Working Group on business and human rights, established by the Human Rights Council to succeed the SRSG,[117] to take up expressly in this regard what Ruggie left insufficiently acknowledged and conceptually underdeveloped.

---

[117] UN Doc. A/HRC/RES/17/4 (2011) (establishing a 'Working Group on the issue of human rights and transnational corporations and other business enterprises, consisting of five independent experts', to continue the SRSG's work by promoting the dissemination and implementation of the Guiding Principles and assessing them on the basis of information received from all relevant sources).

# List of Authors

**Signe Andreasen** is a political scientist from the University of Copenhagen, Denmark. She works as an advisor on CSR at the Copenhagen based consultancy firm GLOBAL CSR. Signe is specialised in Responsible Supply Chain Management as well as more broadly in CSR in the context of economic developing countries. She contributed to *Changing Course – A Study into Responsible Supply Chain Management*, a 2011 report drafted for the Danish Ministry of Foreign Affairs.

**Samantha Balaton-Chrimes** is a PhD candidate at the School of Political and Social Inquiry, Faculty of Arts, Monash University. Her research focuses on both empirical and theoretical aspects of citizenship, citizen empowerment and human rights, particularly in the context of developing economies. She has collaborated in research projects encompassing broader aspects of statelessness, ethnic politics, livelihoods, land rights, labour rights, private regulation of human rights in the context of global business practices, and consumer perceptions of ethical product certification schemes. She received a Layne Beachley Aim for the Stars Foundation grant in 2009. In 2008 and 2010 she was awarded the AFSAAP Postgraduate Prize, and in 2008 from Monash University the Rufus Davis Memorial Prize for Honours (Politics).

**Meg Brodie** was the inaugural National Human Rights Institutions (NHRI) Fellow at the Raoul Wallenberg Institute for Human Rights and Humanitarian Law (RWI) from 2010–2011. Meg's research leveraged RWI's programmatic NHRI work to focus on thematic areas directly relevant to the NHRIs with which it partners. For example, she published on the international accreditation procedures for NHRIs including a case study of Sweden's 2011 application. Meg is completing a PhD at the University of Melbourne on the power of NHRIs to create change, focusing on national inquiry methodologies. Her research has included fieldwork with the Mongolian, Indian and New Zealand Human Rights Commissions. Meg has worked as a corporate lawyer, in the development and not-for-profit sectors, and lectured in human rights.

**Karin Buhmann** is Associate Professor of Law at the University of Copenhagen (the Institute of Food and Resource Economics). Dr. Buhmann holds degrees in law and East Asian Studies and a PhD from the Department of Law at Aarhus University

(Denmark). She has published widely on legal and regulatory aspects of CSR and business responsibilities for human rights, which she approaches from the perspective of public regulation at international and national levels. She was admitted to the Danish Bar in 2002 and previously worked at the Danish Ministry of Foreign Affairs as an in-house advisor on human rights and good governance in development, and the Parliamentary Ombudsman, and in charge of a Danish government project to promote CSR.

**Mary Dowell-Jones** is a Research Fellow at the University of Nottingham Human Rights Law Centre and an independent consultant. Her work focuses on financial market stability, systemic risk and financial crises, and how these affect the enjoyment of socio-economic rights. She is currently part of an Australian Research Council-funded project at the University of Sydney on finance and human rights. She has also worked in risk management for commercial and investment banks. Her publications include 'Minding the Gap: Global Finance and Human Rights', *Ethics & International Affairs* (with David Kinley, 2011) and *Contextualising the International Covenant on Economic, Social and Cultural Rights: Assessing the Economic Deficit* (Martinus Nijhoff Publishers, 2004).

**Nicolas Hachez** (LLM (NYU); JD (Louvain)) is a Research Fellow at the Institute for International Law and at the Leuven Centre for Global Governance Studies, University of Leuven. His research interests include international legal theory, international human rights law and international investment law. He published on various issues connected to those disciplines, such as corporate social responsibility, the role of non-state actors and of private regulation in global governance, and the relations between international investment law and other branches of international law. Formerly he worked as an attorney in the Brussels office of an international law firm, where he focused his practice on international investment law and European Union law.

**Fiona Haines** is a Criminologist and Associate Professor at the School of Social and Political Sciences at the University of Melbourne and Fellow of the Research School of Asia and Pacific at the ANU. Her expertise lies in the areas of globalisation, risk, regulatory theory and regulatory reform. She has published extensively, including most recently *The Paradox of Regulation: What regulation can achieve and what it cannot* (Edward Elgar, 2011). This work on risk is currently being extended to explore the intersection between financial and climate regulation. Fiona Haines is co-editor (with Nancy Reichman (Sociology), University of Denver) of the leading international journal in regulation: *Law & Policy*.

**John Howe** is Associate Professor and Director of the Centre for Employment and Labour Relations Law at the Melbourne Law School, where he teaches in the areas of labour law, corporations law and corporate social responsibility. John has written extensively on labour law as a form of labour market regulation, and on the intersection between diverse forms of state-based regulation and corporate self-governance of employment practices. He is co-editor of the book *Labour Law and Labour Market*

*Regulation* which was published in 2006, and his book *Regulating for Job Creation* was published by Federation Press in late 2008.

**David Kinley** holds the Chair in Human Rights Law at Sydney University and is an Academic Panel Member of Doughty Street Chambers in London. He is author or editor of eight books, including *Civilising Globalisation: Human Rights and the Global Economy* (2009), and is currently writing a follow-up to this book on the intersections between human rights and global finance. He has previously held teaching and visiting positions at other universities in Europe, the United States, Hong Kong, South Africa and the South Pacific, as well as Australia. He has worked for many years on human rights matters with governments throughout South East Asia, and for the UN, the World Bank, Friedrich Ebert Stiftung, and a number of transnational corporations.

**John H. Knox** is a Professor of Law at Wake Forest University, in North Carolina, where he teaches and writes about human rights, international environmental law and trade law. From 1988 to 1994, he served as an attorney at the US Department of State. He is a member scholar of the Center for Progressive Reform and a special counsel to the Center for International Environmental Law. His recent scholarship addresses environmental human rights, the extraterritorial application of US law, and the duties of non-state actors under human rights law.

**Karin Lukas** is a senior researcher and head of team at the Ludwig Boltzmann Institute of Human Rights. She is also a member of the European Committee of Social Rights of the Council of Europe. She has been a consultant for various national and international organisations, such as the UN Development Programme and the Austrian Ministry for Foreign Affairs. She has done research as well as project-related activities in the field of human rights, in particular women's rights, development cooperation and business, since 2001. She currently works on the issue of labour rights in global production networks, including its gender implications, which will result in a work to be published in 2011, and is project leader of the junior partner Austria in the EU Twinning project "gender equality in working life" in Turkey.

**Kate Macdonald** is a Lecturer at the School of Social and Political Sciences at the University of Melbourne, having held previous positions at the London School of Economics and Political Science, the Australian National University, and Oxford University. Her research focuses on social, labour and human rights governance arrangements in the global economy and their implications for developing countries. Previous publications include: 'Globalising justice within coffee supply chains? Fair Trade, Starbucks and the transformation of supply chain governance', *Third World Quarterly* (2007); 'Non-Electoral Accountability in Global Politics: Strengthening Democratic Control within the Global Garment Industry', *European Journal of International Law* (with Terry Macdonald, 2006).

Radu Mares (LLD (2006), LLM (1998)) is senior researcher at Raoul Wallenberg Institute of Human Rights and Humanitarian Law, in Lund, Sweden, specialised in the area of business and human rights. His work focuses on ways to strengthen the protection of human rights and good governance in the Global South. His preferred approach is to deliberately keep in the picture both governmental and private entities, so that the interaction between law, public policy and corporate practices can be studied, synergies captured, and their effectiveness enhanced. Dr. Mares has written on the justification of the corporate responsibility to respect human rights, on the relation between law and self-regulation, and on CSR in the mining industry and supply chain contexts.

**Errol Meidinger** is Professor of Law, Director of the Baldy Center for Law & Social Policy, and Vice Dean for Research and Faculty Development at the Law School of the State University of New York in Buffalo. He is also an Honorary Professor at the University of Freiburg, Germany. His current research focuses on innovative transnational governance arrangements for promoting environmental conservation, social justice and public safety. These include regulatory initiatives such as forest certification, fair labour standards and food safety programmes. He is particularly interested in how these programmes compete and coordinate with each other and with state programmes, and how the larger governance ensembles that are being formed may reshape international law.

**Tara J. Melish** is Associate Professor of Law and Director of the Buffalo Human Rights Center at the State University of New York, Buffalo School of Law. With degrees from Brown University and Yale Law School, she has served as Staff Attorney and Legal Advisor to the Center for Justice and International Law, Associate Social Affairs Officer at the UN Department of Economic and Social Affairs, and Disability Rights International's UN representative in the drafting negotiations of the Disability Rights Convention. She has likewise served on the law faculties of Notre Dame, Georgia, George Washington, Oxford, and Virginia and been the recipient of professional fellowships and research awards from the John D. and Catherine T. MacArthur Foundation, the Yale Law School and the Fulbright Foundation.

**Christine Parker** is Professor of Law at Monash University Law Faculty and Centre for Regulatory Studies. Before that she was at the Melbourne Law School, University of Melbourne, where she was also an Australian Research Council Australian Research Fellow. She conducts socio-legal research on strategies of business regulation and enforcement, internal corporate responsibility systems, legal ethics and the regulation of lawyers. Her books include *Explaining Compliance: Business Responses to Regulation* (forthcoming); *The Open Corporation: Self-Regulation and Corporate Citizenship* (2002); *Regulating Law* (co-edited, 2004); and *Inside Lawyers' Ethics* (with Adrian Evans, 2007). She is co-chair of the Law and Society's Association Collaborative Research Network on Regulatory Governance.

**Sune Skadegaard Thorsen** heads the consultancy GLOBAL CSR. With a background in international corporate law, Mr. Thorsen has specialised in CSR/Corporate Sustainability since 1996. GLOBAL CSR advises a range of leading transnational corporations, governments and organisations as experts on social sustainability. He was expert advisor to Mary Robinson's Business Leaders Initiative on Human Rights since inception (2003–2009). He continues as expert advisor to the Global Business Initiative on Human Rights. His honorary positions have included: Chair of the Danish Institute for Human Rights, Director of the Danish Centre for International Studies and Human Rights, and member of a range of CSR initiatives and advisory boards, the Danish Section of the International Commission of Jurists, and the Danish Peace Foundation. He frequently speaks at international conferences and publishes widely.

**Rory Sullivan** (PhD) is a Senior Research Fellow at the University of Leeds and Strategic Adviser to Ethix SRI Advisers. His previous roles include acting as the investor lead on the Oxfam Better Returns in a Better World project, and chairing the Amnesty International (Australia) Business Group. Rory is an internationally recognised expert on responsible investment, human rights, environmental and development issues, and has written seven books and over 400 papers, reports and articles on these issues. His books include the newly published *Valuing Corporate Responsibility: How Do Investors Really Use Corporate Responsibility Information?* (2011), and the edited collection *Business and Human Rights: Dilemmas and Solutions* (2003).

# Index

## A

Accountability, corporate 10, 11, 19, 23, 35, 36, 61, 68, 72, 99, 165, 218, 225, 227, 304, 318, 320
Adjudication 4, 18, 26
Aid, development 37
Agriculture 23, 117, 118
Alien Tort Claims Act (US) 18, 19, 27, 51, 62, 72, 76, 183
Amnesty International 22, 47, 67, 92, 99
Association, freedom of 24, 46, 123, 135, 140, 160, 161, 225
· See trade unions
Audit, social 115, 132, 138, 293
Australia 15, 16, 99, 164, 246, 261, 291
Banking sector 21, 27, 38, 155, 195, 198, 211, 218, 295, 297

## B

Benchmark, in CSR 4, 11, 29, 197, 198, 223, 321
Best (good) practice 3, 11, 29, 130
Bribery (corruption) 116, 117, 147, 197, 217, 226, 296
Business Leaders for International Human Rights (BLIHR) 11, 234, 242, 303
Buyer company 13, 41, 44, 119, 131, 136, 145, 154, 161, 169, 177, 184, 320
· See supply chains; parent company

## C

California 14, 184, 202
Certification 21, 61, 118, 123, 125, 290, 320, 325
Child labour 21, 38, 88, 140, 265
China 100, 123, 132

Civil society (groups) 7, 9, 12, 13, 25, 29, 33, 35, 36, 37, 41, 44, 60, 65, 79, 83, 90, 93, 99, 133, 166, 253, 269, 274, 283, 290, 299, 303, 315, 317, 328
Code of conduct 5, 6, 22, 30, 109, 114, 116, 118, 131, 159, 233, 300
Codification, progressive 26, 29, 114, 116
Collective action 26, 306, 310
Columbia 20, 44, 184
Community (local) 17, 117, 170, 179, 200, 268, 320, 322, 331
Companies Act (UK) 16
Company law 2, 14, 26, 39
Compliance 21, 24, 27, 28, 62, 90, 105, 115, 124, 137, 160, 226, 230, 284, 307
· Creative compliance (symbolic conformity, 'decoupling') 34, 36, 117, 160, 232, 288, 294, 311, 329, 332
Complicity ('aiding and abetting') 3, 10, 19, 39, 41, 42, 45, 52, 72, 75, 156, 161, 174, 184
· See Knowledge
Conflict zones 13, 46, 82, 146
· See Kimberly Process
Constructivism 306, 310, 326
Consultation 3, 7, 14, 30, 65, 78, 85, 101, 230
· See Participation
Consumers 14, 87, 123, 166, 190, 225, 290, 299
Contract 2, 12, 21, 33, 37, 43, 141, 156, 163, 184, 190, 275, 284
Corporate governance 14, 40, 194, 223
Crimes against humanity 41, 57
Culture, of companies 4, 18, 21, 31, 111, 306
Cumulative progress/effects 31, 35, 47
Customary international law 54, 60, 67, 71, 73, 219

## D

Democratic Republic of Congo 13, 224
Directors, of companies
  · See Duty of care (of managers, in company law); Discretion, managerial
Disabilities, persons with 58, 267

Discretion, managerial 16, 18, 275, 278, 291, 298, 308, 316
Discrimination 54, 140, 194, 201, 265, 266, 292, 294
Displacement of communities 44
Donors (development cooperation agencies) 145, 190
Do no harm 41, 43, 107, 177, 232
Dodd–Frank Act (US) 13
Draft Norms on the Responsibilities of Transnational Corporations (UN) 2, 3, 6, 8, 9, 10, 11, 24, 34, 41, 43, 53, 60, 63, 68, 85, 96, 187, 229, 234, 276, 304, 334
Due diligence 4, 10, 13, 22, 27, 34, 46, 116, 155, 165, 195, 203, 230, 236, 275, 289, 292, 295, 300
  · Due diligence defence 27, 232, 282
Duty of care (of managers, in company law) 17, 19, 26, 220
Duty to protect (of states) 4, 6, 7, 25, 26, 32, 37, 56, 62, 64, 144, 170, 191, 195, 207, 214, 257, 268, 284
  · See Inconsistencies (in state practice)

## E

Ecuador 20
Education, right to 117, 140, 193
Environmental protection 13, 15, 16, 21, 29, 87, 110, 116, 120, 121, 162, 166, 179, 221, 265, 268, 275, 320
Equator Principles 39, 127
Ethical Trading Initiative 127, 133, 325
Ethics 15, 29, 153, 231, 240
European Commission 7, 14, 21, 23, 190, 228
European Court of Human Rights 38
European Parliament 14, 228
European Union 7, 14, 15, 18, 21, 164, 222, 316, 323
Expectations, societal 65, 192, 218, 225, 234, 274
Export credit agencies 21, 39, 275, 284
Export processing zones (EPZs) 144

Expression, freedom of 24, 98, 140, 225
Extractive industries 13, 46, 171, 181, 224, 265, 268, 295, 324, 334
Extractive Industries Transparency Initiative (EITI) 223
Extraterritoriality (of state duty to protect) 7, 25, 37, 41, 52, 78

## F

Fair Labor Association 133, 325
Fair-trade 110, 115, 118, 124
Food, right to 56, 80, 140, 193, 265
Forced labour 21, 88, 170, 184
Foreign direct investment (FDI) 10, 217
  · See Multinational enterprises
Framework agreements, global 110

## G

Gender equality 24, 55, 56, 58, 122, 135, 140, 202, 294
Global administrative law 95
Global Compact (UN) 12, 35, 61, 98, 101, 116, 147, 151, 197, 251
Global Reporting Initiative 23, 117
Ghana 143, 265, 268
Governance 12, 24, 28, 29, 134, 237, 304, 315
  · Decentralised 2, 8, 18, 22, 32, 33, 36, 135, 279, 284, 316, 317, 325, 326
  · Gaps 5, 25, 35, 41, 292, 305, 310, 328
  · Global 30, 36, 305

## H

Health, right to 22, 80, 117, 140
Health and safety, occupational 110, 122, 135, 140, 161, 165, 194, 217, 268, 295
High Commissioner for Human Rights (UN) 3, 5, 10, 11, 60, 81, 151, 261, 272
HIV/AIDS 22, 222, 223
Home states 6, 19, 25, 37, 78, 82, 88, 191
Homeworkers 160, 165, 167
Host states 6, 20, 25, 190
Hours of work 124, 135, 137, 161, 162
Housing, right to 117, 119, 122, 140, 195, 200
Human Rights Council (UN) 1, 3, 7, 10, 11, 23, 35, 46, 67, 71, 175, 265, 304
Human Rights Watch 35, 44, 65

## I

Impact assessment (human rights) 3, 48, 66, 135, 190, 212, 243, 283, 318, 330, 335

Inconsistencies (in state practice) 6, 32, 284, 291
· See Duty to protect (of states)
Incremental approach 46
India 22, 46, 110, 264
Indigenous people 64, 101, 110, 179, 265, 334
Indonesia 44, 46, 183
Institutional investors 15, 38, 190, 203, 218, 239
Institutionalism 309, 330
Insurance industry 14, 17, 190, 205, 211, 214, 217, 284
International Chamber of Commerce 92, 98, 99, 102
International Commission of Jurists 17, 154, 161
International Covenant on Civil and Political Rights 4, 55, 59, 79, 160, 262
International Covenant on Economic, Social and Cultural Rights 4, 55, 58, 79, 160, 194, 262
International crimes 25, 31, 52, 54, 67, 69, 158
International Criminal Court 57, 59, 70, 157, 166
International criminal law, 2, 57
· See International crimes; War crimes; Crimes against humanity
International Finance Corporation (IFC) 7, 13, 22, 23, 39, 116
International human rights law 2, 24, 37, 51, 55, 59, 242, 276, 325, 332
International Labour Organization (ILO) 125, 133, 263
· ILO Declaration on Fundamental Principles and Rights at Work 4, 23, 87
International law 2, 4, 19, 24, 57, 70, 281, 304
International Organisation for Standardisation (ISO) 7, 23, 116, 319, 321

## J

Joint (criminal) enterprise 42
Joint ventures 42, 183
Justice, access to 20

## K

Kimberley Process 45, 61
Knowledge (of impacts, circumstances, conduct) 11, 40, 157, 181, 225, 239, 292
· *Mens rea*, in complicity 19, 75

## L

Labour standards 12, 21, 22, 54, 136, 139, 159, 263, 325
Labour inspectorates 45, 120, 161, 180, 291
Laggards, corporate 28, 29, 30, 36, 227
Law 12, 91, 176, 185, 188, 195, 207, 219, 287, 299
· See also Company law; International criminal law; Global administrative law; International human rights law; International law; Securities law; Tort law
Leading companies 29, 30, 167, 227, 240
Legal separation of entities (limited liability) 41, 173, 187, 190
Legitimacy 90, 108, 117, 121, 123, 144, 177, 185, 190, 204, 236, 241, 249, 257, 267, 276, 283, 300, 309, 316, 318, 331
Leverage 6, 12, 14, 19, 21, 22, 32, 44, 112, 113, 138, 141, 145, 154, 156, 158, 190, 191, 217, 242, 274, 284, 315, 320, 328, 335
Lobby 29, 68, 89, 92, 101, 116, 117, 147, 209, 226, 314
London Stock Exchange 15
Living, standard of 193
Living wage 46, 120, 121, 161, 327

## M

Management system 4, 11, 116, 118, 162, 211, 275, 293, 321
Markets 12, 26, 30, 31, 162, 190, 194, 238, 287, 305
· Financial markets 19, 194, 214
Materiality (of information on risks and liabilities) 13, 26, 225
Medicines, access to 22
· See health, right to
Microcredit 201
Migrants (workers) 135, 179
Mitigation (of harm, risk) 4, 30, 46, 66, 130, 155, 157, 195
Monitoring 9, 52, 54, 132, 159, 162, 237, 267, 269, 289, 311, 319, 321, 329, 331
Multinational enterprises (transnational companies) 6, 10, 15, 19, 20, 23, 35, 37, 41, 53, 78, 86, 110, 124, 126, 136, 151, 159, 165, 175, 262
Multistakeholder initiatives 11, 27, 28, 30, 31, 44, 46, 109, 133, 324

## N

National Contact Points (OECD) 88, 251, 262

· See OECD Guidelines
National human rights institutions 27, 245, 260
Negligence 42, 178, 183
 · See Tort law; Reasonable person
Nigeria 20, 44, 73, 181, 261
Nike 44, 45, 149, 161, 162, 166
Norms (social, human rights) 23, 28, 29, 33, 36, 62, 91, 111, 115, 123, 174, 226, 248, 285, 307, 310, 313, 325, 335

## O

Obligations (of corporations) under international law 2, 6, 9, 11, 24, 26, 51, 60, 61, 72, 89, 101
Ombudsman, global 27
Omissions (inaction) 20, 44, 172, 178
Organisation for Economic Co-operation and Development (OECD) 7, 14, 46, 103, 116, 130, 262
 · OECD Guidelines 23, 35, 41, 88, 262
Overtime
 · See Hours of work
Outsourcing
 · See Buyer company

## P

Parent company (core company) 20, 37, 38, 41, 170
 · See Buyer company
Participation, of civil society 34, 297, 305, 316, 328, 330
 · See also Stakeholders; Civil society
Partnership (public-private) 116, 130, 144
Pensions 15, 38, 194, 217, 240
Pharmaceutical industry 22
 · See Access to medicines; Health, right to
Playing field, level 29, 30, 164, 227
Poverty reduction 13, 193, 201, 210, 213
Pragmatism, principled 7, 8, 12, 18, 105, 168, 186, 229
Principles on Responsible Investment (UN) 197, 224
Privacy, right to 24, 140, 194, 235
Privatisation 26, 289
Profitability 16, 18, 177, 207, 220, 226, 278, 294, 321
Public procurement 14, 21, 26, 275, 288, 291

## R

Rating agencies 204
Rational choice 306, 309
Reasonableness 27, 38, 108, 114, 118, 157, 174, 181, 191, 236
Reasonable person, care (in negligence law) 182, 188, 282
 · See Negligence
Remedies (access to) 3, 4, 27, 35, 43, 172, 180, 202, 213, 263, 283, 312, 332
 · Judicial 27, 58, 186, 246
 · Non-judicial 27, 88, 165, 258
Remuneration, of workers 46, 119, 121, 126, 135, 137, 165
 · See Living wage
Reporting, corporate 4, 17, 18, 26, 300
 · See also Transparency
Reputation, corporate 17, 155, 158, 221, 278, 331
Retailers 14, 138, 165
Risk 13, 16, 28, 138, 144, 180, 183, 201, 225, 237, 275, 298
 · Assessment 40, 158, 207
Role of states (in CSR) 3, 6, 12, 18, 29, 31, 37, 148, 284
Role of law (in CSR) 11, 12, 31, 33, 35, 299
Role of business (in society) 31, 63
Rule-making, process of 9, 23, 25, 47, 86, 90, 234

## S

Sarbanes Oxley Act (US) 15
Securities and Exchange Commission (US) 13
Securities law 2, 17, 39, 284
Security-providing industry 41, 181, 184, 225, 269
Self-regulation, corporate 28, 112, 159, 242, 275, 289, 293, 329
Sentencing Guidelines (US) 18, 21
Shared responsibility 40, 44
Shareholders 16, 17, 19, 27, 40, 211, 221, 222
Shell 13, 44, 98
Slavery (human trafficking) 14, 55, 59
Socially responsible investment (SRI) 39, 224
 · See Institutional investors
Soft law 15, 16, 18, 22, 29, 40, 61, 64, 191, 278, 316
Sovereign funds 40, 218, 219
South Africa 20, 22, 44, 100, 222, 259
Sphere of influence 3, 53, 99, 152, 158

Stakeholders 5, 10, 15, 17, 18, 92, 101, 238, 251, 269, 294, 300
Standard-setting 33, 34, 119, 123, 324, 325
- See International Organization for Standardization
State-owned enterprises 26, 257
Sub-contractors 116, 141, 153, 157, 160, 163, 167, 238
Supply chain 13, 14, 21, 22, 39, 44, 88, 116, 117, 151, 171, 206, 213, 296
Systematic (serious, severe) human rights violations 20, 73, 82, 157, 163, 172, 182, 266
- See International crimes

## T

Taxation (taxes, royalties) 13, 46, 98, 116, 164, 222, 269
Tipping point 30
Tort law 18, 19, 51, 173, 180, 185, 189
- See negligence
Torture 44, 58, 72
Trade 30, 37, 46, 284
- Trade barrier 137
Trade union (labour union) 22, 45, 46, 119, 123, 135, 164, 166, 180, 274
- See Association, freedom of
Transparency 11, 13, 14, 21, 90, 204, 224, 228, 291, 321
- 'Comply or explain' 14, 15
Treaty on CSR 2, 7, 8, 9, 11, 25, 29, 67, 68, 82, 165, 219, 234

## U

United Kingdom 14, 16, 289
United States 16, 21, 45, 100, 123, 180, 194, 226, 288
- See also Alien Tort Claims Act; Dodd–Frank Act; Sarbanes Oxley Act; California
Universal Declaration of Human Rights 4, 60, 63, 141, 160, 219, 262

## V

Voluntarism (corporate) 11, 25, 28, 29, 61, 99
- Displaces regulation 29, 34, 68
- Complement regulation 30, 36, 37, 68
- Scaling-up 31, 32
Vulnerable people 179, 186, 189, 193, 199, 205, 213

## W

Wages
- See Remuneration
Wal-Mart 22, 149
War crimes 41, 57